# SPEECH-MAKING

# SPEECH-MAKING

by

### JAMES A. WINANS
Evans Professor of Public Speaking
Dartmouth College

With a chapter on Voice and Speech

by

### CHARLES K. THOMAS
Assistant Professor of Public Speaking
Cornell University

## D. APPLETON-CENTURY COMPANY
INCORPORATED

NEW YORK                                          LONDON

To

The Memory of My Father

JAMES ADDISON WINANS

who never made a public speech except under
extreme provocation

# PREFACE

This book cannot justly be called a revision of my *Public Speaking*. Very few paragraphs are completely unchanged, and a great part of the book is new writing.

For several years I have been making notes for a preface in which I should explain why I have done this and not that, included this and excluded that, anticipate criticisms sure to be made, and generally "carry the war into the enemy's country." But dog-day weather and a wishful look in the eye of my editor make all that seem less desirable. So I am just saying: Here is the book; I have worked long and hard on it; it is the best I can do just now, and I hope you like it.

I will permit myself just one comment: If you do not find in this book certain topics, such as the special forms of speeches, it is because I find that brief, dogmatic discussion and scanty illustration of after-dinner speeches, occasional addresses and the like are rather more likely to be misleading than helpful, and a textbook of reasonable size cannot be an encyclopedia.

After all speech-making is speech-making. What the student needs chiefly is practice based upon an understanding of fundamental principles. If a teacher wishes to stress particular forms and feels the need of help, he can find a plenty in special books. If not, I hope I may yet supply the lack with a book, companion to this, in which I plan to treat of special problems and illustrate their solutions somewhat elaborately.

I am happy to place in the Appendix for those who wish to pay some attention to parliamentary procedure a chart prepared by Professor Garrison of Amherst College. Brief though it is, it has cost a good deal of work. For the privi-

lege of reprinting it, my best thanks. A chapter brief enough
to include in this book could hardly be of more service. For
those who wish to stress parliamentary law the better way
would seem to be to use one of the inexpensive manuals on
the market.

It is with great pleasure that I include a chapter on Voice
and Speech by Charles K. Thomas. I know no one better
qualified to write this chapter. I particularly admire the sane
balance of his views, and his refusal to set up absolute
standards where no absolute standards exist.

In the matter of thanks for assistance, it is difficult to
know where to begin or to leave off. In the older book I tried
to thank all to whom I felt indebted; but no one can give
credit to all who have helped him. To all to whom I was
indebted then I am indebted now. I owe much to my colleagues past and present; but I have resolved to limit specific
acknowledgment to those who have given me unusual assistance: to Herbert A. Wichelns of Cornell University for
many long discussions of the plan of the book, and for
reading most of the manuscript at an earlier stage, with
many trenchant comments; to Dayton D. McKean of Dartmouth College for reading the greater part of the manuscript
and making many wise suggestions; and to Wilbur S.
Howell of Princeton University for reading the chapters on
persuasion in two editions of the manuscript and making a
remarkably painstaking and constructive criticism. Faithful
are the wounds of friends. To these men I am deeply grate-
ful; but, I hasten to add, they are not to be held responsible
for the faults of this book, for they were dealing with a
somewhat stubborn author.

J. A. Winans.

Lake Placid.

# CONTENTS

The art of Rhetoric . . . is valuable, first, because truth and justice are by nature more powerful than their opposites; so that, when decisions are not made as they should be, the speakers with the right on their side have only themselves to thank for the outcome. Their neglect of the art needs correction. Secondly, [Rhetoric is valuable as a means of instruction]. Even if our speaker had the most accurate scientific information, still there are persons whom he could not readily persuade with scientific arguments. . . . The speaker must frame his proofs and arguments with the help of common knowledge and accepted opinions. . . . Thirdly, in Rhetoric . . . we should be able to argue on either side of a question; not with a view to putting both sides into practice—we must not advocate evil—but in order that no aspect of the case may escape us, and that if our opponent makes unfair use of the arguments, we may be able in turn to refute them. . . . Lastly, if it is a disgrace to a man when he cannot defend himself in a bodily way, it would be odd not to think him disgraced when he cannot defend himself with reason [in a speech]. . . . If it is urged that the abuse of the rhetorical faculty can work great mischief, the same charge can be brought against all good things (save virtue itself), and especially against the most useful things such as strength, health, wealth, and military skill. Rightly employed, they work the greatest blessings; and wrongly employed, they work the utmost harm.[1]

ARISTOTLE.

[1] Lane Cooper, *The Rhetoric of Aristotle*, p. 5. By permission of D. Appleton-Century Company.

# SPEECH-MAKING

## CHAPTER I

### INTRODUCTION

There is no entirely satisfactory term to describe our subject. An earlier work of mine is entitled *Public Speaking*, a term some object to on the ground that *public* limits the field too much, for we are concerned with speeches addressed to groups of any size, whether audiences of thousands in public halls, or small groups in committee rooms or wherever people meet for discussion with closed doors. On the other hand, the term *speech*, favored by many, is too broad for our present purpose since it includes everything involved in "the utterance of meaningful sounds." We are to deal with *speeches*, a term more limited in general usage than *speech*. The word *speeches* is, however, broad enough to be applied to the simplest utterances in conversation and to elaborate orations. So we speak of Daniel Webster's Speech in Reply to Hayne, and also say of a compliment, "That's a very pretty speech."

*Speeches* is therefore somewhat too broad, for we shall not deal directly with ordinary conversation, which is typically made up of a series of short speeches. I believe, however, that much of the work suggested in this book will have a beneficial effect upon conversation. Anything that develops good speech, in the narrower sense of the word, including good diction, enunciation, articulation, pronunciation, voices pleasing and expressive, is surely helpful in private as well as in public speaking. And what could be

I

more helpful in conversation than to be trained to straighten
out facts and ideas into expressible shape, to understand what
is and what is not interesting to others, what are interesting
and effective ways of saying things, and above all to have
drilled into one the habit of adapting what one has to say to
one's hearers, to their interests, their notions, their habits of
thought, to be trained to talk, not for the pleasure of hearing
one's self talk, but with a keen regard for the responses of
one's hearers?  It is a fundamental assumption of this book
that no clear line can be drawn between public and private
speaking.

Our direct attack, however, will be upon that kind of
speaking which involves one person talking rather continuously to several others; and this corresponds well to the
common understanding of the term *speech-making*, although
no doubt it can be used more broadly.  The term will be
used to include speaking to numbers large or small, whether
the speaker stands on a platform or on the same level as his
hearers or sits with them at a conference table, whether he is
speaking with the doors opened or closed to the public, or
possibly is addressing the whole world over the air, or
whether the topic and occasion are more or less important.

Upon the importance of learning to speak well I shall
touch but briefly.  We need not argue the relative importance of talking and doing.  Very often doing includes talking; and usually talking is necessary in inducing others to
coöperate.  The old argument about the relative importance
of the orator in ancient and in modern times need not
detain us at all; for whatever the answer may be to that
question, in these latter days of ever multiplying organizations with their conferences, conventions, and dinners, and
in a country governed by discussion and public opinion, it
has come about that there is greater opportunity and demand

for speech-making than ever before. The average man finds it greatly to his advantage in civic, organization, and business affairs to be able to speak his mind. Thus it comes about that never before have so many ill-prepared men found themselves facing audiences. While many "work out their own salvation," literally with fear and trembling, more have but scanty success.

It would be easy to fill a long chapter with the testimonies of distinguished men from many walks in life to the value of the ability to make a good speech; but to me quite as impressive are the words of those who describe themselves as "plain business men," men very little in the public eye. "It isn't oratory I want," such a man hastens to say, "but just the ability to get up and say what I think when things are being discussed, or to talk to my workmen or my sales force." Of course men do succeed in most vocations without this ability. The just claim is that they find it a help in most callings and indispensable in some.

Not only does the study of speech-making provide a gain in practical efficiency; it is in the broadest sense educational. We are told till we weary of hearing it that one great aim of education is to produce leaders. It will be increasingly evident that most of the principles of good speaking are the principles of leadership. To interest, to inform, to convince, and to persuade, these are the purposes of the speaker. Again, we are told that the leader must be a man of self-control; and we shall see more and more clearly the importance in speech-making of self-control.

Education should also develop individuality, and enable a man to stand out from the mass and on his own feet. A course in speaking takes a student off the back seat, puts him up before his fellows and compels him to do something on his own responsibility, to express his own ideas and to impress them upon others.

But we may go further. William James has declared:[1] "No reception without reaction, no impression without correlative expression,—this is the great maxim which the teacher ought never to forget." Yet in how much of our college work is there encouragement to reaction and expression on the part of students? To sit on the small of one's back, to absorb a little from lectures and assigned readings, to squeeze the mental sponge out on an examination paper— so dry that only a trifle of sediment is left—this too often is education. But whether present methods are right or wrong, it has become highly desirable that there be some courses in which the student has opportunity for self-expression, in which he has an opportunity to formulate and express and thus clarify and develop his ideas. We are told that the father of Woodrow Wilson "believed that nobody had grasped a thought until he could put it quickly and definitely into words. This he did himself and this he taught his son to do."

But should speaking be studied? Some think speaking is a wonderful art, requiring remarkable powers which must be the gift of nature. It is true that a liberal natural endowment is necessary to the great orator; but I have met with few who could not by persistent effort become good speakers. There are others who think that speaking is too simple for study; as if a subject which is concerned at every point with human nature could be simple!

"But is it not just a matter of practice?" some ask. Well, practice and experience are absolutely essential. Without practical experience, no textbook and no course of training is

---

[1] *Talks to Teachers*, p. 33. By permission of Henry Holt and Company, New York.

worth while. It is quite true that many have become good speakers, even orators, without such aids. All book and all school training, in whatever field of endeavor, are subject to the same limitation. Gradually the conviction has gained ground, however, that lawyers, physicians, engineers, and now farmers too, are better for the training of books and schools; or rather that they are best trained by a judicious combination of what the narrowly practical man is apt contemptuously to call "theory," and experience gained, at first, under skilled supervision.

We study everything in these days; mathematics, medicine, and also hotel management and blacksmithing, even sport. It is quite true that a man may have a natural gait which will enable him to win a race over the best trained men; but we all have more confidence in the runner who has both natural ability and training. A runner may train himself, and to a great extent he must, as one must in speaking or anything else; but he gets on faster and more surely with the help of one who has studied running and observed many in their development. The "get-there" stroke sometimes wins a boat race; but those whose stroke is the product of long study of ease and efficiency, most often "sweep the river."

No attempt is made in these pages to reveal a royal road to eloquence. There is no way to make a good speech without having something to say. Attempts to ignore this truth bring speech-making into contempt. But speech-making is a subject in which the confident assertion of half truths leads to much misunderstanding. Some will assert that the form, language, and delivery, are all important; others that the content only need be considered. Truly "fine feathers do not make fine birds," but a bird without feathers is a sorry bird indeed. The analogy can be pressed further: as the feathers are necessary to the life and success of a bird, so the form and method of a speech are an essential part of it. Given something to say, desire to say it, a proper opportunity, and a good speech has become possible; but there is no need of arguing the pretty theory that nothing else is necessary. Surely college students do not need to be told that there are many men who have much to say but cannot say it.

Besides having something to say, a speaker must be able to think; not only to think, but to say what he thinks; not only to say it, but to make others listen to it, understand it and feel the force of it. Some who can do all else, simply cannot deliver a speech. We wish they would write down what they have to say, and let us read it. To take a sane view of this subject we must take account of all that enters into the success of a speech,—the topic, the subject matter, its formulation, and its delivery; and all this, though not all of it can be treated fully in one textbook, comes within the scope of this work.

But what can be done in college classes? This is a question that is best answered by experience. It is a fact that students do learn to speak well in college classes, and learn to speak in such a way that they do not have to unlearn in practical life, but only to go on developing. It is quite true that a student may at times learn more in one evening of experience outside than in a month of work in the class. The soldier learns in his first battle what years of drill could not teach him. And yet the magnificent German fighting machine was trained without actual fighting to a high pitch of readiness. But do not suppose that the parallel is exact; for the practice work of a class in public speaking can be made more real than any mock battle. The class speaker faces most of the problems of speaking: he has to hold the attention of an audience more weary of listening than a general audience outside; he has every need of explaining and convincing; and when he touches upon exciting questions he often finds himself with a real fight on his hands.

The ideal way is to have class work and outside practice also. In class one has the advantage of making one's first efforts along with others in a similar situation, and this eases the embarrassment. Again, while failure always has a weakening effect, it is likely to be less disastrous in class than before other audiences. The student has also the stimulus of working with others who are trying to do the same thing. He has more opportunity for speaking in a variety of ways and on a variety of topics than he is likely to have elsewhere.

But perhaps the greatest advantage is that he can get honest, intelligent criticism by one who is trained to the work and who has had experience in watching the development of many other students. Competent criticism is extremely hard to get elsewhere. There are enough to condemn or ridicule us, and our friends are quick to tell us we do splendidly; but there are few who are candid enough, and fewer still discriminating enough, to tell us the truth. The unskilful will usually touch upon the incidental rather than the essential; they will base their comments upon a very mechanical view of the subject, and they will usually criticize too much. When you do find anywhere a competent critic, "grapple him to thy soul with hooks of steel." He is more likely to be found in one's speaking class than elsewhere. The comments of student on student are not the least of the advantages of such a course.

To those who have an honest fear that this study may develop in them affectations, let me say that all depends upon the way the subject is taken up. If too much stress is put upon technique alone, or if speech-making is viewed as largely a matter of tricks, there is danger. But if we study speaking strictly as a means to an end, as the means of influencing audiences, the danger is slight. It is regrettable that the ends of speaking are often lost sight of in the study of the means; the audience is forgotten. But if we keep a normal view of the purposes of speaking, we can then safely give due attention to any matter which affects those purposes.

I make no apology to those who may complain—not in just these words—that this book is addressed to their intelligence rather than being a book of rules of thumb which tell them just what to do under all circumstances. The only way that promises success in the long run is to become intelligent about speech-making. Suppose we had a book that seemed to provide for all foreseeable situations that may confront a speaker; and suppose further that we had gone through the dreary work of learning the rules. What then? We meet a situation, apply the rule and it works. Well and good. But what if we cannot remember the rule at the right moment? Or, since two similar situations may not look just alike, what if we cannot decide which rule applies? Or, what is more likely in the complexity of human affairs, suppose there is no rule for the situation that confronts us. What to do? Being trained by rules we are lost; we are not really intelligent about speaking; we are simply rule-of-thumb mechanics. But if a speaker is really intelligent about speech-making he can adapt himself to whatever situations develop. He will size up each situation, not trying to recall what some book or teacher said, but solving the problem in the light of the principles and experience he has stored away.

This is not saying there is no place at all for rules. They may be very useful as suggestions, but we should not be dependent on them. We must understand what lies back of them, and always remember that they are subject to exceptions and modifications. What I am asking you to do is admittedly harder than learning rules, and also more interesting. In the words of wise old Solomon, "with all thy getting get understanding." Study principles, consider them in relation to many possible situations and problems, work them out in many speeches. Consider, too, many suggestions and methods that do not rise to the dignity of principles. Train yourself to self-possession and resourcefulness in actual speaking. Drill yourself in good habits; and develop a speaker's mind, a speaker's way of looking at things.

It is rather unfortunate that so many people consider themselves authorities on speech-making. "I heard So and So," says a would-be authority, "and he did thus and so; so I know the secret of success." Perhaps the great secret is a mere trick or mannerism which works well enough with the speaker referred to; or possibly it actually decreases his effectiveness. Or some person succeeds, perhaps because he is really a good speaker and perhaps because he had a situation in which any one could have been effective. At once he may set himself up as an authority; but he is quite as likely as not to ascribe his success to trivial or to wrong causes. What notable speakers have to say on our subject is often very valuable; but to profit by the advice of even the best one needs a developed intelligence in regard to the whole subject. And one should be particularly chary of the dogmas of those who would put the whole secret of success in a nutshell.

No mere skimming of such a book as this will develop the needed understanding; there is need of pondering. If after fully understanding what I say, you disagree, well and good; you will in the process be developing intelligence.

Some statements in any such book are bound to be matters of opinion. Much, on the other hand, is the result of the study, observation, and experience, not of one man but of many. All that any teacher can justly ask is that his teachings shall not be cast aside before they are grasped; and he can justly ask that. Hasty skimming of such pages as those that follow usually result in such fallacious notions as, "All that's needed is just to be natural," or "Always be concrete"—gleanings of a reader more anxious to find positive statements to write on an examination paper than to get understanding.

We shall now turn to a consideration of the nature of speech-making, and particularly to the matter of public delivery, partly because this will serve to establish a conception of the whole subject, and partly because beginners are usually more worried about delivery than about subjects and speech composition.

# CHAPTER II

## CONVERSING WITH AN AUDIENCE

Some seem to look upon speaking in public as a strange and almost abnormal act; and although they have been talking to others all their lives, they either fear to make a speech, or if they do "rise to address an audience," they cease at once to be their normal selves, assume strange tones and speak in stilted language. They hardly conceive of their audience as a group of human beings, listening to ideas; but rather as a monster terrible to face, but possibly to be routed by roaring, or placated by cringing.

Let us imagine all speeches and all memory of speech-making to be blotted out, so that there is no person in the world who remembers that he has ever made a speech, or heard one, or read one; and there is left no clue to this art. Is this the end of speech-making? Here comes a man who has seen a great race, or has been in a battle, or perhaps is excited about his new invention, or on fire with enthusiasm for a cause. He begins to talk with a friend on the street. Others join them, five, ten, twenty, a hundred. Interest grows. He lifts his voice that all may hear; but the crowd wishes to hear and see the speaker better. "Get up on this truck!" they cry; and he mounts the truck and goes on with his story or his plea.

A private conversation has become a public speech; but under the circumstances imagined it is thought of only as a conversation, an enlarged conversation. It does not seem abnormal, but quite the natural thing.

When does the converser become a speech-maker? When ten persons gather? Fifty? Or is it when he gets on the truck? There is, of course, no point at which we can say the change has taken place. There is no change in the nature or the spirit of the act; it is essentially the same throughout, a conversation adapted as the speaker proceeds to the growing number of his hearers. There may be a change, to be sure, if he becomes self-conscious; but assuming that interest in story or argument remains the dominant emotion, there is no essential change in his speaking. It is probable that with the increasing importance of his position and the increasing tension of feeling that comes with numbers, he gradually modifies his tone and his diction, and permits himself to launch into a bolder strain and a wider range of ideas and feelings than in ordinary conversation; but the change is in degree and not in kind. He is conversing with an audience.

In what way is the speaking fundamentally different if on the evening of the next day he responds to an invitation to tell his story before a group of people met by prearrangement in a convenient room? There are differences to be sure; but though the procedure seems less like that of conversation, these differences do not make an essential difference in the act of speaking.

I wish you to see that speech-making, even in the most public place, is a normal act which calls for no strange, artificial methods, but only for an extension and development of that most familiar act, conversation. If you grasp this idea you will be saved much wasted effort and unnecessary worry and embarrassment.

PUBLIC AND PRIVATE SPEECH COMPARED. Let us examine the more important differences which will occur to the reader of this chapter. First, it may be said, a public speaker talks more loudly than one in conversation. Well, a public speaker, just as a private speaker, should speak so as to be heard without strain. If you have occasion to speak to a person at the other end of a long table, you raise your voice. If you wish to speak across a noisy stream, you may have to shout. This would not be ordinary speaking to be sure, but it is still conversation and not at all abnormal. The difference is altogether a vocal one. You speak loud enough to be heard.

Again, one is told, the public speaker does all the talking; in conversation there is a give and take. These statements are misleading. There are many conversations in which one party does all or nearly all the talking. Because an old man talks continuously to a young man who listens respectfully, we do not say the old man is making a speech. Our imaginary speaker talked continuously before he got on the truck, with but little vocal response from his hearers. Nor is it true that the public speaker does all the talking. The audience applauds and thereby says, "We approve." It may hiss and thereby say, "We disapprove." Questions may be asked and encouragement shouted. But all these expressions are only audible signs of what is going on in any audience whether quiet or not. His auditors, if giving attention at all, are thinking answers to the speaker's questions, or asking him questions, or assenting, or making objections; and the experienced speaker has learned to read less demonstrative, but no less certain signs of the thoughts and moods of his hearers. He can tell by attitude and facial expression whether the other party to this conversation is interested or bored, approves or disapproves, understands or is puzzled, and he amplifies a point or touches it lightly in accordance with what he sees. The story is told of how Rufus Choate reiterated the arguments and pleas of one of his jury addresses for hours after eleven men were won, until he saw the stern face of the twelfth juror relax in sympathy. Many a passage of good oratorical prose can be turned into a dialogue by writing out the questions and objections that lie plainly between the lines.

The young speaker can do no better for himself than to fix firmly in mind that *a speech is a dialogue* and to emphasize constantly the part of the audience, anticipating and watching for its response. If he does not he will be a poor speaker, whatever his virtues, just as one in private conversation who does not regard the reactions of his hearers is a poor converser.

I have been told that it is easier in conversation to know what the other fellow thinks, knows, and is. Maybe, if you are intimate with him. But a pretty good argument could be made to the effect that an audience is rather less likely to affect interest or indifference, to seem to agree in order to avoid argument, or to take the other side just for the sake of argument, than is an individual. The upshot of that argument is that it is sometimes hard and sometimes easy to anticipate or to realize the reactions of one's hearers, be they few or many.

A third difference is said to be that the public speaker prepares, while the converser speaks as things occur to him. It is true that a public speaker should prepare when there is opportunity; but he is none the less a public speaker because he is too indolent, or too busy, or is called upon too suddenly. Nor is a man less a converser because he prepares for a private conversation.

Suppose a student is chairman of a committee formed for resistance to the abolition of cherished holidays. This student has an appointment with the President of the University for the purpose of presenting the views of the student body. He talks with his committee. One says, "This is a good argument to use." Another, "That is not the way to put it; this is the way to reach the President." After discussing the arguments, the chairman remembers that the President has promised him but ten minutes. He must cut out some arguments and find brief ways of presenting others; and by the time of his appointment he knows just about what he intends to say and how he will say it. We will suppose that the President says very little, simply listens attentively with but an occasional question. The student talks as directly and pointedly and in as good language as he can and stops on time. Has he made a speech or conversed? Conversed, of course; but he has sifted his ideas, adapted them to his hearer, and has not presumed upon his hearer's time. He has followed a method excellent for a public speaker.

Suppose, further, that at the end of the conversation the President says, "Mr. Smith, I wish you would come to the faculty meeting to-morrow and say there what you have here." At faculty meeting our chairman has fifty or a hundred hearers. He has to raise his voice a bit, he stands up, perhaps no questions are asked; but if he has the good sense and self-control to talk to the faculty in the same spirit and largely in the same manner as when he spoke to the President alone, he will probably make an effective speech. If, on the other hand, he adopts a tone and manner strange to himself, but which he may consider as belonging to speech-making, he may easily be ridiculous.

So we might go on with other objections to the statement that public and private speaking are basically the same; but we should come to much the same results. If we are told that public speaking demands more dignity of manner or of language, the answer is already plain: All depends upon circumstances. Our student, though discussing the same subject, talks to a fellow student in a more free and easy way

than to the President and he talks to the faculty in a manner
different from that in which he addresses a meeting of the
student body.  In a similar way can be met other arguments
made to prove that public speaking and private conversation
are essentially different acts, and that therefore the former
calls for essentially different methods. We are dealing not
so much with essential differences as with adaptations.

However, I do not maintain that public and private speech
are *ordinarily* just alike.  We usually have no difficulty in
distinguishing conversation from speech-making.  Conventional differences, such as that the public speaker usually
stands before a considerable group to talk while the converser
usually does not, make a distinction.  Ordinarily, too, the
public speaker does speak more loudly, does talk more continuously, does make more preparation, and especially he
does have to deal with more minds.  These and other differences may be important.  They may make public speaking
*seem* quite different from private speaking; but since there
is practically nothing true of public speaking that may not
be true at times of conversation and nothing true of conversation that may not be true of public speaking, we can hardly
hold the differences of fundamental importance.  Rather we
shall get on best by thinking of our speech-making as conversation, enlarged and modified but still conversation.  It is,
however, misleading to say, as some do, that we should speak
to a considerable audience as to a single person, if for no
other reason than that we should not be heard.  We must
not forget the necessary adaptation.

If there is any basic difference it must, I believe, be found
in the fact that men in masses may not react just as the same
men would as individuals.  We have, too, such differences,
of degree rather than of kind, as that the more varied one's
hearers the more difficulty there may be in finding common

ground of interest and of belief. This difficulty may confront a hostess at her own dinner table, but may grow more acute with a large general audience. Such differences as these—different in nature from those discussed above—will be considered in the following chapters; but need not trouble us greatly in getting a start. Our first business is to gain the ability to carry into speech-making, more or less public, the mental conditions of good private conversation.

COMMON MISCONCEPTIONS. Before entering upon further consideration of those mental conditions, we may be able to reach a better understanding by dealing with certain misconceptions that often arise at this point.

First, it is not true that a public speech to be conversational need sound like conversation, certainly not like ordinary conversation. Conventional differences may make it sound very different. However, conversation has many different sounds. Much depends upon the hearer, the situation, the subject, and the speaker.

The same man in discussing the weather, politics, literature, religion, may have several different manners. He may be listless while speaking of your hobby, but while talking of his own impassioned. The diction of the commonest man tends to become elevated when he speaks of elevated subjects, even in private conversation. We should note, also, the possibility of getting a distorted conception of the style of a speaker like Webster because most of us read only isolated passages, and the lofty strain of an impassioned peroration may be very different from the body of the speech. Each part is fitted to its place. Nearly all have read Webster's apostrophe to the flag at the conclusion of the Reply to Hayne (the passage beginning, "When my eyes shall be turned to behold for the last time the sun in heaven"); few have read the whole of that four-hour address. Thousands have read Webster's terrible description of the murder of Joseph White for one who has read the whole of that masterly summation speech in the trial of the murderer. The parallel passages below will show how different the same speaker, within the same half hour, dealing with the same set of facts, can sound according to the nature of his purposes. In the first Webster is impressing upon the jury the cruel nature of the crime in order to wipe out any sympathy for the prisoner the defendant's attorney might have created in his closing speech; in the second passage Webster is stating the facts indicated by the evidence as simply as possible in order to prove a conspiracy.

The deed was executed with a degree of self-possession and steadiness equal to the wickedness with which it was planned. The circumstances now clearly in evidence spread out the whole scene before us. Deep sleep had fallen on the destined victim and on all beneath his roof. A healthful old man to whom sleep was sweet, the first sound slumbers of the night held him in their soft but strong embrace. The assassin enters through the window already prepared, into an unoccupied apartment. With noiseless foot he paces the lonely hall, half lighted by the moon; he winds up the ascent of the

Let me ask your attention, then, to the appearances on the morning after the murder, which have a tendency to show that it was done in pursuance of a preconcerted plan of operation. What are they? A man was found murdered in his bed. No stranger had done the deed, no one unacquainted with the house had done it. It was apparent that somebody within had opened, and that somebody without had entered. There had obviously and certainly been concert and coöperation. The inmates of the house were not alarmed when the murder was perpetrated. The assassin had entered without any riot or any violence. He had found stairs, and reaches the door of the chamber. Of this he moves the lock by soft and continued pressure, till it turns on its hinges without noise; and he enters and beholds his victim before him. The room is uncommonly open to the admission of light. The face of the innocent sleeper is turned from the murderer, and the beams of the moon, resting on the gray locks of his aged temple, show him where to strike. The fatal blow is given! and the victim passes, without a struggle or a motion, from the repose of sleep to the repose of death. . . . The deed is done. He retreats, retraces his steps to the window, passes out through it as he came in, and escapes.

the way prepared before him. The house had been previously opened. The window was unbarred from within and its fastening unscrewed. There was a lock on the door of the chamber in which Mr. White slept, but the key was gone. It had been taken away and secreted. The footsteps of the murderer were visible outdoors, tending away from the window. The plank by which he had entered the window still remained. The road he pursued had thus been prepared before him. The victim was slain and the murderer had escaped. On the face of the circumstances it was apparent, therefore, that it was a premeditated, concerted murder; that there had been a conspiracy to commit it.

The second passage above makes it easier to understand the assertion of one of Webster's contemporaries that Webster talked to a jury as if he were a thirteenth juror who had just stepped out in front in order to address them better. Again we must remember that the conversational style of Webster—of whom Carlyle wrote, "No man was ever so great as Daniel Webster looked," and who made the British laborer exclaim, "By Jove, there goes a king"—that the conversation of such a man would not sound like that of more commonplace people. Henry Jones Ford says of

Woodrow Wilson that even in conversation "his thoughts came with their clothes on." [1]   An acquaintance has told me that he was amazed by Roscoe Conkling's ability to pour out impromptu a lofty diction in the Senate or on the stump, until he knew Conkling personally and found that he never let down in his vocabulary.   The grand style was his natural language.

Secondly, when it is said that speeches should be enlarged conversation, do not understand that the suggestion is that they should not be dignified, or strong, or eloquent.   In particular, there is no suggestion that speeches should be delivered in a low, weak tone, or in a careless manner, or couched in other than good English.   Give to your thoughts fitting expression; to plain thoughts plain expression, to heightened thoughts heightened expression.   But dignity, strength, and language have no necessary connection with our present problem.   What I am now urging is that, whatever else you do, you should make your speech communication.   Do not look upon your speech as a performance, but as a genuine dealing with men.

What has been said should make it clear that I am not here advocating any particular *style* of delivery.   One may believe that the so-called "conversational style"—that is, the style which in tone and composition is as near actual conversation as may well be in speech-making—is better adapted to this age than the more sonorous style rather common a hundred years ago; or may take a middle ground on that proposition.   But all that may be left out of our present consideration.   Wendell Phillips, the famous anti-slavery orator, is the most noted exemplar of the conversational style.   Of his speaking, his contemporary George William Curtis said, "It was simply colloquy—a gentleman convers-

[1] H. J. Ford, *Woodrow Wilson, The Man and His Works*, p. 281.

ing." But William Jennings Bryan, the most famous orator of recent years, had slight suggestion of conversation in his style. His constructions were not those of conversation and his delivery had pronounced oratorical cadences. Yet it would be rash to say that either one of these powerful speakers more than the other made his speeches communicative, made his hearers feel that he had business with them. The important matter for us just now is *not conversational style but conversational quality*. So please note that we are not talking in this chapter of "conversational style" or "mode." This may go with conversational quality; but a speaker may have either without the other.

Styles may come and go; but there is no good speaking without this conversational quality. It is true we may be glad to listen to a few men whether they talk with us or not; we should be happy to eavesdrop their soliloquies; but that fact does not make them good speakers. Wendell Phillips, Daniel Webster, Demosthenes, and all speakers great and small, in all ages, have had this communicative quality when they have genuinely spoken, in spite of the fact that some may have sounded like men conversing and some may have intoned. Even the same speaker may vary greatly in style on different occasions, or even in a single speech. I cannot represent here the delivery of a speaker, but we can judge pretty well from the written record.[2]

Another misconception is involved in the easy advice, "Just be natural." This advice is plausible but hardly helpful. What does this advice, constantly used to signify all that is good, really mean? The savage is nearer to nature than the civilized man, yet he is hardly a model. Indeed,

[2] Besides the excerpts from Webster above, read the oration on Daniel O'Connell in *Speeches and Lectures* by Wendell Phillips, Second Series; especially pp. 406-413.

there is much pith in a student's saying that it is easy, following this advice, to "make monkeys of ourselves." The child is more natural than the adult. As Henry Ward Beecher says, if nature were the ideal we should remain infants. It is natural to be bad as well as to be good. It is natural for some to stammer, for others to strut, for others to be afraid of audiences. Indeed, is it not natural for some to be affected? At least affectation comes without effort. It is natural for many to be unnatural on the platform. The advocates of "Be natural" as an all sufficient guide are quite as likely as any to strut and bellow.

It is manifest that we are juggling with various meanings of the word *natural*. It may mean (1) in a state of nature, untrained; (2) unaffected, sincere, not artificial, not exaggerated; or (3) in accordance with nature's laws, normal. The word as generally used is too loose for our purpose. If it is good to be natural in the first sense, then all education must be wrong. We wish to develop nature and remove defects in speaking, as in all else. Too often the plea of naturalness is made as a defense for faults. If your mannerisms are objectionable to your hearers or decrease your effectiveness, they should be remedied if possible, whether "natural" or acquired.

Suppose a speaker is indistinct: this indistinctness may be due to over rapid utterance, to a defect in the vocal organs or in his mental make-up, to lack of proper early training, or to sheer laziness. One may call the cause natural, if one likes; but should the defense, "It is natural for me to speak that way," be accepted if improvement is possible? If a boy needs an operation to make his leg normal, shall we stop to ask if the defect is due to accident or came by "nature"?

Without attempting to draw any sharp line of distinction, we may safely say that much that is defended as natural is merely acquired habit. A speaker may say, "It is natural for me to look most of the time to the right"; but the truth is he has acquired a habitual "stance" that makes looking to the right more comfortable. The plea "It's natural" is commonly an excuse prompted by the natural reluctance to change a habit and improve one's self.

Taking the second meaning of natural (unaffected, sincere), we shall find that while good, it does not go far and is difficult of application for a beginner. Most feel embarrassment; and an embarrassed beginner may unconsciously put on many airs, including the worst of all, an air of indifference assumed to cover nervousness. No mere *don't* will help much; the cure is practice while keeping in mind a normal view of speech-making, as we are trying to do in this chapter.

To find out something of the significance of *natural* will be a large part of our business in this book; and immediately as applied to delivery. However odd the phrase may sound we do need sometimes to learn how to be natural. We need now to learn how to act in accordance with nature and to develop habits that will hold us to the normal under the stress of the platform. Let us look more closely into the nature of conversational speech, in order to learn what we have to develop and adapt to public delivery.

CONVERSATIONAL DELIVERY ANALYZED. Let us turn to a common experience. Why is it that a small boy in school reads "See—the—horse—on—the—hill" without a trace of meaning in his tone, and yet five minutes later on the playground shouts the same words to his playmates with perfect expression? And why is it that if the teacher insists that Johnnie read over his sentence and get its meaning before reading it aloud, he will read with far better expression? And why, if the teacher then asks him to stand facing his class and read or tell the story to them, does he read with really good expression? The reason for his first improvement is apparent: in his first reading all his mind is given to recognizing words as words. They are without content for him; they bring no meaning, no picture to his mind. His expressionless voice is a true index of his impressionless mind; or rather, to be strict, his high, strained tone expresses truly the anxious strain of his attention to the symbols before him. When he grasps the meaning, expression comes into his voice. He not only understands, but if he has a marked success, he has more than bare understanding: the objects and incidents of which he reads are present to his imagination. The horse is to him a real and significant object at the instant he speaks the words. He has approached the conditions of his playground conversation. He is "thinking on his feet"; *he creates, or re-creates, the thought at the moment of delivery.*

But our small boy is still more successful in his reading when he is made to feel that he is reading or telling his story to his classmates. To throw the statement into a phrase we shall make much use of, the boy succeeds when he reads or speaks with a sense of communication. On the playground he has the most perfect expression of all, when with no thought of how he says things, he uses perfect tone, emphasis, and inflection. Still the advice, "Forget your delivery," will be of little aid to the embarrassed beginner. We can forget only by turning our attention to something else. Forget embarrassment then by holding your mind to your subject matter and your business with your audience. Hold firmly to the conception that you are there to interest them, not in your speaking, but in your ideas; to convince or persuade them. Look for their response. Stand behind your speech, and embarrassment will disappear. As soon as you can carry out these injunctions, whatever your faults, you will be a speaker. Until you can, whatever your virtues, you are not a speaker.

WHAT TO DO. To summarize, then, you will have carried over into your public delivery the most desirable qualities of conversational speaking when you maintain upon the platform—

(1) *Full realization of the content of your words as you utter them,* and

(2) *A lively sense of communication.*

When the first element is lacking we may characterize the delivery as *absent-minded;* when the second is lacking we may describe the delivery as *soliloquizing, indirect,* or *not communicative.*

Put so simply these directions may strike some as needless. They may ask, "Do not all sensible speakers think as they speak, and do they not realize that they speak to communicate?" These natural questions must be answered in the negative. Absent-minded speaking and soliloquizing speaking are very common.

REALIZATION OF MEANING. Mind you, no half grasp will do; there should be full and sharp realization of content. And this includes more than bare meaning; the implications and emotional content must also be realized. The reference here is not merely to those striking emotions commonly recognized as such, but also to those attitudes and significances constantly present in lively discourse: the greater or less importance of this or that statement, the fact that this is an assertion and this a concession (with an implied "granted" or "to be sure"), this is a matter of course while this has an element of surprise, and so on through all possible changes. Context and situation color statements. *It is now ten o'clock*

may mean just that and no more; but if there has been a
threat that some dire event would take place before ten, then
the sentence may be filled with relief; or if a man has promised that if he accepts your proposition he will appear before
ten, then the words may express disappointment. The full
significance should be in mind as one speaks. Realization of
meaning is not the same as knowing one's subject thoroughly,
desirable as that is. One may know his subject and yet
speak with a blank mind. (This topic is developed further
in Chapter XX.)

SENSE OF COMMUNICATION. To fail of contact is a fault
very common indeed. Young speakers too often look upon
public speaking as an exhibition; and older speakers frequently fall into a perfunctory manner, especially those who
speak frequently and in a routine way. Moreover, many of
those who do in a measure fulfil the conversational conditions suffer from a wrong start. The man who begins his
career as a speaker because he "has something to say which
he wishes very much to say," and continues for the same
reason until his habits are fixed, and who has no false notions
of speaking, may come naturally to a genuine delivery. But
if a speaker begins with the notion that he speaks to make
an exhibition of his delivery, or that delivery is an external,
mechanical thing to be manipulated according to rule, or in
imitation of a model, he will probably develop a conventional tone and other bad habits that will resist the force of
even a strongly felt message and an eager audience. Unfortunately, many of us have made a wrong beginning with
our reading and speaking, and have the habit of perfunctory
delivery. We began to read with all our attention on pronunciation, and to "speak pieces" we did not understand, in
order to make admiring aunts and jealous neighbors say,

"How splendid! I heard every word!" when our delivery was really an abomination, neither song nor speech.

The distinction between communicative and non-communicative speaking is easier to feel than to put into words. We hear a speaker, we perhaps follow his thought, yet we do not feel he has business with us; we are "listening in" while he talks to himself. If he asks questions we do not feel provoked to reply even mentally. We are not participants but idle spectators. There is no challenge to our attention. With another speaker we feel contact.

While we *may* follow from a real desire to get his ideas a speaker whose delivery lacks communicative quality, such attention is more tiring than it should be, and can hardly be expected from the average audience. The thought may be worthy, the language fitting, the delivery otherwise good, the voice clear, pleasing, and well modulated; and yet lacking communicative quality the speaking does not reach and grip. It may be the speaker is thinking intently, but as he lacks touch with his audience, his speech is only soliloquy. We say of another speaker, "He talks over our heads"; and this points to more than character of thought or vocabulary. The speaker may literally talk and look over our heads; or, though his eyes are turned toward us, he may be practically unconscious of our presence. Some advance from soliloquy to monologue and talk at us, or thunder at us.

But true speech is a dialogue; better even than talking *to* us is talking *with* us. It is conversation with an audience. The audience is conceived of by the speaker as responding, asking questions, approving and disapproving. He dwells on an idea till he is sure of the response. He never follows his own train of thought to the ignoring of the thoughts of his hearers. This conception brings into the speaker's voice the tone we call *communicative*.

While it is difficult to tell just what this sense of communication is, since it must be experienced before it is really understood; on the other hand it is no mystery, for it is experienced every time we join in alert conversation. I have used the word *sense* because it is not something we *think about* while speaking; rather we *feel* we are in touch, we have contact, we and our hearers are in communication.

We should make sure in our efforts to bring this communicative tone into our delivery that it springs from mental attitude; for it, no more than other tones, should be assumed as a trick of delivery. The attempt to assume it is likely to result in an over familiar, confidential, or wheedling note which is most objectionable.

As you rise to speak try to keep uppermost in mind what you have to say, try to tell it to your hearers so that they will listen and think. (It is obvious that the more interesting your speech and the better your grasp of it, the easier it will be to carry out these suggestions.) Look for your hearer's reactions. When you have finished, ask yourself, Was I really talking with them, or just talking?

It takes self-control to speak straight to an audience. This is not because of embarrassment merely, but because of the necessity of commanding and directing the thoughts of many. There are times when the speaker feels that it is his will against the combined wills of his hearers. The point was well put by a former student who, from being a rather weak speaker in college developed a direct and effective style while preaching to Western cowboys: "I tell you, when your congregation may jump out of a window or dance in the aisle if you lose control, you have to *grip* them!" If the speaker weakens and retires within himself, he quickly loses control and a restless inattention ensues almost as distressing as these "wild and woolly" extremes. Sometimes the inertia of an audience is still harder to overcome.

We should emphasize in connection with directness, the *effect of the eye*, which is quite as important as the voice in maintaining contact. The speaker should look at his hearers squarely. No dodging will do; no looking just over their heads, or down the aisle, or at a friendly post. The speaker who meets the eyes of his hearers—not merely looks toward them but definitely sees them—will rarely see their eyes turn away from him and he will rarely lose contact. But the temptation is often strong upon the young speaker to turn away; not merely because of nervousness, but also because the necessity of thinking tempts him to drop his eyes to the floor, or raise them to the ceiling. But the time for meditation has passed; his facts, arguments, and conclusions should be clearly arranged in his mind. His thinking now should be of that objective sort that is best stimulated by contact with his audience. Of course a speaker who has had no opportunity to prepare has some excuse if he fails to follow this suggestion, and one dependent upon notes cannot fully; but the loss of force is readily noted.

While a speaker should avoid a constantly shifting gaze, he should neglect no part of his audience. The part directly in front should receive most attention. Many speakers develop a bad habit of addressing one side of an audience nearly all the time, with but glances at the other. The neglected side soon grows restless. Do not let an habitual posture cause you to neglect any part of your audience. Make all feel that you are talking with them. "I wonder," said a freshman, "why Prexy preaches all his sermons at me." "Why," replied his friend who sat on the other side of the chapel, "I thought Prex. aimed them all at me!" It must not be inferred from the above that a speaker should stride forward with a fierce gaze and an I-am-going-to-make-you-listen air, or fall into a gunman's crouch. It must be strength with ease and self-confidence with respect for others —"a gentleman conversing."

RESTRAINT AND HALF-DIRECTNESS. Many beginners speak in a half direct way. They are not entirely lacking in the sense of communication; but they do not come out of themselves and vigorously take command of their hearers' attention. Sometimes they defend themselves against criticism by declaring that they do not like noisy, demonstrative speaking, thus showing that they mistake the critic's point. It is true that one may be effective without noisiness. There is a quiet directness which is highly effective; but we should not, as some do, make mere quietness an end in itself. A quiet delivery which fails to hold attention is certainly not desirable. We wish always to have our words listened to and accepted, and usually there is needed a display of frank earnestness. Quiet force is good; but be sure there is force, not indifference. Self-restraint is not the same as self-control; freedom is consistent with dignity. Act like one with business to transact.

The beginner, moreover, is rarely able to command the quieter force. He gets on much faster if he throws off restraint. As a result he may speak with unnecessary loudness and exaggerated action; but if he will keep trying to communicate and impress his ideas, he will soon acquire the feeling of direct contact with an audience, and will find that he can preserve this as he tones down to a more composed manner.

THE CONVERSATIONAL ELEMENTS IN VARIOUS FORMS OF DELIVERY: *In reading aloud.* Perhaps it is more common to read than to speak absent-mindedly and indirectly. The minister, for example, reading hymn or scripture lesson, with his mind on his sermon, or on who has come to church, may proceed with but the vaguest consciousness of the meaning of what he reads and with no feeling that he is reading to answering minds. He may pronounce the words in a sonorous ministerial tone. And his congregation? How rarely do they really listen! If indifferent, they think of business or fashions; if devout, they piously feel it is all good and true and are affected by the sound regardless of the sense, like the old lady who always wept when she heard "that blessed word, *Mesopotamia!*" Whenever a speaker in court or on the platform begins to read a quotation, the audience is likely to suspend listening until the speaker explains the meaning of what he has read. But one who reads with mind intent on meaning and with a sense of communication can read so as to command attention.

*In speaking from manuscript.* As in reading the words of another, so in speaking with manuscript in hand one is liable to fall into the mere pronunciation of words, because it is so easy for him to do so. He can get along after a fashion without thinking at all, for nothing is easier than to recognize and pronounce words without consciousness of their meaning. Yet there are times, especially in those cases in which an accurate and well balanced statement is particularly important, when reading is the only practicable method. And speaking from manuscript can be lively and communicative if the speaker exerts himself to think and keep in touch with his audience. He is helped in this by becoming very familiar with his manuscript so that he can frequently lift his eyes from his paper.

*In speaking from memory.* The reading speaker is not popular, but by no means all readers carry manuscripts to the platform. The speaker who memorizes should succeed better than the speaker with manuscript; for he can better keep in touch with his audience.  As compared with the extemporaneous speaker, he is freed from the harassing necessity of choosing ideas and words from the many offering themselves, and from the necessity of determining order.  He can, therefore, give all his mind to presenting his thought to his audience.  Probably, much as we admire the ability to speak extempore and necessary as it is to the well equipped speaker, a large proportion of the great speeches have been delivered memoriter.  But too often one who delivers a memorized speech really only reads and reads badly, from a manuscript before his "mind's eye," giving all his mind to recalling the words.

Some declare that a speech committed to memory cannot be delivered with spontaneity.  So in Ian Hay Beith's *First Hundred Thousand* we read of a soldier up before his captain for misconduct: "Corporal Mather clears his throat, and assuming the wooden expression and fish-like gaze common to all public speakers who have learned their orations by heart, begins. . . ."  But this sweeping statement is by no means justified.  Thomas Wentworth Higginson tells us that Wendell Phillips usually spoke extempore, but adds:

I remember that after his Phi Beta Kappa oration, in which he had so carried away a conservative and critical audience that they found themselves applauding tyrannicide before they knew it, I said to him, "This could not have been written out beforehand," and he said, "It is already in type at the *Advertiser* office." I could not have believed it.[3]

Whitefield, one of the most effective of English preachers, declared that he was at his best the fortieth time he delivered a sermon.  The lecturers of the lyceum and Chau-

[3] *Hints on Writing and Speech-Making*, p. 62.  Permission of Longmans, Green & Company, New York.

tauqua platforms may repeat their addresses hundreds of times and yet deliver them with freshness. Again, when weary or indifferent, the best of them may give you as little sense of personal contact as a phonograph. I have heard Mr. Bryan illustrate both of the preceding sentences. The book agent repeats his "spiel" in house after house, but if he keeps his mind alert and is keen about his business, he will not remind you that his talk was taught him by his company. Inveterate story-tellers repeat their stale yarns with gusto whenever they can corner a fresh hearer.

Nor can it be said that ability to deliver well a memorized speech is limited to a few. It is a matter of re-creating the ideas, and of keeping up a sense of communication. If one does keep these conversational conditions he will not have a "wooden expression and fish-like gaze," or a merely declamatory tone, for his mind will be active.

The method of memorizing is also important. In learning the words and in practice, as well as in final delivery, hold yourself to the thought and avoid the parrot-like repetition of words; and, further, do not learn in small bits, but fix the line of thought clearly in mind and learn in large sections. This will prove easier and will establish the connections firmly in mind. When memory fails it is nearly always at transitions. If you keep the thought uppermost the words will readily come to associate themselves with the ideas. No doubt it is harder for some to memorize than for others; but if you will follow these suggestions you will not be likely to enroll yourself among those who weakly say, "I cannot memorize." Experience with thousands of students indicates that, given the will, there are extremely few who cannot memorize well and deliver effectively.

And when you memorize, do it thoroughly, for if you are struggling for half memorized words you cannot think of anything else. It has been said of George William Curtis, one of the ablest speakers of the last half of the Nineteenth Century, that "he practised that perfect memorization which has the virtues of extemporization without its faults."

*In speaking extempore.* In this book the terms *extempore* and *extemporaneous* are applied, not to speeches without preparation, which we shall call *impromptu*, but to speeches that have been prepared but without being written out in full. But what is said of the extempore speech applies to the impromptu with still greater force.

Extempore speaking his its faults and its virtues; but it is to be noted here that not even this method is free from the faults under consideration. We must all know from observation that it is as possible to make an extempore speech without well controlled thinking as it is to converse without "knowing what we are talking about." Any experienced speaker knows how possible it is to talk on without knowing at the end of a period what he has been saying. Extraneous thoughts come—an engagement forgotten, the train to be caught, disturbances in the audience—yet the speaker talks on, probably forming grammatical sentences, but rambling and marking time. Again, the effort of thinking out a point not thoroughly mastered before, or consideration of a point now first presenting itself, may throw him into a reflective frame of mind; his thought loses the objective character needed. As a result he breaks contact with his audience and soliloquizes.

The extemporaneous speaker, therefore, needs quite as much as others a firmly fixed habit of always holding his mind firmly to the matter in hand and of speaking directly to his audience.

CONVERSATIONAL QUALITY NOT ALL OF GOOD DELIVERY. There is a tendency to assume at this point that when a speaker can "think on his feet" and maintain a sense of communication, then his delivery will be perfect, or "good enough." There is no good delivery without conversational quality, but many faults may exist along with it. It is plain that if one's conversation has defects, some of these may appear enlarged in his enlarged conversation. Faulty pronunciation, indistinct enunciation, nasal or provincial twang, throaty tones, lack of range or of agility of voice, are but examples of faults that may be transferred to the platform. A rational study of technique may be beneficial after the first success is won. A rational study of technique requires that the student shall never look upon technical matters as of first importance, though they are often very important indeed. I am only insisting in this chapter on putting first things first.

We were speaking in the last paragraph of faults of delivery. There are of course many other reasons why a speaker whose delivery is thoroughly conversational may yet be a poor speaker. He may have a weak vocabulary, or careless habits of thought and composition; he may lack information and ideas, or understanding of audiences; he may be deficient in imagination, earnestness, and strength; he may have an unpleasant personality.

It should be pointed out, however, that many of these faults tend to disappear when public speaking is thought of as a larger conversation. For example, one earnestly reaching out for the understanding of his audience will make more effort to be distinct than in ordinary conversation; and often effort is all that is needed. Nervousness may cause a speaker to use his voice badly; but it is clear that he is less liable to this fault when he looks upon public speech as a larger conversation, calling for a normal use of his voice, than if he assumes strange tones. If a speaker talks too rapidly—and no fault is more common with beginners—a direct attempt on his part to slow down often results in increase rather than decrease of rate. But if a speaker holds himself to a full realization of the content of his words, he will pause much of necessity; and if he is earnestly striving to talk with his audience, he will soon realize that an audience cannot be carried so rapidly as one listener. Deliberation will be the natural result. Again, if a speaker comes into intimate contact with his hearers, he is more likely to observe what manner of persons they are and adapt his message to their understanding, beliefs, and feelings.

The preceding discussion may serve to clear away some misconceptions and do something to establish a sound notion of speech-making; but the teaching can be fully grasped only by experience.

Much practice is needed. Habits need forming and re-forming. The student speaker can profitably practise much by himself, or with a competent adviser. The vanity of notable speakers may make them wish to conceal the fact that they practise; but many of them do, or have practised in their earlier days. There is no more reason for being shamefaced about practising speaking than about practising jumping; and no less reason for doing so if we wish to do well. We do both by nature; we can improve both.

But still more important is the actual making of speeches before whatever audiences are available; and this is especially important in the early stages of training in order to gain a "realizing sense" of the nature of speech-making. One who waits to learn a great deal about speaking before he begins to make speeches is not likely to learn much. We shall proceed presently to consideration of the preparation of speeches, but it will be assumed at this point that any student can prepare some sort of speech.

The first thing a beginner has to do is to accentuate the mental conditions of alert conversation. If the speaker succeeds in doing this he will succeed in giving expression to his ideas, more or less well. If at first he does not succeed very well, he must keep on trying. The chief remedy for failure to express is more thinking, a firmer, more complete grasp of the ideas, and more effort to talk with his hearers. He must not let mere words fill his mind. Words he must have, but they must remain subordinate to the thought. *He must establish the habit of speaking no phrase until its meaning is distinct in his mind.* And, as has been said and will become more clear as we proceed, the thinking indicated in this chapter is not a mere dry, cold process, but is to be taken broadly as including imagination and feeling.

Do NOT BE MECHANICAL. It will be seen that there is no place in our scheme for consciously and mechanically pausing, inflecting, and emphasizing, or determining what tone to use. To think of one's delivery in this way is to introduce a process quite foreign to normal expression, and to negative the whole teaching of this chapter. And it is, of course, quite unnecessary. The voice reflects the mind with remarkable fidelity. "Expression," says Cicero, "is always perfect." A clear thought is clear in expression, and a hazy thought is hazy in expression. Our voices respond promptly and instinctively to our changing thoughts, feelings, and moods, and to the varying situations in which we find ourselves. As a rule we take no thought of emphasis, pause, inflection, and tone; yet the expression comes true. When we do take thought of it, it is most often not to express ourselves better, but to conceal indifference, eagerness, dislike, fear, or other mood. Wrong emphasis is due to failure at the moment to discriminate values; wrong pausing is due to failure to distinguish the units of thought; the wrong tone is prompted by the wrong feeling. The remedy is complete thinking and sincere feeling. "But how can I deliver that sentence correctly," protested a student, "unless I know which words are emphatic?" The answer was pat: "How did you ask that question with so much meaning and feeling?" Why should not the response of voice be as true in public as in private speech, provided we can maintain upon the platform conversational mental conditions?

And, of course, you do not need to imitate the delivery of another speaker. Not only is this quite unnecessary; it is a positive evil. First, because it, like other mechanical methods, takes the mind off content and interferes with the sense of communication; and, secondly, because imitation too often leads to a style of delivery unfitted to the imitator. It is the usual fate of the imitator to catch the mannerism and miss the spirit. If a person with an awkward walk tries to imitate the gait of the most graceful walker he knows, he will probably produce an amusing caricature. He should try to improve his own walk. In doing this he may need to study walking in order to find out what produces and what interferes with ease; and in this he can find help in considering the poise and mental and muscular conditions of good walkers; but that is very different from imitation. Or, shall we say, he should imitate qualities, not manner and style. Fight against it as we may, there is nothing better for any one of us than his own individuality developed and improved. Most of us give this doctrine lip service; yet many in this matter of delivery demand that some one "show them how." And I have often discovered that a beginner speaking in some absurd manner, either pompous or affectedly careless, was trying to imitate some admired speaker.

In saying this about mechanical methods I am not saying they have no place in the training of a speaker. After a speaker has gained a considerable ability in thinking on his feet and in talking with an audience, certain mechanical defects may be treated by mechanical methods. Then the fact that we may not in conversation use a wide range of voice and tone color may make certain vocal exercises desirable. The wise teacher may at times make good use of imitation. When and how much such methods should be used is so dependent upon the needs of the individual student that I leave the matter to his teacher. In a later chapter I shall go as far into the technique of delivery as I deem prudent in print.

It should be noted that in the development of range and power of expression, to which reference has just been made, we should not depend upon pure mechanics. The better part of such training comes from expressing a wide variety of ideas and sentiments, using both our own productions and those of others which we have assimilated. In such practice we should always seek the right expression by means of a firm grasp of content and the effort to communicate directly to auditors, real or imaginary. (An imagined audience is very patient and helpful for practice purposes.) As a result, we shall find the response of voice to mind growing more prompt, certain, and satisfying. And since, on the other hand, the effort to express develops that which we seek to express, we shall find in such practice that harmonious development of thought, feeling, and voice which is the truest vocal training. To this may be added the physical training of breathing and other exercises for strengthening, purifying, and freeing the voice, or in any way bettering the response of voice and muscle to the mind. When mechanical methods are used they should be strictly subordinate; exercises should be treated as just that and should have no part in what we may call one's platform consciousness. When one is speaking to an audience he should very rarely indeed think of how his voice goes. He has other use for all his thinking power.

REGARDING NERVOUSNESS. I add a few words about nervousness, not because one need look upon making a simple speech as a trying ordeal, but because some beginners are as a matter of fact nervous. To a great extent this trouble disappears with practice; but relief will come sooner if one can look upon speaking to a group as the entirely normal act which it is. The assurance that one is well prepared is also a great help. I will add some excellent advice entitled,

### THE MOMENTS BEFORE TAKING THE PLATFORM [4]

"1. The plan of the speech is the strongest support that the speaker can find. Keep the plan in the foreground of consciousness and you will have a sense of control of your material.

"2. Have it in the back of your head that your task is only to tell your ideas to persons not very different from yourself.

"3. Deep breathing and erect, rather than slumped, posture tend to reduce nervousness.

"4. Don't expect to avoid all tension.

"5. In the first speeches at least, avoid last-minute changes either in plan or in details.

"6. The man who acts as if he were alert, at ease, and in control of his subject, will tend actually to be so."

I add another don't: Do not try to cover up nervousness by an affectation of indifference. The suggestion just above

[4] From *Manual for an Elementary Course*, by H. A. Wichelns, G. B. Muchmore, and others, p. 19.

of acting as if at ease is accompanied by suggestions of acting alert and like one having something to say.

If you can also see that your hearers are actually listening to what you have to say, initial nervousness will tend to disappear.

"Don't expect to avoid all tension." An experienced speaker may feel great tension (and nervousness too) on important occasions, just as one may be keyed up at the beginning of a game or of any undertaking that seems important, especially if several people are present. It is not even desirable that a speaker should be entirely free from tension. A phlegmatic speaker will awaken little response. But the tension I speak of is quite different from the mere stage fright we have been considering.

One meets a few cases of those whose nervousness in speaking is so great that expert treatment is needed, possibly the services of a psychiatrist; but for most the suggestions here given are sufficient.

GESTURE. This topic is close enough to the theme of this chapter to deserve brief mention here. Beginners often ask, "Shall we gesture?" Yes, by all means, if you mean by gesture genuine self-expression through action. The answer is no, if you mean formal, planned motions. Gesture, but do not *make* gestures. Let your gestures spring from the impulse common to all expression through action. Gesture from the beginning because (a) gesture is a useful means of expression, particularly in indicating those attitudes and significances beyond the bare meaning of words; and because (b) to gesture is instinctive, "natural" in the best sense of the word, and to yield to the impulse to gesture is a help in freeing one's self from nervousness (which is partly due to restraint), and in getting into a normal state of mind before an audience, and hence in thinking clearly and in becoming communicative. Repression of this natural instinct to express through action tends to produce lifeless, indirect speaking.

On the other hand, the effort to execute planned motions tends to increase self-consciousness and embarrassment. Whatever can be done profitably by more detailed, even mechanical work on gesture will be taken up in a later chapter; but it is not for the beginner. For him the first step is to fix in mind that gesture is a normal and useful means of expression, not a means of exhibition. The next is to get an understanding with his muscles that it is all right for them to take a part in expression, to do what they, in the absence of repression, would do as a matter of course. Then he must trust those muscles. They know more about gesture than he does.

But, perhaps, because of habitual repression, these muscles need encouragement. First, they should have the encouragement that comes from good bodily *poise*. Gesture is often checked by the restrained or the slouchy position in which one stands. To be poised is to stand easily erect, without limpness or rigidity and without waste of muscular effort. The chin is neither thrust forward nor drawn in, the chest is up, giving the sensation of being the center of activity, the hips thrust neither forward nor backward, the weight of the torso carried directly over the hips, and all resting chiefly upon the balls of the feet. The weight may be borne on both feet, or on one foot, but there should be no sagging in either hip. The feet should not ordinarily be held together, or on a line, nor yet far apart. Don't "spread yourself," or adopt the before-the-fireplace, or the soldier-at-attention stance. In an active, ready-for-business posture, it is possible to transfer weight from one foot to the other without effort; hence one is free to turn or step in any direction without "walking over one's self." And this freedom is of first-class importance to good action.

Though I have brought in poise as an aid to gesture, it is a direct aid to communication between speaker and hearer. It gives the speaker a feeling of alertness and wars against any tendency to retire within one's self. The attitude of a well poised speaker says to the audience, "I have business with you." So poise itself may be said to be an excellent gesture. Lack of poise is an unfortunate gesture, saying, "I am scared stiff," or, "I am scared and yielding to my fear," or, perhaps, "I don't care whether you listen or not, but rather hope you won't."

The beginner can further encourage himself in gesture, if he gets no results otherwise, by putting out one or both hands and at the same time speaking vigorously. Put them out, not a few timid inches, but with a full, free movement. Such free movements will tend strongly to result in expressive action. Put your hands out to the audience. Let the arm *swing from the shoulder*, not merely from the elbow; and let the action *reach to the finger tips*. Then, if you are in poise, with feet free, the *whole body* will join in the movement, though the "body sympathy" may be too slight to be noticeable. Awkwardness of gesture is due largely to restraint, which causes the pump-handle effect of arms moving independently of the body, angular elbow movements, doubling up of one or more fingers, repressed thumbs, and petty little movements which do not seem to take in the audience. Such restrained movements are far more likely to attract attention to themselves as mere motions than are easy, freely expanded movements.

Do not worry about where to gesture. If you are trying to express your ideas, the gestures—which are a means of expression and particularly of emphasis—will come naturally upon the more important points. The man who says his speech has no places for gesture is saying he has no points to make. He is probably under the delusion that gesture must picture something. Gesture can picture effectively, but we may well pass that aspect of the subject for the present.

To summarize, do not try at this stage to do particular things; but get into a bodily condition that makes action easy, a positive, well balanced attitude; speak vigorously and encourage yourself in full, free movement. And practise. Perhaps this will be all the instruction in gesture that you will need.

Just a few words for the objectors: First, there is the man who says, "I never gesture." He is fooling himself. Everybody gestures in one way or another. Gestures are not limited to hands and arms. Attitude is a gesture; a nod or the lift of an eyebrow may be very expressive. No doubt some gesture more than others; but all gesture. Students even while assuring me that they never do, have used excellent unconscious gestures. If you gesture little, it is because you do not freely express yourself, or because you consciously check this native tendency, or have in the past established the habit of repression. If you do not like to express your ideas, I see little present hope for you as a speaker; if you consciously repress, stop doing so; if you have the habit of repression, break it and get "back to normalcy."

For the beginner who objects to gesturing for fear of being absurd, there is this word: You cannot help gesturing. If you set yourself against it, your whole body will cry aloud, "I won't gesture!" If you slump into a posture that discourages gesture, your appearance will declare, "I am indifferent." Or your hands will show rebellion against repression by fussing with clothing, digging deep into pockets, fumbling with papers, or rubbing ears. How much better to gain at once the power to act like a purposeful, free, expressive, mature human being—all over. The chances of being "funny" are much worse for the speaker who represses himself.

Any tendency to overdo gesture is easily checked, but it is hard to do anything for the man who will not let himself go. And it is my experience that students of speaking rarely make much progress until they get into action and use every means of expression. The student who does this from the beginning soon outdistances those who yield to restraint.

In this chapter I have considered conversational quality chiefly as a matter of delivery, but it goes deeper than that. Much depends upon what ideas are expressed, much upon how they are put into words, and very much upon how they are related to the interests, understanding, beliefs, and sentiments of those addressed, considerations that will occupy a large part of this book. We shall turn now to the primary matter of subjects to talk about.

# CHAPTER III

## SELECTING A SUBJECT

Preparation of a speech involves considering its occasion, audience, and purpose, selecting a subject, gathering material, analyzing the material, planning the speech, and preparing it for delivery. To speak of these processes as distinct stages of preparation, to be attended to one at a time and in a certain order, is misleading, although we have to separate them somewhat in our treatment. There is no necessarily best order for our consideration, but since for a beginner the first problem is often, What shall I talk about? we will take up subjects first.

SEEK A SUBJECT. If a subject does not occur promptly, go after one. Little will be gained by asking one's self, What in the world can I talk about? or by waiting for a bright idea to come along.

*Seek a subject early.* A subject determined upon early will save both work and worry. Ideas and materials seem to come to one who has a topic fixed in mind; and while the subject of a speech is important, a pretty good subject in time is better than an ideal subject found too late for adequate preparation. It will be evident as we proceed that a speaker has sometimes to discuss topics in which he has little initial interest, and we shall consider how interest can be developed; but we shall see that the methods have little promise for one who grabs a topic at the last moment without time for gathering and assimilating ample materials.

*Mull over the possible subjects.* Failure to find a topic promptly is often due to running over the possibilities too rapidly. When you find a topic of even slight promise, dwell upon it. Let imagination play over its different aspects; think over the concrete facts and situations, the people and the principles involved in the solution of the question, the arguments and applications that can be made, the attitudes of your hearers toward the matter, what they know about it, and what they may wish to know.

Suppose you have studied Chinese civilization. You see an article headed "China Breaks with Her Past." But, perhaps you reflect, can a nation break with her past? How far is that possible? What characteristics of China are bound to persist under new conditions?

Perhaps this topic will emerge: Is communism consistent with Chinese character? Can you adapt this topic to your occasion and audience? Would it prove interesting?

Or take the triumphant proclamation often made to teachers, who are not supposed to know this truth: "Education is not all in books." Instead of letting it pass as an axiom, ask yourself, How much truth is there in that statement? What does it really mean? And what about it anyhow? What changes does it suggest?

With such treatment even dull-seeming subjects may sprout interesting possibilities. Less looking and more thinking is needed.

*Questions that may suggest topics.* A positive attack can be made on the problem of finding a subject by asking yourself certain general questions, of which the more important are:

Does the occasion suggest an appropriate theme?

What subject will best serve your purpose?

What are the interests of your audience?

Is there a topic your audience will be especially glad to have you discuss?

Is there a subject that especially interests you?

What are your hobbies?

Have you known any interesting characters?

Have you had any unique experiences?

Have you lived in a place of peculiar interest? Etc.

What is suggested by the affairs of your community? your town?   your college?

What is suggested by current events?

What can you draw from your studies?

Do you know some book, play, or poem that will give you a start?

*Questions that will aid in testing your topic:*

Will you be able to interest your hearers in this topic?

Will you be sufficiently interested to make a good presentation?

Is the topic suited to the occasion?

Will it serve your purpose?

Is there some reason of tact or policy why you are the wrong person to speak on this topic?

Can the topic be properly treated in the allotted time?

Should the topic be narrowed?

Can it be?

Is the topic suitable for oral presentation, under the circumstances?

*Does the occasion suggest an appropriate theme?*   There are times when the demand is simply for a speech; as often at a dinner, or when a teacher is asked to speak at a student club, and the chairman says, with seeming generosity, "Oh, we shall be glad to hear anything you care to say."   A student of speech-making who is to speak at a meeting of his class or speaking club cannot draw much inspiration from his occasion, except at those times when a special topic for the meeting is assigned, or a mock occasion is planned.

But outside of practice speaking the speaker's topic is often suggested, sometimes dictated, at least in a general way, by the occasion. The body to be addressed may have met to consider a certain problem, or for the celebration of a certain event. Often celebrations present a wide range of choice; and sometimes the usual themes have become very hackneyed, as those most common on Memorial Day or Lincoln's Birthday. Mere appropriateness, though often a major consideration, is not enough. A speaker can sometimes take a suggestion from the theme of the hour and apply it to another theme, as when at a Lincoln dinner a speaker pays tribute to certain of Lincoln's qualities and then raises the question, What would Lincoln, possessing such qualities as these, do about this problem of ours?

We should be chary, however, of wrenching an occasion too violently from its natural trend and disappointing the expectations of the audience. If people have gathered to honor a hero or an event, they may resent your failure to render due honor. The less keen and personal the feeling of your hearers toward the occasion, the more liberty they will allow in theme and treatment. Washington's Birthday has become merely a holiday; but we can hardly say the same of Lincoln's.

An audience may gather to hear a certain theme discussed, not merely because it is the theme of the hour, but more because of a desire to hear a certain speaker on that theme. One may have good reason for refusing to meet such a desire, but it is not lightly to be ignored.

*What are the interests of the audience?* If a Democratic

club invites a politician to speak during a campaign, he knows they expect something about candidates, issues, methods of carrying the election, or the prospects of victory. There is a presumption that an advertising club wishes talks on its specialty, or at least on business. But illustrating the fact that one cannot always go on such presumptions, there is a notable advertising club in New York that invites to its luncheons celebrities of all sorts, and it can hardly wish to hear about advertising from the aviator who has made the latest record for speed. Women's clubs do not wish to hear about women's problems all the time; rather they seem to be seeking enlightenment on all sorts of subjects. Students are seeking education, but experience shows that many educational problems do not interest them at all.

We should remember that, besides specialized interests, we have those of a sort deeper and more constant because they arise from common human experience, as the problems of marriage, religion, racial frictions, and human relations in general. So worn a problem as the relations of parents and children suggests many possibilities: How should we train our parents? How far should we accept their advice? To what extent should we sacrifice for their happiness? Mistakes in dealing with the old. A mistake I shall not make with my son. That hoary subject, How to succeed in life, disguised under many titles (as "Big Blunders," "What's to Hinder?" "Seven Keys to Success," "Acres of Diamonds") is the theme of many popular lectures and of a tremendous amount of writing.

*Is there a subject that especially interests you?* The self-centered person who assumes that what interests him will interest others is a too common figure, both in public and in private speaking. Equally common is the young speaker who assumes that his familiar interests cannot interest others;

or assuming that every one has had the same experiences as himself, never thinks of them as sources of themes. And not rarely one meets a student who declares he is interested in nothing. This startling statement must mean, nothing that will make a topic for a speech. However that may be, his best speeches will be made on topics close to his own interests; that is, out of what he has been doing, observing, reading, and thinking before his search for a subject began. There is no better promise of interest in a speech than the speaker's own interest. If you as speaker are interested, I as listener am hopeful of being interested; if you are not, why should I bother to listen? My interest in stamps is slight, but I have enjoyed hearing an enthusiastic philatelist talk on his hobby.

What are your hobbies? What do you get warmed up about in conversation? What will keep you arguing into the small hours? What subjects will catch your eye in paper or magazine? What studies will keep you working overtime?

Have any of your favorite institutions or beliefs been under attack of late? Is there any abuse, any mistaken notion, or any improvement you would like to express yourself on?

Have you known any interesting characters, lived in a place of peculiar interest, or had unique experiences? If not directly, perhaps through reading?

Sometimes objection is made that one is likely to seem conceited in talking about his own experiences. Plainly there are topics too personal for public discussion; but one should not let reticence bar all his genuine interests. After all, the impression of egotism lies largely in the treatment of a topic; and one may easily seem more egotistical in speaking on Manchuria than on My Experiences on a Southern Plantation.

Among the speeches that stick in memory out of the thousands I have heard is one on tips by a student who had been porter in a summer hotel, another by an ex-aviator telling how to sight objects to be bombed, another by a summer canvasser on the ethics of high-pressure salesmanship, a speech by a college golf champion on the art of putting, and one by a quarterback on inside football.

Many tell me their lives present nothing whatever of peculiar interest. Certainly one should not strain to make out a unique experience, and one should bear in mind that some experiences interesting to go through may not be susceptible of interesting description. Especially in a short talk a good deal of skill is required to work in those colorful details that make the hearer share one's experience. Nevertheless most of us have in our experiences the "makings" of good speeches. Or if an experience in itself seems insufficient it may serve as an illustration to light up some theme.

At the time when Tom Johnson was attracting wide attention by his novel measures as mayor of Cleveland, a student replied to my random questioning that he lived in that city. "What do you know of Tom Johnson?" I asked. "Oh, I know a lot about him; I'm related to his family." "Interesting man, is he not?" "I should think so!" "By the way, what about your 'Golden Rule' Chief of Police?" The student grinned. "Why, I never thought about those things. Got two or three subjects now." He was never again at a loss. When called on for an expository speech he, the best tennis player in the university, explained various serves.

Another, quite hopeless, chanced to remark that he had spent most of his winters in Charleston, South Carolina. Now what could be more interesting to a Northern audience than first-hand information about the life of that once belligerent city? He knew old Confederate majors and old plantation Negroes; his family from antebellum days had owned a plantation near the city, on which could be studied many of the South's problems. He knew the Southern view and the Northern view; yet he did not wish to talk about Southern problems, he said, because he did not know enough about them. He did not; but he had a splendid *foundation* for several interesting speeches.

*What subject will best serve your purposes?* I have been stressing interest in subjects because interest is always a primary concern, and because an interesting speech is a great help to a beginner; but we must note that speakers have other purposes, as informing and persuading. As has been said, *the speaker chooses an object rather than a subject,* and then he chooses a theme that will serve that object. A stump speaker, for example, has as his object the winning of votes; but he may choose any one of many topics to serve his purpose—farm relief, control of corporations, which party has the worst bosses, or economy. Even when a speaker's general theme is prescribed by the occasion, he still may make the theme serve his own purposes. Thus on Lincoln's Birthday, one may honor Lincoln's memory while using his authority to support a policy, or to condemn the party he helped to found. George William Curtis was able to grace with his oratory all sorts of conventional occasions, such as dedications, commencements, and the banquets of societies, and at the same time to preach effectively a high type of civic righteousness. Without a serious purpose occasional addresses are likely to be bombastic, dreary, or absurd. The Gettysburg Address is masterly in the way Lincoln makes his more evident and his more important purpose serve each other.

To determine definitely one's purpose may also determine what the theme should be.

*What is suggested by the affairs of your community?* The town or city government, local taxes, the streets, the schools, the town's history, its needs and possible development—any of these might suggest themes. Is a local election imminent? Is some notable visitor coming to town, and do you know, or can you learn, more than your audience knows about him? Or his coming may suggest certain themes apart from his personality. Say the visitor is famous for explorations of the South Polar region. Most of us have a vague notion that such work is very fine and heroic, but few could give an intelligent answer to the challenge: What good is it? A speaker of scientific turn of mind might try to answer.

For the college student talking to students *campus topics* have advantages, especially to begin on. Being, if well chosen, of first-hand interest to both speaker and hearer and also familiar topics of conversation, they help a beginner to escape a feeling of strangeness in facing his class. But it is a mistake to suppose that these topics can be well treated without labor. Too often a speech on a campus topic is no better than the speaker could have made impromptu; for, although he has some first-hand knowledge of his subject, he has only the superficial information that floats about the campus, often incorrect and already common property. But if a student will, by searching college publications, by talking with the well informed, and by analysis, gain better than the common knowledge and do straighter thinking than the student body is doing, he may make a speech that will command attention, even on a worn theme. He will not then exhibit that vice known as carrying coals to Newcastle.

A student wished to speak on the threadbare topic, Our Need of Dormitories. He was asked, "Why don't we have them? All agree we need them, and the University has funds which might be used." He began an investigation.

Publications offered little; so he went to the treasurer, who gave him the facts ascertained by a committee of the trustees. The student came back convinced that the trustees would not be justified in using the funds for dormitories, which would make but small financial return; and he made a speech worth hearing.

Here are some themes that have been used successfully: What is college for? General college course as a business training. Is it worth while for one looking forward to a business career to work his way through college? Is table-waiting a good way to earn money in college? Should one borrow to go through college? To what extent should a college assume responsibility for students? The four-year residence requirement. Should the coach direct the game? Delayed rushing for fraternities. The distinction between major and minor sports.

The usual faults of speeches on campus topics are more a matter of treatment than of topic; but since experience shows that such speeches do not furnish the greatest development after a start has been made and since it is best to use various kinds of topics, the use of campus topics may well be limited, once a class is well launched, to those instances in which there is promise of ideas and material well above the average.

There are subjects of especial interest to students which are not strictly campus topics. Genuine interest may develop over such topics as professional and amateur sport, betting on games, refusing to serve in the next war, the place of women in modern life, chaperones, the proper attitude toward money-making, questions arising from the drama and moving pictures, the new generation, and many another phase of modern life.

*What is suggested by current topics?* Here we are thinking of events in the larger world. Their advantages are so obvious that I prefer to comment on their limitations. In the first place, it is not safe to assume because an event has occupied much space in the newspapers of late that the majority of your hearers are interested. Do we all read about a great international conference, even we who think we are educated and intelligent? The event may be a good subject nevertheless, but the initial advantage is not so great as is often supposed. There is usually, however, a moderate advantage in the fact that most hearers have at least a headline knowledge of the event, know that it is important and appropriate for discussion, and perhaps feel they should be better informed.

In the second place, if the speaker is selecting his subject, as he should be doing when feasible, well in advance of his occasion, he must consider whether the newsy topic will still be interesting when he speaks, whether the measure will have been voted on, or the event past and practically forgotten. The speaker who chose "Who will win the election?" for a speech to be made two days after election, had yet to get his eyes open on speech-making. It is a rare topic that "holds the front page" for more than a week, and the nine days' wonder may soon be as "dead as last year's bird nest." In general one should avoid the more evanescent sort of news topics and use those of more enduring interest which now and then spring into prominence. Racial prejudice is an instance of a topic which may have its ups and downs as news, but because of its genuine importance a specific outbreak of such prejudice may suggest a good topic.

No one should choose a current topic (or any other) *unless he is willing to make himself better informed than any of his hearers is likely to be*. To be corrected by one's hearers is always painful; and this is peculiarly likely to happen with a current topic because it is current. No one should ever suppose that the reading of one article, or worse, a digest of articles and opinions, fits him to speak on a topic. He should "read up" thoroughly on the topic, if possible read into its background, and throw in a goodly amount of reflection on his own part.

And no one should seize upon a current topic—or any other for that matter—which does not genuinely interest him, simply because he thinks it "will do." Only if the topic connects with an established interest is it likely to prove good.

And this suggests what is probably the best use of current events as speech topics: Take them not so much as topics as suggestions for topics. Does the news item suggest a problem or a principle more important than itself? A document published to-day may have an important bearing upon the causes of the World War. Perhaps an item will associate itself with your interest in some question of politics, sociology, or science.

The following dispatch from London to American newspapers inspired Glenn Frank to write an interesting article, which needed only delivery to make it a good speech, on the Perils of Respectability:

When Charles Edward Bond, who began his career as a carpenter and joiner, applied to be ordained as a priest of the Church of England, there was a protest on the ground of his lowly origin from a section of the clergy.

Bond was summoned a short time ago before a committee of bishops for examination. When questioned about his former humble calling, Mr. Bond replied simply, "I believe there was once a carpenter—" and the examination ended there.

It is not, in general, the business of a speaker to tell the news of the day, though he may need to recapitulate facts on which to base his remarks.  Of course, if one has a personal relation to the events, as in case of an explorer telling of a recent expedition, or a member of the team telling How we won, we may gladly hear his story in detail.  We may also appreciate the service done by one who straightens out for us a confused set of facts scattered through the newspapers.

*What can you draw from your studies?*  There are, of course, no end of topics in economics, such as labor problems. Most of them are too large for short speeches, but they admit of subdivision.  Political science suggests numerous topics, such as City managers, Bossism inevitable? Tammany Hall, How far should democracy be carried?  Sociology is even more fruitful of topics, such as can be drawn from the problems of social welfare, philanthropy, prisons, eugenics; for example, Should we give to beggars?

History presents many characters of high interest, and many subjects that can be related to present-day interests. The enfranchisement of the Negro has a present-day bearing so obvious as to make interest easy.  Usually matters of purely historical interest should not be attempted unless the speaker sees a way to give the historical situation a degree of dramatic interest.  I recall a speech on the Battle of the Nile which was a distinct success.

The law, science, engineering, architecture, agriculture— in fact every field of study offers something if only one can recognize it and will keep in mind the interests and limitations of his hearers.  A law student, wishing to utilize his knowledge of contracts, found a point of contact with his audience, drawn from all colleges of his university, by speaking of rooming contracts.  One student gloomily said that his major was Latin, and no one could get a subject out of Latin. "But why," he was asked, "are you studying Latin in this age and place? Are you not ridiculed by your friends who are so wise and practical about engines and chemicals and soils?" He made a speech that held the attention of his class.

Unless a student, however, has done a good deal of work in a field, there is little hope that he will have got his bearings in it sufficiently to deal justly with a topic drawn from it. He will do much better with a theme from a study taken last year than from one just begun, however interesting. I regularly reject, for example, topics from the general subject of socialism when offered by those just taking up that large and confusing problem.

A special warning should be given against mere résumés of lectures or of certain pages in a book.

It is folly to attempt to "get across" in a brief speech what a teacher has taken an hour, or several hours, to explain. Attempts to do this produce the dreariest of speeches, bare, meaningless as a table of contents,—a remark that may be extended to all merely "boiled down" material. There is a condensation that improves, but it is not likely to be done by one who knows the material less well than the original author. Instead of merely condensing the matter of a lecture or an assigned reading, or reproducing with minor changes a detail of the course, the student speaker should treat his course as background. . . . Remember that several members of your class may have taken the same course, and a mere résumé or repetition will not appeal to them. You should make sure that you are better informed than your hearers; and the best way is to specialize on some topic touched upon but not much developed in the course in question. . . . Proceeding in this way you gain the very real advantage of a subject from such a source; that is, with your general knowledge of the subject you will not exhibit the rawness, uncertainty, and half-baked quality which are the usual marks of a speech on a subject merely "gotten up" for the occasion.[1]

It may be observed further that making a résumé is not very profitable training, since the search for and the analysis and arrangement of material is an important part of our work; and also that such a procedure does not meet the demand for an original speech.  (But originality will be considered in the next chapter.)

*Will some notable book, or a favorite play, novel, or poem give you a suggestion for a topic?*  Attempts at reviewing books or other pieces of literature usually prove futile in brief speeches; but one can often get a good theme out of a work of the sort that provokes independent thinking.  It is useless to attempt a list of such works here, but many are recommended to students in their various courses.

There are now several books put together with a view to stimulating thought on the part of students who have to produce speeches and essays.  Drummond and Hunt's *Persistent Questions in Public Discussion,* or its later and somewhat more popular form, Drummond and Wagner's *Problems and Opinions,* Blanks's *Essay Backgrounds,* and Taft, McDermott and Jansen's *Contemporary Thought* may be noted as good.  The first two named give helpful suggestions for deriving topics.

The chief moral of these remarks on finding subjects is that one need not wait for a subject to come to him.  Consider your occasion, your purpose, and your audience.  Look about you and look in yourself for topics.  It may be true that some of our best subjects seem just to occur to us, but they occur to us *as subjects* because we get into the habit of

[1] *A First Course in Public Speaking,* Winans and Hudson, p. 34.  Permission of the D. Appleton-Century Company.

looking for them and learn to recognize them when we see them; we develop what some one has called "the theme eye." There is no end of interesting subjects, just as the woods are full of interesting phenomena which only the naturalist sees.

Form the habit of jotting down subjects as they present themselves, along with any related facts and ideas that occur to you. This was the practice of the famous preacher Henry Ward Beecher, his son-in-law tells us; and it went far to explain the brilliance with which he could preach with seemingly slight preparation on almost any subject requested. A filing case of subjects and hints may be a life-saver.

TESTING THE SUBJECT. Assuming now that you have several subjects in mind as possibilities, we will proceed to certain tests of their availability.

Some of these tests need little or no discussion. As regards *suitability to occasion,* in addition to what has been said, we may consider congruity with the spirit of the occasion. To be sure, harmonizing is often more a matter of treatment than of subject; still when one undertakes to eulogize the leader of one faction at a meeting of a hostile faction, or starts an argument as to which faction is right at a harmony dinner, or takes up the tariff seriously or attempts to raise money for the suffering orphans of the Near East on some festive occasion, the vice is primarily in the theme. Again, I have more than once seen an audience intent on getting at the right of some political issue disappointed by discussion of trivialities or by mere buffoonery. There is merit in the old motto, "A place for everything and everything in its place."

*Will the topic serve your purpose?* In considering purpose the speaker may ask himself if there is any object to be served by discussing the topic under consideration before the prospective audience. Are my hearers already in hearty agreement that we should have an ice-making plant in the hockey rink? If so shall I gain anything by urging the need, or should I go forward and show a feasible plan for obtaining the plant? The student help at the Main Street Cafeteria should have a rebate on their meals, is a theme likely to cause the hearer to retort, Tell it to the manager.

There are, of course, many times when the audience is quite content to be interested. In particular, students in speaking classes need not take this test too seriously; yet even in such classes, since we wish our speaking to be as real as possible, it is well to give some thought to this test question. A writer in *The Nation* complains that speakers at Phi Beta Kappa dinners are always talking about the conscience and duty and responsibility of the scholar. Why, he asks, do they "exercise their great powers of moral persuasion upon the ninety and nine just men who need no repentance? . . . It is like talking to a life-saving crew about the importance of learning to swim." Don't describe the campus to the students who live on it; but a competent discussion of the architecture of one or more of its buildings might be interesting.

*Will your audience wish to hear this topic discussed by you?* It will be recognized that either in public or private, tact and good taste require us to avoid certain topics in certain places. Just as the man who has just given his family a piece of his mind will turn his wrath against a neighbor who says the same things, so we do not wish to hear a Harvard man speak on the shortcomings of our institution. Also we may resent advice, however good, from one whom we consider our inferior in standing or experience. The newcomer to a community may well keep his criticisms to himself. But apart from certain touchy questions, we are usually willing to hear almost any subject discussed by any one, provided he seems reasonably well qualified to treat it. One may well consider, however, if it is good policy for him to attempt before a body of experts to speak on their specialty. I have heard some painful efforts by college presidents in welcoming groups of specialists. Unless the president, or mayor, or whoever gives the address of welcome, is really well informed on the subject before the body addressed, he does well to confine himself to an expression of interest and welcome. Governor Alfred E. Smith, speaking at the semi-centennial of Cornell University, did not attempt a learned address; but made a happy speech in which he kept to felicitations and an assurance that the State of New York would continue its generous support of the state schools in the University.

In a class in speaking there is great freedom of choice, for all are to a great extent on a common footing. If your class learns that you are likely to be worth listening to, its members will welcome you on almost any topic. Yet even here the suitability of your topic for you is worthy of attention. An underclassman should be pretty sure of his qualifications before taking up taxation before upperclassmen who have majored in economics, and a young salesman should think twice before attacking a question of management before a speaking club including several experienced executives. But either, if he is sure he has something worth while to say, may go ahead.

There may be, however, as was suggested before, a topic on which you would be especially welcome as a speaker. A student who had been an aviator in the World War was listened to with rare interest and questioned at length. A similar experience may await the chairman of an important committee who tells of its work. When General Lord,

Director of the Budget at the time, told us of his efforts in Washington to save the people's money, many agreed with the business man who said, "It is a great satisfaction to hear a man talking of what he knows at first hand."

But do not feel hopeless because you can think of no unique qualification. You will be exceptional enough in your class or club if you reveal some mastery, though gained at second hand, of almost any subject you choose. A speech on the methods of chemists turned out well, although it would have been a poor topic for one who had not specialized in chemistry. A student who has studied biology sufficiently to be qualified to speak on the theory of evolution to-day will be listened to, if he makes a good presentation.

*Can the topic be treated properly in the allotted time?* Whether the time is arbitrarily limited or not, there is a length beyond which, for reasons of policy or because of a decent regard for the rights of others, a speech should not go. If a speaker is not allotted a limited time, he should determine his own limit, taking account of the whole situation, the nature of the occasion, the number of speakers, and his own part and importance in the scheme of things; and then he will do well to keep within the limit.

In a speaking class most speeches must be brief.

Now most topics can be treated briefly or at great length; but some suffer greatly in a brief discussion. Some require much preliminary explanation with a given audience, as a proposal for the relief of Western farmers before an audience in an Eastern city. Some proposals can be supported by one or two weighty arguments, but some require a large number of arguments. Attempts to speak briefly on Sino-Japanese relations will usually result in bare, unimpressive talk. Some topics depend for their effect upon a wealth of detail, as usually when the aim is to make the hearers realize a character or share in imagination an experience. Experiences as counselor in a boys' camp does not work out well as the topic of a five-minute speech.

Many bad speeches are due to a desire to tell all one knows on a subject. Again, subjects too broad are chosen sometimes because it is easier to run over a large topic, using merely general, superficial information, than to give a thoroughgoing treatment to one phase of it. Most of us could talk a while about prohibition or Russia without any preparation at all; but we might run out quickly on the Swedish system of liquor control, or the soviets and the kulaks. So we have many speeches in which many incidents are touched but none made vivid, many ideas and motives are mentioned but none pressed home.

There may be times when it is important to cover a broad subject in a short speech, but usually it is better to confine one's self to a part that can be well treated in the time allowed. There is a natural feeling that if one shows an evil he should bring forward a remedy; but what if he fails to establish either?

It is true, of course, that a topic may be too narrow for even a short speech. Lifting our hats to President Hopkins would serve better as an example in a speech on college manners than as a speech topic. But a hundred topics too broad are submitted for one too narrow.

As an example of what can be done in dividing a general topic into several more limited, take cheating in college work and notice some of its possibilities. What is "cribbing"? Does the presence of a proctor in a room justify cribbing? Does the fact that the student thinks the examination too hard? That he has been ill? That he has been on a team? That he is working his way through college? (Probably some of these would combine well into one speech as involving the same principles.) The pure honor system. The system with machinery for enforcement. Should students under an honor system be required to report cheating done by others? Should the honor system be extended to include reports and other work done outside of class? What is right and what is wrong when two students prepare reports together?

Or take the subject of socialism: One can limit it with regard to the period to be considered, as socialism to-day. One may limit as to place, as socialism in England. Or one may find so many brands of socialism in one time or place that it will seem best to limit the theme by the definition of one writer, as Marx, or of one school, as the Fabian, or by the platform of one party. But if one's speech is to be short, one may find that socialism of any time, place, or type has so many elements that he had better cut down to, say, ownership of the tools of production, or of natural resources, or to socialization of the coal mines. And with increasing knowledge he may prefer to go still further with subdivision.

If one wishes to speak on experiences as counselor in a boys' camp, he may choose a few characteristic incidents and these may prove more interesting and enlightening than the whole long story. So a few typical incidents from a man's life may give a better notion of his personality than all his biographical data.

The more we know about a subject the more we can narrow it. The fear expressed by many beginners, that if they narrow their subjects they will be unable to talk long enough, need not trouble one who knows his subject as he should. As a matter of fact, even the rawest beginners are with difficulty kept within time limits.

In trying to limit one's theme to meet the very real difficulty imposed by a small allowance of time when one wishes to speak on a large topic, one should give attention to the particular audience anticipated. What information has it already? What does it believe? Speaking to a group of people who were grown up in 1914 one might assume that they have some knowledge of the superficial facts of the World War. Speaking to a group of students who have studied the history of that war, one might assume that they know the facts better. Perhaps your audience, or a majority of it, is already convinced that the evil you are to deal with exists, and you can proceed with little or no argument to the remedy; or possibly if you can convince your hearers that there is an evil, the remedy will be obvious; or perhaps there is one argument that will draw others with it, or one motive that is all sufficient. If you wish to argue for an honor system of examinations and you know that most of your hearers would favor it were it not for the requirement of reporting cheating observed, you can narrow you theme to argument for that requirement; or, if your belief lies that way, you can argue for a system that does not include that requirement. These are very obvious suggestions, perhaps, but they are often overlooked, as by a speaker who persisted in arguing for prohibition before a prohibition convention, when what he should have done was to argue the method of prohibition.

*Is the topic suited for oral presentation, under the circumstances?* Subjects may be too intricate and difficult to put into speeches, especially into short speeches. Some philosophical and scientific subjects are not available before general audiences, though much depends upon the skill of the speaker, as is evinced by Huxley's lectures before working men. The differential of an automobile, without an actual model to exhibit, the fourth dimension, the gyroscope compass, the non-Euclidean geometry have not proved practical under classroom conditions. Much depends, of course, upon the preparation of your audience for hearing. Variations of swimming strokes can hardly be made clear to a general audience without an actual demonstration, but might be to a group of swimming instructors.

In considering your theme and its limitation, you have probably put down certain notes in regard to occasion, audience, and your plans for a speech. The work sheets, or cards, bearing these notes should be kept in a folder, or case, for reconsideration and additions at later stages of preparation.

# CHAPTER IV

## GATHERING MATERIALS

When one has settled upon a subject and has some notion of what he wishes to do with it, his immediate concern is with the materials, the stuff out of which his speech is to be woven. He must have ideas and data with which to hold attention and to make and impress his point. What apparently is not so obvious to all is that he needs a wealth of material to build up and sustain his own interest in his topic. These statements will have more meaning as we proceed through the discussion of interest; and everything we learn will impress the truth that nothing is more fundamental to the interested as well as the intelligent handling of a subject than ample knowledge well assimilated.

REVIEWING WHAT ONE HAS. Many of us who have come up through the schools have been sent so continually to books as the source of all knowledge, that we turn almost automatically toward the library when need arises. To go to the library is excellent, but it is not in most cases the first thing to do. The first question should not be the usual "What can I find on this subject?" but "What have I in store?" Or, as a student put it, the first thing to do is to "take an inventory." You may find you have more, or less, than you supposed. Anyhow find out what facts you have and what you think about them.

If you sit down and frown at a piece of paper, you are not likely to accomplish much. You must do something with such material as you can bring to mind. Look at it in as many ways as possible; ask yourself questions about it. Which facts seem to belong together? Which are related as cause and effect? Into what divisions do they fall? Which are major and which subordinate points? What different classes of interests or people are concerned? Suppose your general subject is Lincoln and you have not yet narrowed down to your particular theme. You think of Lincoln in various characters: as a boy on the frontier, as laborer, student, lawyer, politician, stump speaker, Congressman, President. You ask yourself how he became educated with such meager opportunities, the secret of his success as a lawyer, of his hold on the people, of his success in a terrible crisis. You may not be able to answer all these questions; but you are at least on the trail of some facts and ideas and have "got the subject on your mind." There is a good chance also that half-forgotten facts and ideas will come back to you, and that pertinent matter will present itself as you go about your affairs.

Furthermore, this stage of work makes for independence and originality of thought, for you start with ideas of your own. The late Senator Beveridge, himself an orator of power, declared, after urging comprehensive reading, "But, as you value your independence of mind—yes, even your vigor of mind—do not read other men's opinions upon the subject *before* you have clearly thought out your own conclusions." [1] It may be you will abandon every supposed fact, every opinion, every bit of analysis, as a result of further study; still you will not "swallow whole" what you read, but will use discrimination since you have something as a basis of comparison. You will also save time in the end; for

---

[1] Introduction to *Modern Eloquence* (1923), Vol. I, p. xxxiii. By permission of P. F. Collier & Son Corporation.

knowing what you lack and what some of the elements of the subject are, you can read to more purpose, looking for definite things rather than reading hit and miss—although, when time permits, just browsing around in one's subject is an excellent practice.

In this process of mulling over what you have, do not refuse a fair look at anything at all; the most futile seeming scrap of data may develop possibilities, or at least may suggest something of value.

You will find a mechanical device of great benefit in this work: write each idea on a separate slip of paper or a card. First, this serves to objectify your idea, to get it out where you can view it more as if it were another's. The very process of writing it down may show you its futility or make it bloom into a better idea. Expression both clarifies and develops. In the second place, this method is better than writing in a notebook, because of greater ease of arranging and rearranging until the fruitless ideas are rejected and the remainder brought into a system which shows their relations.

OBSERVATION AND INVESTIGATION. Whether the next step after self-examination should be reading or not depends upon the nature of one's subject; but, let us note, reading is not the only resource. Information gained at first hand is likely to be especially interesting to both speaker and hearer. Often, as in dealing with a campus or other local topic, one can gain this first-hand information by visiting a place spoken of, watching in shop or factory a process to be described, attending town-meeting, visiting a prison or other institution, or interviewing people concerned.

CONVERSATION. A form of investigation that deserves special notice is talking with those who know the facts. On any college campus there are men who have intimate knowledge of the history of the institution. They know how such and such a tradition grew up, what conditions made a certain regulation necessary; they know the ideals of the founders and how these have been adhered to or abandoned, and they know the heroes of the college. How could one get a better understanding of the background of the college's problems to-day than by talking with a man who has spent forty years on its campus? Before damning some policy of the athletic council, talk with some of its members. And the same things, in substance, can be said of municipal affairs. Or before making rash statements about changes that have taken place in manners and morals, talk with those who were adult before the War. Some things cannot be found in print, and some things in print need checking against the experience of those who have been through the mill.

But talk also with those not especially well informed, with several kinds of people. They are likely to suggest ideas, to show you what will need explaining, what objections are to be overcome, and in general what reactions to expect. Whatever you glean, the process of talking over your subject is likely to prove stimulating.

As a result of your investigations you are likely to have numerous new cards to add to your store of notes. It is well to keep these sorted into some sort of order, even though you have not reached a final analysis.

READING. If Richter said, "Never read until you have thought yourself empty," he added, "never write until you have read yourself full." Both statements may be rather extreme, but they are worth thinking about. After all, for many topics the principal source of accurate information and the best means of finding out what has been said and thought, what has been established and what exploded, is the printed word. And this is true although you can by no means believe all you find in print. And in spite of what has been

said above about those who rush at once to books, there are
many who neglect reading. One should strive to have individuality and originality; but it is folly to neglect the best
sources of information and ideas.

FINDING THE BOOKS. The efficient use of libraries is an
art that requires, for its adequate treatment, a volume written by an expert. Brief treatment of the subject will be
found in many textbooks.[2]

A few suggestions will be made here. If some of them
seem too elementary, the excuse is that many lack just such
elementary knowledge, a lack to be attributed, perhaps, to
the fact they most often go to the library to read books to
which they have been directed rather than to find materials
for themselves. Yet is there any one ability an educated
man should have more surely than the ability to utilize the
riches of books? Certainly the speaker needs this.

Make a beginning by going into the best library within
reach and browsing around, with the definite view of finding
out how to find the books you want. Acquaint yourself with
the methods of cataloguing. If the library publishes a
descriptive pamphlet, obtain a copy. Note the method, for
instance, of cataloguing books whose authors have compound
names, or titles of nobility, or have used pen names.

You are likely to find in the card catalogue of your library
that books are entered in two ways: under the author's
family name and under the subject; and that only a few
are entered under their titles. See if it is not true that under
a given subject heading the general, unclassified works are
placed first, alphabetized according to the author's names,
and that after these are placed, in distinct alphabetical lists,
books under various subheads. Give a few minutes to ob-

---

[2] Among others see *Public Speaking*, J. A. Winans, p. 369; or better,
*Argumentation*, Winans and Utterback, p. 262.

serving the use of guide cards; that is, the cards that stand up above the catalogue cards. On an author card, sometimes on the face, sometimes on the back, you will usually find the subject under which the book is classified; and this will aid you in finding other works on the same subject.

A reference librarian tells me that the chief cause of failure to find works on a given subject is the tendency to look in the catalogue under the single word the searcher has in mind as representing his subject. One might find nothing under Reformatories; but then he should turn to Prisons, and if he does not find that, keep on with other related words. And note the "see" and "see also" references. For example, under Penology you may find "See Prisons, Punishments, Reformatories." A certain library catalogue under Penology has twenty-four "see also" references, among which are Criminal Law, Pardon, Detectives, Insanity, Police power, William Shakespeare, and Suicide.

As regards periodicals, every student should be familar with *Poole's Index*, the *Cumulative Index*, and the *Reader's Guide*. There are also special indexes, as *The Dramatic Index*, *The Industrial Arts Index*. For finding articles in the newspapers we may turn to the yearly indexes published by the London *Times* and the *New York Times*. These may be used for other papers by taking the dates as clues.

There are many other works for helping one find out about legislation, investigations, committee reports, government activities in general, historical, biographical, and literary facts, and one does well to form an acquaintance with these time-savers.

The special cyclopedias, such as *The Encyclopedia of Social Sciences*, are likely to prove useful.

One of the quickest ways to find material is to ask an expert in the subject; or the reference librarian. He is there to serve you; but he cannot be expected to know everything, or to do your work for you.

WHAT TO READ. In ideal preparation a speaker should read everything available; in practice he should read as much as time and opportunity permit. Unless he already has a good general knowledge of the general subject from which his theme is drawn, he should do some general reading upon it, lest he present distorted views. For example, one could not speak justly about Lincoln the lawyer if he knew little of the rest of Lincoln's career. After some general reading the speaker should direct his reading to his particular subject.

Any book or article on your subject may be worth reading; if not for its information and arguments, at least for its viewpoints. But when there is a great mass of material at hand, it is usually wise to pick and choose. In any case, you will do well to read the better works first. How shall you know which are the better works? You may ask a specialist in the subject. From your searches through catalogues and indexes you will gain some impressions as to who are the important writers on the subject. From articles read you can gain some idea of the names which are generally respected. You can infer something of their standings by observing the character of the publications which accept their articles. Sometimes one can find a bibliography which attempts to evaluate the books and articles listed. You can learn from title pages and from *Who's Who* or *Who's Who in America* of the works produced and the positions held by your authors. You can judge from the date of publication whether a work represents the latest views—a matter of much more importance in some subjects than in others. None of this evidence is conclusive, but any of it may be helpful in determining whether a book is authoritative and what discounts to make. When in regard to such a remarkable history as that contained in

Prince's *Dissociation of Personality*, I ask a psychological friend if it is to be taken at face value, and am told, "Yes, so far as facts go," I know how to read the book. Of course, the final test of a book is the book itself; but the less versed one is in a subject the more one needs aid in selecting reading upon it.

In any case, do not be satisfied with reading a careless article, or with reading one article or book. Read enough to gain a comprehensive view of your subject, and to learn the various opinions held in regard to it. In particular, do not be satisfied with reading a mere digest of articles; the value of such digests for the speaker is largely in giving him suggestions and clues for further reading.

Do not in any case feel that you have necessarily wasted effort if you find later that you have gathered materials that you cannot use. It is worth while to discover that seemingly related matters are not pertinent; and as for matter which, though related, is not usable for your particular theme, you will always benefit by knowing your subject clear to the edges and beyond. The man who wishes to make the best trail through a forest will succeed best if he knows the whole region. Do not be content with a skimpy knowledge of your subject; usually you should be able to reject more material than you use.

How to read. In taking up a book, examine title page, preface, and introduction. These will enable you to understand the book better, because you will know better what the author has tried to do, the scope of the work, its point of view, and its limitations. You will be better able to decide, too, whether it is an impartial statement of facts, or a statement of facts manipulated to establish a thesis. Look at the table of contents to get the plan of the chapters; and look over the index, or the index volume if you are dealing with a set of books. Time spent in getting acquainted with a book will save time.

As for the actual reading, what better can be said than was said long ago by Bacon? "Read not to contradict and confute, nor to believe and take for granted, nor to find talk and discourse, but to weigh and consider." Read, that is, open-mindedly, not with awe of the printed page, not simply to find support for your own views, ignoring or rejecting all that refutes them, and not simply to find pat quotations or something to fill up with; but with mind alert for all the truth and with critical judgment. Read and think, and think more than you read. Compare what you read with what you already have in mind. Keep in mind as you read any special bias of the writer; for example, in reading *Macaulay's History of England*, remember that he wrote as a Whig.

Bacon continues: "Some books are to be tasted, others to be swallowed, and some few to be chewed and digested; that is, some books are to be read only in parts; others are to be read but not curiously [carefully]; and some few are to be read wholly, with diligence and attention." Ability to skim books wisely is needed by every reader; but it seems that students to-day are sent through so many books in haste, in the preparation of so many ill-digested papers, that there is danger that they will never gain the ability to master, or exhaust the possibilities of a page. "Beware of the man of one book," says a proverb, and like most proverbs this expresses a great half truth. The man of one book is likely to be narrow and to overlook the possibilities of the opposition; but his complete mastery of one view of a subject makes him a dangerous antagonist for the man of vague ideas and information. While a speaker should read rather widely that he may know all sides of his question, and thus be honest with himself and his audience, and also know what to expect from the opposition, he should "chew and digest" some of the best works on his subject.

TAKING NOTES. At times one may read just to soak himself full of a subject, and wish few notes; but most often he wastes time if he does not pin down what he reads. The ideas which seem perfectly clear as he reads grow hazy and slip from memory; the facts which he is sure he can remember, or turn to when he needs them, quite elude him. He may wish to use them a long time after his reading.

Some may prefer to read a book through before taking notes; others to take notes as they read. A good method is merely to jot down on a slip (do not mark the book unless it is your own!) the pages on which usable matter is to be found, and then make complete notes after finishing the book. As for the manner of taking notes, the following additional suggestions are offered:

1. Use cards of uniform size, the size you determine is best for your card index.

2. Place on a card matter relating to one sub-topic only.

3. Quote from the original source, if possible.

4. Always make an exact reference to the source at the time you make a note. You may wish to state this in answer to a challenge, or to return to the book for verification or additions.

5. Always quote exactly and mark quotations in the standard manner. Be careful to avoid any confusion of quoted matter and your own comments. If you summarize make the fact clear.

6. When you omit a passage indicate by dots, thus . . . .

7. If you supply words, put them in brackets, not parentheses.

8. Give each card clear headings, both main subject and sub-topic.

9. Put down the date of the publication from which you take a note—not the date on the title page, but the date of the copyright.

---

PERSUASION                            THEORY

James, *Psychology: Briefer Course*,[3] p. 452. (1892)
"We thus find that [Italics J's] *we reach the heart of our inquiry into volition when we ask by what process . . . the thought of any given action comes to prevail stably in the mind.*"

---

Do not imagine these suggestions are intended to make extra work; followed out they will save much time and labor.

As a conclusion to this topic I set down here the wise words of Phillips Brooks, one of the great preachers of the latter part of the Nineteenth Century. The application of them is by no means limited to preaching.

One preacher depends for his sermon on special reading. Each discourse is the result of work done in the week in which it is written. . . . Another preacher studies and thinks with far more industry, is always gathering truth into his mind, but it is not gathered with reference to the next sermon. It is truth for truth's sake, and for that largeness and ripeness and fulness of character

[3] Published by Henry Holt and Company, New York. Quotation by permission.

which alone can make him a strong preacher. Which is the better method? The latter, beyond all doubt. In the first place, the man of special preparation is always crude; he is always tempted to take up some half considered thought that strikes him in the hurry of his reading, and adopt it suddenly, and set it before his people, as if it were his true conviction. Many a minister's old sermons are scattered all over with ideas which he never held, but which held him for a week.[4]

This quotation bears, also, upon our next topic.

## ORIGINALITY

This topic, touched upon earlier in this chapter, needs further attention. The speech-maker is understood to be making an original speech, unless a statement is made to the contrary. What is the meaning of the term *original* as here used? A speaker criticized for merely boiling down an editorial, retorted, "What more can one do?" And it is often said, "You have to get it somewhere." It is certainly true that we cannot expect many brand-new ideas from ordinary mortals, and most of the facts in speeches have to be gleaned from the works of others; but would you tell a man that because he has gathered his materials from many sources, or has even torn down another house for materials, that he cannot build a new house, even a unique house?

No satisfactory definition of originality can be given, but one can arrive at a working conception. George P. Baker speaks of "the reaction of an individual mind on the material." [5] Esenwein puts the matter thus:

How does my mind work when it receives a new truth?
Does it enjoy the truth, and then give it out again unaltered,

---

[4] *Lectures on Preaching*, p. 157. Copyrighted by E. P. Dutton and Company, New York. By permission.
[5] *Forms of Public Discourse*, p. xix.

exactly or substantially in the same words? That is quotation, if credit is given to the author; otherwise it is literary theft.

Does my mind feel stimulated, upon receiving truth, to produce other thoughts, and yet utter the received thought without change? That is expansion.

Does my mind not only receive a stimulus from new truth, but also assimilate it, transform, clarify, and amplify it, so that in uttering that truth I utter it stamped with my own image and superscription? That is originality.

. . . An original thought is a new birth, the fruit of a union of truth from without and of thought from within.[6]

Originality may consist in finding a new phase of a subject, in working out a new analysis, or a new point of view; or in applying an old truth to a new situation. Each age must adapt old knowledge, the product of earlier ages' experience, to its new, or seemingly new, circumstances, and restate it in terms of the new day.

"A thought is his who puts new youth in it," says Lowell. Certainly we do not demand an absolutely new thought; for, as has been said, one absolutely new thought to a century is a high average. It is enough that an individual has really reacted to the old ideas. That is a high degree of originality when one has come to a clear realization of a truth as the result of experience, even though the truth was in his first copybook. The burnt child has an original idea when he first learns by experience that fire does burn. I recall a student who came in with a great desire to write on Compensation, a thought which had come to him from a certain experience and which he supposed really new. It was honestly original, though as old as the first thinker, and in spite

[6] From Esenwein's *How to Attract and Hold an Audience*, p. 51. Published by Noble and Noble, New York. Used by permission.

of the fact that the student had probably met the idea in
forgotten reading.

We admit a degree of originality, also, in one who gives
an old idea freshness of treatment and puts it in a superior
way.

> For we call a thing his in the long run,
> Who utters it clearest and best.[7]

Lincoln's famous "government of the people, by the people,
for the people" is simply the best statement of an idea that
had been expressed in somewhat similar terms many times.

Negatively, we may say that one who sits down to make
an abstract of an article or a chapter, taking out topic sentences and changing a few words, is not doing original work.
Nor is he though he does not use a single sentence from his
author, so long as he adopts the author's ideas and standpoint. To paraphrase may be a very good exercise, but it is
not meeting a requirement for an original speech. The case
is somewhat more hopeful when one reads two authorities,
compares them and writes a speech based upon both. But
we cannot establish any rule for originality based on the
number of works read. *It is the thinking, assimilating, and
reacting that count.* We may safely say that if one will
follow the directions in this chapter in regard to the stages
of preparation, he will be fairly original.

There is a moral aspect to this question of originality,
which seems to demand attention. One sometimes finds
astonishing views prevailing. A student took an oration,
transposed some sentences, struck out here and there a clause,
presented it as an original speech and defended his action.
I recall hearing a man of some distinction, in an address to

[7] *Franciscus de Verulamio sic cogitavit.* Lowell's Works. Vol. IV,
p. 197.

arouse martial spirit, declaim eloquently without acknowledgment large sections from a speech by Wendell Phillips. A
friend of mine holds in his hands proof that a certain college
president preached a baccalaureate sermon taken largely
from the printed sermons of another college president. Does
not the moral sense of mankind condemn such practices?
The natural anxiety of the friends of the president first
mentioned that the proofs of his plagiarism shall not be
made public indicates that there is a moral obligation upon
a speaker to be original in some fair sense of the word.

On the low ground of expediency plagiarism is inadvis-
able. There were at least two persons who heard the speaker
declaiming from Wendell Phillips who were able to "give
him away." A preacher assumed that no one read printed
sermons; but one little woman did, and she forced him to
the humiliating confession that he had preached a sermon by
Lyman Abbott.

I find no reason to suppose that the standard of originality is lower for speakers than for writers. We must, of
course, consider in a given case what is understood by the
audience: there may be times when a speaker is understood to
be but a mouthpiece. He has been sent to represent another
person or an institution. Again, speakers under certain circumstances will be understood to have used certain authorities.

A speaker should be quick to acknowledge his indebted-
ness, when acknowledgment is due. He will not lose by so
doing, but gain in the respect of his audience. When
acknowledgment is due cannot be laid down definitely; but
the honest man will make sure he goes far enough in this
direction. One is not bound to give credit for ideas taken
from the great common stock, even though he knows that a
certain writer has expressed them, unless he is borrowing

that writer's form. For example, I was told that a suggestion I had made in regard to tact in giving information the
audience should already possess, had been made by Poor
Richard. Possibly I got it from him; but I feel no obligation to give credit for such a commonplace, though I might
wish to cite so strong an authority as Benjamin Franklin.

There is no use in trying to lay down rules about originality. The unscrupulous man will cheat any rules in such a
subject. The honest man will keep himself from fraud when
he realizes what honesty demands; and he can best do it by
thorough mastery of facts and genuine thinking.

# CHAPTER V

## WORKING THE MATERIAL—ANALYSIS AND BRIEFING [1]

The processes of analyzing, arranging, and planning which you have already carried on to some extent should now engage your attention more definitely.

Before a speaker can make more than a tentative plan for his speech, he should have an analysis of his subject, for this process may give new meaning to his material, and even change his notion of what he wishes to do with it. Now *analysis resolves a subject into its parts, discovers the central idea, and relates the parts to it and to each other.*

If your theme is argumentative *the central idea* will be formulated as a proposition—what you think and propose to prove. The supporting material, your reasons for thinking as you do, will be formulated as sub-propositions. Each sub-proposition may have its own supporting facts and ideas, until you come down to ideas so plain, or facts so well known, as to need no clarification or support. At all stages the principle is the same: you separate what you think from why. If you are working out an exposition the central idea is the truth, object, or operation to be explained, and analysis will discover and relate to this those parts and details which are necessary to understanding of the central idea.

[1] Teachers who prefer to pass over this chapter until their students are better established as speakers will find no difficulty in so doing; or in omitting from the heading "Briefing," or from "Subject sentences," to the end of the chapter.

### HELPS TO ANALYSIS

Analysis is sometimes a difficult process. In making certain suggestions I have no desire to dictate, here or elsewhere, any procedure as best for all at all times; but most are helped by certain methods, and students will do well to learn these and give them repeated trials. Some of the suggestions may seem too elementary; yet it often happens that one sits and stares at a mass of material without making progress, and devices such as the most simple of these may get one's mental machinery past the dead center which is holding it motionless.

USE OF NOTE CARDS. The process of analysis is much facilitated by the use, recommended in the preceding chapter, of cards bearing jottings of ideas and data. Go over the cards you have now and complete their orderly arrangement, trying to bring together in each pile those items which seem most closely related. If, for example, your subject is the forward pass, you will probably find one pile builds up around the pass from the spectator's point of view, another about the changes worked in the game by the pass, and so on. Then you will probably find that each group tends to break up into smaller groups, and perhaps that all tend to group themselves about some central idea, as that the forward pass has improved football. Or it may be seen that certain parts group about one central idea and certain parts about another, either of which might be a good speech subject. Thus if your material concerns Lincoln you may find part of it grouping about Lincoln's education, another part about Lincoln the statesman, or the lawyer, or the orator. Also some of your materials may be support for more than one of these ideas, as Lincoln's education and his skill as a speaker; while you may find that some of your material has no real bearing on your subject, or any phase of it you are likely to choose.

In this process of sorting you may find that you have a great deal of material on some minor point and are short of material needed for a more important division; that is, you see what is to be rejected and what is yet to be sought, and you are gaining for the subject a sense of proportion.

As you go through this process it will be helpful to write out short statements embodying the idea of each division of your material. These will help in clarifying your ideas, and may serve later as heads and subheads in your brief, and possibly in the speech itself.

If you have not done so already, you should now determine, at least tentatively, the central idea of the speech you are to make. Make an effort to put into a sentence what you think; decide what you will drive at in your speech. To put it another way, write out what you would wish a listener to say after your speech, if asked to state the gist of it in a single sentence. Would he be able to make a clean-cut statement like one of these?

The speaker's canoe trip on the St. Lawrence was a harrowing experience.

A college coöperative store saves money for students.

A coöperative store should be established in our college.

Cement is made by burning a mixture of clay and limestone.

When the speaker has found a central idea, suitable to his purpose and the occasion, he has determined the type of his speech; whether narrative, expository, or argumentative in its aim. He has also determined its scope. For example, if his speech is to be argumentative, he has determined whether he will argue only that certain facts are true, or that action should be taken with regard to those facts, as in the examples above based on the coöperative store; whether he will argue only the existence of an evil, or proceed to a proposal to remedy the evil. He has limited his scope in another way; for example, he has determined whether he will argue for the whole policy of his party, or for only one of its proposals. Since he has now limited the theme and scope of his speech, he can simplify his material, perhaps laying some of it aside as not relevant to his purpose. Most important, he has found a point of view; he has something to steer by, or toward. Once the central idea is found, the speaker is no longer floundering about in his subject, but is able to move purposefully among his materials, selecting and arranging those that will support this central thought. In selecting and arranging his supporting material, it is important to organize his ideas so that they shape up into a pattern satisfying to the mind. A mere miscellany of facts or reasons is hard to remember, makes little impression, and goes only a little way in making things either clear or satisfying; while a good analysis enables a speaker to present his material in organized, systematic fashion, and once found is an aid both to the speaker on the platform and to the audience. What we now have to discover are *aids to analysis*, patterns into which our thinking often falls; or ways of dividing subjects.

The case is simpler when one knows from the beginning just what he wishes to do and by what means he will do it; but even then he will be more likely to take a sound view of his subject and less liable to fall into fallacy, or to omit some needed element of his reasoning or explanation, if he goes through a rather definite scheme of analysis.

PATTERNS OF ANALYSIS. As suggested above, the natural divisions of a subject may reveal themselves on inspection.

Again one may have to look for the lines of cleavage. *Temporal relations* may be the clue, as in considering the method of nominating a candidate for the presidency one naturally thinks of the stages in the order of their occurrence. So with the details of a story one thinks in terms of chronology. But instead of telling the story of the Norman Conquest, one may divide the material into effects of the Conquest on the character of the population, effects on the political system, effects on the language, and so on, with probably another division, outside of this system but related to all the divisions noted, having to do with the characteristics of the Normans and of the English. Such an arrangement may be called *topical*.

*Spatial relations* may be the basis of division and arrangement, as the exterior and the interior, the foundation, the walls, and the roof, or east and west. If one had been working in the fall of 1932 on Franklin D. Roosevelt's prospects of election, one might have considered the East, the South, the Middle West, and the Pacific Slope. But one might also have proceeded topically, considering *the elements and interests affected*, as the so-called "Wall Street interest," the manufacturers, the laborers, the farmers, the veterans, the "wets" and the "drys." Probably one making an extensive survey of the probabilities would have combined the two systems and considered various elements in different sections, so that one main division would have dealt with the farmers, with subdivisions for farmers in each section.

A question of policy worked out on the basis of the elements and interests affected is illustrated by: The proposed rushing system should be adopted, for it will be good for the freshmen, it will be good for the College, and it will be good for the fraternities.

*Causal relations,* or the relations of cause and effect, may furnish the pattern. Perhaps the central idea is that the

N. R. A. was the chief cause of such recovery as we enjoyed in 1934, or that disarmament will bring peace to the world, or that jealousy prompted Roe to kill Doe. In each case the central idea is stated as an assertion of cause and effect. We are led to ask such questions as these:

1. Does the alleged cause really exist?
2. Is the alleged cause strong enough actually to produce the effect?
3. Are there other forces at work which might better explain the effect, since they have a closer connection with it?

Thus in showing that jealousy prompted Roe to murder Doe, we must show that Roe was jealous of Doe, that his jealousy was very strong, and that no other explanation of Doe's death will serve. In dealing with the N. R. A. we find ourselves concentrating on the second and third questions above, and asking, Could regulation of industry account for recovery in a country still agricultural to so great an extent, and might not improvement be traced to currency manipulation, or to world-wide improvement, or to government spending?

If we start with the effect, We are paying exorbitant taxes in this city, the questions may be, Are the taxes due to unusually good service? No, the service is poor. To the building of better streets, schools, etc.? No, there have been no improvements. To a cumbersome system of city government? Yes, at least in part. To lack of centered responsibility? Yes, in part. To graft? Yes, in part. Then the remedy will be found in the city manager system, for this will remove each of the causes named.

In this example we have traced a given effect to its causes, and then have forecast an effect from a given cause. In this second use of the analysis by causal relations, where the argument is that certain benefits or evils will result from a given change or failure to change, we ask such questions as these:

1. Is the alleged cause adequate to produce the effect?

2. Has it been known, under similar circumstances, to produce the effect?

3. Would a different cause, if set into operation, more surely produce the effect?

*Elimination,* as has been seen already, figures largely in this sort of analysis. When the possibilities are plainly limited in number, then the choice of the most favorable possibility is made by eliminating each of the others in turn. Thus, if we are considering the future of government in this country, we may eliminate unregulated capitalism as no longer feasible, fascism as not suited to America, communism as not suited to America; and so arrive at the central idea, We should look to a system of strict governmental control of our economic life.

For questions of future policy there is no more helpful pattern than what is sometimes called the "disease and remedy" analysis, already exemplified in the discussion of causal relations. In its simplest form we ask the questions, Is there an evil? and What is the remedy? These questions may be elaborated into many, but the following, combined with those just suggested for cause and effect, are usually sufficient to give a good start:

Is there anything wrong with things as they are?
If so, what are the causes of the evil?
Will the proposed change remedy the evil?
Will it remove the causes of the evil?

Are the objections to the proposed remedy sound?
Is it the best feasible remedy?

What other remedies are offered?
Does any one of them reach to the causes of the evil?
What objections to these remedies?

With a little practice one comes to run over these questions very rapidly. Not all of them need detain in every case. There may be general agreement that there is an evil, even that the proposed change would remedy it, possibly even that there is no better remedy; so that the only question is whether the remedy is worse than the disease; as, Is it worse to pay heavy taxes or to endure the poor streets? Or, Admittedly the republican form of government is not very efficient and a dictatorship would give us greater efficiency; but are the ills of a dictatorship greater than the ills we have?

The questions suggested, *when turned into declarative answers,* may form the headings in the brief that analysis is preparing for; and I will use now, in order to save needless repetition, the declarative forms.

The questions of the "disease and remedy" pattern are usable whether one decides to speak in advocacy of, or in opposition to, a proposed policy; but the answers will, of course, differ widely. The speaker in opposition will, as a result of his analysis, arrive at *one or more* of these assertions as the basis of his argument:

The present condition of things is satisfactory.
The proposed change would not cure such evils as exist.
The proposed plan is not feasible.
The proposed change (plan, policy) would result in greater evils than we now have.
There is a better remedy (plan, policy).

We may illustrate with a homely example:

### Central Idea

Let's go swimming, for

### Argument

I. We are all suffering from the heat.
II. A good swim would cool us off.
III. There is no other way to cool off so satisfactory.
IV. The objection that dressing and getting back will leave us hotter than we are now, is not sound.

The opposition may state the central idea in the negative, and support it with these two sub-ideas:

I. We should be hotter than ever by the time we were back.
II. The better way is to avoid all exertion.

The foregoing examples of the "disease and remedy" pattern involve positive evils to be removed; but the general scheme is applicable even though one is proposing only to improve a tolerable condition; for example,

Our profits would be greatly increased by the proposed advertising campaign.
No better plan has been presented.
The objections are not sound.

The *theory and practice* pattern is very simple, taking this general form:

The proposed policy is sound in theory.
The proposed policy works out in practice.

It should be noted, however, that unless the matter you are dealing with is in fact simple, a simple pattern of main heads only postpones the real difficulties, which have still to be solved in the subheads; and this theory and practice pattern can hardly be said to do more than to jog one's mental machinery. But it may be helpful by doing just that.

Most of the preceding illustrations have been drawn from arguments. The analysis of expository subjects will be given further attention in Chapter XI.

*Combining patterns.* As has been noted, it may be desirable, and it may even be necessary, to employ more than one method of analysis with a single topic. So the introductory part of a brief in advocacy of the city manager system might well be based upon a definition of that system, while the body of the brief might be based upon the "disease and remedy" pattern. Care should be taken in combining patterns to avoid the confusion that analysis is aimed at. Confusion will usually be avoided if those headings in a brief which are of the same order, or bear the same relation to the central idea (or in the case of subheads, bear the same relation to a superior heading) are all parts of one pattern; and they can usually be kept to a single pattern. At least they can for short speeches.

It would be possible to offer many more variations of patterns of analysis; but those offered should suffice. Such devices certainly will not solve all difficulties, or take the place of hard thinking; but they can help in getting started. At any rate there are far too many speeches that present mere miscellanies of ideas and facts, without structure, unity, coherence, or definiteness of impression. Such speeches are not likely to be made by a speaker who has made as part of his preparation a logical analysis of his subject and material, and embodied this analysis in a brief.

A brief presents the results of analysis in graphic form. The brief is good if it sets forth the analysis boldly to the eye, revealing the pattern of thought with its supporting material, all so correlated that the relation of point to point is manifest. The whole scheme of headings, indentations, numerals, and connectives is designed to give the pattern "high visibility." Though it is a condensed statement its meaning should be unmistakable to the reader.

The following will illustrate an argumentative brief based upon the "disease and remedy" analysis:

## Central Idea

The Athletic Council should hire competent persons to do the work now done by competitors for managerships.

## Proof

I. The present system is unsatisfactory, for
  A. The work is inefficiently done, for
      1. Correspondence is not well done.
      2. There is confusion in attending to the details of the work.
  B. Competitors give too much time to the work, for
      1. This is inevitable, since
          a. The competitor who does the most work is most likely to win.
          b. They must be continually hanging around for a job.
      2. Competitors often fail in their college work.

II. The proposed change would eliminate the evils, for
  A. That the work would be better done needs no argument.

      B. That the harm now done to competitors would be removed is obvious.

III. The objections to the proposed change are unsound, for
      A. The objection that it would deprive competitors of a valuable business training is not justified, for
         1. Athletics are not run on a business basis.
         2. A large part of the work is manual.
         3. Only the most successful reach work that may have a slight value as business training.
      B. The objection that the Council cannot afford to hire people to do the work is not justified, for
         1. It would be cheaper to have the work well done by a few efficient workers than to have it bungled by competitors.

This brief has been fashioned to bring out the pattern. It is true that in this particular argument the brief might be quite as useful if simplified. The matter under II may seem unnecessary; but in most cases there is need of definite proof that the proposed policy will remove the evils. At any rate, it is well, at least in one's early briefs, to use the full form, for in so doing one is more sure to consider all the elements in his case.

Since expository briefs seem most often to make trouble, a somewhat elaborated example is added. You might wish to explain—not to argue for or against, but just to explain—coöperative stores as they are run in many colleges; and your material is covered by these statements:

Stockholders get limited dividends.
The operation of the store is not, superficially, unusual.
Customers pay cash at current prices.
The store is run for the benefit of the customers.

A coöperative store is an effective means of combating the high cost of living.

A trained merchant manages the store.

Its appearance is that of an ordinary store.

Various colleges have had success with the plan.

Sales slips are issued with each sale; and when signed and deposited by the customer, these form the basis for calculation of a rebate.

Customers whose purchases amount to, say, two dollars receive rebates at the end of the year.

Rebates depend upon (a) the net profits of the business and (b) the amount of a given customer's purchases.

The differences between the coöperative and the ordinary store are found in the financial plan.

*The New English Dictionary* says that a coöperative store is "a store or shop belonging to and supported by a coöperative society, with the purpose of supplying themselves with goods at moderate price, and of distributing the profits, if any, among members and regular customers."

Before going further, ponder this material with a view to bringing it into a coherent system. You may notice, first, that certain items may be laid aside as having no part in an expository brief, although they might be useful in making the speech itself interesting, or in making a brief on the proposition that a coöperative store should be established. You may then note that the remaining statements tend to group about two main ideas: the financial plan of the store and the daily operation of it. The definition looks like a good condensed description of the institution to be explained and can stand as a statement of the central idea, with the other usable material falling into the following topical pattern:

### THE COÖPERATIVE STORE

*Central Idea*

A coöperative store is a "store or shop belonging to and supported by a coöperative society, with the purpose of supplying themselves with goods at moderate price, and of distributing the profits, if any, among the members and regular customers."

*Explanation*

I. The operation of the store is, in the main, that of an ordinary store, in that
  A. The store is open to all who wish to buy.
  B. A trained merchant is in charge.
  C. Customers pay cash at current prices.
  D. A sales slip is given for each purchase.
  E. The chief unusual feature is that customers sign and deposit the slips.

II. The important differences between the coöperative and the ordinary store are found in the financial plan, in that
  A. Members of the society buy shares.
  B. The shareholders as such receive limited dividends.
  C. Each purchaser of goods amounting to two dollars receives, at the end of the year, rebates based upon
    1. The profits realized on the total business, and
    2. The amount of his purchases.

In these briefs we have not only analyses but syntheses of our speech materials, expressed in coherent and graphic form. We may need other matter, as illustrations and colorful details, to impress the points and make them interesting, but a brief presents the basic stuff for a speech.

TESTS OF THE BRIEF. I will indicate here, in the form of test questions, the minimum requirements of a good brief. The rest of this division will explain what is here dogmatically set down, with some additional suggestions.

1. Does the sentence embodying your central idea clearly and justly express it?

2. Do the main heads, taken together, constitute sufficient proof, development, or clarification of this central idea?

3. Does each main head relate directly to the central idea?

4. Are your main supporting statements actually in the main heads and not obscured by being placed in a subhead?

5. Considering each main head with its subhead as a separate system, will the headings bear tests similar to those applied above to subject sentence and main heads?

6. Can *for*, or *in that, to enumerate*, or other subordinating phrase, justly be used to connect a heading with each heading placed as subordinate to it?

7. Can *and, or, but*, or other coördinating phrase, justly be used to connect two heads given equal rank?

It is desirable, but not always feasible, that an affirmative answer should be possible to this question:

8. Do your main heads reveal *by their wordings* their relations to each other, and constitute a clear system?

And it is highly desirable, but again not always feasible, that an affirmative answer should be possible to this question:

9. Does each heading express a single idea?

SUBJECT SENTENCES. The statement of the central idea is called in an argumentative brief the proposition, but a term satisfactory for all types of briefs is *subject sentence*. This statement should be as crisp as a just statement of the idea permits, and should, wherever feasible, *contain but a single assertion*. If more than one assertion is made in the subject sentence there is danger of confusion as to which a given main head supports; and one chief purpose of a brief is to make the relation of point to point manifest. (That word *manifest* should be taken seriously. In the ideal brief nothing is left to inference or oral explanation, or to be puzzled out. Every relationship is unmistakable, standing forth to eye and understanding.)

It must be recognized, however, that in practical speaking resolutions may be multiple; as Our city should meet its financial crisis (1) by enforcing tax collections and (2) by rigid economy. The common practice in discussing such propositions of a "motion to divide," providing for taking up one part at a time, is evidence of the danger of confusion. It is well for students of speaking to avoid that sort of proposition in the short speeches to which circumstances usually confine them. The vice of the double proposition can hardly be said to exist, however, in a resolution containing two proposals that in common acceptance are bound to go together, as the manufacture and sale of beer.

Do not include details of the development in the subject sentence, and especially do not include a reason for the assertion. These belong in the body of the brief. Tipping is an evil and should be abolished, is the equivalent of, Tipping should be abolished because it is an evil, and therefore offends against the principle stated early in this chapter, that what one thinks should be separated from why one thinks so. In this case the fault may be little more than waste of words, but Tipping should be abolished, is the clean-cut proposition. Then if it seems that there is need of argument that tipping is an evil, that statement may be made a main head in the proof.

More dangerous was this subject sentence (used while prohibition was still an issue): To allow the manufacture and sale of light wines and beer would change prohibition from a failure into a success. That statement involved the assumption that prohibition was a failure. For some that needed proof; by some it would have been accepted; but in any case the sound proposition was, The prohibition laws should be amended to allow the manufacture and sale of light wines and beer.

Avoid placing your main idea in a subordinate clause; as, It is believed that . . . , President Roosevelt asserts that . . . , All will agree that . . . . We do not set out, usually, to prove that *So and So declares* that government ownership of coal mines would result in cheaper coal, but that government ownership of coal mines would result in cheaper coal. Instead of writing, Washington advised Americans to avoid entangling alliances, one should write, Americans should avoid entangling alliances, and place Washington's authority with the supporting material; unless, indeed, the whole point of the speech is to be that Washington took this position.

The subject sentence, like all headings in a brief, should be *as short as is consistent with clearness*. The wordings objected to just above are objectionable also on the ground of unnecessary length. Many of the remarks appropriate in a speech serve only to clutter up a brief. For example, Maple sugar is produced by complex methods, is better than, Maple sugar, once made by a simple process, is now produced by complex methods. The latter form could be defended only if the brief-maker is looking forward to making his speech a running comparison of old and new methods.

Many wasteful expressions are found in briefs, even in the briefs of those who complain that an adequate brief has to be very long; as, "A college student without a vocational goal is not wasting his time, money, or college opportunities, as many people make him out to be."

*Do not put your subject sentence, or any other heading in a brief, in the form of a question.* Avoid, too, "live" figures of speech; that is, those that retain much of their figurative quality. Both questions and figures of speech are useful in addressing an audience, but the purposes of a brief are best served by *precise, literal language and declarative sentences.*

The logical position for the subject sentence is *just before the first main head* of its proof or development. It may be preceded by whatever is needed to clear the way for initial understanding, as comment on the history of the question, definition of terms, elimination of matter which, though irrelevant, is commonly confused with the issue, statement of admitted matter, or analysis of the issues. For an abbreviated example:

I. It is assumed that most of my audience will agree that prohibition in the United States is a failure.

II. The "Quebec" system of liquor control has these principal features:
   A. . . . . . . . . . . . . . . . . . . . . . . . . .
   B. . . . . . . . . . . . . . . . . . . . . . . . . .
   C. . . . . . . . . . . . . . . . . . . . . . . . . .

III. (Subject sentence) The United States should adopt the Quebec system in its main features.

The formation of subject sentences is sometimes difficult in briefs not argumentative. In exposition a definition will sometimes serve the purpose; as "Burglary is breaking and entering the dwelling-house of another in the night time, with intent to commit some felony in the same"; or, A gyroscope railway is a "single rail railway upon which each car is kept erect by the rotary force of two gyroscopes in rapid opposite motion."

Most difficult of all seem to be subject sentences for briefs explaining a process. Sometimes a condensed exposition is possible; as, "Cement is made by burning a mixture of clay and limestone." Rather unwieldy is, "Polo is a game played on horseback, usually with a light wooden ball and with mallets having long flexible handles, with four players on a side, whose effort is to drive the ball through their opponents' goal posts at the opposite end of the field," but this is the best the editors of a famous dictionary can do, and on the whole more satisfactory than Polo is "a game at ball, played by persons on horseback." "I propose to show how my wrists, arms, and body work in making my approach shot in golf," is hard to improve upon for the particular sort of speech indicated.

Less difficult are the subject sentences of explanations which not only give information, but have also a point of view or seek to make a particular impression; as, "Altering a T-model Ford into a racing machine requires that it be practically rebuilt"; or, "The blocked kick results from carefully planned defensive plays."

For a narrative which embodies a thesis or moral we may have such a subject sentence as, This is a tale of the conflict of conscience and ambition. If the narrative has no definite pattern and aims at no definite impression, we may be driven to such subject sentences as, This is the story of my experiences in the War; but it is doubtful if students of speaking should indulge in such speeches. The last remark may be applied also to the talk which is a general commentary, as What will the next Congress do as regards the tariff, foreign debts, farm relief, and so on? Leave such talks to returned heroes and elderly statesmen. No one needs to practise rambling.

There is, to be sure, an artistic rambling in which a speaker without seeming purpose does make a definite impression. Back in war time I heard Hendrik Van Loon tell his experiences on the Western Front in a seemingly rambling talk that might have had for its subject sentence, War is a nasty, unheroic business. But note that the seeming aimlessness was in the speech; back of it may have been a firm brief. But this type of speech is beyond the skill of most, though simple rambling is distressingly easy.

A clear, simple subject sentence (which, we recall, is a statement of the central idea), is of first-class importance. It organizes the whole. *All that precedes leads to it; all that follows looks back to it and supports it.*

THE MAIN HEADS. A main head in the discussion bears the same relation to its subheads as the subject sentence bears to the main heads; and to save repetition it may be stated that nearly all that has been said above of the subject sentence applies to them. In addition it may be said that the chief considerations are: (a) that each main head shall state clearly the idea of a main division of the theme, (b) that each shall reveal an unmistakable relation (without need of explanation or inference) to the subject sentence, (c) that this relationship shall be one of subordination, and (d) that taken together the main heads, being themselves developed, shall suffice to develop and support the central idea as expressed in the subject sentence. It is also highly desirable that the main heads should constitute a system or pattern, revealing as clearly as may be their relations to each other.

THE SUBHEADS. Each set of subheads bears the same relation to its main head as the main heads to the subject sentence; and the same statement applies when a subhead becomes the main head of lower subdivisions.

METHODS MAKING FOR CLEARNESS AND COHERENCE. In the first place, it is well to set up for your standard, *not a brief clear to yourself merely, but one readily grasped by another who may read it*. This may seem an arbitrary standard, but there are good reasons for it. First, such a brief gives your critic a good chance to help you. In certain respects he can help you more at the briefing stage than later, for he can more readily "size up" your material and its analysis, provided he does not have to spend his available time puzzling out your meaning. Secondly, what you have made clear to another is more surely clear to yourself. Very often one who has made a confused or vague brief has no clear idea of what he wishes to say.

*Write only complete sentences in your brief.* No mere captions, catch-lines, or half sentences should be used. Do not omit either the subject or the predicate of a sentence however evident it may seem. Do not write "Sales slips" for "A sales slip is given with each purchase"; or—

I. Tipping and employers.
 A. Little interest in work which brings no tips.

But do write—

I. The custom of tipping is bad for employers, for
 A. Employees take little interest in work which brings no tips.

NOTE.—In this chapter examples of poor briefing that are displayed like the above and not run into the paragraphs, will be put into smaller type to distinguish them from examples that are good, improved, or in the main satisfactory.

It is true that abbreviated statements may sometimes be clear; but they are so often ambiguous and so often fail to make relations clear, that it is best to avoid them altogether. Too often they represent hazy thinking; and one who writes them in his brief will often fail, on being questioned, to explain what he means, for the reason that he does not exactly know.

As a rule, *each heading should be able to stand alone.* The student who wrote in a brief on the George Junior Republic—

  I. The Republic develops
    A. Democracy,
    B. Races and sexes,

would surely have seen that he was bringing together unrelated matters and writing nonsense, if he had written—

  I. The Republic develops desirable qualities, for
    A. It develops democracy among its citizens.
    B. It develops races and sexes.

Let each heading be clearly and sharply *limited by its phrasing to the points it is to cover.* Do not write *omnibus headings;* that is, headings that can cover anything without discrimination; as, Some arguments in favor of professional coaches, Some arguments generally overlooked. Such statements obviously mark no advance in analysis, furnish no test of the soundness of analysis, and are of no assistance in the further stages of preparation. All the work has still to be done.

When feasible, the coherence of a brief—that is, the relation of part to part—is plainer when headings of equal rank are put in similar terms and constructions, as in—

I. The proposed tariff measure would injure the manufacturers.

II. The measure would injure the laborers.

III. The measure would injure the farmers.

The clearness and coherence of a brief are much enhanced by consistency in the use of the mechanical details of its construction—indentations, numerals (including letters used as numerals), and connectives. Uniformity helps carry out the idea of a brief as a chart of analysis. And while no one system is necessarily best, there is an advantage if all members of a class use the same one.

It is usually best to write in the appropriate connective words between main heads and their subheads (and frequently between headings of equal rank), for such words furnish an excellent test of correlation. If one finds that the relation between two statements is justly expressed by *and, but, yet, or, also, again, further,* or other coördinating phrase, then one knows that the statements are of equal rank and stand in the same relation to a superior heading. One cannot be subordinate to the other, and they take the same order of numerals and the same indentations.

(To say that two headings are of equal rank is not to say they are of equal importance. Two captains are of the same rank, yet one may be of less value to the army than a private, while the other may be of more value than the general.)

If one finds that the relation between two headings is expressed justly by such subordinating phrases as *for, since, because, in order that, to enumerate, in that, to explain, to illustrate, namely,* then one knows that the clause governed by one of these phrases is subordinate to the other; and the form of the brief should indicate that subordination.    The following is an illogical arrangement:

1. Democracy needs leaders.
    a. The colleges are training schools for leaders.

The arrangement declares as plainly as words could that the second statement is subordinate to the first; but if you supply the right connective, *and*, you find they are coördinate. The correct arrangement is—

I. Democracy needs leaders, and
I'. The colleges are training schools for leaders.

(Note the use of the prime (') to indicate that though neither of the statements is subordinate to the other, still they are peculiarly dependent upon each other.)

I. A federal censorship of moving pictures would create a uniform standard of censorship.
    A. A benefit to the producer who now has a hard time trying to meet the demands of many boards.

This is poor in several ways, but its worst fault is in making the major statement subordinate to the minor.    What connective would you use?    This is better:

I. Federal censorship of moving pictures would benefit the producer, for
    A. He now has difficulty in meeting the demands of several boards, and
    A'. With federal censorship he would have to satisfy but one.

It is a well established custom in briefing always to *place a main head before its supporting statements;* and one who attempts to arrange them in the reverse order, if the brief is much elaborated, will find the convention has reason back of it. At any rate it is well to follow the custom for the sake of uniformity. So we may say that if we find that a statement, in the body of the brief, is properly introduced by *hence, therefore, thus it will be seen,* or other phrase implying that the support precedes the statement, we may consider the order wrong. It is an offense against the convention, but only that, to write—

> A. Employees take little interest in work which brings no tips; therefore
> I. Tipping is bad for employers.

But if the headings are arranged in this way—

> I. Employees take little interest in work that brings no tips; therefore
> A. Tipping is bad for employers—

then the offense is not against form only, for this arrangement places the major statement in a subordinate position where its relation to the subject sentence (Tipping is an evil) is obscured.

The proper *phrasing of the refutation of an argument, or the correction of an error,* so often proves difficult that it deserves some special attention. The following is objectionable first, because A does not go to prove but to disprove I, and, secondly, because A, 1 is not, as the form implies, subordinate to A:

> I. The World Court can settle important international disputes.

A. It is argued that in an important dispute the losing party will not abide by the decision; but
    1. This is not true, for
        a. World opinion would force acceptance.

This is sound:

I. The World Court can settle important disputes, for
    A. The argument that in important disputes the losing party would not accept the decision, is not sound, for
        1. World opinion would force acceptance.

Other useful forms can be illustrated thus:

The argument that capital punishment has lowered the crime rate is based on a misinterpretation of the facts.

The argument that the Eighteenth Amendment lacks the support of the people is irrelevant to this question.

The common belief that leaves change color in the fall because of frost has no scientific basis.

FINALLY. No matter how much this subject of briefing might be elaborated, it would still be true that nothing will take the place of ample information and hard thinking.[2] I have seen many briefs splendid in appearance which covered only ignorance and superficial analysis. Nevertheless, it is true that a brief worked out faithfully in accordance with the suggestions made above will be a great help to one who wishes to "know what he is talking about."

[2] In *Argumentation* by Winans and Utterback, and in several other works on argumentation, can be found fuller treatment of the analysis and briefing of arguments.

# CHAPTER VI

## PLANNING THE SPEECH

No one who listens to speeches thoughtfully can be unaware of the fact that many of them are rambling and that they fail of definite impression. An important reason for these failures is that the speaker has fixed in mind no definite objective. Having no goal he reaches none, or the wrong one, or an inconsequential one. Or if he has a goal in mind, he fails to consider carefully the means of reaching it.

The man who objects to making a plan for a speech should, to be consistent, object to making a plan for a house. It is true that one might build a very delightful house without a plan; but the chances are that he would waste much money in buying his material, and in making the changes necessitated by the fact that the chimney cut off the stairway and that the bath room could be reached only through the kitchen. And when he was done he would be likely to find that his work of genius had neither form nor utility. It may be very delightful to start from one's hotel and walk to the station, with only the general notion that it is "over that way." One may have a fine time watching the crowd and looking in at the shop windows, or he may meet an old friend; but at train time he may be far from the station.

So a speaker may ramble about, perhaps enjoying himself hugely, but never accomplish any purpose. And the speaker must consider his audience, the people with whom he has to do business. There are some speakers we gladly listen

to as they ramble about in their stores of information and
their memories; but we know most such talkers are bores.
Certainly the speaker who has to do business in a limited
time should not adopt the haphazard method.

We now assume a topic, a supply of materials, and an
analysis worked out into graphic form; and we proceed to
more definite planning of the particular speech to be made.
Adaptation of material to occasion will be considered throughout this book, and has already been touched upon in Chapter III; but it will be well to note here certain considerations.

At this point take up your worksheets and reconsider your
first notes as to time, place, audience, purpose, and theme.
Looking at your brief in the light of those notes, will it
serve your purpose? Do you need other material for proof
before the particular audience? For explanation? Or would
it perhaps be well, after analyzing your material, to modify
your theme, or even your purpose?

*Which of the several arguments in your brief are best
adapted to your particular audience?* Which are your
hearers most likely to accept? Which have they accepted
already? What are their strongest objections to your conclusion? What should be especially stressed? Assume you
are arguing for an honor system of examinations. Do most
of your hearers already believe the present form of the
proctor system should be displaced? Do they go so far as to
agree that some form of honor system should be introduced?
Do they differ with you as to which form; or have you only
to arouse them to take steps toward a change?

*From what interests of theirs can you derive interest for
your speech?*

Coming closer to the actual construction of the speech, the
next question is, *How shall you approach your audience?*
or, How can you best introduce your subject? Obviously

the answer will be much affected by the situation in which the speaker expects to find himself. Will interest be aroused in advance, or must you awaken it? Will your hearers anticipate being interested by you? Or will they be wishing to get to other business or entertainment?

Does the probable situation suggest a means of awakening interest? In the association of your theme with some local interest, with some recent event, or with some interesting person? Will an illustration of one of your points serve at the start both to arouse interest and to introduce your theme?

Will your audience understand your proposition at once, or must you explain it? Do they have more than a hazy idea of interallied debts? Do they know football only as a spectacle, or do they know enough of the strategy of the game so that you can go at once to an explanation of the Warner shift?

Will there be prejudice to overcome? Distaste for the topic? Hostility to the proposition? To the speaker? Will starting with your most effective argument, or a story, win a friendlier attitude?

What, to put the matter briefly, will form the best connecting link between your subject and the state of mind of your audience?

It would be unwise to attempt to discuss these suggestions at this point, and some of them need no discussion; but at any rate remember that the approach to your audience and subject is not to be looked upon as a perfunctory matter for which any commonplace is good enough. Your way of beginning may have a pronounced effect upon the attitude of your audience and the success of your speech.

It is not necessary to decide finally upon your opening first, however; you may be able to think of a better introduction for your speech after it is more fully developed.

And while it is usually best for an inexperienced speaker to know in advance pretty definitely even the phraseology of his opening, he should keep in mind the fact that the actual situation at the time of speaking may make it advisable to change his planned approach.

*What is the best order in which to marshal the points?* This may be the order of the brief; or it may seem that the audience in view would better follow another order. In some cases a certain logical or chronological order may seem necessary, but in more cases the order is a matter for the speaker's discretion. In presenting the matter in the brief on coöperative stores the decision might turn on which division of the subject-matter is the more likely to arouse interest.

If one has a brief in which the main heads to support the proposition that tipping is an evil are: I. Tipping is bad for patrons, II. Tipping is bad for employers, III. Tipping is bad for employees, the order of the speech might be determined by whether the audience will be composed chiefly of patrons, employers, or employees. If a general audience, the speaker would be likely to begin with patrons since every one is at times a patron, and as such may have some feeling on the subject. If one is advocating a measure to which his hearers have a strong objection, as that it will cost too much, one considers if he will tackle the objection at once, or wait until opposition may be weakened by a presentation of the beauties of his proposal. A somewhat similar problem arises if one is opposing a proposition to which the audience is strongly attracted.

Usually it is best to proceed from the known to the unknown, from the interesting to the less interesting, from the acceptable to the less acceptable; but it is not safe to make a rule to that effect. Each case must be judged by itself.

Often the order of climax is best; but with an indifferent or a hostile audience it may be necessary in order to gain a hearing to put the strongest point first.

A question sometimes arises as to whether to state early one's proposition, or to delay until a part or all of the supporting arguments have been made. Usually the early announcement is better as giving more significance to the arguments as they are made; but because delay may awaken curiosity in an indifferent audience or avoid hostility in an opposed audience, there is sometimes virtue in holding back one's proposal. It may also be true that an audience is in no mood for argument at the beginning.

Occasionally it is unwise to state one's proposition at all, as when a political candidate wishes to prove, but not actually to state, that his opponent has lied, or when one feels that the time is not ripe to state his proposal, but wishes to lead his hearers to deduce it for themselves. So a student whose proposition is that our system of college athletics should be supplanted by the Oxford system might content himself with an attractive description of the latter.

At times, to gain interest and avoid an argumentative tone, a speaker may decide to cast his description, exposition, or argument, not into a topical form, but into a narrative which will accomplish his purpose. So one can explain coal mines by telling the story of a trip through one, or coöperative stores under the title, A Visit to the Coöp. at Columbia, or argue against independence for the Philippines by telling the story of the American occupation, or against tipping under My Experience as a Bellhop.

*The conclusion* deserves careful planning, for it is the final chance to impress the point of the speech. Very short speeches, or those in which the line of thought is easily held in mind, may close with the last main head, provided this is a strong point; but most often something more is needed. This may be a recapitulation of the main points of your discussion, a forceful restatement, or a vivid illustration of the main thought, or it may be a plea for action. Whatever form the ending takes, it should be a genuine conclusion, a real outgrowth of the speech, not something tacked on at the end.

These, out of innumerable suggestions that might be made, are set down here as particularly useful to beginners. They have value in themselves; but their greatest use will be in cultivating the invaluable habit of considering the demands and possibilities of one's situation, instead of following the common practice of just going ahead regardless, putting things as they come to mind, or in any way that appeals to the speaker himself. We must fix in mind early the truth that the audience is a large element in a speech.

### THE SPEECH OUTLINE

All these considerations set down under the head of planning the speech, and many others, affect the formation of the outline of your speech, which is a sketch of the trail you plan to follow to your goal. It indicates where you are to start and where to stop, by what roads you will travel, into what stages you will break your journey, how these will be connected, and gives some sketchy idea of the terrain you will traverse.

The brief is an orderly and logical arrangement of the materials one has for presenting a theme; it is an aid to the speaker in gaining a mastery of these materials, any or all of which he might present on a variety of occasions. The outline sets forth these materials, or such parts of them as he wishes to use, *adapted to a given occasion*. It is in this adaptation to the particular occasion that the chief difference between the outline and the brief lies; and in such adaptation the speaker has an opportunity to show his highest skill.

Because of a question often asked, let me say that briefs and outlines are not to be distinguished by length. Either may be very long. Length depends upon how much material is included and into how many orders of headings the analysis is carried.

What form the outline shall take is less certain than in case of the brief. Probably there is no one form best for all speeches. The best I can do is to present the form which experience indicates is best in the majority of cases, and certainly best for most of the speeches that students of the art should be making.

QUALITIES OF A GOOD OUTLINE. First let me set out the qualities that must be present in any outline if it is fully to serve its purpose.

1. No outline can be good that does not make the line of thought stand out distinctly in coherent form. Major points and subordinate points should be proclaimed such by the form; and so with what is probative, explanatory, refutative, illustrative, and so on.

2. A good outline will reveal what is to be stressed and what is to be passed over quickly.

3. The outline should not only be a guide to what you wish to say, but should also be a test of your preparation for the particular speech; that is, it should by its form aid you in determining whether you have a satisfactory order, whether it has coherence and "all hangs together," whether you are including in your plan what is needed to make your point effectively, or perhaps are including matter that is not helpful.

OUR STANDARD FORM. To meet these requirements the best general purpose form is an outline which in some respects resembles the brief, but with greater freedom as regards order, and in general more freedom of expression. For example, questions may occasionally (but sparingly) be used as headings, and there may be more freedom in the use of phrases to indicate the color to be given a statement, as *unfortunately, as we all know, admittedly*. This form, like the brief, has complete sentences and a system of numerals, indentations, and connective terms to encourage precision of thought and definiteness of relations, and to make easy their recognition. It has, therefore, in a high degree the first quality of a good outline; and also, as well as any possible form can have, the second and third qualities set forth above.

Occasionally the brief itself will make a good outline, though it will usually need headings to indicate opening and closing remarks. But the suggestions already made (and others that will be made as we go through the study of interest and persuasion, especially with regard to adapting material to a given occasion) should make it clear that in the majority of cases the outline should be a paper distinct from the brief.

Some of the possible differences between brief and outline can be illustrated with an outline for a speech based upon the brief of the proposal concerning athletic competitors on page 95. A student planning to make this argument before an audience to whom it may seem heresy may decide to hold back his proposal until he has argued the evils of the present system, but still to give some hint of a radical proposal to come. He may also prefer not to proceed in the proposition-proof order in some division, if only for the sake of variety. He may then decide that it will be good persuasion to elaborate and make ridiculous the ways in which competitors spend their time (I, B, 1 in the brief) by word pictures; and he indicates this elaboration in his outline by going more into details. And finally he decides that if he covers all the main heads in his brief he will not have time to elaborate his best points sufficiently; and so determines to cut out the division numbered III, A, as the part least effective with his particular audience. He comes out with something like this for his outline:

## AMATEUR SLAVES

### *Introduction*

I. We have all accepted the hurried, worried, important looking "compet." as a part of the necessary order of nature.

II. Is our system of selecting managers for athletics working well?

### *Discussion*

I. Their work is not efficiently done.

A. There is confusion in carrying out details.

B. Correspondence attended to by competitors is not neat or well expressed.

---

(Turning now to the student's side of the question—)

A. Since, as is well understood, the amount of work done is an important element in winning,

B. Since competitors must be continually hanging around for a stray job, and

C. Since they must spend a great deal of time in—

1. Pushing rollers,

2. Carrying towels to athletes,

3. Running back hammers and javelins,

4. Writing letters, we conclude that

II. Competitors give too much time to athletic competitions.

    D. As further evidence, we know that competitors often fail in their studies.

*Subject Sentence:* The Athletic Council should hire competent persons to do the work now done by competitors.

III. The argument that the Council cannot afford to hire people to do the work is not sound, for

    A. A few efficient workers could do the work of many competitors.

    B. It would be cheaper to have the work well done by a few paid workers than to have it bungled by competitors.

### Conclusion

Since the present system is profitable neither to the Athletic Council nor to the competitors, it should be abolished. If we cannot abolish it, let us at least keep out of it.

Some may say the brief in this case is as good a speech outline as the outline itself. That is as may be. The purpose of the example is to illustrate possibilities. It is safe to say that the more one studies his material with reference to his audience, the more likely he will be to make his outline differ from his brief; and the skilful speaker who has succeeded with one audience will usually, in presenting the same thesis to a different sort of audience, make still further changes.

It will readily be seen that if a speaker explains a co-operative store by a narrative of a visit to one, his outline will depart widely from his brief.

The brief back of the next outline would need none of the introduction except the subject sentence, and might without harm omit from the explanation some of the headings marked with Arabic numerals. The outline was made for a speech to be delivered to an audience that had some superficial knowledge of the institution discussed, but not much interest in it or understanding of its character, and the introduction was planned as the basis of remarks which should both awaken interest and prepare the way for the discussion.

WHERE GOOD CITIZENS ARE MADE

*Introduction*

I. The George Junior Republic was established in 1895 near Freeville in Central New York, by William George, a New York business man.

II. It was the outcome of his experience in conducting, during his summer vacations, camps for "fresh air" children.

   A. He found difficulty in conducting his camps, in that

      1. The children showed a tendency toward pauperization.

         a. They were greedy for gifts but unwilling to work.

      2. They had small regard for the property rights of others.

   B. He found a partial solution of his difficulties in two measures:

      1. He refused to give out clothing until the recipient had done work on the camp road.

      2. He introduced a measure of self-government.

III. He resolved to embody his discoveries in a permanent colony for training youngsters of from 14 to 18 years of age.

IV. Good citizenship has always been the guiding aim.

*Discussion*

I. The Republic trains for the civil duties of citizenship, in that
  A. It is governed by laws made and executed by its citizens.
  B. Its form of government is adapted from that of the greater Republic.
      1. It has executive, legislative, and judicial departments.
  C. Citizens learn by experience the need of protection to person and property.
  D. They learn also the evils arising from bad laws and from inefficient and corrupt government.
  E. The powers reserved to the Director are sparingly exercised.
      1. He prefers to use personal influence and suggestion when control becomes necessary.
      2. Even needed reforms are left to the initiative of the citizens.

II. Citizens are trained for citizenship industrially, in that
  A. Each citizen is impressed with the duty of self-support.
      1. The motto and policy of the Republic is, "Nothing without labor."
      2. A vagrancy act is enforced.
  B. Each citizen learns how to support himself.

*Conclusion*

To-day hundreds of "alumni" look back to the "G.J.R." with gratitude for the training it has given them.

I will add an example of the sort of outlines that many find most difficult—outlines for explaining a process. It is the work of a student, and I give it without improvement. It has at least one flaw; but if you will first try to put into sound outline form a bit of football strategy, or some similar matter, you will realize that this was not easy.

### INSIDE FOOTBALL

#### Introduction

I. The blocked kick is not an accidental occurrence in modern football.

II. It results from carefully planned defensive plays.

#### Discussion

I. In one play the center and guards work together to block the kick.
   A. The right guard pulls the opposing center out of the way.
   B. The left guard pulls the opposing right guard out of the way.
   C. The center is left a clear path to the kicker.

II. In another play the tackle and fullback try to block the kick.
   A. There are two possibilities that this play will work.
      1. If the quarterback stops the tackle the fullback can block the kick.
      2. If the quarterback blocks off the fullback the tackle is left with better chance to block the kick.

III. These plays, perfect in theory, depend on individual skill and cunning for effectiveness.
   A. If one man fails in his duty the play is spoiled.
   B. Variations in the play of opponents must be matched with variations in the play of the defense.

C. The surprise element must be maintained.
  1. Plays must be alternated.
  2. Hidden signals are used.

This outline was accompanied by charts to be used in the speech, indicating the positions and movements of the players. The third division of the Discussion is the least satisfactory. Can you spot any fault? And correct it?

THE PARAGRAPH OUTLINE. As was said earlier, there are speeches, or talks, which have but a superficial unity, and which, while not advised as training, are proper enough under certain conditions. For these the form of outline here presented may at times prove too strict; and the "paragraph" form, a more loosely bound series of statements, each made a paragraph, with no distinction of rank (no main heads and no subheads), may be substituted.

Also when one wishes to change a division of his speech from the so-called deductive order in the brief to an inductive order in the outline (as in heading II of the outline on athletic competitions) one may, if he finds the arrangement in the standard form becoming too complicated, drop into the simpler paragraph form. *This practice should be indulged in but sparingly* lest the many advantages of our standard form be lost. Still it is relatively *safe for one who has first worked out a faithful brief*.

HOW COMPLETE SHOULD AN OUTLINE BE? This question cannot be answered by a rule. We may say, in general, that *everything you intend to say in your speech should be provided for in your outline;* that is, it should fit in under some heading. Further, it is better for the beginner to err on the side of fulness rather than of scantiness. It is not true, as is sometimes complained, that the sort of outlines here advocated requires one to "write the whole speech."

An outline is a condensed statement, comparable to a skeleton, necessary to the symmetry and beauty of the body, but in itself bare, ugly, and needing much covering. Usually one can without crowding put a good outline for a ten-minute speech on one page of 8 × 10 paper, often on less; but this statement assumes genuine economy of words—not leaving out needed words but making all count.

It would be a waste of space even to attempt to discuss and illustrate all the problems that may arise in outlining; but the preceding discussion will furnish clues for the solution of most difficulties. Give this whole matter of analysis, briefing, and outlining careful attention early in your training, study and follow the forms until you have mastered them, and you will find that they help in clear thinking and effective presentation; that is, if you wish to do something better than just to talk. Of course, for one who wishes merely to develop the "gift of gab," this whole chapter is waste; but for one who wishes to learn to speak to the point, to know when he has made his point, and so avoid confusion, doubling on his tracks, and rambling on in the hope of yet reaching some point, briefing and outlining are helps in doing work that must be done. They do not increase labor; they save it. The habit of following out these methods is soon established, and it enables one to proceed with preparation without waste of time and effort. Experienced speakers, one a distinguished ambassador of the United States, have testified to me that readiness in casting their thoughts into familiar logical forms has proved a "life-saver" when they have been called upon to speak with but little chance for preparation.

USE OF THE OUTLINE. We should recall here the use of the term *extempore*, as explained in Chapter II.

I shall not give much space to the much debated question

of whether a speech should be delivered extempore, or written in full and either delivered from memory or read from manuscript. This is a question over which people are peculiarly liable to lose their sanity. It is absurd to say that all speeches should be made this way or that way. Each method has its merits and its defects, its uses and abuses. One who asserts that extempore speaking is the only method for a practical man may be asked how many of the speeches we hear by radio are delivered without manuscript, or how many important speeches in a Presidential campaign are not written, and even handed out in advance to the press. (And one does not have to run for President to meet occasions when it is important to say things just right.) Memorized speeches are delivered far more often than is popularly supposed. On the other hand, the speaker who will not venture away from a written speech may be asked to consider how limited must be his part in a court room, or in offhand debate in a board of directors or the meeting of any sort of organization. The well balanced view is that there are times for every method of speaking and the well equipped speaker is able to employ all of them.

The practice of all methods will also be better for a speaker's development. One who writes only is liable to produce speeches that are over-formal, lacking in conversational flavor and adaptation to audiences; or that, as the phrase runs, "smell of the lamp." He should vary his practice with extempore speeches. On the other hand, the speaker who rarely writes is likely to develop a style loose, rambling, and repetitious. He should write a speech now and then; or at least he should keep a check on himself by having some of his speeches recorded for later review. However, it is usually best for the beginner to start with extempore speeches and occasional impromptus, because these are nearer to his ordinary speaking from which he is to build up.

Whether a speaker writes his speech or extemporizes, he should not feel bound to follow his outline slavishly; but he is wise to follow it until he has good reason for departure from his carefully ordered plan, for the chances of becoming entangled and lost are large. It may be added, however, that the man who has made such a plan is just the one who can most safely venture off the trail; for he has gained in the process of analysis, briefing, and outlining, if only by trial and error, a knowledge of the possible routes through the subject to his goal. In general, there should be an intelligent, not a blind, use of the outline. The experienced speaker finds out what methods are best adapted to himself.

Some speakers prefer to take their outlines to the platform; and this procedure may be best upon important occasions for those of treacherous memory. One may write out cues on a card, which is more easily handled and is less tempting to the speaker's eyes. This last point is not inconsequential, for many speakers lose one of the chief advantages of extempore speaking by gazing needlessly at any sort of aid before them. Austen Chamberlain tells us that, although Disraeli sometimes went so far in preparing speeches as to rehearse them before a *Times* reporter, yet he feared to have notes while speaking lest he "should lean upon them." At any rate, when a speaker feels he must have some sort of guide before him, the points should be set down so boldly that he can catch his cue quickly and turn completely away from his notes to his hearers; unless he is dealing with statistics, a quotation, or other matter that should be stated with unusual exactness. And whatever you have, do not try to hide it from your audience; they will know when you are looking at notes. (Watch the next speakers you hear from the news reel.) Place your notes on the desk without concealment, if there is a desk. If not, hold them in one hand. Most awkward method of all is to put them in your pocket to pull out from time to time.

For nearly all students of speaking, especially before they acquire a good degree of communicativeness, it is better to speak without notes of any kind; for beginners are too likely to talk to any paper before them and so lose contact with their hearers. Perhaps an exception should be made for the rare person, say one in a hundred, who has extreme difficulty in controlling his thoughts before an audience.

For *the final preparation*, the final steps between outline and delivery, it would be difficult to find better advice than this:

"The problem is to transfer the plan (speech outline) to your mind and to become so thoroughly familiar with its sequence of ideas that one will automatically call to mind the next. The process of memorizing combines with that of rehearsal; the stages of the joint process may be divided as follows; each step, of course, will have to be repeated several times.

"1. Read through the written plan; ignore the subheads, but fix in mind the succession of main points.

"2. Read through again, this time concentrating not only on the succession of main heads, but on the details supporting each.

"3. Still referring to the written plan, speak through the speech in whatever words happen to come. Talk out loud, not under your breath. It helps to stand up and face an imaginary audience. Get through the whole speech; perhaps you will at first bungle a certain part; go right on to the end without stopping to straighten out the troublesome section. Attend to that when you have finished the speech.

"4. Without using the plan or any memorandum, stand up and speak through the speech as before. If you can find a patient auditor, so much the better. At each rehearsal, seek better expression of your ideas; more vivid terms, more forceful development of illustrations, clearer transitions.

"5. When you can get through fairly well, time yourself, and adjust the speech to the stated requirement. It is important to acquire a sense of time on the platform, and the habit of keeping within the agreed limits." [1]

IN CONCLUSION. It may seem to some that I should have told just what to put in the introduction, what in the discussion, and what in the conclusion. I might have told you that the introduction should arouse interest, clear the ground by explanations, put you on common ground with your hearers, make them willing to hear your case, and start them thinking in the right direction, that the body of the speech should make the argument, explanation, or whatnot, that the conclusion should clinch the point, deepen the impression, or arouse to action; and I should not have been misstating the truth more than one usually does in sweeping statements. But I fear the matter is not so simple. In the first place, few such statements should be made so absolutely; "circumstances alter cases." In the second place, the divisions of a speech are not so distinct as these statements imply. It is desirable that all parts of a speech should be interesting, all parts persuasive; explanations may be needed at many points in a speech; common ground is a needed element everywhere. In the third place, to say that a certain part of a

---

[1] From *Manual for Public Speaking*, I, p. 22, by H. A. Wichelns and others (1932).

speech should be explanatory, interesting, or persuasive is
not to say much. What we need now is to study into the
principles and methods involved in interesting, informing,
and persuading audiences.

# CHAPTER VII

## INTEREST

That stress should be put upon the obvious necessity of interesting audiences may seem strange; and yet as a matter of fact the necessity is often ignored. This is not so surprising, however, when we think of the number of those who in private conversation talk on about their own affairs, their ideas, their "game," their children, calmly ignoring the yawns of their hearers. This tendency to think mostly of our own interests is probably encouraged by the requirement all the way up through school of essays, which are usually written without thought of interesting the reader. Who ever thought of interesting the wielder of a blue pencil? The average student of speaking needs to rid himself of the "composition" attitude of mind and fix firmly the conception that a speech is to produce effects upon the hearer; and first to interest him.

An audience always holds it a natural right to be interested; often it asks nothing more. The speaker himself may at times have no purpose beyond interesting; that is, entertainment. More often the speaker has a purpose beyond this, as explaining a problem, inducing belief, or influencing conduct; but whatever his purpose, the demand for interest he must satisfy, for he must have attention. A "polite hearing" is rarely genuine; and very few members of the average audience will listen by sheer will power, nor is it desirable that they should.

Another reason for seeking to interest is that few speakers are able to go energetically through a speech without evidences of response from their audience. Without such evidence one feels a great load on his spirits. It is sometimes worth while to take pains to interest a single person in order to have his sympathetic following; but unless a speaker has a majority of his audience following with easy attention, he cannot often do well. When practically the whole audience listens with keen interest, then he finds his greatest freedom in speech.

There are times when the speaker has the advantage of an aroused interest in his audience. There are times when he can rely on this interest, even abuse it; but such times are rare, and even strong initial interest is usually easily lost. I have seen 2,000 eager listeners, come together to hear a potential Presidential candidate, bored into helpless irritation by an inept address. The young speaker will find few occasions indeed when he can safely ignore the means of interesting.

The speaker standing before his audience faces a very practical problem: How can he gain and hold attention? No matter how noble his purpose, how splendid his rhetoric, how clear his explanation, how sound his arguments, if he is not listened to. There they sit, his potential hearers. Presumably most of them are willing to be interested; but unless they are interested, they will think of their own affairs, sink into bored endurance, or become restless. Consider how easily and ruthlessly the dull radio speaker is turned off. The speaker must grip attention, right at the start, and he must hold it.

How CAN ATTENTION BE WON? In the first place, it does little good to tell one's audience that the theme is interesting. Speakers are constantly defending their dull efforts with "They ought to be interested in that"; but the question remains, Are they interested? It is only the speaker of high prestige with his audience who can depend, even for initial attention, upon an assertion, or an assumption, that his matter is interesting. It should promptly appear to be interesting.

We see at once that the question, What does interest audiences? is too complicated for brief and final answer. We do not advance much, so far as answering our question goes, when we say, what is profoundly true, that *the speaker should have something to say worth saying;* for that really means something the audience thinks worth hearing, and that is much the same as saying something the audience finds interesting. Hence we are where we started. Perhaps we can, however, establish a few principles and become intelligent in applying them to various situations. Luckily we do not have to go into the warring psychologies and ask why people are interested, or precisely what in scientific terms interest is; we wish to know *how* people are interested. Or, in other words, what they attend to.

USE OF TERMS. It will be convenient to use the word *attention* as well as *interest* in this discussion. They are not synonymous terms; but, as William James said, "What-we-attend-to and what-interests-us are synonymous terms." Interest and attention are related as cause and effect, and either may be the cause of the other. It is evident that to be interesting is more than to be pleasant to attend to, or entertaining, although it includes that. A blow in the face, or information that one has a fatal disease is interesting, but not entertaining.

ATTENTION MAY REQUIRE MORE OR LESS EFFORT. We know that some things are hard to attend to, some are easy, and some command our attention. We know further that some things once hard to attend to are now easy. You can recall, no doubt, some school subject which at first seemed impossible. After a brief effort other matters would slip in and carry away your thoughts. But by main force you did hold your mind to the subject and gradually found that you could attend to it with only moderate effort; and it may be that in time you found it hard to turn away from that very subject. It became your hobby.

The subject that gains such a hold on a man may be his life's study or vocation, as rocks for a geologist or stock reports for an investor; or it may be of lesser importance to him, as stamps for a philatelist; or it may be a temporary interest due to his immediate situation. He may have ordinarily but small interest in the variations in automobiles, but when about to buy a car he may find the vehicles parked along Main Street so interesting that he forgets his errand downtown.

To distinguish this involuntary or effortless attention which we come to give to subjects which do not at first command it, from the native effortless attention we give to sensations such as loud noises and sharp pains, we may call it *acquired effortless attention.*

*Applications to speech-making.* Plainly enough acquired effortless attention is of much importance to the speaker. He does, to be sure, make use of the primary or native attention of his hearers, as by change of voice, movement, and by various sensational methods; but these alone will not sustain attention long to ideas that have in themselves slight interest for his hearers. And he may be sure that forced attention will soon flag; besides, he wishes them to use their mental energy in thinking about what he says, not in mere effort to overcome boredom or to fight off distracting ideas. He strives, therefore, to present his matter so that the mere listening, if not effortless, is made as easy as may be.

Again, the speaker himself should be free from effort in keeping his mind on his theme, so that amid the distractions of the platform his mind will be able to work on his material, selecting, arranging, and adapting it to his hearers, without worry or waste, but with the efficiency of a smoothly running engine. But to save confusion in our consideration, this aspect of the matter will not be treated until later.

Our question has now become: How can we develop and handle facts and ideas so that they will command effortless, or nearly effortless, attention? Or, How can we add to their interest?

INTEREST GROWS WITH KNOWLEDGE. It is plain enough that we attend to what interests us; but fully as significant for us is the correlative truth that "things are interesting because we attend to them." [1] The quoted statement is true because "interest grows with knowledge, and, in fact, is made by knowledge." [2] "One's permanent interests, one's tendencies to attend, are largely dependent upon what one has, on one's permanent store of knowledge. Ordinarily if one fills his mind with a subject he will become interested and attend to it." [3] "In order to develop interest in a subject, secure information about it. . . . The typical university professor or scientist . . . is interested in a certain subject of research—infusoria, electrons, plant ecology,—because he knows much about them. His interest may be said to *consist* partly of the body of knowledge that he possesses. He was not always interested in the specific, obscure field, but by saturating himself with the facts about it, has developed an

[1] From *Attention* by W. B. Pillsbury, p. 55.

[2] *Idem*, p. 54. By permission of The Macmillan Company, publishers.

[3] From *Human Nature Club* by E. L. Thorndike, p. 73. By permission of Longmans, Green & Company.

interest in it amounting to passionate absorption, which manifests itself in 'absent-mindedness.' " [4]

DERIVING INTEREST. Interest grows with knowledge because as we learn about a subject we find out interesting things about it; and that means we find out things which are related to what, because of native tendencies and experience, we have come to consider interesting. Derived interest, or interest one subject gains by being associated with another, is explained in a classic statement by William James:

Any object not interesting in itself may become interesting through becoming associated with an object in which an interest already exists. The two associated objects grow, as it were, together: the interesting portion sheds its quality over the whole; and thus things not interesting in their own right borrow an interest which becomes as real and as strong as that of any natively interesting thing.

. . . There emerges a very simple abstract programme for the teacher to follow in keeping the attention of the child: Begin with the line of his native interests, and offer him objects that have some immediate connection with these.

Next, step by step, connect with these first objects and experiences the later objects and ideas which you wish to instill. Associate the new with the old in some natural and telling way, so that the interest, being shed along from point to point, finally suffuses the entire system of objects of thought.

If, then, you wish to insure the interest of your pupils, there is only one way to do it; and that is to make certain that they have something in their minds *to attend with*, when you begin to talk. That something can consist in nothing but a previous lot of ideas already interesting in themselves, and of such a nature that the incoming novel objects which you present can dovetail

[4] From H. D. Kitson, *How to Use Your Mind*, Chicago: J. B. Lippincott Company, pp. 173-174.

into them and form with them some kind of a logically associated or systematic whole.[5]

Here then is a major secret, which, like most great ideas, is just plain common sense: To make a dull subject interesting associate it with something already interesting. To interest yourself in a dull topic, force attention to it until you find out interesting things about it; that is, things you can connect with your existing interests. The suggestion is pat for interesting others. Tell a boy that in physics can be found the explanation of a baseball's curve or of radio, and you may change an idler into an eager student.

We see now, not only why increasing knowledge brings increase of interest, but also why it is easier to interest a well informed man than an ignorant man; the well informed man has so many more points of contact for a subject. As some paragrapher has said, "Ideas die quickly in some minds; they cannot stand solitary confinement." And we can see also that what is needed to increase interest in a subject is not a mere mass of information, but knowledge organized and effectively related to existing interests.

*Applications.* How derived interest can be employed in speech-making is already apparent. Suppose the Professor of Greek is invited to speak before the Rotary Club, an organization of business men, who are perhaps hoping that Professor Smith will "keep off that old stuff." Professor Smith, however, determines to show them that the ancient Greeks were not just figures in a book; and he chooses for his theme, How the ancient Greeks carried on business; or, perhaps, Olympic games old and new; or, Where the architect got his ideas for our new Court House. And he might

[5] From *Talks to Teachers*, pp. 94-97. By permission of Henry Holt and Company.

be able to carry the interest of his hearers on to aspects of Grecian civilization not so immediately interesting to them.

Problems of deriving interest arise every day in a speaking class, and this is especially true in a university where members of the class may represent widely divergent interests. If one's subject is What is the matter with the football team? there is a fair presumption that there is a common ground of interest and there is little use in seeking aid from related topics, but we cannot stick to such topics. A student in agriculture had some good ideas on the common complaint that too much time is spent in teaching theory and too little on practical applications. Two-thirds of the class, not being students in agriculture, evinced little interest. The speaker might have gained general interest by first taking up the question as one that arises in all courses, and illustrating with the course he knew best. A student in architecture, speaking in a class including no others from his college, kept up interest by selecting his examples from the college buildings. A student in chemistry who started with our interest in automobiles carried us far into a discussion of substitutes for gasoline.

All this implies that a speaker will consider the interests of his audience, what they have to "attend with," and how "natural and telling associations" can be set up. It should not be understood that any sort of association with any existing interest will be effective. The connection must not seem far-fetched, it must be made in a skilful way, and the interest from which one seeks to derive aid should be one readily awakened. A student about to make what proved to be a dull speech on the Cape Cod Canal reported to his instructor that he was depending upon our interest in taxes and in legislation. Unfortunately our interest at the moment was less keen in taxes and legislation than in the Canal itself.

There were in this attempt to use derived interest three faults: 1. The interests appealed to were not, at the moment in the particular audience, sufficiently lively for ready response. 2. No effective connection was made. 3. The relation seemed too remote, for the questions of waste and corruption were not pertinent to the speech as made.

*Methods in deriving interest.* There is usually no need for a direct statement that there is a relation between the speaker's theme and the interests of the audience; it is enough to reveal the connection. Professor Smith need not tell his audience that a comparison of ancient business methods with modern methods is interesting; but he may in his speech draw out the comparison at some length, or he may decide that his hearers will be more interested to note for themselves the likenesses and unlikenesses which he makes obvious.

Sometimes the existing interests of one's hearers may be enlisted by starting with one of these and leading into the desired topic. So in wartime a blockade may be used to lead into international law. Again, one may start with a phase of his subject which will soon reveal a relation to existing interests, as by taking up the rights of neutrals and so coming to blockades. The connection is often made by the illustrations used. A stump speaker addressing now farmers, now railroad men, now salesmen, will usually try to vary his illustrations to fit each group. We should not suppose, however, that any class of people is interested only in its own specialties.

By whatever method one proceeds one should not expect an audience to listen long without seeing how the topic is related to something they consider interesting. And this should not be thought of as a matter of the introduction only; as the speech goes on one should continue to link new

matter to that already made interesting, "so that the interest, being shed along from point to point, finally suffuses the
entire system of objects of thought." One may be able, also,
to connect the speech with other interests than those first
touched. It is easily conceivable that in a single speech one
might, with perfect unity, associate the subject of Greek life
with interest in athletics, in temperance, in education, in
art, and in religion. And each of these interests might serve
as posts to which to moor the new subject.

Here, as in many places, we can see the advantage to a
speaker of acquaintance with men of many kinds.

NEW AND OLD AS ELEMENTS IN INTEREST. We know that
anything strikingly new or different will attract attention.
But we must not overestimate the importance of mere novelty. It may catch, but cannot hold attention. "Curiosity
will give us a start," says Woodworth, "but is too easily
satisfied to carry us far." [6] Indeed, the extremely novel has
less holding power than the moderately novel. It is uninteresting because we have no points of contact with it,
nothing to compare and identify it with, nothing from which
it can derive meaning and interest; hence our minds are
baffled, and in most cases we simply ignore it. The fact that
Hebrew is read from right to left does not interest a man
who knows nothing of reading.

It is well-nigh impossible to present anything absolutely
new to an educated adult; he at once begins to find points
of contact. Primitive man furnishes us with examples.

Some Indians brought to a large city remained stolid at the
sight of mechanical wonders of bridge, trolley, and telephone,

---

[6] *Psychology* by Robert S. Woodworth, p. 258. By permission of
Henry Holt and Company.

but were held spellbound by the sight of workmen climbing poles to repair wires.[7]

If we move among strange ideas we are happy to return to the home feeling of our usual topics. Listen to the comments of people coming out from a weighty lecture, even in a "learned" community. Unless the lecturer has skilfully linked his matter with the familiar interests of his hearers, you will hear a few discussing the subject with interest, more talking about it in such vague terms as, "Fine, wasn't it?" and "So improving!" and many more saying in a tone of relief, "Think it's going to rain?" and "How about a little contract?"

The interest which can be gained from novelty, then, depends upon our power to assimilate it. If the more novel were the more interesting, we should not pass by so many objects with scarce a glance, provided they do not obstruct or annoy or alarm us; nor should we pass over so many new facts and ideas in periodicals just because they seem so remote from our interests, and turn to the most familiar topics, as sports and markets. But we know we are keenest about the things we know most about. These are our "interests."

I am not myself presenting a novelty, but rather an almost proverbial truth, as is evidenced by the expression "busman's holiday." A man who knows says that "a railroad man on a holiday spends most of his time down at the yard watching them get No. 8 ready." Are the so-called brain-workers very different?

But, on the other hand, we all know the dullness of the over familiar, of monotonous, unchanging ideas and experience. "The same old thing" is our common expression of

---

[7] *How We Think* by John Dewey, p. 120. By permission of D. C. Heath & Co.

boredom.  How shall we reconcile this with the fact that we do dwell a great deal, and unnecessarily, on the same round of ideas?  The answer has already been suggested: interest is keenest when we have the novel and the familiar in due proportions; and in the compound the familiar should have the larger part.  As William James said:

> It is an odd circumstance that neither the old nor the new, by itself, is interesting: the absolutely old is insipid; the absolutely new makes no appeal at all.  The old *in* the new is what claims attention—the old with a slightly new turn.[8]

The new derives interest from association with the old; and this interest is strongest, of course, when the old with which the new is associated is itself interesting.  Yet it seems that association with any existing knowledge awakens some interest; we know how a person languidly viewing his friend's snapshot will come to attention if he chances to recognize the scene, although that scene has never before aroused his interest.  We should beware, however, of establishing associations with anything considered tiresome or in any way distasteful.

Interest is, generally speaking, strongest in old things in new settings, looked at from new angles, given new forms and developed with new facts and ideas, with new light on familiar characters, new explanations of familiar phenomena, or new applications of old truths.

*Applications.*  The application of the foregoing to speech-making will almost make itself.  We should seek a judicious mixture of old and new.  When we offer new ideas to an audience we should present them so that their relation to familiar ideas is apparent, so that they can be readily com-

[8] *Talks to Teachers,* p. 108.  By permission of Henry Holt and Company.

pared and identified; and when we present old matter we should give it new aspects, relations, and applications.

Travel lectures, which have great vogue on lyceum and Chautauqua platforms, illustrate these truths. They furnish a pleasant opportunity for comparing and contrasting, and discovering the familiar in the seemingly unfamiliar. "What an odd way to do!" we hear a listener say; that is, how different from our way of doing some familiar act. "What a queer looking place! Why it's a kind of store, isn't it? How interesting!"

A group of housewives may be interested in hearing an explanation of the familiar phenomenon of the rising of bread. I was interested in learning from a speech by a student of architecture of the notable accomplishment of Thomas Jefferson as an architect, while the student had become interested in the statesman who was also an artist.

Speakers err in both directions. We in college are familiar with the visiting lecturers who "shoot over our heads," assuming that we are all learned; and we are even more painfully familiar with those who tell us such elementary and familiar things that we feel our time is wasted. In speaking classes we have the industrious fellow, keen for new facts and ideas, who tries to put into his speech as much new matter as possible, quite regardless of our understanding and interest; and then is surprised, and possibly a bit superior, because we are not eager for his offering. Then there are those who will tell us how the campus is arranged, or that Presidents are elected by the Electoral College. In one institution I heard about the shortcomings of the gymnasium until, given the start, I could give the rest of the speech. Any sophomore could make the speech without preparation. Yet I heard one speech on that same gymnasium and its deficiencies, which combined with the familiar matter so much new information and such an individual point of view that it was genuinely interesting.

And there we might let the matter rest were it not for the disquieting fact that while the absolutely familiar is said to be insipid, beyond doubt there are times when people like to hear familiar ideas and even like them put in a familiar way. Indeed, they may dislike any marked departure from the usual. We know that partisan audiences love to gather on Jackson's or Lincoln's Birthday to hear again the familiar praises of party and party heroes. Gatherings of school and college alumni and of old soldiers do not weary easily of familiar themes and eulogies. It was said that the veterans from North and South at the great gathering at Gettysburg in 1913 did not take kindly to President Wilson's attempt to talk to them of the duties of the present; their minds were full of the past.

Now this is in apparent conflict with the fact that no criticism is more common or damning than that a speech was trite, stale, worn out with much repeating. Plainly enough it behooves us to get a clear idea of *triteness*.

The reconciliation of this criticism with the liking for the familiar may be sought, *first,* in the kind of subject used in a given case. It may not have been one considered important by the fault-finder. Some one has well said, "No truth ever is or can be trite to one who uses it." Old problems still pressing for solution do not become trite, though we may temporarily weary of them. The old, old Negro problem can still provoke an interesting discussion in my classes. Again, the subject may not have been one dear to the hearts of the audience. We may note that the themes which people love to hear about in the old way are those concerning which they have warm convictions and strongly emotional associations.

*Secondly,* much depends upon the occasion. The old recital is especially welcomed at gatherings which awaken old and emotional associations. Then the old is congruous with the hearer's mood. The old soldiers gathered at Gettysburg were very different from the same men at home, with business uppermost in their minds. In political and religious meetings of certain types, rallies, or any meetings that bring people together in enthusiastic accord and lessen the critical spirit, they love to hear speeches emphasizing what they hold in common. (And, conversely, such stress on common views increases harmony.) As a student once put it, "Triteness is saying the old thing in the old way at the wrong time."

*Thirdly,* the treatment of the old topic may have been dull, confused, or inferior to what the audience was accustomed to. To fall below the expectation of the audience, based on memory of other speakers, is especially unfortunate.

*Fourthly,* much depends upon the presumption with which the old matter is presented. If old information is presented as new, or old arguments are made as arguments which the audience has not before understood, resentment may be provoked. "Does he think we don't know that?" is sometimes heard.

It is well in preparing for a given audience to note that people differ in their relish for novelty. The differences arise not only from temperament but from training. In a very general way, we may say that the educated are more ready, if only because they are more experienced, in taking up new ideas than the uneducated.

Most persons will expect, on most occasions, to gain something from hearing your speech. They usually hope for new information, or to get new light on an old problem, or perhaps to receive reassurance and inspiration. Excepting the unusually serious-minded, few will take stock afterward of what they have gained, provided they have been interested. But if you have not succeeded in interesting them they will grumble that their time has been wasted, that it was "the same old stuff," and that they have heard it much better put before. Usually we should aim to give something new in material or something new in treatment; or, better, something new in both.

FUNDAMENTAL INTERESTS. It becomes pertinent to inquire what are some of the common, abiding interests with which we can profitably associate our topics. We may put first a group of interests which plainly are desires, or what we usually call motives.[9] These have much to do with persuasion, but may be briefly noted here. First we may place *life* and *health*. The vast deal of matter on health that is printed and spoken over the radio presumably supplies a demand; but when we consider how readily we sacrifice health, and even life, we conclude that these topics do not normally occupy a large place among our interests. *Property* is one of the surest interests to which a theme can be linked; and this interest is not limited to our own pocketbooks. Stories of success and failure in business have a large place in popular periodicals.

But since we both spend and give away our money rather readily, there must be interests still greater. Men are interested in the means of *acquiring power* and *reputation;* and in what touches their *sentiments,* as in regard to social welfare, good of country, honor (by whatever names these abstractions may be called). They are interested in what touches their *affections,* as the welfare of their children. And they are interested in all that gives them *pleasure,* as sports, adventure, comforts, music, drama, literature.

[9] Those familiar with *Effective Speaking* by E. A. Phillips, will know that I am adapting here his "impelling motives."

This catalogue of interests, rough-and-ready as it is, and intended to be suggestive rather than complete, may be of more use to us than a more scientific list requiring much definition and explanation.  This list can be tested by every-day experience, and added to as experience and observation suggest.  Some of the interests named may be derivatives of others and some may be compounds, but all are real.

*How this list can be used.*  It will be well to say some-thing here of the use of this list, and other interests and methods of interesting to be discussed farther on.  First, such a list impresses a truth that must grow increasingly familiar; we must study audiences, study human nature, observe that men are many-sided in their interests.  This suggestion is of special value to the self-centered speaker; and many of us are self-centered.  Then the list may help us in observing whether we habitually appeal to but one or two interests; always, for example, harping on profit and duty, and never presenting anything in the light of an adventure, or failing to use a judicious mixture of duty, pleasure, and profit.

Now notice, please, that I am not suggesting that one preparing a speech should say to himself: Now a little health, now a dash of property, now spice up with adventure.  But I do suggest that one planning a speech may well consider what interests he will appeal to, and whether, for example, he might throw his speech, or a part of it, into a narrative of adventure.  To use again the Philippine problem as an example, an argument might be cast into the form suggested by the title, An Adventure That Failed.  With some subjects illustrations involving adventure can be used.

I suggest further that if one has prepared a speech that threatens to be dull, he may well go over his list of funda-mental interests to see if interest cannot be derived from one or more of these sources.  Such practices (and the same may be said of many of those suggested in this or any other book on the subject) may aid a speaker in establishing good habits in his early efforts, and may at any stage of his development furnish a valuable means of self-criticism.

It should be noted that the interests named are not put forward as themselves, in their abstract form, interesting topics to speak on.  Nobody wishes to hear talks about honor, reputation, humanity, or health; but we may be interested in specific instances of, say, honor or dishonor, and are sure to be if the case touches our personal honor or the honor of the group to which we belong.

In many instances, of course, a speech rests inevitably upon one or more of these fundamental interests, as when one is urging a plan on the ground that it will be profitable.  In other cases the question is whether it is worth while to derive interest from a source not strictly necessary to the discussion; as in awakening interest in the ancient Greeks by stressing their athletics.

There are fundamental interests which are not so obviously motives.

*Interest in human beings.*  Any one of the interests we are considering will commonly be found mingled with others; and this is particularly true of the so-called human interest. It is very often associated with our interest in activity, but our interest in people is not limited to people in action; and similar remarks might be made of our interest in mystery and in conflict.  It is close to the interest in celebrities; but we are interested in "just folks"—men, women, and babies. This interest in human beings is one of the most dependable. "Man is perennially interesting to man," says Carlyle; "nay, if we look strictly to it, there is nothing else interesting." Mr. Dooley said that we were not so much interested in the poles as in the fact that men could discover them. It has been said that a complete revelation of the life of the simplest man would make the most interesting book ever written. This may be the "language of enthusiasm," but it is an attempt to express a profound truth: personality is always interesting.

So a speaker will often find it to his advantage to state his ideas in terms of persons—flesh-and-blood individuals, so presented that they seem real, not mere bundles of qualities. We may be impressed by generalizations or by large numbers, as when we are told that because of the depression there are thousands of boys who in normal times would be in school or at work, now on the road as hoboes; but we shall be more interested in, and remember longer, the stories of one or two so told that we feel we know them.

To illustrate the difference between speaking merely of a person's qualities and giving him flesh-and-blood interest, we may recall a story told of Thackeray. When he was thinking of putting Washington into a book he asked an American friend to describe the great man. The American began with a list of the qualities commonly ascribed to Washington, his integrity, sagacity, etc. "No, no," said Thackeray, "not that. Tell me, did he take snuff and did he drip it down his coat?" That was Thackeray's vigorous way of saying he wanted the real man. For a century Washington was to most people a figure on a monument, on the base of which was carved, First in War, First in Peace, and First in the Hearts of his Countrymen. To-day he is emerging from history as a human being, not so perfect as once supposed, but far more interesting.

The interest in men leads us to demand heroes and villains in public affairs. An experienced newspaperman has declared that people are never interested in reform but in its heroes, and more in its villains. The obvious suggestion is that you describe your evil in terms of its villains; hitch your cause to the man who represents it; state your principle in terms of the man who embodies it. Boss Tweed and the Looting of a City, George William Curtis and Civil Service Reform, Grover Cleveland and Honesty in Government, are more promising titles than Corruption in City Government, Civil Service Reform, and Honesty in Government. The same principle holds, of course, for subjects other than public questions, as Theodore Roosevelt and the Strenuous Life.[10]

In speeches that are not biographical in form, it is often possible to introduce the human interest by means of numerous illustrations. (We may refer here to "Acres of Diamonds" by Russell Conwell, which is probably the most famous of all popular lectures, and which was delivered over 6,000 times. It is replete with stories of the great and of the humble.)

*Interest in activity*. The simplest sort of movement takes our eyes. "I have seen a roomful of college students suddenly become perfectly still to look at a professor of physics tie a piece of string around a stick which he was going to use in an experiment, but immediately grow restless when he began to explain the experiment."[11] Says John Dewey:

It is a commonplace that what is moving attracts attention when that which is at rest escapes it. . . . Mere change is not enough, however. . . . The changes must (like the incidents

[10] As examples of the interest, and also of the persuasive force, that personality can give to an argument, one can study two speeches by Wendell Phillips: "Toussaint L'Ouverture," frankly an argument for the high quality of the Negro race; and "Daniel O'Connell," not so obviously, but in great part actually, a defense of agitation. There are, of course, many other elements of interest in these speeches.

[11] From *Talks to Teachers* by William James, p. 92. By permission of Henry Holt and Company.

in a well-arranged story or plot) take place in a certain cumulative order.[12]

The appeal of action, sometimes utilized in speeches by the use of apparatus, regularly by the use of gesture and a measure of acting, can also be utilized by narration of events and description of animated scenes. I have seen a class held intently interested by a description of the animated life the microscope reveals in a pail of water; and I remember after many years a speech which skilfully combined contrast, imaginative appeal, and activity. We were taken to the shores of a little lake in the Canadian woods and shown a scene of the utmost stillness. No wind stirs leaf or water. Overhead a hawk sailing high and a fleck of cloud that scarce seems to move. But as we gaze slight rustlings are heard; tiny creatures are moving; a spider pounces upon a fly, and a bird upon the spider; a fish breaks water, a deer bursts from the forest, and all at once the scene is full of life and movement. Told with just a few incidents, with no clogging details, with words apt to express movement, such as *rustlings, breaks, bursts, pounces,* the speech held the sharp attention of a class blasé and weary at the noon hour.

It was only a class exercise, but it was nevertheless an effective part of a good speech with the theme, Come out into the woods. Something might have been done to enliven a dull speech I heard recently in advocacy of middle lanes for speed in main highways. Suppose the speaker, in addition to the presumably valuable information he gave us, had described a trip the first part of which was on ordinary, cluttered-up roads, the rest on free middle lanes.[13]

[12] From *How We Think,* pp. 194-195. By permission of D. C. Heath & Co.

[13] Interesting examples of activity, and its related quality, movement of style, can be found in Webster's "Defense of the Kennistons," Phillips's "Toussaint L'Ouverture," and in Ingersoll's speech nominating Blaine.

*Interest in conflict.* We have an instinctive interest in conflict. We may hate it or joy in it, but are rarely indifferent to it, whether it takes the form of a dog fight, of athletic struggles, of war, of business competition, or of a struggle with nature. We also like stories of conflict, so told that through imagination we become spectators of or participants in the struggle.

At times a speaker can utilize this interest by throwing his speech, or a part of it, into a narrative of the conflict with the forces of the opposition, whether those forces consist of men, as in war, politics, and commerce, or of natural obstacles, as in building a canal or overcoming disease. No doubt interest is keenest where the conflict is with men, where passions are aroused; but enmity is not necessary. The story of the heroic period of an enterprise or reform will usually hold attention.

For more than a century the standard speech for the Fourth of July was in great part the story of the struggle between the American colonies and the mother country; and these descriptions were so colored with hostility to England that they were spoken of as "twisting the British lion's tail." The practice of employing "fight talk" as a means of attracting attention, and possibly distracting attention from one's own shortcomings, is not unknown to our politicians.

Even a Presidential campaign does not arouse much interest until a fighting spirit is generated; and interest is keenest if the conflict takes on a personal tinge. A contest of principles, or even of specific measures, is not nearly so good a "show" as a contest of persons. However regrettable the fact may be, we like to "see the fur fly," and will throng where it is likely to fly. Applause becomes more spontaneous the moment a candidate begins to chastise his opponents, and one of several reasons why candidates often write their speeches is the fear of going too far under the stimulus of such applause. Challenges to opponents to answer questions also increase fighting spirit.

It should not be inferred that the clash need be ill-natured. Indeed, while the encounter may be sharp, ill nature is felt to be poor sportsmanship and mars the enjoyment arising from a lively tussle of wits.

A dangerous but effective way of arousing interest is by *antagonizing the audience*. Dangerous because it may turn your hearers against your proposal; effective because we cannot be indifferent to that which arouses our combativeness. Bernard Shaw is sure of a hearing whenever he speaks, and partly because he is sure to say something startlingly antagonistic to his hearers, even abusive, as when he begins, "My dear American boobs." Archibald Henderson, Shaw's authorized biographer, declares that Shaw deliberately speaks in an irritating way, holding that the best way to arouse attention. That it succeeds is evident. If we were considering the effect upon his influence, the question would be more difficult. The public, apparently understanding his stage play, chuckles; but probably for most of us good manners are both more becoming and more effective.

This interest aroused by antagonism can be used without abusiveness. I heard a distinguished clergyman, preaching in a college chapel, say in a frank but friendly tone: "You have often been told that you are to be the leaders of the future. I have some doubts about that." The students laughed and sat up. A plain but courteous statement of beliefs contrary to those of the audience, or condemnation of their customs or heroes, usually will be enough to arouse attention.

Sometimes a speaker can startle a sleepy audience into attention by a sweeping statement which he later modifies.

A conservative audience was held in considerable trepidation by a speaker who devoted the first half of his speech to the best possible arguments for anarchy; and then the audience listened with relief while he toppled over those same arguments. There would have been little interest in an orthodox refutation of anarchy before an audience already convinced of its awfulness. A student preaching to other students the benefits of "student activities" would get better than usual attention if he first stated fairly the arguments against them. There need not be even the momentary deception involved in the speech on anarchy; for he will get much the same arousal if he begins by simply repeating the attacks that are made on such activities; as, It is asserted that we are a lot of nitwits rushing about at this and that without serious purpose, etc. Now is this true? Better yet, if he can name some well-known person as making the assertions.

(I consider here only the question of interest. I assume that a speaker will ultimately say, in one way or another, what he means. I recognize, too, that one may antagonize an audience for other reasons than awakening interest.)

One can often note the hush of strained attention when a speaker so much as approaches certain touchy questions, as those involving racial, religious, or sectional prejudices. This sort of interest is illustrated in a college class when certain fraternity questions are brought up.[14]

[14] The speeches of Henry W. Grady in the North, and the speeches of Booker T. Washington will illustrate. Cyrus W. Field's "Story of the Atlantic Cable" illustrates interest in man's conflict with nature. *Modern Eloquence* (1923), Vol. IV, p. 99. Speeches illustrating the interest of conflict in its simplest aspect are, of course, numberless.

# CHAPTER VIII [1]

## METHODS OF INTERESTING

HUMOR AND INTEREST. This is not the place to treat the philosophy and methods of humor, or the nice distinction between wit and humor, subjects that fill whole books; but a few observations practical for speakers can be made. We all know that an audience will listen as long as it is amused, and that a good laugh may banish weariness or hostility. So true is this that ability to make an audience laugh becomes a dangerous temptation. Unless the story or witticism serves the purpose of the speech it is likely to distract attention. The practice of going out of one's way to "be funny," dragging in stories with only a fictitious connection, though very common, is one to "make the judicious grieve." It comes within the spirit of Hamlet's condemnation.

Let those that play your clowns speak no more than is set down for them; for there be of them that will themselves laugh, to set on some barren quantity of spectators to laugh, too; though, in the meantime, some necessary question of the play be then to be considered: that's villainous, and shows a most pitiful ambition in the fool that uses it.

It is usually far better to use wit and humor as a spice, a relief, and as a means of emphasizing and "making stick" the ideas of one's speech. A good test of a speaker's humor

[1] The entire discussion of interest is a unit, and is rather arbitrarily broken up only because many prefer short chapters.

is this: Does it help to make the point? and when it comes back to mind later does it bring back the point? The next time some one tells you of the great joke So and So got off in his speech, ask what the point was; and if your informant cannot tell you readily, you may assume that the humor did not serve the speaker's purpose, unless his purpose was simply to be amusing.

Speakers, and especially American speakers, will do well to note that the repetition of stories is not the only way to add humor to a speech. In spite of all I say here in warning, I gladly welcome real humor in student speeches; but I rarely dare suggest the lightening-up of a speech for fear the reaction will be, "Where can I find some funny stories?" But humor can spring from the turn of a phrase, from placing in juxtaposition an opponent's incongruous arguments, from a comical bit of description or narration, without going at all outside of the proper materials of the speech, or checking its movement. Take this from a student's speech on athletics:

Unconsciously we have made a huge caricature of the whole business. . . . We train up our athletes as did the colonial cavalier his fighting cocks, or as does the modern millionaire his racing horse; we specially feed them, transport them in special trains; we yell for them, bet on them and weep over them. If it were not so serious it would be highly humorous, the sight of our five-thousand dollar coaches and trainers—intelligent men for the most part—running around after their charges, coddling them and denying them, looking solicitously after their appetites, seeing that they are properly rubbed down, tucking them into bed, turning out the lights, aye, and report has it, even praying for them in a fashion all their own.

The amusing anecdote no doubt has its uses as well as its abuses. Two pertinent questions in any particular case are:

Is it in point, and can it be told quickly and effectively? A Columbia debater, wishing to stress the inconsistencies in the case of his Cornell opponents, told the story of the farmer who was sued for damages to his neighbor's sap kettle. The farmer made three defenses: First, he never borrowed the kettle; second, it was cracked when he borrowed it; third, it was all right when he returned it. This story not only brightened up the debate, but was telling in its effect because the parallel was well justified. But the debate was printed and the story appeared in many of the debates of the league for the next ten years, regardless of fitness.

Even if a speaker has the gift of making an audience laugh, and can also make humor serve his ends, still it is not best to keep an audience "convulsed with laughter" all the time. Even the comedian whose only purpose is laughter knows there are limits, and tries to mix grave and gay. The most common purpose of a serious speaker in using humor, beyond impressing a point, is to give relief, to refresh the hearer for more serious attention; but if the hearer is kept laughing too much he becomes incapable of genuine listening.

CURIOSITY. We are turning gradually (gradually because there can be no clear line of distinction) from those elements of interest which depend primarily upon the matter put into a speech to those that depend primarily upon the handling of the matter, and among the elements of the second class is curiosity. An audience will always listen when its curiosity is aroused. Curiosity may be aroused at times by announcements, as that the inside story of the traction franchise will be told by So and So in his speech tonight; or by a curious title, as "Jelly Fish and Equal Rights," or "Technocracy in Heaven." It is usually better, however, to give some clue to one's real subject in one's title, as "The Sincere Hypocrite," or "The Younger Generation Grows Older."

Curiosity may be aroused during the speech by keeping the hearer guessing as to the speaker's real position. Sometimes tricks are played upon the audience, as when a speaker displays a mysterious document, to which he may or may not refer. Unless, however, the speaker, having caught attention, really interests his audience in something else, or in opening up his mystery satisfies them that their attention has been repaid, they may resent the trick; as one feels peevish to find that a great secret he has been called aside to hear is but trivial. If Mark Antony had not had a real sensation after holding back Caesar's will so long, his own might have been among the houses burned by the mob. One remembers, too, the fate of the boy who cried, "Wolf, wolf!" when there was no wolf.

A preacher in a country church had trouble on hot summer Sundays in keeping the weary farmers awake. One morning he announced that he would not give his text until the end of his sermon, and suggested that his hearers might consider as he went along what the text should be. His congregation, very familiar with the Bible, kept awake. One cannot be sure they listened in the best possible way, but their listening was better than sleeping.

So close to curiosity that the words are often interchangeable, and examples of one will often serve as examples of the other, is *suspense,* that element that carries us on to the conclusion of a novel and which makes most thrilling the game which is in doubt till the final whistle. We have already noted the speaker who began with what seemed a defense of anarchy. But it is not necessary to put an audience "on tenterhooks"; it is enough if they are sufficiently in doubt to wish to know the conclusion. Sometimes the material of a speech can be thrown into the form of a narrative which has suspense as an element.

It is not blank inability to foresee any issue at all that is most provocative of interest; rather the chance to anticipate, to make a shrewd guess at the outcome. This is why many keen minds delight in detective stories. More than this, we take great pleasure at times in looking forward to a known outcome. We enjoy plays although we know before entering the theater what the end will be.

If it were noised about the campus that a prominent student was going to make important proposals at the next student assembly, many would go to hear him although they knew substantially what he was going to say. All this assumes, of course, that the matter anticipated has something in it of emotional interest; we do not necessarily flock to hear Professor Blank's public lecture on the subject we have been studying with him for a semester.

SENSATIONAL METHODS. Almost any method of gaining attention can be used in a way that will be called sensational; very plainly conflict, curiosity, and activity. In a sense a speaker uses sensational methods when he suddenly lifts his voice, or uses a striking gesture or epigram; but the term is applied when a speaker departs very markedly from the usual; as when an evangelist advertises, "Hell to-night at the Presbyterian Church!" or leaps upon the pulpit, or makes violent attacks on prominent members of the community. Between these extremes there are many grades of sensationalism.

Sensationalism may lie in startling actions, as when "Billy" Sunday impersonated David, going forward with his sling and hitting Goliath "in the coco, right between the eyes" and then fell, as the giant, full length upon the platform; or when a trial lawyer and his assistants, using the bloody exhibits, act out a murder. Or sensationalism may lie in such mild actions as hand-slapping and desk-pounding.

Sensationalism may lie in the use of words. I have twice heard an eminent Scottish divine use expressions in the pulpit that in the mouth of a layman would be considered strong profanity. Sensationalism may also lie in a general luridness of language. And some forms of expression without any shocking or incongruous quality may be used with sensational effect, as interjections or apostrophe, as may be seen in Webster's famous address to Warren in the First Bunker Hill Address. The resources of delivery may, of course, be added to produce startling effects.

Much depends upon the time, the place, and the man. A partisan passage that would pass as normal in a campaign speech might be sensational in an inaugural address. This suggests, as do many examples of sensationalism, that incongruity, especially incongruity that becomes bad taste, is often a large element in startling effects; and this is one reason why *sensational* as applied to speeches, and especially to sermons, has a sinister meaning. Another is that a sensational speaker is tempted into loose, extreme, or abusive statements.[2]

Sensational methods cannot be condemned out of hand. Even rather extreme forms are at times justified, perhaps when an audience is peculiarly inattentive because of stupidity, or weariness, or anger as in case of a mob, or because their attention is strongly drawn to other attractions, as is often the case in outdoor speaking. We also have audiences resistant because they are present by compulsion, whether of law or of moral force. Such can be found in churches, prisons, and classrooms. We have to remember that no speech can accomplish its purpose unless listened to; and

---

[2] See the passage in Wendell Phillips's "Idols" in which he flays Rufus Choate. For a speech involving a question of taste, see Mark Twain's "A Littery Episode."

while we cannot say that any method that secures attention is justified, for after all the heavens will not fall if our speeches are ignored, yet we can say that before giving up a hard situation it is well to try a bit of sensationalism.

It would be useless to attempt to draw a line between the justifiable and the unjustifiable; but one may advise against false, or needlessly offensive statements, especially personalities. It is always well to avoid any extreme method that is not needed.

Much indulgence in extreme methods brings its own punishment: when a speaker's public becomes accustomed to his antics it will not listen contentedly when he wishes to employ simpler methods. A quiet old lady, of Quaker origin and Presbyterian practice, went to hear "Billy" Sunday at an afternoon meeting. She came home disappointed, for Sunday had preached "just like any one else." Then extreme methods are like other stimulants: the dose has to be increased. If you turn a physical or mental handspring to-day, you will be expected to turn it backward to-morrow.

As with humor, the chief danger of sensational methods for a serious speaker lies in their tendency to defeat their legitimate purpose of drawing attention to one's ideas, by drawing attention to themselves; they too often "steal the show."

Something may be said, however, for experimentation in sensational methods on the part of students of speaking; for used in moderation, they may aid him in gaining contact and freedom. A student who had spoken many times without realizing "what it was all about," in delivering a sensationally partisan declamation was almost overwhelmed, and then delighted and inspired, to find that his hearers were actually responding with laughter, hisses, and applause. That day for the first time he was a speaker. I recall another who began his speech by baaing; and then went on to tell his startled mates that Baa, baa, baa! should be their college yell, for they were just a flock of sheep following in opinion and conduct a few bellwethers. Now this silly beginning plainly came under the condemnation of unnecessary sensationalism, for there were enough spicy elements in the speech without such a device. Nevertheless the speaker benefited, for this was the first time he had let himself go in a speech and probably the first time he had experienced the delightful sensation which comes from a keenly attentive audience. There is always hope for a speaker who is willing to try at least some things once. I must admit, however, that most attempts at sensationalism in my classrooms have done more to create excitement than to impress ideas. And it would be unfortunate for a student to develop skill in sensationalism at the expense of skill with more dependable means of interesting and impressing.

IMAGINATION AND INTEREST. An audience will listen more readily and longer to discourse that stirs imagination than to that which is couched in general and abstract terms; for imagination properly gives to thought both vividness and clearness of outline. It is hard to keep one's eyes on objects that waver uncertainly in a fog; and it is hard to keep one's mind upon objects of thought that take on no imaginative reality.

We attend most easily to sensations, to what reaches us through eyes, ears, etc.; next to mental representations of sensations or mental images; and with most difficulty to abstractions. But even that statement needs modification in favor of imagination; for, as Dewey tells us, physical objects do not attract long unless presented so as to stimulate imagination.

When a speaker indulges in much abstract discussion most

of us—all but those who have had a considerable philosophical training—soon cease to follow and wait for the welcome,
"Now to illustrate." It is an old saying that "the road to
hell is paved with abstractions"; and the reason must be
that they befuddle understanding or are too uninteresting
to hold attention. I quote from another distinguished American philosopher.

The term *imagination* is most conveniently used as a name for
the sum total of the mental processes that express themselves in
our mental imagery. When used psychologically the word imagination conveys no implication that the mental imagery in question
stands for unreal or fantastic objects.[3]

Now a reader familiar with psychological language may
find that quotation easy reading, but many will not. One
unaccustomed may get no meaning at all. Such a one may
find the following excerpt hard, or may get an erroneous
meaning from it:

The imaginative is not necessarily the imaginary; that is, the
unreal. The proper function of imagination is vision of realities
that cannot be exhibited under existing conditions of sense-per-
ception. Clear insight into the remote, the absent, the obscure is
its aim. History, literature, and geography, the principles of
science, nay, even geometry and arithmetic, are full of matters
that must be imaginatively realized if they are realized at all.
Imagination supplements and deepens observation; only when it
turns into the fanciful does it become a substitute for observation
and lose logical force.[4]

[3] From *Outlines of Psychology* by Josiah Royce, p. 161. By permission of The Macmillan Company, publishers.

[4] From *How We Think* by John Dewey, p. 291 (revised ed.). By
permission of D. C. Heath & Co.

This valuable passage would be easier for most if it were illustrated; for instance, the clause about geometry. Compare these quotations with the following passage written by a psychologist for those of uncertain training in his subject, in which after speaking of *visual images,* or what one sees in his "mind's eye," and *auditory images,* or what one hears in his "mind's ear," the author continues:

I call up a former experience in which I was playing football. . . . I feel in imagination the straining of the muscles as I attempted to push against the line. I imagine the terrible struggle, the twisting, straining and writhing of every muscle, tendon, and joint. As I imagine it, I find the state is reëstablished and I am unconsciously leaning toward the goal as if the experience were a present one. *My motor imagery* of the football game is almost as distinct as the motor perception of moving the table. . . . In my imagination I feel a fly slowly crawling up my nose—I have a *tactual image* of it—and the image is so strong that I have to stop and rub my nose. I ate a peach this morning. . . . As I think how it tasted, my mouth waters—I have a *gustatory image* of the peach. . . . As I think of how the gas factory smelt yesterday when I passed it, I have an *olfactory image* of the gas. . . . As I think how it felt when I stepped on a rusty nail, I have a *mental image* of the pain.[5]

The need of touching imagination in one's hearers is plain as one runs over the sources of interest that have been mentioned; for instance, without imagination there can be no appreciation of activity not taking place before our senses. It is plain, too, that most of the facts and situations which are involved in speeches must be realized, if at all, through imagination. The character of a person, an historical event, the justice of Japan's attack on Shanghai in 1931, the prob-

[5] From Scott's *Psychology of Public Speaking,* p. 16. Published by Noble and Noble, New York. Used by permission.

able working-out of the farm bill, the relative advantages of the old "cutthroat" system of rushing for fraternities as compared with the new system—these are typical examples. And we may be sure that the facts pertinent to these subjects will be just dull, heavy data unless they are imaginatively realized, first by the speaker and then by his audience. One writer has gone so far as to say: "A man who cannot translate his concepts into definite images of the proper objects is fitted neither to teach, preach, nor to practise any profession. He should waste as little as possible of the time of his fellow mortals by talking to them." [6]

*Imagination and the materials of the speech.* As already intimated, one does not have to introduce special material for the purpose of arousing imagination, but can use the necessary materials of the speech. If you are speaking of Lincoln you can weave the facts of his life together so as to make him stand before us a living man; or the facts upon which you base an argument for or against the four-hour day, or a new method of handling traffic, can be so put as to make conditions real. If you were discussing the Russian kulaks, the causes of the World War, the safeguarding of deposits in banks, the business future of your town, the best kind of power plant for a certain factory, you might, with a gain in both clearness and interest, so group your facts that your hearers would imaginatively realize situations, conditions, persons, and events.

Some speeches will naturally fall into narrative or descriptive form, while others will more naturally take an argumentative or expository form. These latter, however, may need narrative and descriptive passages, as in explaining or arguing about the Monroe Doctrine. Besides these neces-

---

[6] From Halleck's *Psychology and Psychic Culture*, p. 188, Copyright. Used by permission of American Book Company, publishers.

sary passages which are addressed to imagination there is also opportunity for enlivening discourse by anecdotes.

You will have noticed from the illustrations used that I am not thinking chiefly of the imaginative appeal in lofty poetic passages. It may lie in a description of the best way to cook beans in camp as well as in the great passages of Burke. And it should not be understood that long passages are necessary to imaginative appeal. It is often strong in single words; and is notable in this sentence Booker T. Washington addressed to his colored brothers: "The opportunity to earn a dollar in a factory just now is worth infinitely more than the opportunity to spend a dollar in an opera house."

*Imaginative appeal through illustrations.* Illustration in one form or another is the very life of speech. The two common forms are examples and analogies.

*Examples* hardly need explanation; and will be sufficiently treated later under the head of "Suggestions for the use of illustrations."

Under *analogy* I am including all expressions of "resemblances between things somewhat different." As a means of holding attention they can be considered a phase of derived interest; and it will be readily understood that the best results will follow when comparison is made with something already interesting. Analogies are commonly divided into literal and figurative.

We use the *literal analogy* when we compare two objects, situations, ideas which are in the same class and literally resemble each other; as when one explains polo by certain resemblances to hockey, or argues that commission government will work well in X City because it has worked well in Y City, and the two cities are similar in size, industries, and character of population. The literal analogy is much used in exposition and argument; but is used also for impressiveness, as when a coach between the halves of a football game urges a seemingly beaten team to remember the eleven of three years ago that triumphed in spite of an even greater handicap.

In drawing literal analogies, the more points of resemblance found between the objects, situations, or concepts compared the better. There would be little point in comparing two cities differing widely in size and general character, or two games more unlike than like.

The case is quite different with the *figurative analogy*, for "part of its appeal lies in the novelty, or unexpectedness, of the comparison; and if the objects compared are strikingly unlike in all points except in the point made by the comparison, so much the better."

Woodrow Wilson, discussing college "activities," declared that the sideshows were crowding out the main tent, and the analogy has been quoted thousands of times since. Huxley gave freshness to the familiar thought that education should prepare for life, by saying:

Suppose it were perfectly certain that the life and fortune of every one of us would, one day or other, depend upon his winning or losing a game at chess. Don't you think we should all consider it a primary duty to learn at least the names and moves of the pieces; to have a notion of a gambit, and a keen eye for all the means of giving or getting out of a check?

The famous passage of which this is a part develops this analogy with an elaboration which cannot often be carried through successfully, for the longer we dwell upon an analogy the more the unlikenesses tend to obscure the likenesses. It is an old saying that comparisons "never go on all fours." Moreover the pleasure of the hearer wears off if the elaboration becomes, as it often does, rather forced.[7]

The speeches of successful popular orators abound in analogies. Every one recalls the magnificent conclusion of the speech generally ranked as the greatest in American history, Webster's Reply to Hayne, but as good in its way is the humorous opening, intended to relieve the intense strain of the occasion:

When the mariner has been tossed for many days in thick weather and on an unknown sea, he naturally avails himself of the first pause in the storm, the earliest glance of the sun, to take his latitude and ascertain how far the elements have driven him from his true course. Let us imitate this prudence and, before we float farther on the waves of this debate, refer to the point from which we departed, that we may at least be able to conjecture where we are. I ask for the reading of the resolution before the Senate.

Or take this homespun analogy from Webster's speech to the jury in the Knapp-White murder case:

The key which unlocks the whole mystery is the knowledge of the intention of the conspirators to steal the will. . . . It shows the motive which actuated those against whom there is much evidence, but who, without knowledge of this intention, would seem to have had no motive. . . . If one desirous of opening a lock turns over and tries a bunch of keys until he finds one that will open it, he naturally supposes he has found the key of that lock.

"A man conversing in earnest," says Emerson in his essay on Nature, "if he watch his intellectual processes, will find that always a material image, more or less luminous, arises

[7] An example of a speech that carries one analogy throughout is "Smashed Crockery" by St. Clair McKelway, found in O'Neill's *Models of Speech Composition* and in *Modern Eloquence* (1900), Vol. II, p. 807.

in his mind contemporaneous with every thought; which furnishes the vestment of the thought. Hence good writing and brilliant discourse are perpetual allegories." Sometimes this fondness for figure, and especially for metaphor, which has been called the orator's figure, tempts a brilliant speaker to overload a passage to the extent that the hearer is kept so busy interpreting that he misses something of the impression intended. This criticism might be made on the following from Wendell Phillips's famous Phi Beta Kappa address, in which he condemned the scholarly class for its aloof and critical attitude toward problems of democracy:

Let us inaugurate a new departure, recognize that we are afloat on the current of Niagara, eternal vigilance the condition of our safety, that we are irrevocably pledged to the world not to go back to bolts and bars—could not if we would, and would not if we could. Never again be ours the fastidious scholarship that shrinks from rude contact with the masses. Very pleasant it is to sit high up in the world's theatre and criticise the ungraceful struggles of the gladiators, shrug one's shoulders at the actors' harsh cries, and let every one know that but for "this villainous saltpetre you would yourself have been a soldier." . . . "Very beautiful," says Richter, "is the eagle when he floats with outstretched wings aloft in the clear blue; but sublime when he plunges down through the tempest to his eyry on the cliff, where his fledgling young ones dwell and are starving." Accept proudly the analysis of Fisher Ames: "A monarchy is a man-of-war, staunch, iron-ribbed, and resistless when under full sail; yet a single hidden rock sends her to the bottom. Our republic is a raft, hard to steer and your feet are always wet; but nothing can sink her." If the Alps, piled in cold and silence, be the emblem of despotism, we joyfully take the ever restless ocean for ours,—only pure because never still.[8]

[8] *Speeches and Lectures*, Second Series, p. 361. By permission of Lothrop, Lee & Shepard Company.

George William Curtis replied to Phillips's charge in a passage full of figure, but with less tax on the hearer. An extract follows:

Gentlemen, we belong to the accused class. Its honor and dignity are very precious to us. Is this humiliating arraignment true? Does the educated class of America especially deserve this condemnation of political recreancy and moral cowardice? Faithless scholars, laggard colleges, bigoted pulpits, there may be; signal instances you may find of feebleness and pusillanimity. This has always been true. . . .

But remember what Coleridge said to Washington Alston, "Never judge a work of art by its defects." The proper comment to make upon recreant scholars is that of Brummell's valet upon the tumbled cambric in his hands, "These are our failures." Luther, impatient of the milder spirit of Erasmus and Colet and Sir Thomas More, might well have called them our failures, because he was of their class, and while they counseled moderation, his fiery and impetuous soul sought to seize triple-crowned error and drag it from its throne. But Luther was no less a scholar and stands equally with them for the scholarly class and the heroism of educated men. Even Erasmus said of him with friendly wit, "He has hit the Pope on the crown and the monks on the belly." If the cowled scholars of the Church rejected him and universities under their control renounced and condemned him, yet Luther is justified in saying, as he sweeps his hand across them and speaks for himself and the scholars who stood with him, "These are not our representatives; these are our failures."

So on our side of the sea the educated body of Puritan Massachusetts Bay, the clergy and the magistrates, drove Roger Williams from their borders—Roger Williams, also a scholar and a clergyman, and, with John Milton, the bright consummate flower of Puritanism. But shall he not stand for the scholar rather than Cotton Mather, torturing terrified old women to death as witches! I appeal from Philip drunk to Philip sober—from the scholarship that silenced Mrs. Hutchinson and hung Mary Dyer and pressed Giles Corey to death, to the scholarship that argued with George Fox and founded a political commonwealth upon soul liberty. A year ago I sat with my brethren of the Phi Beta Kappa at Cambridge, and seemed to catch echoes of Edmund Burke's resounding impeachment of Warren Hastings in the sparkling denunciation of the timidity of American scholarship. Under the spell of Burke's burning words Hastings half believed himself to be the villain he heard described. But the scholarly audience of the scholarly orator of the Phi Beta Kappa, with an exquisite sense of relief, felt every count of his stinging indictment recoil upon himself. He was the glowing refutation of his own argument. Gentleman, scholar, orator—his is the courage that never quailed; his the white plume of Navarre that flashed meteor-like in the front of battle; his the Amphion music of an eloquence that leveled the more than Theban walls of American slavery. At once judge, culprit, and accuser, in the noble record of his own life he and his class are triumphantly acquitted.[9]

The danger of overloading in student speeches seems to be slight; perhaps because students think of analogies as something for orators on great occasions. But unpretentious analogies are very useful. Lincoln, wishing to characterize a slippery argument by Douglas in their debates, declared that by the method of Douglas one could prove that a horse chestnut is a chestnut horse. Many of the parables of Jesus, the fables of Æsop, the sayings of Poor Richard, in fact, a great part of the sayings that stick in the memory of men everywhere, are analogies and often in homely terms, as "A rolling stone gathers no moss," and the easy retort, "Who wants to be a mossback?" Much of our pungent slang and many slogans show the force of homely metaphor. Of the extreme abolitionists Beecher said, "They are trying to drive

[9] From "The Leadership of Educated Men," *Orations and Addresses*, Vol. I, p. 318. By permission of Harper & Brothers.

the wedge into the log butt-end foremost, and they will only split their beetle." And Robert Collier said of Beecher, who broke through the traditional theology of his church, "He was an oak planted in a washtub; it was hard on the tub."

It is well to give attention to analogies; for whether one wishes to use them or not, one cannot well avoid them, and there are dangers in their careless use. They are frequent in our commonest talk. Even if a speaker says he will "leave such flowery stuff to the wind-jammers and hot air artists," he is using analogies. Some one has said that language is but a nosegay of faded metaphors. "*Attention* really means a *stretching out toward.* . . . *Apprehend* is nothing more than Latin for *catch on.*"[10] We see more plainly the figures in *daybreak, wild ideas, flight of time, break the ice, fret, grit.*

*Suggestions for the use of illustration.* I wish now to make certain suggestions applicable to a great variety of illustrations.

*First suggestion:* Take care that each illustration adds its strength to that which deserves emphasis in your speech, and does not obscure that by unduly emphasizing minor points. Resist the temptation to use a good story or striking picture for its own sake, regardless of the worth of the idea that it strengthens. Do not "work illustrations in" if they are not strictly pat, no matter how amusing, or stirring, or beautiful. Your hearers will either puzzle over the relation which should exist, or they will be drawn off to the thought the illustration really illumines. A speaker who is privileged to hear the comments of his auditors will often be pained at the number of instances in which their attention has been

[10] From a valuable discussion in *English Composition* by Barrett Wendell, p. 248.

caught by some idea incidental to an illustration used, while the main thought has escaped them. You may expect your illustrations to be remembered longest; they should therefore be of such a character that they will recall to mind your major ideas.

*Second suggestion:* Use only illustrations which are congruous with the spirit of your speech and of the occasion. Beware, for example, of frivolous illustrations on serious occasions and of such as will seem pretentious and over serious on lighter occasions. It should be noted, however, that illustrations, especially of a narrative character, are useful in gradually changing the spirit of an audience. I have already noted the purpose of the opening of Webster's Reply; and note below what is said of the effect of the opening of Conwell's "Acres of Diamonds."

*Third suggestion:* Do not use unnecessary details, but choose those needed to make the picture. To give every detail is to stifle imagination; as a photograph may suggest less than a few strokes of an artist's brush. The street urchin I heard replying to his chum's question, "How is the ice?" with, "Fine; so clear you can see a snake on the bottom!" could not have improved the picture of good skating with any number of details. Do not let needless preliminary details take more time than the incident. A formal introduction is not always necessary, not even "To illustrate." Avoid a long preamble, as, This reminds me of a man who used to live in our town, who had a son named John, who would not go to school. So the father decided he would find a way to impress the desirability of school upon his son. So one morning he said to John, at the breakfast table, says he, "John, etc." Instead of all this rigmarole, it would be better to say, As a father said to his son who would not go to school, etc.

*Fourth suggestion:* On the other hand, there must be details. How many it is useless to attempt to say: enough to serve the purpose. If needed details are omitted the audience may make no imaginative effort; or may supply wrong details.

If you wish them to imagine a scene of great animation, you must give enough details of life and movement to prevent their imagining a lifeless scene. However, it is generally true that fewer details are needed when you wish to convey merely an impression than when you wish your hearers to form an image correct in details. A few details will suggest the picture of a fussy merchant bustling about his store. A great many may be needed if you wish a board of directors to know the proposed arrangement of a factory, or a jury to realize exactly how the parties to a tragedy were grouped. There may be times, also, when elaboration is desired simply to hold attention upon the illustration longer, in order to deepen the impression.

Sufficiency of details is often consistent with brevity. Much is gained by using specific words. If instead of saying *building,* you say *tower* or *church,* your hearers have the right image at once, and no further detail may be needed. It is not necessary to give each detail a separate statement. To illustrate both this and the preceding hint, if you say, The army was moving along a stream, you still need several details, lest your hearers see a creek when you mean a considerable river, and see the army on the left bank going north, when you wish them to see the army on the right bank going south. But if you say, General Jones was hurrying with his cavalry division down the right bank of the Delaware River to reach the ford at X, several essential points have been economically conveyed, and yet given sufficient prominence.

The quotations a few pages back from Phillips and Curtis may be studied in this connection. And note the quickness with which Dr. Charles E. Jefferson made his picture in this bit, and try to say it some other way:

> No man has the right to do things which encroach on the rights of others. The old peasant woman who walked down the middle of a business street in Moscow soon after the Russian revolution, with a bucket in each hand, saying, "We have had a revolution and I am going to walk where I please," was driven from the street because she held up traffic.

It should not be understood, however, that all illustrations must be brief. I recall an excellent speech that was practically all one illustration. The subject was yellow journalism. The speaker began with a sedate family newspaper which gave such news as the editors considered fit for a respectable family to read, and as accurately as possible. But one morning the paper's readers were astounded to find on their breakfast tables a new *Courier:* It had "screaming" headlines; divorce, scandal, and crime held first place while city, state, and national affairs were pushed off the front page, and the doings of Society were treated chiefly for their scandal value. This developed with specific detail, made the speech; and at the end the speaker said only, "That is yellow journalism." Perhaps we should have had clearer ideas if the speaker had shortened his illustration enough to permit a statement in more general terms; but the speech certainly left more with us than an abstract discussion alone could have done. And, it may be noted, this illustration could not be effective without a good bit of detail.

Whether an illustration is worth the space needed to give it its best effect can be decided only with reference to a particular case. The story with which Conwell opens "Acres of Diamonds" would fill five pages of an average textbook. Briefly told it is the story of Ali Hafed, a prosperous Persian farmer, who being told that diamonds might readily be found by searching, sold his farm, left his family behind, and went hunting in Africa and Europe for the precious stones; until after years of searching, money gone and hope fled, he ended his life by jumping into the waves at Barcelona. In the meantime the man who bought Ali Hafed's farm found a diamond in the garden; and thus was discovered the Golconda, one of the richest diamond mines in the world, right on the farm Ali scorned.

Conwell tells the story with a wealth of detail, introducing several characters, with prologue, entr'actes, and epilogue. Was the length justified? I think so. He is giving a long lecture, and no one in his audience is in a hurry to reach the end. In the second place, this story carries admirably the central idea of the speech: Look about you where you are in seeking success; you may be surrounded by opportunities. In the third place, the story creates the desired atmosphere for the speech. It has something of the "once upon a time in a far-off land" spirit, and yet it is true. The speaker is to tell us of many wonderful discoveries such as we are prone to think mythical; but this happened in Persia, a land where anything might happen. Now why not nearer home? It is notable that Conwell's other stories (and the speech has many) are told with comparative brevity.

Some stories require space for effective telling, and some will not bear spinning out; but many can be told at any length. Conwell's five pages can be cut in half merely by the omission of unnecessary details, and that with hardly a change in his language. It can be cut down to: A Persian farmer sold his farm and left his family, to go seek for diamonds. After years of failure he died a suicide. The man who bought his farm discovered on it one of the richest diamond mines in the world. You could give it any length between that flavorless fragment and Conwell's profusion. Undoubtedly it loses color and effectiveness when cut low. So far as the moral goes, what the farmer's name was, where he lived, where he searched and where and how he killed himself do not make the slightest difference; and yet such details are needed to make the picture and give the story a tangibility that will fix it in one's mind.

*Fifth suggestion:* The success of any piece of word painting will depend much upon *order* of details. It has been proved that the time taken by an experienced mechanic in assembling a machine can be cut down two-thirds by providing him a rack which presents the parts to his hands in the best order. Somewhat similar is the increase in your hearers' imaginative effectiveness when you give them details in the right order. If some needed detail is not given in time, your hearers may be at a loss, or may supply it wrongly, and then have to "reassemble" the whole. Often as one listens in conversation to a description or narration, he is puzzled until some missing detail is given. "Oh," he says, "that is what bothered me; now it begins to clear up." One who listens to a speech is rarely able to reassemble details. (The illustration above based on the movements of an army can be adapted to this point.)

There is need of care, also, in arranging details so that the story will tell well, especially with regard to climax, or so that "the kick comes at the right place." Can you improve on the telling of this really interesting and significant incident?

When Theodore Roosevelt was Police Commissioner of New York, back in 1896, an anti-Jewish agitator came to the city and arranged for a meeting. The Jews of New York were aroused, and friends of the agitator asked Roosevelt for special police protection. T. R. sent up a squad that bore the most pronouncedly Jewish features that could be found in the force. When the speaker launched his tirade there was an uproar and trouble threatened; but when the police scattered through the audience and Jews were seen protecting an anti-Jewish agitator, wrath passed away in a gale of laughter, and the speaker was allowed to speak undisturbed. This incident illustrates Roosevelt's understanding of human nature.

*Sixth suggestion:* Consider your audience in choosing illustrations. First consider what illustrations your audience will understand. The speeches of Curtis are marred by allusions to history and literature that only the especially well read can appreciate—a mistake rarely made by Bryan. I refer here to brief allusions. If time permits and the illustration is worth it, sufficient explanation to make it intelligible may, of course, be given. Secondly, when you use illustration for the sake of interest, you should draw from fields which interest your hearers. Thirdly, you should consider what associations you may be stirring up. You can get the interest of old soldiers by illustrations drawn from the Civil War; but in your Memorial Day address in the North you had better not confine yourself to Bull Run, Chancellorsville, and other defeats, nor in Georgia would you choose Sherman's "bummers" to illustrate reckless daring.

An illustration, though apt and applied to a major idea in the speech, may be too interesting, whether the feelings it arouses be pleasant or unpleasant. If a speaker in a college classroom in November uses a football analogy, he risks losing attention, for football may arouse associations that will carry the audience far away. A speaker denouncing war propaganda referred to appeals based on the *Lusitania* incident in a way that implied he thought the sinking justified, and so started an argument with his hearers on a topic quite foreign to his purpose.

*Seventh suggestion:* In adapting your illustrations to your audience, be sure you know your ground. Railroad men may like to hear you draw illustrations from their work, if you can do so easily and naturally; but they will be amused or bored by a strained attempt. Of a preacher who tried to talk to an audience of sailors in their own terms, one of his hearers said: "There are two things he doesn't understand, navigation and religion."

# CHAPTER IX

## COMPOSITION AND INTEREST

SPEAK IN TERMS THAT MAKE ATTENTION EASY. "When we hear the words *table, chair, stove, coat,* we do not have to reflect in order to grasp what is meant. The terms convey meaning so directly that no effort at translation is needed. The meanings of some terms and things, however, are grasped only by first calling to mind more familiar things and then tracing out the connections between them and what we do understand." [1] Note especially in this quotation the words, *"no effort at translating is needed."* Your language should have instant intelligibility. We may know the meaning of every word in a given passage and yet have to make an effort not unlike that necessary in reading a half-mastered foreign language. *Kilometer* is to many of us as much in need of translation as the Greek *parasang*. Even with many well-educated people such terms as *electron, chemical affinity, conditioned reflexes, social consciousness, laminated, desiccated, mercantile theory, undivided middle, modicum, umbrageous,* register their meanings only indirectly. I am thinking of learned words as opposed to popular words or words that "belong to the people at large, and are not the exclusive possession of an exclusive class." [2]

[1] From *How We Think* by John Dewey, p. 136. By permission of D. C. Heath & Co.

[2] Greenough and Kittredge, *Words and Their Ways in English Speech*, p. 19. Their third chapter is an excellent reference in this connection.

We are rarely much impressed by the content of a passage we laboriously translate. The reason has been best put by Herbert Spencer in developing his theory of economy as the basis of a "philosophy of style." If too narrow a basis, it is at least true in itself:

A reader or listener has at each moment but a limited amount of mental power available. To recognize and interpret the symbols presented to him requires a part of his power; to arrange and combine the images suggested requires a further part; and only that part which remains can be used for realizing the thought conveyed. Hence the more time and attention it takes to receive and understand each sentence, the less time and attention can be given to the contained idea; and the less vividly will the idea be conceived.

*Speak in familiar terms.* The most obvious characteristic of words that register meaning without translation is that they are familiar. It makes no difference where they come from, whether they are Anglo-Saxon, French, Greek, or Latin in origin. *Army, card, catch, city, chimney, hour, letter, pencil, river, table,* are from the French; *act, animal, auction, agent, circus, collision, cucumber, different, fact, horrid, joke, medicine, single, student, use, vest, vote,* are from the Latin; *anthracite, aster, athlete, attic, chemist, hector, panic, telegraph, tonic,* are from the Greek; but all are familiar. *Divide* is more familiar than *cleave, castle* than *burg, travel* than *fare, remain* than *abide, defend* than *shield, firm* than *steadfast, prophet* than *soothsayer, fate* than *weird, resist* than *withstand;* yet in each pair the second term is Anglo-Saxon and the first is not.

Most familiar and most readily handled are those words we have heard and used since childhood. Next come those we use in our daily affairs. Now these will, no doubt, be to a considerable extent Anglo-Saxon in origin. They will tend also to be short words, but that fact also is not very important so far as we are concerned at the moment. It is by no means true that short words are always better than long words. It may be noted that the Gettysburg Address is not remarkable for the absence of either long words or of Latin derivatives.

The safest principle that can be laid down is that suggested by the quotation from Dewey and also by that from Spencer: use words that convey your meaning with as little translation as is feasible. There may, of course, be excellent reasons for not using the most familiar words, reasons of accuracy, of dignity, of tact; but as a general guide the principle holds good.

While some familiar words may not suit the dignity of certain occasions, we all know that simple, familiar words may have the utmost dignity. The common example is the prose of the King James version of the Bible. Webster is accounted our greatest American orator. He was, I fear we must admit, at times pompous; but not often, taking into account his occasions, the style prevailing in his period, and the innate bigness of the man; but anyhow at his best magnificent. His language was always dignified. Let us look at one of his most magnificent passages, already quoted in Chapter II. Would any word in that excerpt cause waste effort to the simplest juryman, even though that juryman might not himself use every word? Now compare again the parallel passage. The second is matter of fact and less rhythmical; but can it be said that there is any marked contrast as regards the familiarity, derivation, or length of the words used?

We have been thinking primarily of the general audience. It is evident that a vocabulary familiar to one audience may be "all Greek" to another. To the garage worker the language of automobiles is familiar, while the scholar may find it more difficult than the language of science and philosophy. One who speaks to a special group should, of course, take account of its language. It does not follow that he should attempt to speak as they do, unless he is well accustomed to that way of speaking. He would probably be absurd in any such attempt; and audiences do not like to feel that a speaker is talking down to them. A speaker should try to talk to his audience in language which they are accustomed to hear, with which they feel at home, whether they use it themselves or not; and for most groups that is simply standard English. Bryan was certainly, in every sense of the word, a popular speaker. I have never noted in any of his speeches that I have heard or read any attempt either to talk down, or to talk up.

Of technical terms it may be said that one who is qualified to speak to specialized groups on their specialties will employ such technical terms as are needed; but before a general audience he will use discretion in this regard. One reason why specialists, and among these we may include college professors, are not as a rule good speakers for general audiences is that they become so accustomed to a specialized language that they forget that it is strange to others. I have noted, too, that students who are specializing in subjects they present to their classes in speaking are often too fond of technical verbiage; and this is especially unfortunate when they have only partially mastered it. When a specialist like Huxley trains himself to interpret scientific discoveries to laymen, he learns how to translate technical terms into standard English.

Using discretion in regard to technical terms does not mean that they are to be avoided entirely before general audiences; and particularly it does not mean that one should refer to a carburetor as a "thingumbob," or a radiator cap as a "doodad," or say "thing-on-top-of-the-column" for *capital*. Many precise technical terms are fairly familiar, or are self-explanatory, or can be explained in a word or two without checking one's discourse, as, the capital, or head of the column. Certainly nothing is gained by the what-do-you-call-it manner of speaking. If any unfamiliar technical term is needed, and especially if it is to be used several times, it is often best to take time to explain it; but an audience cannot be expected to master many new terms during a single speech. When possible it is well to put new terms before eyes as well as ears, as on a blackboard. Often one has a choice of synonyms. Whether to say *façade* or *front, antonym* or *opposite* is to be decided with reference to the particular audience.

*Use concrete words. Concrete,* in its standard usage, is the antonym of *abstract.* "A concrete name is the name of a thing, the abstract name is the name of a quality, attribute, or circumstance of a thing." *Tall man, tall tree, tall monument,* are all concrete terms, but *tallness,* denoting a quality drawn out, or abstracted, from them, is abstract.

We have already considered abstractions in speaking of imagination. While abstract ideas are of great importance and we need abstract words to express them, still we should beware of letting the abstract element predominate in our speech; for there is no doubt that concrete language is easier to listen to. In the first place, concrete words, generally speaking, are more familiar than abstract words, they are the words we learned earliest; although it is true that many abstract terms, such as *law, honesty, vanity,* come to have an equal familiarity. In the second place, concrete words tend to bring up images in our minds.

Gardiner [3] says we must expect abstractions from two classes of men: "First the great thinkers whose intellectual powers work, as it were, by leaps and flights; in the other extreme from people who are too lazy to think their subject out in specific detail." Speaking of general words (which are of much the same nature as abstract terms, and are often identified with them), Hill sums up [4] their advantages and disadvantages, saying that the general term covers more ground but is less definite than the specific. It serves to classify and, as it were, store up knowledge. General words are of service in writings intended to popularize science, enabling the writer to avoid technical terms. General expressions are sometimes more striking than specific ones; as when we say of something, "It is perfection," or when Byron spoke of a "sublime mediocrity." General words are a resource of those who seek to disarm opposition, or to veil unpleasant facts; but also of those who seek "to hide poverty of thought in richness of language, to give obscurity an air of cleverness and shallowness the dignity of an oracle, to cover the intention to say nothing with the appearance of having said much, or to 'front South by North,' as Lowell's 'Birdofredum Sawin' did. They abound in the resolutions of political parties, 'appeals' of popular orators, 'tributes to departed worth,' second-rate sermons, and school compositions."

We are all familiar with the ignorant but pretentious man who will talk loudly of liberty, wonders of science, or philosophy, without definite meaning behind his words. He will explain a scientific marvel with a comprehensive gesture and one word, "Electricity," or problems of mental phe-

[3] *Forms of Prose Discourse*, p. 52.
[4] From Hill's *The Foundations of Rhetoric*, p. 187, Copyright. Used by permission of American Book Company, publishers.

nomena with, "That's psychology," or, "That's just suggestion." Unfortunately we all tend to accept too much from teachers and books in the form of mere language which we never think out in definite concrete forms. Just as we grasped years ago the truth that two and two are four by adding two blocks to two blocks, so other conceptions should be translated into realities. At any rate much futile speaking is done by those who fail to do this. I recall a speech on the Federal Reserve Bank. The speech sounded very learned, but left only a vague impression. Questions were asked and the speaker answered with an air which implied that we were very dense; but still we did not understand, and persisted in questioning. Finally the speaker threw up his hands and exclaimed, "I don't know anything about it; it's just words to me."

It may be said that if a speaker exercises his imagination on his material and uses illustrations freely, he will tend to speak in concrete terms, and this is true; but it is good practice for a student of speech-making to make a definite effort in this direction. He may well review his own productions to see what his tendencies are, and try the effect of substituting here and there concrete for abstract expression.

*Use specific terms.* Many writers of high authority use *concrete* and *specific* as synonyms; but more strictly a specific term is the opposite of a generalization, and a generalization can be expressed in concrete terms, as "All men are liars." William Smith is a liar, is both concrete and specific. Plainly enough a specific term is still more vivid, more likely to provoke a sharp image, than a term merely concrete. Herbert Spencer, in developing his principle of economy of attention, tells us we should avoid such a sentence as, "In proportion as the manners, customs, and amusements of a nation are cruel and barbarous, the regulations of their penal code will be severe," and that we should say, "In proportion as men delight in battles, bullfights, and combats of gladiators, will they punish by hanging, burning, and the rack."

The examples suggest a limitation on the use of specific terms: it is necessary that one's hearers know the specific things referred to. There are degrees of specificity; thus *mammal* is more specific than *animal*, *horse* than *mammal*, *Dobbin* than *horse*. And the further one goes in this direction the more he narrows the imaginative appeal. If all know Dobbin, that term brings the sharpest image, not otherwise; and it may be better to let each hearer visualize that horse which his associations bring to mind. A poet could not stir us by a rhapsody about flora, but on the other hand,

> I think that I shall never see
> A poem lovely as a tree—

has a wider appeal than a poem about pines, or palms, or fig trees. This is assuming, of course, that it is not important to our discourse that any particular tree be brought to mind.

We have also to consider the possibility that one's hearers may fail in a given instance to deduce from a specific statement what one wishes to leave with them; for example, it is not certain that the second of Spencer's sentences just above would carry all his meaning. The impression would be surer if we made a combination of the two forms:

In proportion as the manners, customs, and amusements of a nation are cruel and barbarous, the regulations of their penal code will be severe; nations that delight in battles, bull-fights, and combats of gladiators, will punish by hanging, burning, and the rack.

For vividness and consequent interest it is often well to follow with specific expressions even generalizations that are clear enough in themselves. If one says of a man that he has known many of the great of his time, one may add that he has met and talked familiarly with Gladstone, Bismarck, and Cavour. So Macaulay writes:

> Down went the old church of France, with all its pomp and power. The churches were closed; the bells were silent; the shrines were plundered; the silver crucifixes were melted down; buffoons dressed in surplices came dancing the carmagnole, even to the bar of the convention.

It may seem that to be specific requires a voluminous style not always possible in short speeches. However, it may be observed, first, that there is not much use in any form of expression that does not carry its idea effectively to the hearer, no matter how admirable it may be in precision and compactness. It may be better to say less and say it effectively. In the second place, the specific expression may be quite sufficient in itself and often briefer. The enumeration of details is not the only way to be specific. If you say *maple* instead of *tree*, *Sam Adams* instead of *one of the Revolutionary Fathers*, or *It snowed* instead of *The weather was bad*, you have not increased the number of words. Indeed if you are ultimately to reach the specific statement, to use the specific term at once is the briefer way. *He staggered down the street* is shorter than *He went down the street and staggered as he went*. Consider both the economy and the vividness of such substitutes for *went* as *walked*, *ran*, *marched*, *paced*, *trotted*, *ambled*, *shambled*, *plodded*, *hurried*, *sauntered*, *slunk*, *strode*, *swaggered*.

In this discussion we cannot forget, what is true of most that can be said about any aspect of expression, that nothing is sure, nothing always true; "circumstances alter cases." There may be excellent reasons for using abstract, general, and unfamiliar terms; but we can say with as much assurance as we say anything in this subject, that a speaker should cultivate the habit of speaking in terms that make listening easy, in terms that need as little translation as may be, in words familiar, concrete, and specific.

SUSTAINING ATTENTION. Plainly enough the more interesting a discourse is the longer we can keep our minds upon it, for less effort is required. But though involved in all that has been said about interest, the problem of sustaining attention once gained needs some special consideration. The problem arises from the fact that at any instant innumerable objects, sensations, and ideas are battling for attention, and from the further fact that attention is mobile, exploratory. Uncontrolled by will or interest it wanders constantly to new things.

It is impossible to keep one's mind upon an unchanging idea, just as it is impossible to keep one's eye upon an unchanging object. "The subject must be made to show new aspects of itself; to prompt new questions; in a word, to change." [5] You cannot think just *Edison;* you have to think *about* Edison—"news-butcher," telegraph operator, inventor, phonographs, electric lights, artificial rubber, tremendous worker, friend of Henry Ford, etc. In other words, the only way to keep one's mind on one thing is to think of its different aspects and of other things in connection with it. Plainly enough attention is bound to be a rather shifty affair, and the only way to control its errant tendencies is to confine its wanderings within narrow limits. "Sustained attention is not glued to one point, by any means,"

[5] *Talks to Teachers* by William James, p. 104. By permission of Henry Holt and Company.

says Woodworth,[6] "but is simply confined to a given object or theme, within which its motion is as lively as ever."

*Variety.* For us at this point, having dwelt so long on interest, the most important fact is that one can listen longer to discourse that presents a goodly variety; and we will take up here some of the ways of avoiding monotony.

The first suggestion is the obvious one: deal with the various aspects of the subject. If Lincoln is your theme, you can view him in the many phases before suggested. If you have narrowed down to Lincoln's tact, you can consider his tact in the law court, in politics, in dealing with his generals, with diplomats. If you speak on "Honesty is the best policy," you can treat it first theoretically, then practically; and then you can consider honesty in social life, in the practice of law or medicine, or in selling goods. And you can add much variety by means of illustrations. Again, you can consider your problem as it is viewed by, or as it affects, different classes of people. If the lynching of Negroes is your theme, you can consider how it affects the ignorant Negro, how the intelligent Negro views it, how the North looks upon it, and how different classes of Southern whites view it. It is not necessary to take up so many phases of the subject, however. The better you know your subject the more variety you can find in one part of it.

And not only in subject-matter can variety be provided, but also in method of statement. For example, you can consider the possibilities of putting your ideas so as to appeal now to the interest in activity, now to the interest in conflict, now to the interest in people; of putting them humourously, or so as to arouse curiosity or anticipation. Again, monotony can often be much relieved by changing merely the form of one's sentences; as from assertion to question, or to sentences begining with *if* or *suppose*. The long excerpts from Phillips and Curtis, above, have interesting variety in sentence construction.

This topic links closely with those following.

*Amplification.* The suggestions just made apply to many kinds of speeches, including those that move rapidly forward from point to point. But often single ideas need to be dwelt upon. It is evident that for clearness and for conviction, information and evidence must be introduced; but there are other reasons for amplification. Some ideas are too difficult for a hearer when put into condensed statement. Moreover, if you succeed in setting your hearer to thinking, he needs time to consider and assimilate; or, as DeQuincey says, time "for the intellect to eddy about a truth, and to appropriate its bearings." [7] This important truth the inexperienced speaker, accustomed as a student to tell things to those who know them better than he does, often fails to appreciate. And many older speakers fail to grasp effectually the most profound truth of all: that what the speaker says is not the most important thing about a speech, but rather what as a result happens in the hearer's mind.

There may be need of restatement of an important point because some distraction has taken the attention of part of the audience, if only the confusion caused by late arrivals. As a matter of fact, on ordinary occasions few listen continuously.

There are not infrequent cases in which a speaker wishes to dwell upon an idea for an appreciable time without going forward at all, either for the reasons suggested above, or to emphasize the idea, or because out of varied expressions of a thought some may prove more significant to one part

[7] See his essay on Style, Part I.

of his audience and others to another part.   Wise restatement is not "idle repetition."

There is, to be sure, restatement which is a mere marking of time, a filling of space because one has nothing to say, or a playing with phrases for the speaker's own pleasure. A distinguished United States Senator, speaking back in war days, apparently became, in the phrase Disraeli applied to Gladstone, "intoxicated with the exuberance of his own verbosity":

> I submit to you that there can be no future as to these war profits, because they are fleeting, ephemeral at best, lasting alone with the war, with the exigency, with the strife, and with the conflict, ceasing the very moment the war ceases, and the very moment the conflict is at an end.

There is no gain, just "vain babbling."   Such speech kept up for a considerable time would be less likely to impress ideas than to beat one's hearers into insensibility.

But study this from Carlyle's *Past and Present:*

1. In this God's-world, with its wild, whirling eddies and mad, foam oceans, where men and nations perish as if without law, and judgment for an unjust thing is sternly delayed, dost thou think that there is therefore no justice?  It is what the fool hath said in his heart.  It is what the wise, in all times, were wise because they denied and knew forever not to be.  I tell thee there is nothing else but justice.  One strong thing I find here below: the just thing, the true thing.

2. My friend, if thou hadst all the artillery of Woolwich trundling at thy back in support of an unjust thing, and infinite bonfires visibly waiting ahead of thee to blaze centuries along for the victory on behalf of it, I would advise thee to call halt, to fling down thy baton and say, "In heaven's name, no!"

3. Thy "success"?   Poor devil, what will thy success amount

to? If the thing is unjust, thou hast not succeeded; no, not though bonfires blazed from north to south, and bells rang, and editors wrote leading articles, and the just things lay trampled out of sight—to all mortal eyes an abolished and annihilated thing. . . .

4. For it is the right and noble alone that will have victory in this struggle; the rest is wholly an obstruction, a postponement, a fearful imperilment, of the victory. Towards an eternal center of right and nobleness, and of that only, is all confusion tending. We already know whither it is all tending; what will have victory, what will have none! The heaviest will reach the center. The heaviest has its deflections, its obstructions; nay, at times its resiliences, its reboundings, whereupon some blockhead shall be heard jubilating, "See, your heaviest ascends!" but at all moments it is moving centerward, fast as is convenient for it, sinking, sinking; and by laws older than the world, old as the Maker's first plan of the world, it has to arrive there.

5. Await the issue. In all battles, if you await the issue, each fighter has prospered according to his right. His right and his might, at the close of the account, were one and the same. He has fought with all his might, and in exact proportion to all his right he has prevailed. His very death is no victory over him. He dies indeed; but his work lives, very truly lives.

6. An heroic Wallace, quartered on the scaffold, cannot hinder that his Scotland become, one day, a part of England; but he does hinder that it become, on tyrannous terms, a part of it; commands still, as with a god's voice, from his old Valhalla and Temple of the brave, that there be a just, real union as of brother and brother, not a false and merely semblant one as of slave and master. If the union with England be in fact one of Scotland's chief blessings, we thank Wallace withal that it was not the chief curse. . . .

7. Fight on, thou brave, true heart; and falter not, through dark fortune and through bright. The cause thou fightest for, so far as it is true, no further, yet precisely so far, is very sure

of victory.    The falsehood alone of it will be conquered, will be
abolished, as it ought to be; but the truth of it is part of Nature's
own laws, coöperates with the world's eternal tendencies, and
cannot be conquered.

Now this excerpt can be summarized in the statement that
justice will triumph in the end.    Each paragraph says that;
yet each says it with a difference, and each adds significance.
To summarize paragraph by paragraph:

1. In spite of appearances to the contrary justice will triumph in the end.    (Denial of the obverse, followed by
affirmative assertion.)

2. No matter what available force and what assurance of
success you may have in an unjust cause, do not attempt it.
(Denial of the obverse put into the form of a dramatic
hypothetical example.)

3. No matter how great a success you may seem to have
won in an unjust cause, it is not real.    (Same comment as
for 2.)

4. For justice is the law of the moral universe as gravita-
tion is of the physical; and in spite of delays it is always
working toward its consummation.    (Thesis supported by
an analogy.)

5. Therefore wait and you will see that all the justice in
a man's cause triumphs finally, whatever becomes of him.
(Idea put more precisely and a possible misunderstanding
removed.)

6. The story of Wallace illustrates the final triumph of
justice.    (Example.)

7. Therefore fight on, regardless of temporary success
or failure, since all the justice in your cause must, because
in harmony with the law, win in the end.    (Restatement in
form of exhortation.)

Whatever else may be said of the passage, it will not be called monotonous.

*Ways of restating.* If we are to carry out the purposes of dwelling upon an idea, we must, of course, maintain interest; and the less variety there is in the matter the more there need be in the manner. We have already noted some of the ways of restating, and shall note others farther on. It will be well to give a partial list here—with the suggestion that the student add others as they occur to him. No rigid attempt to avoid overlapping terms is made.

Abstract statement; concrete statement; general statement; specific statement.

Illustrations: examples; analogies. (These, of course, may be of the utmost variety according to their sources.)

Restatement in synonymous terms.

Repetition in the same terms, immediately or after an interval.

Quotations embodying the same idea.

Quotations from authority. (This adds an element to the preceding. A quotation may be effective because it expresses an idea well, or because its author's opinions are respected.)

Denial of the obverse.

Statement with limitations, modifications, or exceptions.

Statement with applications to different persons, institutions, and actions.

Questions.

Illustrating several of these, we may say: What we learn by experience is learned best and sticks best. "Experience is a great teacher." We learn little of the practical affairs of life from any other source; only "the burnt child dreads the fire." Does any man learn from physicians to care for his health, before he has suffered from the effects of carelessness? No; through suffering he comes to wisdom.

Now it is not to be supposed that any one will use a great number of those devices in one short passage, or that he will stand on the platform checking them off as he uses them; but the list may be useful for self-criticism with a view to breaking up monotony, or relieving bareness of style. It is an excellent practice, also, to make a few trial speeches in which you attempt definitely to use many ways of stating an idea. If no good theme for the purpose occurs to you, take a fable, a proverb, or any pithy saying as a starting point.

BREVITY. But, it may be said, all this conflicts with the much praised virtue of brevity. In the words of Shakespeare, "Brevity is the soul of wit, and tediousness its outer flourishes"; and again, " 'Tis better to be brief than to be tedious." We are told that the average composition would be bettered by cutting out half its words. Too many words and phrases, circumlocutions, useless repetitions—all these clog movement and make style tiresome. Brevity is an essential ingredient, along with surprise, in many pithy sayings; as, "Verbosity is cured by a large vocabulary," or "Do not mistake perspiration for inspiration." Stories are told of the effectiveness of short speeches. When Judah P. Benjamin, Senator from Louisiana before the Civil War, made a brilliant four-hour defense of slavery, Senator Ben. Wade of Ohio blasted its effectiveness by just raising his arms and exclaiming, "An Israelite with Egyptian principles!" And finally we know that audiences like brevity; that is, they like short speeches.

Granting all this, and more, still we must not overestimate mere brevity. It is better to be brief *than to be tedious.*

To be tedious is a cardinal sin, and the sooner a tedious speech ends the better; but it is quite easy to be brief *and* tedious, and also to amplify at length and be interesting. "The briefer the better," like all short, sweeping assertions, needs a deal of qualification. If this confident assertion were accepted at its face value, many of the greatest books, essays, and poems should be condensed into a few sententious sayings. I ask on what basis a student should be marked, and am told, "On accomplishment." That seems to mean something; but try to apply it, and you find my oracle is as vague as the Delphic. About all that can be said on this subject of brevity boils down to this: Say enough but not too much. But is that helpful?

The late Senator Beveridge wrote a long passage to elaborate his dictum, "Condense, condense, condense." The Gettysburg Address is pointed to as a marvel of brevity; but if the utmost brevity is good, this speech is verbose. Short as it is, it contains words not necessary, and even repetitions. Moreover, the times prepared the audience for the speech, and Edward Everett, who spoke before the President, had in a long discourse reviewed the history which formed a background for Lincoln's address. And after all, there is strong evidence that the audience were not so much impressed with the speech as we are. It was too short for a hearer, who lacks the reader's opportunity to deliberate. When Lincoln debated with Douglas he usually took his full hour and a half.

A good thing should not be made a fetish. Serious writers recognize the limitations as well as the virtues of brevity; only some, impressed by the undoubted force of condensation properly used, grow lyrical on the subject and lose their sense of proportion.

What then is the truth? Am I urging you to be as long-winded as you like? Heaven forbid! Short speeches are usually best and brevity is frequently necessary. Verboseness, that is, using more words than are helpful, is to be condemned. How can we reconcile these statements with the need for amplification?

*How to be brief.* First, we must consider the circumstances and the needs of our audiences. Matter which is easy to comprehend because of its nature or of its familiarity may often be cut short. Secondly, consider whether you are amplifying a thought that deserves emphasis, or are spinning it out simply because it is pleasant to talk about, or perhaps is important *per se* rather than important in the development of your theme. A simple illustration may be found in a speech on the making of cement in which the speaker spent so much time on the processes of getting the limestone to the mill and crushing it—essential processes but not peculiar to cement-making—that he had left too little time for the actual making of cement.

Thirdly, waste no words. A distinguished United States Senator used in an address perhaps forty times the phrase *United States of America. United States,* or *This country,* would have served as well in every case; and in most instances no phrase at all was needed because we could not possibly have supposed he was referring to any other country. Many modifiers can be cut out with a gain in strength. When Hamlet says of his father, "He was a man, take him for all in all," he could not have strengthened his praise by adding adjectives to *man.* Perhaps no one ever seriously called a spade an "agricultural implement frequently utilized for purposes of excavation," but the expression only caricatures a too common style of speaking. What was said of the directness of specific terms applies here. It is a beneficial practice to study your own speeches to see where you can with as great, or greater, effectiveness, put your idea in fewer words. But being economical with words is not the same as being niggardly; economy with words as with money includes wise spending. Do not cut till the effect is bareness. Does a word in question serve a good purpose? As an old lawyer has said, "The number of a man's words should be like the length of a blanket: enough to cover the bed and to tuck in besides."

Fourthly, in order to combine needed amplification with shortness of speeches, *we should narrow our themes*. There are but few occasions when we are required to cover a large subject in a few minutes. On the occasion of Lincoln's second inauguration there were many topics crying for attention, but he did not feel obliged to speak of them all that day. His speech was brief because he limited his scope. This is the brevity audiences like, that of a well-developed but limited idea, not that of a bare, hard-packed address.

Finally, remember that no one complains of the length of a speech that he finds interesting.

UNITY IN VARIETY. I have emphasized the need for change and also the need for dwelling upon important ideas; and now I emphasize the need for unity, which demands that each speech should "group itself about one central idea." We must make a distinction between merely holding attention through a given period and holding attention to those ideas which, properly impressed, will accomplish our further purposes. It may be possible to hold attention, if that is all that is desired, by a series of disconnected "hits," whether these be jokes, stories, "purple patches," epigrams, passages of sheer beauty, or any other resource of composition and delivery; but all this is a waste for a speaker with a purpose, unless he has used all to produce a unified impression. The importance of unity will grow upon us as we study and practise speech-making.

There is need for *unity of thought*, and this is the unity usually emphasized in the texts. Whatever is said, however many ideas are advanced, all should be subordinated to one central thought which all serve to develop. There is also a *unity of feeling*. However many emotions are touched, all should blend to produce the desired mood. Both these unities enter into and are subordinate to *unity of purpose;* that is, all that goes into a speech should bear the test of promoting understanding, inducing belief, or influencing conduct, according to the speaker's aim in a given speech.

Due attention to unity does not preclude variety. *Variety in unity* James declares "the secret of all interesting talk and thought." Other writers say, "Variety in unity is the secret of sustained attention." Unity you need; variety you need; there is no conflict. While you must turn attention from one aspect of your theme to another, you should turn to aspects of that part which is under consideration. And also, as indicated above, you gain variety by stating the same idea in different ways. Fix this in mind: Change does not require jumping from one topic to another; or even to another part of the same subject than that under consideration. Nor is a higgledy-piggledy turning from point to point within your proper scope suggested; rather an orderly, coherent procedure, such as will encourage the efforts of your audience to see the relations of part to part.

To illustrate the foregoing we may turn back to the excerpt from Carlyle. Certainly there is both unity and variety. Each paragraph serves to give a new point of view; yet each serves the central thought and turns attention to it again and again. So evident is the central thought in each paragraph that careless summaries of the paragraphs will be much alike and will really be summaries of the whole.

Lincoln's Gettysburg Address (printed in full in Chapter XX) is a remarkable example of unity with progress and variety. There is unity of thought: all serves to develop the proposition, Popular government must be preserved in the world. Our fathers established a free government; this war is testing the durability of such government; we have met to honor those who have died that it may endure; we cannot honor them, but we can catch inspiration from them and solemnly resolve that free government shall endure. Almost every sentence directly echoes or amplifies the central thought. There is unity of feeling: veneration for the fathers because of the work they wrought for free government, sorrow for the dead, pride in their courage and gratitude for their sacrifices, and with all a glorying in the conviction that this is a struggle for human liberty— all these blend into high resolve to continue the struggle. That is to say, there is also unity of purpose: Lincoln wishes to honor the occasion and more to honor the dead; but these purposes accomplished serve the grand purpose of inspiring his hearers and the country to greater sacrifices.

There is a very real temptation to attempt too much in a single speech, and the speaker often feels that his hearers ought to be capable of understanding several major thoughts in one period, and so often they are; but still experience proves that no audience is likely to carry away from a discourse more than one important thought, that where there is not proper limitation, elimination, and subordination of all to one central thought, the audience carries away little that is clear and well impressed, and that little as often the least important as the most important. In exposition, in argument, and particularly in persuasion, there is need of "pounding in" a single idea. The hearer, we must always remember, cannot, like the reader, review and ponder and so impress many thoughts on his mind. The speaker must consider that he has done well if he has clearly and forcefully expressed one thought; very well indeed, if next day his hearers are able to state justly his main idea.

A few specific warnings may assist in securing unity. Do not let yourself be led astray by mere association of ideas, such as guides most conversations. Each sentence may be related to its neighbors, and yet unity of the whole be lacking. To give an exaggerated example:

Speaking of California, I am reminded of her great prune orchards. Now prunes properly prepared are an excellent food. I do not mean as boarding-house keepers prepare them. Boarding-house keepers are trying to give as little as possible for their money. One can hardly blame them, either, what with the high cost of living, which does not seem to have been much lowered by the depression. We have had high hopes of better times since the new Administration came in; but it's too soon to tell. But speaking of California, they have better things than prunes out there—oranges, and football teams, and tennis stars; but I don't think they can always keep on beating the rest of us, etc., etc.

All one has to do is to let the "associational process" do its work to produce that sort of stuff. Too absurd, do you say? No one would make a speech like that? But is it worse than the following speech described in a student's report?

I was at a dinner of musicians last night. Mr. H., of the H. Music Store, tried to make a speech. First he talked about the Musicians' Union. Then that reminded him of unionism in general. He talked of that for fifteen minutes, and then was re-

minded of Americanism.  Then he made a transition to inter-
nationalism; and having reached the zenith, was suddenly
reminded of a story about two Irishmen.  Then he was reminded
successively of seven more stories about Irishmen.

And yet one does not doubt that, if Mr. H. had average
skill, he slipped from point to point with some appearance
of continuity.

We have noted that illustrations may tempt a speaker
from the path.  A speaker whose theme was the position
of the lawyer in various lands and times, touched upon the
lawyer in Ancient Greece, in Rome, in England, and finally
in America.  Here he chose Daniel Webster as an example.
He then told us of a humorous passage in one of Webster's
legal speeches; and then turned to Webster's humor in
general, and ended by reading us a passage from a speech
which Webster probably never made and which certainly
contained no suggestion of Webster the lawyer.  The lawyer
in history had become the "forgotten man."

Again, do not think you have unity because all you say is
or can be related to one subject.  You might say a thousand
things about Franklin D. Roosevelt that are not clearly
related to the particular theme, Roosevelt's preparation for
the Presidency.  Perhaps many of those things could be
twisted into some semblance of a relation to his preparation;
yet upon the whole they would not serve to develop your
main thought, or the right mood, or make for the end in
view.  Unity requires elimination as well as subordination,
and many an interesting fact, or seemingly brilliant thought
or expression, must be ruthlessly sacrificed.  Unfortunately
few of us have the courage of our judgment in this sort of
self-sacrifice; but the practical question is, Does this detail
serve the purpose?  When in doubt, omit.

The speaker, then, should ordinarily narrow his theme and strive to hold attention to a single idea. If this results in monotony or tiresome repetition, it is because the speaker is not skilful; he is not profiting by the lesson of variety in unity. It is also probable that his mind is not "richly furnished with materials," and that for lack of sufficient analysis he has not viewed his subject in its various aspects and relations.

COHERENCE. Closely related to unity is coherence. To cohere is to stick together. In coherent composition the relation of each part to its neighbors and to the central thought is unmistakable. This might seem to be the requirement of unity, but the emphasis is upon *unmistakable*. Not only should every sentence and paragraph have a proper relation, but this should be made plain, in order that attention shall not be wasted.

In securing coherence, much is gained by making a clear plan, with main heads showing clearly their relation to each other and to the theme, and with each subhead clear in its relation to its main head. Most stress is laid by the authorities, perhaps, upon clear sequence of ideas, as shown by clear transitions from sentence to sentence and from paragraph to paragraph. A review of "college orations" shows that a too common method of seeking force, a sort of snapping, cracking force, is by trimming out connective words and phrases. These have been called the "hooks and eyes of style," and cannot be dispensed with. In listening to such speeches one has difficulty in seeing the relation of sentences while keeping up with the speaker; and often one finds on examination that this disconnected method of composing has encouraged the speaker in stringing together "snappy" sentences which are not well related. For example:

On Virginia's historic soil has been proved the fact that Revolution may be but a stepping stone for Evolution. Man is the center of all evolution. His moral growth or decay is irresistible. Innumerable problems of human progress are the unwelcome inheritance of every generation. To ignore these problems is fatal. America is rousing from a moral lethargy; a thrilling spirit of reform typifies the present age. The fundamental evil of American society is the industrial basis upon which it stands. The State, institutions and men are judged from the standpoint of the almighty dollar. What are the results of this standard, what does it involve, and what is the remedy?

We shall dwell in Chapter XX upon the effect of *echo*, or reference to an idea already expressed, in binding together a speech. (Its use is especially notable in the Gettysburg Address.) Another means is the use of *parallel constructions;* that is, giving similar form to phrases of similar significance. Wendell speaks of "the amazing value of parallel construction," and he illustrates with the Lord's Prayer. A study of a master of speech composition, like Wendell Phillips, will reveal much use of connective words, echoes, and parallel constructions. I have chosen the following passage, not because it is the most remarkable for coherence that could be found, but because it combines coherence with the abrupt force sought in the excerpt above.

In this mass of ignorance, weakness, and quarrel, one keen eye saw hidden the elements of union and strength. With rarest skill he called them forth and marshalled them into rank. Then this one man, without birth, wealth, or office, in a land ruled by birth, wealth, and office, molded from these unsuspected elements a power which, overawing king, senate, and people, wrote his single will on the statute-book of the most obstinate nation in Europe. Safely to emancipate the Irish Catholics, and in spite of Saxon-Protestant hate, to lift all Ireland to the level of British citizenship—this was the problem which statesmanship and patriotism had been seeking for two centuries to solve. For this blood had been poured out like water. On this the genius of Swift, the learning of Molyneux, and the eloquence of Bushe, Grattan, and Burke had been wasted. English leaders ever since Fox had studied this problem anxiously. They saw that the safety of the empire was compromised. At one or two critical moments in the reign of George III, one signal from an Irish leader would have snapped the chain that bound Ireland to his throne. His ministers recognized it; and they tried every expedient, exhausted every resource, dared every peril, kept oaths or broke them in order to succeed. All failed; and not only failed, but acknowledged they could see no way in which success could ever be achieved.

O'Connell achieved it. Out of the darkness, he called forth light. Out of this most abject, weak, and pitiable of kingdoms, he made a power, and dying, he left in Parliament a specter which, unless appeased, pushes Whig and Tory ministers alike from their stools.[8]

EMPHASIS. A large element in speech-making, as regards both composition and delivery, is emphasis. Emphasis attracts attention, and right emphasis attracts attention to what should be especially noted. The term might be extended to cover much in this chapter. In its narrower sense emphasis is often a matter of *proportion*, giving due space to the different ideas of a speech and holding attention longest upon what is chiefly to be impressed. For this purpose we use amplification. In this connection Baldwin has an interesting discussion of the Gettysburg Address. After pointing out the ways in which Lincoln gives fine proportion to his speech, Baldwin continues:

[8] From "Daniel O'Connell," *Speeches and Lectures*, Second Series, p. 392. By permission of Lothrop, Lee & Shepard Company.

Now suppose this due emphasis of space changed. Suppose the speech, keeping the same number of words, to have dwelt longer on the past, and on the present more for itself than for his message.

Fourscore and seven years ago our fathers brought forth upon this continent a new nation, conceived in liberty and dedicated to the proposition that all men are created equal. This principle of democratic free government is our heritage. To establish it, many of the fathers laid down their lives; to secure it, the others united under the Constitution. Now we are engaged in a great civil war, testing whether this nation, or any nation, so conceived and so dedicated, can long endure. For this is the meaning of this terrible struggle. The older nations of Europe long ago prophesied that such a government could not endure. Democracy is on trial. We are met on a great battlefield of that war. The ground on which we stand trembled with the shock of armies. We have come to dedicate a portion of that field as a final resting place for those who here gave their lives that that nation might live. It is altogether fitting and proper that we should do this. Where they fought, there we secure their memory and mark our gratitude. But in a larger sense, we cannot dedicate, we cannot consecrate, we cannot hallow this ground. The brave men, living and dead, who struggled here, have consecrated it far beyond our power to add or detract. The world will little note, nor long remember, what we say here, but it can never forget what they did here. It is for us, the living, rather to be dedicated here to the unfinished work which they who fought here have thus far so nobly advanced.

The obvious inferiority of this form is due partly, of course, to the substitution of other words for Lincoln's; but it is due mainly to the throwing of the whole out of proportion. If Lincoln himself had arranged his speech so, however eloquent his words, he would have made his speech weaker. His clearness of thought and his training in public address led him to pass rapidly over parts which, however important they might be for another purpose, were for his present purpose subordinate, and to spend upon that present purpose the greater part of his time.   He dwelt, not upon the past, nor upon the present for itself, but upon the deep significance for the future.[9]

We cannot, however, make the simple rule that the more important should always have more space; for some subordinate but still necessary matter may require much space because of its complicated nature, while some more important matter may be stated in a few words and be of a character to impress without elaboration.

*Position* is of importance in securing right emphasis.   That the beginning and end of a sentence, paragraph, or whole composition are the strong positions, and that generally speaking the final position is strongest, is a commonplace, but a commonplace often ignored by inexperienced speakers. They are particularly likely to sink their principal idea in the middle of a long opening sentence where only forced delivery can bring it to the surface.

The resources of delivery are, of course, available for making a speech coherent and giving due emphasis to its parts; but the speaker should not compose sentences and paragraphs which throw a burden of labored stress, inflection, and pause upon delivery.   "One of the tests of good style," says Newcomer,[10] "is the ease with which a reader, reading the work aloud without previous acquaintance, will properly stress and intone the different sentence elements."   It is the test which I regularly give written speeches submitted to me; only the question in my mind is not, Is it good style?

---

[9] From *Composition Oral and Written* by C. S. Baldwin, p. 21.   By permission of Longmans, Green & Co.

[10] From *Elements of Rhetoric* by A. G. Newcomer, p. 192.   By permission of Henry Holt and Company.

but, Will it speak? Says Genung, "Seek so to place words that they shall emphasize themselves." [11]

Often a clause which one wishes particularly to attract attention can be *built up to* by explanation, arguments, or by a series of statements of which it is the climax. Would the final clause of the Gettysburg Address have become a universal possession if the sentence in which it occurs had been built this way?

It is rather for us to be here dedicated to the great task remaining before us—that from these honored dead we take increased devotion to that cause for which they gave the last full measure of devotion—that we highly resolve that government of the people, by the people, for the people shall not perish from the earth—that these dead shall not have died in vain—that this nation, under God, shall have a new birth of freedom.

Sometimes the best way to throw a statement into bold relief is to give it strong *contrast*.

*Climax,* which may be considered an aspect of emphasis, is even more important in speaking than in writing. It is the natural expression of one who warms to his work; but it also answers to an instinctive demand of the hearer. Genung explains:

It is more a principle than a process, being merely the rhetorical embodiment of the law that a thought must grow, must have progress; which indeed it must, not only to reach a natural culmination by increase of interest, but also for the reader's sake, to make up for the mental energy that the advance of the discourse is all the while using up.[12]

[11] From *Practical Elements of Rhetoric* by J. F. Genung, p. 179. By permission of Ginn and Company.

[12] From *Working Principles of Rhetoric* by J. F. Genung, p. 292. By permission of Ginn and Company.

Anticlimax, when it is not humorous, is weak, as can be seen in the distorted conclusion of the Gettysburg Address above; and much the same effect as anticlimax arises from proceeding without increase of force. Says Baldwin,[13] "A strong sentence goes up hill; a weak sentence goes down hill." As a rule the order of climax should be followed within the sentence, in the paragraphs, and in the whole speech, though, as has been noted, there may be good reason for a different order.

*Avoid overemphasis.* To give an idea too much stress is as bad as to give it too little; for not only does stress on the less important reduce the emphasis on the more important, as is seen in Baldwin's distorted version of the Gettysburg Address, but also, and especially when the undue stress takes the form of strong language—humorously described as "taking a sledge hammer to kill a fly"—the effect may be absurd. This effect may be noted in the conversation of the young girl who "just loves," and apparently equally, all things she does not hate with a perfect hatred.

But even if the ideas expressed do deserve strong expression, it is tiresome to hear a speaker who in composition or delivery continues at the top of his power. That does not mean that any part should be weak; anything worth saying at all is worth saying firmly. But there should be variation in force. Discourse that is uniformly strong must be considered seriously defective, for emphasis ceases to be possible. In an army where all are generals there is no distinction in being a general. Strong monotony is as truly a fault as weak monotony. Hence we find that the best speakers often follow very strong with milder discourse. Wendell Phillips, though often making outrageously strong

[13] From *Composition Oral and Written* by C. S. Baldwin, p. 125. By permission of Longmans, Green & Co.

statements, knew well how to do this. In his Phi Beta Kappa address he said to a body of scholars:

Wycliffe was, no doubt, a learned man. But the learning of his day would have burned him, had it dared, as it did burn his dead body afterward. Luther and Melanchthon were scholars, but were repudiated by the scholarship of their time, which followed Erasmus, trying "all his life to tread on eggs without breaking them:" he who proclaimed that "peaceful error was better than tempestuous truth." What would college graduate Seward weigh, in any scale, against Lincoln bred in affairs?

Hence I do not think the greatest things have been done in the world by its book-men. Education is not the chips of arithmetic and grammar,—nouns, verbs, and the multiplication table; neither is it that last year's almanac of dates, or series of lies agreed upon, which we so often mistake for history. Education is not Greek and Latin and the air-pump. Still, I rate at its full value the training we get in these walls. Though what we actually carry away is little enough, we do get some training of our powers, as the gymnast or fencer does of his muscles: we go hence with such general knowledge of what mankind has agreed to consider proved and settled, that we know where to reach for the weapon when we need it.[14]

*Antithesis.* Antithesis is based on contrast, with the force of which we are familiar. Genung says [15] that, like climax, antithesis "is really a universal requisite of literary utterance, whatever its stage and scope." Antithesis,[16] "shown on its narrowest scale as a pointed balance of word and structure . . . from this may extend to whole masses of thought,

[14] From *Speeches and Lectures* by Wendell Phillips, Second Series, p. 341.   By permission of Lothrop, Lee & Shepard Company.
[15] From *Working Principles of Rhetoric*, p. 292.   By permission of Ginn and Company.
[16] *Idem,* p. 271.

to contrasted scenes, situations, characters, and events." To illustrate:

A soft answer turneth away wrath; but a grievous word stirreth up anger.—*Proverbs*.

The puritans hated bear-baiting, not because it gave pain to the bear, but because it gave pleasure to the spectators.—*Macaulay*.

It is because Shakespeare dares, and dares very frequently, . . . simply to be foolish, that he is so preëminently wise; the others try to be always wise, and, alas! it is not necessary to complete the antithesis.—*Saintsbury*.

On a larger scale antithesis may be illustrated by the Gettysburg Address, in which, says Cooper,[17] "The balance in thought and phrase is easily detected by both eye and ear, and the use of antithesis is obvious, as in the contrast between then and now, birth and death, the living and the dead," and, it may be added, between what "in a larger sense" we cannot do and what we should do. Both antithesis and climax are among the elements of interest in the famous introduction to Lincoln's Springfield speech (1858):

If we could first know where we are, and whither we are tending, we could better judge what to do, and how to do it. We are now far into the fifth year since a policy was initiated with the avowed object and confident purpose of putting an end to slavery agitation. Under the operation of that policy, that agitation has not only not ceased, but has constantly augmented. In my opinion, it will not cease until a crisis shall have been reached and passed. "A house divided against itself cannot stand." I

[17] From the *Rhetoric of Aristotle*, by Lane Cooper, p. xxxiii. By permission of D. Appleton-Century Company. The Introduction contains an extended discussion of the Gettysburg Address in Aristotelian terms.

believe this government cannot endure permanently half slave and half free. I do not expect the Union to be dissolved; I do not expect the house to fall; but I do expect it will cease to be divided. It will become all one thing, or all the other. Either the opponents of slavery will arrest the further spread of it, and place it where the public mind shall rest in the belief that it is in the course of ultimate extinction, or its advocates will push it forward till it shall become alike lawful in all the states, old as well as new, North as well as South.

*Asking questions.* Says Phelps: [18]

Few expedients of speech so simple as this are so effective in giving vigor to style. Composition comparatively dull may be made comparatively vivacious, and so far forcible, by a liberal sprinkling of interrogatives. Is a declarative utterance of a truth tame? Put it as an inquiry. Ask a question which implies it, and the silent answer may be more impressive to your hearer than any words of yours. . . . Put it to your hearer as if he must sharpen it by a response.

I do not like the term *rhetorical question* with its usual definition, "a question not intended to elicit an answer, but intended for rhetorical effect" (in which "rhetorical effect" apparently means embellishment). No doubt there are such, but the questions I am talking about are intended to provoke answers, whether spoken audibly, expressed by visible action, or only thought. The peculiar virtue of the question in commanding attention is in its prompting of the hearer to answer, to think for himself rather than passively to accept the statements of the speaker. Such questions are a challenge; they "put the matter up to you."

The question is a powerful weapon in argument; and as

[18] From *Rhetoric: Its Theory and Practice* by Phelps and Frink, p. 158. By permission of Charles Scribner's Sons.

it is much used to drive one's opponent into a corner, it often adds the interest of conflict. Patrick Henry's speeches have many questions. In opposing the adoption of the federal Constitution in the Virginia convention, early in his first speech he attacks the framers of the new constitution for exceeding their powers—as they undoubtedly had; and goes on: "I have the highest veneration for those gentlemen; but, sir, give me leave to demand, what right had they to say, 'We, the People'? My political curiosity, exclusive of my anxious solicitude for the public welfare, leads me to ask, who authorized them to speak the language of 'We, the People,' instead of We, the States"? But the question in argument may also be the language of reasonableness. One-twelfth of the sentences in Webster's summation in the Knapp-White case are questions, and while some are of the more belligerent sort, many are simply a means of holding the attention of the jury and of taking them into partnership with the speaker.

The question is much used to keep hearers alert in listening to explanations. In the simplest way, we have such questions as, What shall we understand by behaviorism? Now do you see the connection? How is the spark made to synchronize with the compression stroke of the piston? As such questions strike the teacher note, care should be taken to avoid the gently patronizing tone of "Now, children, what did Peter Rabbit do next?" But properly used the question is useful; as in this from one of Thackeray's lectures on "The Four Georges":

What is it to be a gentleman? Is it to have lofty aims, to lead a pure life, to keep your honor virgin; to have the esteem of your fellow-citizens, and the love of your fireside; to bear good fortune meekly; to suffer evil with constancy; and through evil or good to maintain truth always? Show me the happy man whose life exhibits these qualities, and him we will salute as gentleman, whatever his rank may be; show me the prince who possesses them, and he may be sure of our love and loyalty.

*The effective phrase.* All means of heightening expression are subject to abuse. If carried too far they defeat their purpose by becoming themselves monotonous, or by attracting attention to themselves; and, especially in the form of epigrams and clever sayings generally, they may seem too artificial. There have been college students who were too fond of highly wrought phrases, and no doubt there are still those who try to make expression take the place of thought; but in these days of "practical" courses there are more who despise careful attention to phraseology. I could wish sometimes that my students would overdo expression, for one can check overdoing; but what can one do for those who never try to express themselves well? "What's the odds if people only get it?" they demand; and do not see that they beg the question. If one's words do not fit the thought, or are offensive to the taste of one's hearers, if one's constructions are weak and cloudy, if one's discourse is for any reason hard to listen to, then one's hearers do not "get it," or not with full force. Those who can appreciate good form in pulling an oar or driving a golf ball, or efficiency in laying brick, should not be indifferent to the manner of expressing ideas; or damn as "flowery" every attempt to escape the utterly commonplace.

Is it not a false idea of sincerity which lies back of the notion that a man should not try to say things well? "If a man has a worthy thing to say," exclaimed Henry Van Dyke, "shall he not think it worth while to find a worthy way to say it?" We overlook the fact that as soon as we go beyond the simplest statements, "just to tell the truth is consummate art." What is it we instinctively object to? I do not believe the man lives who does not respond to really good expression. Is not our objection to the effort to make a commonplace idea sound profound, the use of the "feeble forcible" in an effort to make a puny thought startling? The refusal to say a simple thing simply produces bombast, against which we properly react. There are those, also, who carefully avoiding the "highfalutin," and even honest eloquence, yet indulge in so much cleverness that one feels they are trying to be "smart." They attract attention less to their ideas than to their way of expressing them. And this, like a showy gesture, is both ineffective and in bad taste. It is neither the "big bow-wow," nor affectedly clever expression, that is urged upon you; but just an honest effort to give effective, fitting expression to your thoughts and feelings, so that without waste they shall hold and impress the attention of your audience. And if your words, without attracting attention to their beauty and rhythm, give your audience pleasure, so much the better.

And we must remember that the very effort for clear, vigorous expression reacts to clarify and strengthen our thought. We should remember, too, that we are students, not masters; and that if we are to be ready in the crises we look forward to, when with smoothly working minds, and ready command of ample vocabularies, we shall meet unexpected emergencies, we shall have to train ourselves well. A student may well put aside this extreme fear of artificiality and strive to express himself as well as he can; strive to put into each speech at least one sentence that will arrest attention and stick in the minds of the audience.

*Slang.* There are some who seem to have no forceful way of expressing themselves save in slang. Slang is a matter to be treated with common sense. We must admit that its use is not a crime and that it is sometimes effective. Nevertheless, I advise the young speaker against any considerable indulgence in slang. First, we must recognize that there are going to be many times when slang will be unwise and inappropriate. Yet we are such creatures of habit that, if we use it habitually, we shall with difficulty avoid slang when we stand up to speak extemporaneously. And the effort to do so will greatly restrain our freedom. We shall be at a loss for words. Our sentences will frame themselves for their customary slang, which will either pop out in spite of us, or we shall have to hem and haw and start anew. If we cannot leave off our slang altogether, let us at least make a practice of leaving it out of our speech upon the platform; let slang have no part in our platform consciousness. At most, let us use slang only when we are sure that no good English expression will do as well.

In the second place, we must recognize that the constant use of slang limits our vocabulary. The English language has resources never dreamed of by the slangy person. Let us listen to the sane old Autocrat (substituting for his antiques more modern phrases, as "good egg" for "brick"):

I have known several genteel idiots whose whole vocabulary had deliquesced into some half dozen expressions. All things fell into one of two great categories,—*fast* or *slow*. Man's chief end was to be a *brick*. When the great calamities of life overtook their friends, these last were spoken of as *a good deal cut up*. Nine-tenths of human existence were summed up in the single word, *bore*. These expressions come to be the algebraic symbols of minds grown too weak or indolent to discriminate. They are the blank checks of intellectual bankruptcy;—you may fill them up with what idea you like; it makes no difference, for there are no funds in the treasury upon which they are drawn. . . . Don't think I undervalue the proper use and application of a cant word or phrase. It adds piquancy to conversation, as a mushroom does to a sauce. But it is no better than a toadstool, odious to the sense and poisonous to the intellect, when it spawns itself all over the talk of men and youth capable of talking, as it sometimes does.[19]

In the third place, we must recognize that what seems very effective to some may be very ineffective and even repulsive to those of better taste and judgment. That one may get a laugh by an atrocious bit of slang does not mean that it has served his real purpose. There are many atrocious ways of drawing a laugh from an audience—sometimes a laugh from the more vulgar portion while the rest shiver. We should notice, of course, that there is slang and slang; that some is almost necessary in discussing certain themes in certain places, and that in any case there is a wide difference between such mild slang as "something doing" and such a senseless vulgarity as "feed your face." But one who indulges greatly in slang is not likely to have a fine taste in the matter. And we may note, further, that such effectiveness as slang has diminishes with frequency of use.

[19] From *The Autocrat of the Breakfast Table* by Oliver Wendell Holmes, No. XI.

# CHAPTER X

## INTEREST OF THE SPEAKER

We have to consider not only the interest of the audience, but also the interest of the speaker. We have noted that the speaker needs to be keenly interested in what he is saying. If he has, or develops, interest in his subject, his preparation will not be a boring task; and if he has strong interest when he comes to speak, he will consume less of his energy in merely keeping his mind to its work, and his speaking will be far more likely to have alertness and communicativeness, for what interests him he will enjoy telling to others.

If a speaker could always choose subjects in which his interest is keen, no problem would arise; but, as we have noted in the chapter on subjects, he may have to treat topics in which his initial interest is not keen. The occasion, or the interests of his audience, may demand a certain theme of no special interest to the speaker; or circumstances may demand a speech from him when he "has nothing on his mind," or when the subjects that are taking his mind cannot be spoken about. The more prominent a man is in his community the more often he will be dragged in to say a good word for this and that cause, or to make this and that occasion a success. A clergyman, or a man in official position, as the mayor, is subject to calls for all sorts of occasions, not all of which interest him.

Sometimes to carry out his own purpose a speaker has to take a subject he cares little about; as in a political campaign he may have to talk of farm relief or water power when his real interest is in international relations. The dean of a college, or the supervisor of a working force, may have to say things which, because they must be said time after time, become very tiresome. The pretty notion that one should speak only when his soul is bursting with a message does not work out well in practice. We will hope you will not often have to speak on subjects of no interest to yourself; but there are likely to be a good many occasions when you will start with less interest than is desirable.

The answer to the question, What can the speaker do to increase his interest in his subject? is to be found in the preceding pages; and it will not be necessary to go over all the ground again. It is to a considerable extent true that if a speaker prepares his speech so as to make it interesting to his audience, he will also make it interesting to himself; but certain points will bear further consideration.

The primary step in increasing interest is to increase knowledge of it. The suggestion is so good that the very phrases in which it is couched have grown trite: "Fill yourself with your subject," "Soak yourself full of your subject," "Steep yourself in your subject." But we know that an intelligent procedure requires more than just "soaking," though that may be good at an early stage. We have in Chapter IV considered the gathering of information, and in Chapter V the analysis of this material and its synthesis into orderly systems. Following the suggestions of those chapters will build up interest.

Then as the speaker reads and mulls over his material he can make a definite effort to assimilate it, associating the uninteresting with his existing interests, the new with his existing knowledge and experience. He can "state the new in terms of the old," the old in terms of the new.  He can develop derived interest.

Let us take an extreme case, and assume that Tom Brown, intelligent about the affairs of to-day but indifferent to the past, has been assigned (very unwisely, I will admit) to speak on some phase of Greek archeology.  He barely knows what the term means, but decides to make the best of a bad job.  What to do?  First, by applying forced attention Brown proceeds to find out something about the ancient Greeks.  He discovers that they had sports, Olympic games in fact; and that we are imitating their sports to-day.  In a museum of casts he finds the Discus Thrower and the Wrestler, and is led to take notice of Greek art.  He reads of the Greeks as a military people who fought battles important in the history of civilization.  He finds further that the Greeks had industries, commerce, sciences, and that among them were great lawyers, physicians, playwrights, poets, and philosophers, and that we have derived much from them.  He learns of interesting characters, as Socrates, Diogenes, Alcibiades.  He is naturally led to compare some of the Grecian ways and ideas with ours.  From one or several of these lines of information Brown derives an interest which he finds it no hardship to follow up; and he becomes able to speak on some aspect of his general subject with interest to himself, and probably to his hearers.

In following this study Brown has applied not only the first method for developing interest—that is, he has gained knowledge and associated this with his previous knowledge and interests; but he has also applied another method: "In order to develop interest in a subject, exert activity toward it."  He can also follow this method profitably by talking and writing about the subject.  He can make speeches about it (with or without listeners)—an excellent method not only for developing interest, but also for clarifying his ideas and finding words to express them, and also a means of getting his material out of the bookish and into the speech-making atmosphere. And, of course, among the standard ways of doing something with the material, or exerting activity toward it, are analyzing, briefing, and planning and outlining.

IMAGINATION IN PREPARATION. Throughout preparation the speaker should utilize imagination, "the instrument of reality." See in your mind's eye the persons, things, acts, and conditions with which you deal. If you are trying to understand a person, begin by visualizing him as clearly as you can; not as a mere *homo*, but as tall, dark-haired, ruddy-complexioned, dressed in a sack suit, or whatever the facts about his physical appearance may justify. Encourage all kinds of imagery, as sight, sound, and motor. Put yourself into a situation, taking part in the action and conversation. So Brown might attend the Athenian agora, listen to the speeches, cast his vote, talk with the citizens. Of course, this requires information and time for brooding. A student whose chief interest was engineering, and who had some knowledge of the Pyramids, wrote:

Suppose we were making a speech on the Construction of the Pyramids of Egypt. . . . We may never have even seen them. However, if we bring imagination into play, we can picture the vast armies who built them, the huge, cumbersome carts used in carrying the stones, the hundreds of sweating, babbling slaves who were made to haul them, the harsh overseers who drove the slaves on to work, the inclined planes up which the stones were dragged by sheer might; and in time we could make the whole scene be so real to us that we could almost imagine ourselves to be the designers and engineers. In this way the subject would be made alive to us, and when we talked it would be with the conviction that we were talking on *something we knew about from our own experience,* and not something taken out of a few dusty old books and here merely something to talk about.

This teaching is quite as good if you are dealing with simpler and present-day situations, as traffic control or the use made of Muscle Shoals. It may be noted that it is sometimes important that imagery be as true as possible to fact, as when an engineer is preparing to make clear to an audience of capitalists the situation of a proposed power dam; but more often it is sufficient that imagination build forms essentially true to reality, true in impression.

If one is to speak on a more abstract subject, say arbitration, imagination is still more needed. The young speaker is prone to deal with such a subject with too little basis in concrete facts. For a man of long diplomatic experience there are so many phases, relations, applications, so many interesting persons connected with the movement for arbitration, such a wealth of material to think with, that the topic readily commands his attention. The young speaker has no such advantage; but by gathering a goodly amount of material and transmuting the data into living forms through imagination, and, of course, linking the new matter to his established interests, such as politics, economics, and sociology, and in these fields to his special interests, as eugenics, he can change arbitration from an uncertain object of attention into a strong, clear concept; and so earn the right to speak.

WORK NOT WASTED. As was pointed out before, it matters not that not all you have learned and thought can be used in your speech. All goes to build up the concept in your mind; you gain in both interest and mastery, and become able to speak with a clearness, a sense of proportion, and an earnestness which constitute the potency of a speaker who is "full of his subject."

We cannot always explain an impression, which nevertheless grows upon us as we listen, that a speaker has nothing back of what he says. In contrast, I have a friend who, when he talks of medieval history, seems quite as much at home as in this present age; and he speaks of historical characters as of intimates of whom he might tell no end of good stories. He makes even an ignoramus interested. A Princeton graduate tells of a lecture in which Professor Woodrow Wilson was saying to his class that Gladstone could make any subject interesting, even a four-hour speech on the budget. "Young men," exclaimed the professor, "it is not the subject that is dry; it is you that are dry!"

BEGIN PREPARATION EARLY. It should be clear by this time why I urged you to get a topic early. That advice is not just schoolmastering, but is based on hard fact. It is not only the time spent in actual work that counts, but also the length of time you carry your topic in mind, provided you do enough with it at the beginning to make it, in a phrase from William James, "bud and sprout and grow." Get the material in mind and then give time for the relations to clear up, for the processes of assimilation and of imagination to work, give time for "unconscious cerebration," or, in homely phrase, for the matter to soak in. We may appropriate what Oliver Wendell Holmes makes the Autocrat say of conversation: "Knowledge and timber shouldn't be used till they are seasoned." When you have put an idea in your mind and return to it after an interval, he says, "you do not find it as it was when acquired. It has domiciliated itself, so to speak—entered into relations with other thoughts, and integrated itself with the whole fabric of the mind."

Beginning early actually saves labor, for the reason just suggested, and also because once we have set our mind for a certain topic, materials, ideas, and illustrations seem to come to us. They existed all about us before, only we did not notice them.

Another good reason for beginning early is that one becomes better able to criticize his own work. We all know that after a struggle over a piece of constructive work, we are not immediately able to judge it. Put it aside for a time, and we can look at it more objectively and can judge better how it will appeal to others. And we find that it is with extreme difficulty that we get any genuine criticism except our own.

Finally the speaker who has waited till the last moment to prepare will lack something of the self-confidence that is needed for good control of his thoughts on the platform. Students often think that it is all the same if they put in a due amount of work as late as possible, but they deceive themselves. Whatever time you have, you will get a better return for the energy spent if you put in a part of that time early.

THESE TEACHINGS ARE PRACTICAL. I know as well as any one that the teachings of this book cannot be carried out fully in every case. I have been speaking of thoroughgoing preparation, trying to tell you how to make a really good speech. But granted that the foregoing suggestions cannot be carried out ideally in every case, it is better to know the best that can be done so that we may not fail to do our best for lack of knowledge of the possibilities. And so far as the limitations of students in classroom speeches are concerned, I should not care to teach, or you to study, in a course that did not look beyond the classroom.

There are several encouraging facts. A student in a class

in speaking may be called up often to speak on simple and familiar topics, just to get him accustomed to speaking; but for some of his speeches he will have time for serious preparation. In the second place, if one does faithfully try to apply the teachings to a few speeches he finds that his facility increases rapidly. To a medical student who showed me the amazing list of questions he was expected to consider in diagnosing a case, I said, "How in the world can you do all that for each case?" He replied, "Oh, with practice one does it very quickly." Thought is swift, and many of the processes indicated go on quite or almost simultaneously. Moreover, the practised diagnostician does not go far without realizing that many of the points on his chart are not applicable to the particular case.

In the third place, the class of speakers for whom this book is written, having lived a considerable number of years and had many years of schooling, do not have to "start from scratch" in every case. They should choose subjects in which they have good grounding. If we may return just once more to a standard illustration, schooled Americans should know a good deal of American history, should have some grasp of the great struggle between North and South, and should know a good deal about Lincoln. So they should have a pretty good foundation on which to build preparation of a speech on the great President. Another encouraging circumstance is that not every speech need be made in a new field. Any subject has many phases, any one of which is likely to prove more than sufficient for a speech, provided the speaker is well informed. The desire to range superficially all over a large subject is evidence of ignorance. Having spoken on one phase of a subject, next time the speaker may take another phase of the same subject, and he will find that the previous study proves helpful. Knowledge, mastery and interest will grow; the speeches will be better and the incidental culture greater than if one touches superficially many fields. This presumes, of course, that the speaker will make real progress each time he speaks, and not go on repeating on the basis of his first preparation. A man may do a great deal of speaking throughout a long career, without tiresome repetition, yet use but few themes and those related. Nearly all that Webster said in his many speeches, if we except those incidental to his law practice and the routine business of the Senate, and including much in those, could be grouped around one subject, the Constitution. A man gains more reputation and produces more effect by limiting his range.

And, finally, it is better to make a few good speeches than many poor ones. Poor speeches do not profit the speaker, even as training; and they certainly do not profit any one else.

THE REPEATED SPEECH. When one has to repeat a speech several times, he should find it growing in interest and improving in expression. This will be true if his knowledge grows and his thinking continues. But if one does find himself stale, the best way to freshen interest is to repeat the steps of the original preparation, going over the data, the analyses, the concrete situations, utilizing imagination; and also finding new data, new illustrations, new applications, combining the new with the old and doing more thinking. Often it is best to prepare a new speech, approaching the subject from a new angle, and thus avoiding the dangers of new wine in old bottles and new patches on old cloth. The process will compel fresh thinking, and that is what is needed.

# CHAPTER XI

## THE EXPOSITORY SPEECH

One of the principal purposes of the speaker is to make clear, to explain. Discourse which has explanation for its chief purpose is called exposition.

There are good reasons why the student of speech-making should give attention to exposition, although to convince and persuade may be his distinctive purposes. First, there are many times when exposition is the speaker's final aim. This is often true in lecturing and in business speaking. Explanation is peculiarly the business of the teacher; but nearly every one is at times a teacher; the president of a company to his directors, the manager to his foreman, the foreman to his workers, the coach of a team to his squad. Secondly, exposition is at the basis of speeches aiming at conviction and persuasion. Many differences of opinion are due to different understandings of facts or different definitions. How often disputes end with one party saying, "Oh, if I had known that that was what you meant!" Sometimes all that is needed to win an argument is to set forth lucidly the facts in the case. It is said that judges would often stop Lincoln after his statement of fact and before he began to argue, with "Now we will hear the other side." To convince a manager that he should adopt a certain machine may require only that you demonstrate its operation to him. Thirdly, the student finds the exposition of subjects in which he is interested quite as good as any other kind of speech for helping him to forget himself.

Obviously the quality peculiarly demanded by exposition is clearness; although we must remember that even perfect clearness will not avail in a speech not interesting enough to be listened to. It is obvious, too, that most of what you have learned of explanation with reference to writing is applicable to speech-making. What I shall attempt here is to set down a few points that will serve as a review of what has been learned in English courses, and to add a few points that are peculiar to speech-making.

SPEECHES PURELY EXPOSITORY. In taking up the explanatory speech, I advise that the first attempt be pure exposition; that is, a speech in which understanding is the final aim. If you choose to explain the air-cooled gas engine, stop with explanation and avoid all argument that it is better than another type. If you choose to explain the ethical doctrine of hedonism, do not attempt to prove it right or wrong. Keep as far from advocacy as if you were explaining the seasons on Mars. This does not mean that you must be dull and cold. You should be highly interested; but your dominant emotion should be desire to make your hearers understand. There is a reason back of this suggestion. If you are using your explanation as an argument, you are likely to neglect clearness and also to warp your exposition in your desire to advocate. You should learn to make the most impartial explanations. Indeed, you should make an impartial explanation even when you are to base argument upon it. Authorities agree to the doctrine, which young speakers find hard to accept and older ones to practise, that the introductory and incidental explanations in debate should be without bias; not only because this is the honest method, but also because it is most effective to give an exposition which the other party must acknowledge to be fair.

ARGUMENTATIVE SPEECHES EXPOSITORY IN METHOD. After one has practised somewhat upon the purely expository speech, one may take up speeches in which exposition is used as a method of convincing or persuading; for example, one may explain the commission form of government in such a way that its virtues become apparent. With very slight changes, the brief on the coöperative store and the outline on the George Junior Republic (found in Chapters V and VI) could serve as bases for speeches in advocacy of those institutions. Indeed, in the second instance it would be rather difficult to keep the tone of advocacy out of the speech, though the outline is, in form and intent, expository.

ANALYSIS IN EXPOSITION. As in all speeches we need an analysis; and this is particularly important in exposition. Now we recall that to analyze is to resolve a subject into its parts and determine their relations to the whole and to each other. This matter has been considered in Chapter V, but it will be well to restate certain points as a preliminary to further discussion.

From the definition just given we see that *analysis turns on the discovery and formulation of a central, unifying idea* for the whole speech.[1] If your subject is the architectural design of a railway station, you may know something about its beauty, its serviceability, its method of construction, its place in the history of the railroad. But to ramble from one of these topics to the next is not to make an organized speech. If you determine that your real purpose is to explain how the building is serviceable, you will have to discard much that you know, and restrict yourself to the central idea selected as the unifying point for the speech. From this the

[1] I am using here, almost word for word, *Manual for Public Speaking I*, pp. 25-27, *op. cit.*

main heads will emerge fairly easily: various uses, or classes
of uses, to which the building is adapted.

It is worth emphasis that the mere impulse to tell about
the George Junior Republic, or the Princeton campus, or
the manufacture of paper, or the philosophy of hedonism, or
the consular service, gives one a subject, but not an organizing idea for a speech on that subject. Failure to find such
an organizing idea frequently comes from not standing far
enough away from the subject to have a point of view on it.
Your point of view may become clearer if you deliberately
try to take a broad view of the subject. Ask yourself what
it is you wish to explain. Is it an institution? a structure? a
process or a mechanism? an historical event? These questions suggest central ideas (embodied in subject sentences)
such as the following; note that in each of them the thing to
be explained is generally characterized or described:

1. The George Junior Republic is an institution for training in citizenship.

2. The Princeton campus is an unsystematic group of
quadrangles.

3. The manufacture of paper is a process partly chemical,
partly mechanical.

4. The Civil War was the outcome of a number of antagonisms, each developed over a long period.

5. A student's registration in college is effected by standing in line at the Dean's office, at the adviser's office, and at
the offices of the departments in which courses are elected.
(True for some colleges.)

(Compare the subject sentences suggested for expository
speeches in Chapters V and VI. In those chapters, also,
expository briefs and outlines are exemplified.)

Then by the process technically known as *division*, we proceed to formulate the main heads of the analysis.

1. If the George Junior Republic is an institution for training in citizenship, in what ways or for what aspects of citizenship does it train?

2. The quadrangles of Princeton suggest a main head for each, probably in such order as a visitor might follow on a tour of inspection.

3. The manufacture of paper may divide into an alternation of chemical and mechanical processes.

4. For the Civil War, each of the antagonisms which brought it about will be a main head.

5. The central idea on registration is nothing but the sum of the three chief factors in the topic, each of which, of course, will constitute a main head. (Note that this type of central idea, secured by summing up main factors, is fairly common in exposition.)

If you have found a point of view from which the subject organizes into a central idea with appropriate main heads, it will not be difficult to cast the material into the required form of brief. It is important to have a definite order and sequence in the main heads of discussion. Some of the modes of progression often available are:

1. Time order (chronological: the sequence of steps in the process, as in the manufacture of paper).

2. Space order (as in explaining a building or a campus).

3. Causal order (as in explaining historical sequences or some mechanical processes).

4. From the familiar to the unfamiliar (as in explaining a novel theory).[2]

[2] End of matter from *Manual for Public Speaking I*.

Division is, of course, one of the fundamental processes of analysis, as the definition of analysis indicates. The "modes of progression" just noted are modes of division.

After resolving a subject into its parts, each is considered by itself, and then all together as to their interrelations; and the synthesis is as important as the analysis. One cannot understand the Princeton campus if the buildings are considered in isolation, or the workings of the Supreme Court without knowing something of its articulations with the lower courts.

Perhaps you should be warned against shifting the basis of division—a mistake made by the student who discussed the population of the Philippine Islands under the headings, Native, Catholic, White, and Moro. Such a division is bound to result in headings that *overlap*. Another kind of overlapping would be illustrated if the duties of the President were discussed under the headings,

I. The President signs bills.
II. The President addresses Congress.
III. The President appoints a Cabinet.
IV. The President executes the laws.
V. The President supports the Constitution.

Here the last two headings practically cover the first three. Dividing on a trivial or irrelevant basis might be illustrated by the division of oak trees into tall oaks, medium-sized oaks, and short oaks. Such a treatment is frequently permissible and valuable in a light or humorous speech. . . .[3]

---

[3] Excerpts in this chapter printed in smaller type and not otherwise credited are from *First Course in Public Speaking* by Winans and Hudson. Nearly all of this matter was written by Professor Hudson, and is used by his permission and that of D. Appleton-Century Company, publishers.

*Definitions and analysis.* Definition is, of course, an important part of exposition, but we are at the moment interested in definition as an aid to analysis. As indicated in Chapter V, a definition will sometimes serve as a statement of the central idea. It may also suggest the pattern of main heads. Burglary, for example, is defined at common law as the crime of "breaking and entering the dwelling-house of another in the night time, with intent to commit some felony in the same." A lecture in explanation of burglary will have its pattern based on answers to these questions: What is breaking? What is entering? What is a dwelling-house? What is intent to commit? What is a felony?

If we are concerned with the specific question, Did John Doe commit burglary at the house of Richard Roe? we may base our analysis, and later our argument, upon modified questions drawn from the same definition: Did John Doe break into the building in question? Did he enter? Was it a dwelling-house within the contemplation of the law? Did he break and enter with intent to commit arson, theft, or other felony?

It should be noted, however, that not every definition is plain and explicit enough to be used in this way; for example, the definition of a contract as an "agreement enforceable at law, made between two or more persons, by which rights are acquired by one or more to acts or forbearances on the part of the other or others," though authoritative, does not make explicit such elements as consideration, form of the agreement, and competency of the parties, some or all of which will be brought forward when a court is deciding if A can be held to his agreement to rent the house of B. All these elements are implicit in the phrase "enforceable at law." One must find a more easily understood definition.

Sometimes one must construct his own definition. Now

the two chief ways of defining, as exemplified in the dictionaries, are by synonyms and by "logical definition." Synonyms may be helpful in the development of an explanation,
"as we might help our hearers to an understanding of the
scope of the study of rhetoric by saying that an old synonym
for *rhetoric* is *speechcraft*," or that "*communication* comes
from a Latin verb meaning *to have business with*, and *exposition* really means *setting forth* or *putting out in the open*."
But plainly synonyms will not help us much in analysis.

The second dictionary method, that of logical definition, is
likely to be more useful. Logical definition embraces two steps
—classification and differentiation. . . . The dictionary defines
*ruminants* as "a division of hoofed mammals including those that
chew the cud." Ruminants are first *classified* as "a division of
hoofed mammals"; then they are *differentiated* as "those that
chew the cud." . . .

Sometimes a definition, at least the part devoted to differentiation, is a somewhat detailed, though very condensed,
description, as in the definitions of polo and the coöperative
store used in Chapter V.

DEVELOPMENT OF AN EXPOSITION: *From a definition*. Of
course a bare statement, such as is the ordinary definition,
may not, however correct, be clear to an audience, and is
rarely impressive. Amplification is needed. Descriptive
details, restatements in varied terms, elimination, examples,
and comparisons and contrasts are some of the standard
means of elaboration. The following passage from Daniel
Webster's speech, "The Constitution not a Compact between
Sovereign States," illustrates how a definition may be amplified:

What is a Constitution? Certainly not a league, compact, or
confederacy, but a *fundamental law*. That fundamental regu-

lation which determines the manner in which the public authority is to be executed, is what forms the *constitution* of a state. Those primary rules which concern the body itself, and the very being of the political society, the form of government, and the manner in which power is to be exercised—all, in a word, which form together the *constitution of a state*—these are the fundamental laws.

In this example it may be noted that not only is it necessary at times to state one's definition in several ways, but also to eliminate certain probable misunderstandings or preconceptions. The rule of reasonable doubt as applied in criminal cases is always hard for juries to understand, especially if their feelings incline them to acquittal. The following represents an attempt to make understandable a rule which in the nature of things cannot be stated in unmistakable terms:

The jury are to bear in mind that they are to acquit the prisoner unless they find him guilty beyond a reasonable doubt. More is required to convict than a mere preponderance of the evidence against him. On the other hand, a mere vague question, such as may arise from the natural reluctance to convict in a capital case, is not a reasonable doubt.

A reasonable doubt is not "the mere doubt of a vacillating mind, without moral courage to decide a difficult question and taking refuge in skepticism." It is not, it may also be said, a doubt arising out of some ingenious speculation not based on the evidence.

Reasonable doubt "is a doubt which a reasonable man, fairly intending to do his duty, after deliberating carefully and judging honestly of the evidence before him, still finds remaining in his mind, arising out of the evidence itself; a doubt which can be expressed, for which a reason can be given, which can be debated."

We should beware of assuming that a mere characterization such as the following is definition, or adds anything to definition as such: Home is the place where after a day of buffeting by an unappreciative world and after walking the streets a nonentity, a man can turn in with the happy expectation of becoming, as he passes the portal, a hero to his children—if they are young enough, and of hearing his wife praise him for his meager accomplishments and declare he is a better man than his carping boss—if she is that good a wife. Whatever the merits or demerits of that sentence, it is valueless in telling what a home is, though it may go part way to explain why most men desire homes.

*Use of examples.* There is small hope, in most instances, of making an exposition either clear or interesting to an audience, unless we go beyond the methods already emphasized and add concreteness. And one of the best ways to add concreteness is to give examples. I have found it difficult to remember the name and the logician's explanation of the fallacy of "incorrect conversion"; but I have been able to point out many a fallacy by means of my professor of logic's illustration: "All horses are animals, but not all animals are horses." I am unable to make a rigorous distinction between civil and mechanical engineering; but the example given me by an engineer serves well enough: "A civil engineer builds a track, and a mechanical engineer builds an engine to run on it."

Our friend may talk to us in high-sounding and fluent words about his conception of school spirit, but we are likely never to understand what he means by it until he gives examples of occasions when such a spirit manifested itself or of how a person having it will act—and perhaps he should add examples of how a person *not* having it will act. Nor does our friend himself have a clear conception of school spirit unless he can give such examples.

A definition will be more helpful to the understanding of the hearer if it is followed by an example, or several examples. Even the dictionary applies this rule—as when it follows the definition of *ruminants* (already quoted) with, "as oxen, sheep, goats, antelopes, giraffes, deer, and camels." When Abraham Lincoln was carrying on his debates with Senator Stephen A. Douglas in 1858, one of his friends had been accused of forging some documents. Lincoln began his answer to this charge by explaining the term *forgery*. His explanation opens, as you will see, with a definition, follows that up with two examples, and then ends with a restatement of the definition. (It may be noted that in the stress of debate Lincoln first worded his definition vaguely and even inaccurately. The second statement of the definition is much more successful. . . .)

What is forgery? It is bringing forward something in writing or in print purporting to be of certain effect when it is altogether untrue. If you come forward with my note for one hundred dollars when I have never given such a note, there is a forgery. If you come forward with a letter purporting to be written by me which I never wrote, there is another forgery. If you produce anything in writing or in print saying it is so and so, the document not being genuine, a forgery has been committed.

It should be noticed that the examples given by Lincoln are *supposed* (sometimes called *supposititious*) examples, introduced by *if*. He might have cited *actual* examples, if any had occurred in his experience, by saying, "A man down in Springfield came forward with my note, etc." In this case supposed examples were to be preferred, as actual examples of forgery might cause offense or, at best, might divert the attention of his hearers from the thing being explained to the examples themselves. At any rate, the use of supposititious examples is a valuable resource of a speaker making explanations. Actual examples are usually preferred in *proof*—in speeches designed to convince or persuade—but in exposition the supposed example is especially useful, if it is carefully chosen and rings true. In the case of actual examples the speaker is not limited to presentation by words, but sometimes he can produce examples of what he is talking about. If you were to explain, "How to catch trout," your best resource might be a collection of trout flies and hooks which you could display to your audience as you talked about them.

We should not overlook the use of the negative example, examples of what you are talking about is *not*, or examples of the opposite of what you are talking about. . . . If you are answering the question, "What is a lyric?" it is quite possible that you will mention "Paradise Lost," "The Wreck of the Hesperus," and "The Lady of the Lake," as examples of poetical types other than the lyric. . . .

*Use of one extended example.* It may happen that your explanation will be more effective if, instead of citing a number of examples briefly, you choose a single good example and develop it in some detail. The use of such an example, either actual or supposed, seems to be especially helpful when one is explaining the operation of a law or principle, or the activity of an institution or system—such subjects as "How the World Court arbitrates disputes," "How the President is elected," "The meaning of Mendel's law of inheritance," "What is a touchback?" and "How the protective tariff protects." Turning again to the Lincoln-Douglas debates, we find that Senator Douglas was very eager to get clearly before his hearers the method by which a territory (such as Kansas was in 1858) might, under the existing laws, discourage or prevent the ownership of slaves. The following passage in his explanation includes his supposed example of how the laws might work:

> Any man has a right to go to Kansas and take his property with him; but when he gets there, he must rely upon the local

law to protect his property, whatever it may be. In order to illustrate this, imagine that three of you conclude to go to Kansas. One takes $10,000 worth of slaves, another $10,000 worth of liquors, and the third $10,000 worth of dry-goods. When the man who owns the dry-goods arrives out there and commences selling them, he finds that he is stopped and prohibited from selling until he gets a license, to pay for which will destroy all the profit he can make on his goods. When the man with the liquors gets there and tries to sell, he finds a Maine liquor law in force which prevents him. Now, of what use is his right to go there with his property unless he is protected in the enjoyment of that right after he gets there? The man who gets there with his slaves finds that there is no law to protect him when he arrives there. He has no remedy if his slaves run away to another country; there is no slave code or police regulations; and the absence of them excludes his slaves just as effectively from the Territory and as positively as a constitutional prohibition could.

Thomas Huxley, when beginning a series of lectures on evolution, wished to explain two kinds of evidence—testimonial and circumstantial. He adapted the same example to the exposition of both:

Suppose that a man tells you that he saw a person strike another and kill him; that is testimonial evidence of the fact of murder. But it is possible to have circumstantial evidence of the fact of murder; that is to say, you may find a man dying with a wound upon his head having exactly the form and character of the wound which is made by an axe, and, with due care in taking surrounding circumstances into account, you may conclude with the utmost certainty that the man has been murdered; that his death is the consequence of a blow inflicted by another man with that implement.

The speech on yellow journalism, described in Chapter VIII, illustrated both the extended example and the negative example.

*Comparison and contrast.* Clear and complete exposition cannot get on without comparison and contrast. Analogies have been discussed . . . in connection with interesting the audience. But these devices are no less important in making matters clear. If you can compare your subject, which is not yet clear to your hearers, to something which is already clear in their minds, you have gone far toward solving your problem. Thus you are transferring the principle of *derived interest* to the field of exposition, and using a method which might be called *derived clearness.* Your hearers may be in the dark as to what sort of an animal a zebra is; but if you say that a zebra is very like a small horse in a convict suit, then the clarity derived from this picture is transferred to the idea of a zebra. The English game of football, says a student, stands between American Association football and basketball. Assuming that this is sound, and that his hearers know the games mentioned, by indicating now the points of likeness and difference, he can give them an understanding of the English game. This is our standard method: This unfamiliar game, form of government, belief, automobile is like this familiar game, form of government, belief, automobile, except in this and that respect.

A famous example is that by Victor Hugo beginning (in the English translation), "Those who wish to form a distinct idea of the battle of Waterloo need only imagine a capital A laid on the ground." The description that follows is well worth looking up.[4] The elevation on which the Northern army lay on the third day of the battle of Gettysburg has been compared to an enormous fish-hook, with Little Round Top hill at the eye of the hook, the cemetery at the begin-

[4] *Les Misérables:* Cosette, Book I, Chapter IV.

ning of the bend, which curves away from Lee's main position, bringing the two wings of Meade's army rather close together.

Both literal and figurative analogies are used in explanation. Webster follows his definition of a constitution, quoted above, with this:

But do we need to be informed, in this country, what a constitution is? Is it not an idea perfectly familiar, definite, and well settled? We are at no loss to understand what is meant by the constitution of one of the States; and the Constitution of the United States speaks of itself as being an instrument of the same nature. It says this Constitution shall be the law of the land, anything in any state constitution to the contrary notwithstanding.

Chief Justice Marshall, in expressing a somewhat elusive idea of judicial construction, gave it greater tangibility by using the following figurative analogy:

There is no express provision for the case, but the claim has been sustained on a principle which so entirely pervades the Constitution, is so intermixed with the materials which compose it, so interwoven with its web, so blended with its texture, as to be incapable of being separated from it, without rending it into shreds.[5]

The analogy is particularly useful in explaining matters beyond the reach of the senses; as, "The number of atoms in a pint of water is far greater than the number of pints in all the oceans of the world." For this particular purpose the figurative analogy is much in use. Even science (or espe-

---

[5] From the opinion in *McCulloch* v. *Maryland* in which the Supreme Court held that the State of Maryland could not tax the notes of the Bank of the United States.

cially science when it seeks to become intelligible to the unscientific) uses figurative analogies. So Lord Kelvin: "Fire an infinitely long-range projectile into the sky and the chances are it will not hit anything." Lord Kelvin estimated that the chances of hitting anything with such a projectile were about the same as the chances of hitting a bird if you fired a gun at random. Again, seeking to make us conceive the great distances between the particles in "solid" matter: "Twenty or thirty gnats in a cathedral would not occupy much space. Now abolish the cathedral and leave only the gnats. Let them fly round and round within the quondam walls and you have a model of what the mental eye sees in an atom of matter."

But we must remember that such analogies are liable to misconstruction, and are often more impressive than clear. Although it would be impossible to express some spiritual truths without them, it is well known that the Bible teems with figurative analogies that have caused endless controversy; as the saying, "It is easier for a camel to go through a needle's eye, than for a rich man to enter into the kingdom of God."

*Explanation by causes and effects.* Sometimes we can make others understand a subject most effectively by telling the *causes* that brought it about, or by pointing out the effects of it. . . . Abolitionism, for example, can hardly be made clear without detailing the conditions that gave rise to it. The statement, Americans of pioneer days were versatile, to be clarified, requires first of all a discussion of the conditions in a sparsely settled region, where men and women had to be ready to turn their hands to all manner of activity, raising food, making clothes, surveying the land, establishing schools and churches, carrying on elections and trials, etc. It is not hard to understand the versatility of individuals bred under these conditions. Any subject of controversy, and the positions held by the sides or parties disputing, are likely to be understood only when facts which preceded the controversy and brought it about are known. Hence it is that in the introduction of a debate, a speaker usually gives a short history of the question or a statement of the immediate cause for the discussion, or both.

These illustrations have most to do with explanation by *causes;* we also understand a phenomenon or an action by its *effects.* "By their fruits ye shall know them." The religious nature of the Puritan can be understood by its effects in Colonial life. . . . Going back to our example concerning the versatility of the pioneer American, we might continue our explanation by saying that an effect of this versatility was a willingness to strike out into new territory where there were none of the conveniences of civilization.[6]

We have been considering causes and effects as a means to the development of an explanation; but, as was noticed in Chapter V, they may also suggest the pattern of analysis. A similar remark may be made about comparison and contrast, which, for example, provide the pattern for the brief on the coöperative store.

*Pictures, charts, samples, and models.* These are a particularly useful means of giving concreteness, or tangibility, and consequent clearness and interest, to expositions, and some explanations are impossible without them, for the strain on imagination would be too great. A plan of battle, a machine, or a building, plainly enough need graphic representation, not only for the sake of accuracy where that is important, but also to enable the hearer to see how the parts are related to each other. We should find it very difficult

[6] Examples of explanation by causes and effects, and also by analogies, can be found in a lecture on "Scottish Traits" by John Watson, in *Modern Eloquence* (1923), Vol. VIII, p. 416; and also in the lecture on "Wit and Humor" in the same volume.

to get a conception of even the broad outlines of our own country without a map. We find too that complicated statistics are better understood when worked out in "curves." Pictures, both still and moving, are having a larger and larger part in instruction. And it is well to remember that an object or scene which seems very simple to one who has actually observed it may be very difficult for a hearer without visual aids.

In using any graphic representation, be sure to have it large and distinct enough for all to see, else it may prove only an annoyance. Superfluity of detail is a common cause of indistinctness. A map with only necessary details and with sharp distinctions in colors is better adapted to speech-making than the most complete publication. It is unwise to embellish a diagram with details which are not needed. These are objectionable, not only as decreasing the distinctness of essential details, but as distracting attention and perhaps provoking curiosity as to where they come into the explanation.

You should, however, put in, perhaps rather sketchily, such details other than those you will speak about as are needed by the audience to orient the salient points in a chart; a map would not help us much in determining the location of Durham, New Hampshire, if it did not indicate the relation of Durham to Manchester, Portsmouth, Boston, or other places known to us.

A speaker who has confidence in his handling of crayons may sometimes find it advantageous to develop his chart from the simplest outlines to its complete form as he speaks. This method gives well the idea of progress and development; as for instance in describing an army's campaign. A speaker who attempts drawing on the platform should know precisely what he is going to do, what details he is to use and what scale is needed. Then he should practise the drawing to make sure he can do it. It is well, if the drawing presents any difficulty, to prepare paper with certain details and points faintly indicated, or with the bare outlines boldly marked.

Often it is better to have a series of charts rather than to exhibit on one several stages in an explanation. Different colored crayons and other devices may help out, but there is danger of confusion. The series of distinct charts keeps before the audience a better means of comparison.

Charts prepared in advance have certain advantages over drawings made as one speaks. First, the prepared charts are likely to be better made. Secondly, drawing upon the platform may attract too much attention to itself. A display of skill may be too interesting and clumsy drawing may be too amusing. Thirdly, drawing which requires much care may take the speaker's attention unduly from his audience. These comments, however, need deter no one from a few strokes as needed. Here, as in all, the speaker's business is to keep attention upon essentials.

Charts drawn upon a blackboard are satisfactory when one is sure of having enough space; but it is likely to be true in classroom speaking that not much space is available for each of the speakers in an hour, and few rooms other than classrooms have blackboards. Charts prepared on large sheets of paper or better, cardboard, are often more satisfactory.

One should resist the temptation to look at any exhibit when not referring to it; and even then a glance is usually enough, after which he can turn back to the audience. A speaker should avoid talking to the blackboard, lest he be indistinct, and also lest he lose touch with his hearers. Further, when the speaker looks at board or exhibit, the audience naturally looks where he does. In fact they are only too ready to look at anything their attention is called to, for the appeal to the eye is stronger than the appeal to the ear. It is often well to keep exhibits out of sight until wanted, and to remove them when their use is ended, unless to do so attracts more attention than their presence.

The speaker should avoid standing between audience and chart when it is in use. He should stand at one side, facing the front as nearly as is convenient, and using for pointing the hand nearest the chart; that is, if he is at the right of his chart he should use his left hand. To use his right would cause him to turn away from his audience and come into the line of vision. A pointer is a help in keeping in position. Very simple suggestions, but many a speech is marred by failure to follow them; for example, failure to keep out of the line of vision may cause a justifiable irritation in one's audience.

Perhaps the worst of methods is to pass around a series of exhibits. This means breaking up one's audience into small groups, each attending to a different thing and very few listening to the speaker. If there are enough copies to supply all, so that all attend to the same matter at one time, the method may be good; but even that has its drawbacks if the should-be hearers are likely to go on studying the exhibit after the speaker is through with it. It sometimes happens, however, that this is the only feasible method, as in dealing with statistical or other elaborate reports. Usually a brief digest will satisfy most.

ADDITIONAL SUGGESTIONS. Whatever methods of explanation are used, certain considerations should be taken into account, which, while not peculiar to this form of discourse, are found to be important in spoken exposition. And, first, a speaker should avoid so far as possible asking an audience to carry in mind a very elaborate mass of details. One hears speakers explaining complicated apparatus, and expecting their hearers to put in order in imagination so many thingumbobs articulating with so many thingamajigs that the audience gives up and politely waits for the end. Even with diagrams and all possible aids some explanations are impossible in speeches, and simply should not be attempted. I instanced in the chapter on Subjects the differential of an automobile and the Australian crawl stroke as topics apparently too difficult for classroom speeches; and of course problems of a more abstruse character and for which no graphic representation is possible are still more questionable as topics.

One can often avoid confusion by explaining a machine, a process, system, or institution in its simplest form. One desirous of explaining the principle of a steam engine to those ignorant of mechanics should begin by presenting the simplest form of steam engine; then, when confident that this form is understood, he can, if he wishes, proceed to a more complicated form, or to some special elaboration. And the chart which he will naturally use in such an exposition should be presented with only the simple form delineated. A speaker whose subject was "Why airplanes fly" was very soon talking about "leakage of air" and why the planes are set just as they are, and his real theme was quickly obscured. Another who began with the simple kite principle and transferred this to the airplane accomplished much more in his five minutes.

It is natural to begin with definitions and principles, and this is all right if the audience, rarely in the best condition for thinking at the start of a speech, can follow and remember; but often it is better to begin with more concrete matter and lead up to definitions and principles. Explaining lithography a speaker began with a definition and stated that the basic principle is the antipathy of grease for water.  He then proceeded to the various materials used and a description of the process.  He had a first-hand knowledge of his subject and stated all clearly; but questions from an intelligent audience at the end of his speech showed that the first two of his seven minutes had produced only confusion in the minds of those who had no idea of the process in advance. A description of the process in chronological order would have succeeded better.

When it seems desirable to start with definitions and principles, it is usually best to repeat them later, as in the conclusion.  In fact, it is usually best to limit one's first presentation as a whole so as to have time for a final review of the salient points.

THE PART OF THE AUDIENCE.  In preparing an exposition, the speaker finds that the terms in which he explains must be chosen with an eye to the knowledge and experience of his audience.  In a way, the audience rather than the speaker supplies the language of exposition. . . . To present the idea of "zebra" . . . to an audience of students of natural history . . . it would be better to use such terms as "equine mammal" and "conspicuously striped," since such is their familiar language; [while "small horse in a convict suit" might be better for children].

What was said in an earlier chapter about technical language is applicable here.  A speaker explaining oil wells spoke constantly of the "sand."  Discussion later revealed the fact that several had been puzzled throughout the speech, especially as to the blasting of sand.  It was then revealed to us that, in the lingo of oil workers, *sand* is *sandstone*.  Another speaker said that in paper making the flowing mixture of pulp and water is "run out on a wire." Whether the wire in question was tight or slack we did not know, but the picture of a fluid running on a wire and drying into paper was too much for us, until we learned that *wire* is *wire cloth*. It will be seen in these examples that the use of common terms not self-explanatory is still more confusing than the use of novel terms. Either need explanation. The audience is helped by having such terms put before their eyes, as on a blackboard with perhaps a few words of written explanation.

This principle of drawing our terminology and our illustrations from the audience must prevail, no matter what method of exposition we are employing . . . and, above all, with comparisons. . . . Unless the game to which I compare English football is familiar to my audience, I only give them two unexplained subjects instead of one.

The rule for the speaker, then, is to begin with the questions, What terms are familiar to this audience? In what field of knowledge and experience can I assume them to be at home? What do they already know to which I can link my subject?

DEGREE OF CLEARNESS. Barrett Wendell defines [7] clearness as "the distinguishing quality of a style that cannot be misunderstood." This sets up an ideal not always attainable; but much more wholesome than the standard of many —a style that *can* be understood. We have to recognize that at its best language is a dull instrument, and that to convey fully an idea to another is something rarely done. A speaker should strive to be as clear as he can; and it will be much better for him if, when he fails to be clear, he accepts the fault as his own instead of saying, as many do when questioned or criticized, "Why, I said so and so," and "I thought anybody could understand that." If fairly intelligent people

[7] *English Composition*, p. 194. Published by Charles Scribner's Sons.

do not understand, the fault is in the speaker; and if his hearers are not intelligent, he is still at fault in misjudging them.

But clearness is a relative matter. Clear to whom? Must one seek to be clear to the youngest or least intelligent person present? No, that might bore a great part of the audience. But on the other hand, to leave any large portion of an audience in the dark is to cause restlessness, and possibly resentment. There is no certain solution of the problem presented by a mixed audience; but if a speaker is simple and concrete in his method, uses simple, idiomatic English, and yet avoids the suggestion of baby talk, he can usually satisfy most of an audience on such topics as are suitable.

One does not necessarily tell a given audience all about a subject; it is sufficient if he makes clear what he undertakes. There are different levels of explanation. A speaker could tell the eighth grade a good deal about zebras, and tell it clearly as far as he went; but he could not tell them all that a college professor would think should be told to his class in zoölogy. It is conceivable that one of the six men in the world supposed to understand relativity could tell an educated audience what Einstein is working at, but he could not make many understand relativity.

Much depends, too, on the purpose of an exposition.

In the course of an argument one may mention a term that will recur in the argument, such as "non-justiciable disputes." It is well that the audience should understand this term; but it is not necessary that they should have an understanding of it as thorough as that of a law student facing an examination. The statement that the town of Tabor is in Iowa would enable a person to address a letter to that place; but it would not enable him to find it quickly on the map. . . .

Consider, in this connection, the difference between an explanation of a gasoline engine addressed to a man buying an automobile, and an explanation addressed to mechanics learning to repair such engines.   A lecturer on the consumers' coöperative movement must decide whether he wishes so to inform his hearers that they could organize a coöperative enterprise themselves, or whether he wishes them merely to understand the argument which he is about to present in favor of the movement.   One makes an explanation clear enough and full enough to serve his purpose.

EXPOSITION AND INTEREST.   I find in a good book on speaking a warning that expository speeches are hard to make interesting.   It is true that the promise of an instructive speech will not excite all of us, and to announce that a speech will be both interesting and educational suggests to some a sugar-coated pill.   Still there are people eager for information, either because of intellectual curiosity or because the information will be of immediate use to them.   Not all are subjected, as we are in the college world, to what one speaks of as "the unrelenting pouring out of data, dates, figures, statistics, facts, near-facts, theories, principles, and opinions."   But even in my college classroom expository speeches seem to be as acceptable as those of any type, although perhaps no expository speech is ever quite as interesting as some arguments.

Much depends, as usual, upon the subjects chosen.   Interesting themes can be drawn from current events, or from our more constant interests.   More, of course, depends upon treatment; and, barring the interest of conflict which is not conducive to clear understanding, all that we have considered about interest is applicable to expository speeches.   In no type can more use be made of derived interest.   At a time when people are interested in inflation as a proposed remedy for depression, many will be eager to hear explanations of money theories, or of the actual working of inflation in other lands. Comparison and contrast can be utilized for both clearness and interest, as in our hypothetical speech on Greek life. In its nature exposition is a blending of old and new. In speaking of a method of treating cancer, or on the working of the stock exchange, or on the playing of a game, one is obviously touching fundamental interests. Sometimes one can make use of our liking for "inside" information, as when a member of the team reveals the strategy used last fall in blocking kicks. Narration is one good method of exposition; and activity can often be employed in explaining. The appeal to imagination is constant. And it will be noted that one does not have to go out of his way to be interesting; the methods of interest and of exposition can be made to blend.

TACT IN EXPOSITION. Although exposition is considered the coldest form of discourse, still the feelings of one's audience need to be considered. Although a speaker may be presenting no issue or proposal, he may have to take some care in approaching an audience with certain explanations. We may be so accustomed to certain ways of thinking, or certain methods, that we object to hearing of any other. There are audiences that would object to the most impartial exposition of communism. They "don't wish to hear anything about it"; they would feel compromised by listening to anything but denunciation. But no one need feel superior; some who scorn such intolerance would be equally intolerant toward spiritualism, or if they did listen it would be with a flippant, pooh-pooh attitude, which would make genuine understanding improbable. Tact may be needed on the part of one who would explain such subjects. Sometimes a narrative method can be employed to disarm prejudice. So an explanation of bolshevism might be woven into the story of the Russian Revolution; or it might be approached through stories, humorous and otherwise, which would reveal the human side of the movement. Conan Doyle, creator of "Sherlock Holmes," might be used as an approach to spirit phenomena.

More often tact is needed to avoid boring, or even offending, the better informed portion of an audience while explaining elementary facts to the less well informed; and more in correcting the mistaken notions of those who think they understand. A speaker need not say that his hearers are ignorant or misinformed; but can present the matter as if reviewing or setting in order what many already know; or he may say that he will present for the benefit of some what many of the audience are probably familiar with.

But usually it is better to say nothing about the matter; just to go ahead with his explanation, and treat his hearers as intelligent people who happen not to have all the information he is giving. Especially to be avoided is any assumption of superiority on the speaker's part; this, hard enough to bear from teachers, is intolerable in one's peers. On the other hand, audiences like the quiet confidence of the speaker "who knows and knows that he knows," and have little mercy for one who gets up to explain a problem which he does not understand as well as his hearers, or about which he makes statements plainly incorrect.

# CHAPTER XII

## INFLUENCING CONDUCT

One of our chief purposes in talking with others is to influence their conduct; and this aim is especially characteristic of public speaking. For communicating detailed or complicated information, or the type of reasoning that requires prolonged reflection, the written word is often superior to the spoken; but when men are to be induced to act, to vote, or to change their conduct, face-to-face talk is generally superior.

The word *conduct* is used broadly here to cover (1) the doing of a specific act or a series of acts, (2) refraining from action, and (3) changing attitude. If you induce a person to go to the theater to-night, to establish the habit of going to the theater, or to resolve never to go again, you have in each instance influenced his conduct. If you induce him to change his attitude toward another person from indifference or hostility to kindly interest, you have influenced his conduct, even though his new attitude does not show itself in overt action. And also you have influenced his conduct if you induce him to take interest in a proposal to which he has been indifferent.

It is obvious that we are approaching a problem both important and common; for to influence conduct is to induce others to change their party, to give labor or capital a fair deal, to do Christmas shopping early, to attend to business, to subscribe to charities, to keep from spitting on sidewalks,

255

to yield race prejudice, and to act or not to act in innumerable other ways.

Much discourse may aim only at entertainment or information; but even discourse which seems to have only these purposes may serve to influence conduct, just as in Russia to-day a great part of the expository and artistic writing serves as propaganda for the soviet state. A lecture on economics may be explanatory in form and yet be calculated to affect the hearer's attitude toward the Administration's agricultural policy. A memorial address may be a tribute to a man and yet serve to inspire better citizenship. The conversation of an alumnus beside the fraternity fireplace may, with or without intention, convince a listening undergraduate that the life of a lawyer or of an explorer is the life for him. Even the jovial banquet speech may serve an aim beyond entertainment.

So it is plain that one who studies the art of speaking cannot ignore the ways and means of influencing conduct.

TERMS EXPLAINED. The traditional term for influencing conduct is *persuasion*; and this word, with its cognates *persuade* and *persuasive*, will save circumlocution. It is well to note, however, that these words cannot be sharply defined. In stricter usage, to persuade is to affect conduct, while to convince is to induce belief. In common usage, however, *persuade* covers both meanings, perhaps because it is often difficult to distinguish belief and conduct. Indeed, some maintain that there is no difference.

*Argument* will be treated as one of the means of persuasion. It is discourse in which logical conclusions are established upon premises and facts. If the logical connections are openly stressed we speak of the discourse as argumentative; but discourse may be a texture of premises, facts, and conclusions although not argumentative in form. Argument, as ordinarily conceived, is far from being all of persuasion, which may spring from other sources, as personal influence or suggestion.[1] Indeed, there may be persuasion in defiance of reason, as when a man is persuaded to buy a car although he knows full well that he should use the money to pay his debts.

REASONS FOR CONDUCT, IN GENERAL. It will be well to consider, at this point, some rather obvious truths concerning conduct, as it may be observed in everyday life.

Why do we do certain acts? Sometimes we say, "We just happened to think of it." We may add, "We couldn't see any objection." Again we may have more definite reasons: we think the conduct will bring us pleasure, or profit, or will protect us against loss or pain. We may act from a sense of duty; it seems to be "up to us" to act. Sometimes we act in imitation of others, deliberately or unconsciously. Often we act because of habit, as a matter of course, without considering the possibility of doing otherwise; sometimes even quite automatically, as in taking a familiar path. But in this discussion we are to consider chiefly conscious, purposive conduct, noting here only that the more in line with our habitual or automatic conduct a proposed act is, the more likely we are to perform it.

Why do we not follow certain lines of conduct? Most often because we do not think of them at all. Or if we do, they do not interest us. One often says, "I just could not keep my mind on it." Or the conduct does not commend itself to us as desirable; or the promise of pleasure or profit does not overcome our reluctance to exert ourselves, or our

---

[1] I do not quarrel with those who believe they prove, by an abstruse course of reasoning, that fundamentally the processes are the same. I simply do not believe that for our purposes it makes any practical difference which view is held.

desire to do something else.  Or our sense of duty or decorum is not strong enough to overcome inertia or conflicting desires.

Or we think of more positive objections: the conduct would be too costly in time or money; it would be dangerous; it would be uncomfortable because against habit; it might bring ridicule, criticism, or ill repute; it is bad form, it is not being done, especially not in our set; it is not right and might prove injurious to others; it goes against our principles, beliefs, sentiments, or prejudices.

Sometimes the action suggested is so far from our usual conduct that, while we may think of it as good, pleasant, or profitable, we do not think of it as action to be performed by us; as, for example, fighting for a better city government, flying the Atlantic, writing an epic poem, or robbing a bank.

Sometimes we are in doubt; the advantages and disadvantages seem to balance, or two courses seem equally attractive.  Then we fall into an unpleasant state of vacillation in which we whiffle or do nothing, like the donkey in the fable that, happening to stop exactly halfway between two equally attractive heaps of hay, could go to neither, and so starved to death.  But ultimately we either push the whole problem out of mind, or something happens to tip the scale, or a hidden wish, potent though unrecognized, leads us to build up the case for one course and belittle that for the other.

A harder question is this: Why do we follow a course which in our better judgment we do not consider wise, or even pleasant?  Sometimes we say we could not keep our minds off this course; it kept coming back until it drove our objections away.  Or the act was habitual and we did it without thinking.  Or it was suggested to us when we were excited, or confused, or when a crisis was at hand, or when we were under the influence of others, so that the objections never came to mind at all, or received scant attention. The man who has come to a conviction that he cannot afford a new car may, one day, at sight of an attractive machine urged upon him by a skilled salesman, forget prudence and debts. Or one who abhors the intentions of a mob may be carried away by its spirit.

In such cases objections that would prevent action are kept or pushed out of mind, or are reduced to comparative insignificance. Obviously, then, to keep from following a course which attracts, one must keep his mind upon opposing or inhibiting ideas; or, better, upon some other conduct; or, better yet, engage in other conduct. If I wish to keep at work this afternoon, I must not think about the game, but must think of the necessity and satisfaction of getting my work done, and keep plugging away.

How, then, does one persuade another to an act or course of conduct? If the other has no positive objection, the task then seems to be to present the proposal so that it will hold attention strongly enough to overcome inertia and the competition of other attractive ideas. If he has doubts or objections in mind, the persuader must remove them, either by enlarging upon the desirability of the course proposed until they are crowded out and forgotten, or by showing, in more direct attack, that the doubts or objections are not valid, or are relatively unimportant, and so causing their dismissal. This is the familiar process of argument.

I have been omitting mention of speech-making in order to make it clear that persuasion is not peculiar to public speaking. However, the conclusions we have just come to are as applicable to public as to private communication.

A TYPICAL AUDIENCE ANALYZED. The foregoing discussion leads us to the fact that, in urging a course upon a general audience, we may have before us those who are already favorable to our proposal, or adherents; we may have those who are neutral, and we may have those already in opposition. Do not understand that I am here speaking of sharply defined groups; the same person may be found in more than one at different times. But a rough classification may aid in the ever-present problem of sizing up one's audience. We may commonly anticipate, then, a number of:

I. *Adherents.* Some of these may be ready for action and waiting only for opportunity and leadership. Some may be lacking a clear notion of what to do and how to do it. They must have direction. Some may not have sufficient interest to overcome their inertia and preoccupation with other interests. They must be aroused. Some may be of what Ralph Waldo Emerson called the "small-pot-soon-hot" variety, enthusiastic while under the influence of a meeting but likely to be as ardent for something else to-morrow. They may be useful for the moment to help in moving the audience, but they are not dependable. Perhaps they can be more deeply impressed by explanation, argument, and illustrations, or their easy enthusiasm can be transmuted into sterner stuff by being set to work at once on some task that will carry them on by its momentum.

II. *Neutrals.* Some of these may be merely indifferent and need only to be interested. Some will vote Aye if others do, and are of the same sort as the adherents of easy enthusiasm. Others may be neutral simply because they know little of the proposal. For them explanation may be enough.

More important are the doubters who have already considered the proposal and are interested but not yet ready to indorse it. They see advantages and disadvantages; or perhaps they think it "too good to be true." Some may doubt the desirability of the end sought by the plan. Others may approve the end, but doubt the efficacy of means suggested, or think the plan too expensive or too difficult. Plainly the doubts of these persons must be removed; perhaps by argument to justify the end or the means, perhaps by discourse that will focus the doubter's imagination upon the desirability of the results until doubts are crowded from his mind. At any rate these honest doubters are worth much attention. They are likely to be open-minded. In political campaigns most arguments are leveled at them, though, of course, much energy goes to keeping partisans in line and arousing them to the voting point.

III. *Opponents and objectors.* This group includes not merely those in active opposition as workers and debaters, but all who have decided against the speaker's proposal. Of the possible subdivisions of this group we will note three:

1. Those in opposition because they do not understand the proposal. Clear exposition may be sufficient.

2. Those who are in opposition because of prejudice. The proposal may offend by its strangeness. "We have never done that." Or the proposal comes from a person, a party, or a social group they do not approve, hence it must be wrong. Or it has been labeled socialistic, capitalistic, aristocratic, bourgeois, radical, conservative, vulgar, respectable, stodgy, or something else abhorrent. Since such objectors have not reasoned out their conclusion they are hard to deal with, for they are slow to grant a fair hearing. They just know they are right.

3. Those who understand the proposal and after thoughtful consideration have rejected it. Upon these doughty opponents, as upon the thoughtful doubters, assertion and enthusiasm are unlikely to have much effect; hard facts and solid arguments are needed. But the reasoning objector

knows that there are two sides to almost any question that comes up for argument; and he probably has some pride in his open-mindedness. And while it must be admitted that in most instances relatively few will be won over, the attempt may be worth while; because when the thinking members of a community are won they are likely to carry others with them, and also if genuinely won they are likely to become steadfast adherents.

Most difficult opponents of all (but hardly a distinct class since they may be found in all opposing groups) are those who see in the proposal a threat to their habits, comfort, positions, or income. Their whole emotional set is against finding the proposal has merit. Here again the greatest difficulty is gaining a fair hearing.

THE PROBLEMS SUMMARIZED. In persuading others to modify their beliefs and conduct, we have to overcome indifference, inertia, habit, lack of persistence, preoccupation with competing attractions, and doubts and contrary beliefs due to misunderstanding, to prejudice, or to reasoning.

OUR PROCEDURE. Since it is impossible to discuss all phases of the subject at once, we shall give attention first chiefly to those hearers who have no positive objections to the course proposed; and later we shall turn to those who have positive objections. It is not to be supposed, however, that the line of cleavage is definite. As for the neutrals, they will be given no more than incidental attention, for their needs will be covered in treating the other two main groups.

# CHAPTER XIII

## PRESENTING THE PROPOSAL

INTEREST AND PERSUASION. It will be seen that what we have learned of the subject of Interest will serve us in persuasion; most obviously in overcoming indifference and inertia, and in quickening the impulse of those already in agreement with the speaker. Keener interest will also help in resolving doubts, and even in overcoming opposition; for an uninterested person will often adopt an attitude of doubt or opposition as a defense mechanism. Our previous study of motives as fundamental interests has an immediate application to persuasion; and nearly all the methods of attracting and sustaining attention are in fact means of persuasion.

It should be borne in mind, however, that in persuasion we are seeking more than attention in the ordinary sense; we must win favorable attention to our proposals. Just to keep people listening is, after all, comparatively easy. It can be done by stunts, by literally or figuratively standing on one's head, slapping the auditors in the face, or being "funny" in any sense of the word. But some methods attract attention to themselves rather than to the ideas expressed, and some arouse unfavorable attention. If in urging a man to vote my ticket I call him a fool for resisting, I shall gain his lively interest, but hardly his favorable attention to my plea.

Whatever means we employ we should keep in mind that primarily we are seeking to induce our hearers to give their minds wholly to our proposal, and to keep out, or drive out, of their minds objections, doubts, hostile feelings, and thought of other courses of action. And we must bring them to realize that the course urged is something not merely academically interesting or something for others to follow, but something to do with their own conduct, something in which they are to take a hand.

PROVIDE A PROGRAM. Often all that is needed is to provide an outlet for willingness already existing. No doubt the amazing readiness of the country to follow President Roosevelt in 1933 was due in no small measure to the fact that he furnished a program at a time when the people were desperately anxious to try something. But quite apart from crises we are often moved by impulses that come to naught because we do not know how to begin or where to go.

The indifferent as well as the willing may be enlisted by an attractive plan of action; and even the doubter may become an adherent when shown a feasible program. His doubt may have rested upon the very point of procedure; but even when he doubts the desirability of the end itself, his hesitancy may be overcome by a plan that clarifies its objectives and brings itself into his imagination as something in which he can play an interesting part. Skilful managers of community chests, by devising interesting plans for raising money, often gain the enthusiastic coöperation of workers who have never before taken an active interest in charities.

Even definite objection to a proposal may be forgotten in the face of an attractive plan. A man may be convinced that his business would go to pieces if he should absent himself during business hours; but when his physician tells him that a round of golf every afternoon is what his health requires, he may lose his conviction.

But quite apart from special attractiveness in the plan, in any deliberative body where there is a feeling that something should be done, the member or the committee that brings forward a clear plan of action has a long lead over a mere opposition. An opposition must bring forward an alternative plan, else it is likely to be floored by the demand, "What would you do?" So we have the saying, "It is hard to beat something with nothing."

BRING THE PROPOSAL HOME TO THE HEARER. As was said before, it is not unusual for a person to think of a line of conduct, even highly approve of it, without at all thinking of it as a course for him to pursue. It may seem too remote, too far beyond his scope, or something others should do. This will be illustrated under the next heading.

BUILD UP CONFIDENCE. A boy in a back community may read wistfully of going to college, flying, or big business; but may think of these as something "they," people quite different from himself, do. Suppose you wish to persuade this boy to go to college. You dwell upon the advantages; but he says, "Yes, I'd like to go; but how can I? None of my people has ever been educated; have I the ability? Anyhow, I am not prepared and our school is poor. I have no money and Dad can't help me."

To bring the proposal into the realm of possibility for him, you follow the standard method of citing examples of men who have started with similar handicaps and made good in college and after. You assure him that average ability is enough and that he has that and more. Then you come to ways and means; you offer him books, and point out that there is a good school a few miles away. You tell him of ways of earning money, and of scholarships and loan funds. If only he can get money enough for one year, he can hope for ways to open to him. And since we are all encouraged by having stages in a journey toward a distant goal, you stress things near at hand and not too difficult for the lad to do at once. Perhaps by this combination of inducements, direction, and faith-building, you win.

The methods just suggested can be applied in urging a community to make improvements, such as better roads or slum clearance. If incentive is lacking, you will try to make the community imagine the satisfaction of the improvements, but you will also try to build up confidence that they are possible, by relieving fear of excessive cost, by showing how the money can be obtained, by stressing the fact that not all need be paid at once, and by telling what similar towns have done.[1]

AWAKEN THE SENSE OF RESPONSIBILITY. Often a speaker runs up against the difficulty that while his hearers approve what he urges, they are reluctant to accept responsibility for it themselves. "Let George do it" became popular slang because the phrase expresses a common human weakness. When a nuisance should be abated or an improvement made, we are prone to demand, "Why don't they fix it?" Members of college fraternities will agree that there are a dozen who complain of conditions for one who will do what is needed. Thousands read with sympathy what Jacob Riis wrote in *How the Other Half Lives* about the tenements of New York and his plans for improvement; but very few,

[1] Dr. Victor G. Heiser's fascinating *An American Doctor's Odyssey* is in no respect more interesting than in its revelation of the difficulty he had in overcoming lack of faith. The officials and business men with whom he had to deal in the Orient, who had every reason to desire the elimination of hookworm, leprosy, plague, and cholera from the native populations, could not believe, even in the face of convincing evidence, that the natives could be induced to change their ingrained habits; and the natives themselves were sunk in fatalistic apathy. "If we die, we die." Dr. Heiser's greatest triumph was in building up faith in all classes.

like the young Theodore Roosevelt, stepped forward to say, "I have come to help." The larger the number affected the slighter the sense of responsibility. Political workers think they have done well if they get forty per cent of the voters to the polls, even for an exciting election; and it scarcely enters into the mind of the average citizen to do more than vote. So often the speaker's most difficult task is to make his hearers realize that the needed action is something that these hearers should attend to.

The most obvious way to make them face the fact squarely is to declare bluntly the responsibility of each one present; and sometimes this is the best way, especially when the speaker can depend upon his personal authority with his audience. But we are rather hardened to such attacks by the urgings of parents, teachers, preachers, bosses, leaders and would-be leaders of all kinds. We are told of so many obligations that exhortations roll from our minds like water from a duck's back. Moreover, bluntness may drive us into sullen rejection, for few of us are so fond of truth that we welcome it in every guise.

Speakers, therefore, seek more tactful devices, most of them well worn, like the familiar argument that no chain is stronger than its weakest link. This is an attempt to overcome the feeling of the individual that his part is too small to matter. Skilful solicitors ask me to contribute, not to a fund to relieve thousands of children suffering the summer heat of cities, but for ten dollars to send Gertie Smith of Second Avenue to the country for two weeks. During the World War many attempts were made to make each of our millions of citizens feel his part to be important. Even the feeble old lady could knit for the soldiers. "Every scout to feed a soldier" was a slogan to promote the growing of vegetables in every vacant space. We as a people were wasteful of food; but, we were told, if each home wastes a single slice of bread a day, that amounts to 1,000,000 loaves, or 365,000,000 loaves a year, consuming the flour from 7,000,000 bushels of wheat, the yield of 470,000 acres. And "Food Will Win the War!" Moreover, the prevention of that waste of a single slice of bread in each home each day would release for other needed services an army of farmers, railway men, mill workers, and bakers.

To make one's hearers feel their individual responsibility, give each a definite share in the work; as to canvass a certain district, keep the records, or attend to publicity. A person of executive ability may be attracted by the chance to make things go and then find himself held by the responsibility that will be forced upon him. Pride may be enlisted; and even the pleased vanity that comes when one is adorned with a badge, or has his name published as member of a committee, may cause some to feel that they are an important part of the enterprise. When William George was struggling with the problems presented by a group of "fresh air" boys, and working out the ideas he later embodied in the George Junior Republic, he found that scoldings and argument were of little avail, but that the best way to stop raids on the farmers' orchards and chicken coops was to introduce a measure of self-government and appoint the ringleader in mischief chief of police.

Under appropriate circumstances a plea can be based upon some special obligation of one's hearers to accept responsibility—something in the nature of *noblesse oblige*. President Wilson, speaking to the graduating class at the Naval Academy in 1916, tried to impress once more a thought that no doubt was very familiar to his hearers:

Once in a while when youngsters here or at West Point have forgotten themselves and have done something that they ought not to do and were about to be disciplined, perhaps severely, for it, I have been appealed to by their friends to excuse them from the penalty: . . . "You know college boys. You know what they are. They are heedless youngsters very often, and they ought not to be held up to the same standards of responsibility that older men must submit to."

And I have always replied, "Yes, I know college boys; but while these youngsters are college boys, they are something more. They are officers of the United States. They are not merely college boys. If they were I would look at derelictions of duty on their part in another spirit; but any dereliction of duty on the part of a naval officer of the United States may involve the fortunes of a nation and cannot be overlooked."

Do you not see the difference? You cannot indulge yourselves in weakness, gentlemen. You cannot forget your duty for a moment; because there might come a time when that weak spot in you would affect you in the midst of a great engagement, and then the whole history of the world might be changed by what you did not do, or did wrong. . . . I congratulate you that you are going to live your lives under the most stimulating compulsion that any man can feel, the sense, not of private duty merely, but of public duty also. . . . I wish you godspeed, and remind you that yours is the honor of the United States.[2]

Every college student knows, however, that the plea based upon special opportunity and obligation is so familiar that it must be especially well put to be effective. But much the same can be said of all standard pleas.

INSIST UPON FACING THE TRUTH. Akin to, and at times identical with, the tendency to dodge responsibility is the reluctance to face facts squarely. The facts may be evident enough; but they are complacently passed over. "Those

[2] From press reports of an offhand speech.

machines have always been dangerous," we may say when a
speaker urges safety appliances; or, "Oh, well, crime, poverty, tuberculosis have always been with us." The speaker
who faces this attitude has to do more than call attention
and show how evils can be eradicated; he has to make his
hearers face the evils as evils, and he has to make the
remedies a matter of personal concern to them.

The difficulty is greater when the condition is obscure or
remote. Something may in fact be lacking in our educational
system, or in a particular curriculum; but negative evils of
this sort are not spectacular, and people respond to urging
that the evils should be remedied by saying that things seem
to have gone pretty well, that our graduates—at least those
we take note of—are successful. Why worry? It is also
true that people do not readily awaken to the need for action
to prevent future evils, such as the effects of neglect of
health, or of certain tendencies in our government. Fifty
years of agitation have hardly yet awakened us to the need
for the conservation of natural resources.

In such cases the speaker must work through imagination; and since he cannot draw much from the experience of
those whom he would persuade, he must draw from the
experience of others. Speaking at the Yale alumni luncheon
in June, 1934, President Roosevelt said that twenty-two
years before, when chairman of the committee on forests,
fires and game in the New York Legislature, he had become
interested in the fact that some of the Adirondacks were
being washed bare. He induced Gifford Pinchot, then Chief
Forester of the United States, to come and speak before the
legislature on forest conservation:

And the thing that sold it to the layman's mind—to the mind
of the average member of the Assembly or the Senate—was not

so much what he said as what he showed, photographs of North China, a region once covered with magnificent forests, a region which today is a desert. We passed our legislation, and that was the first step towards practical government supervised forestry, so far as I know, in the eastern part of the country.

By means of his famous analogy comparing life to a game of chess, Huxley impressed upon his audience of English workingmen the dangers of living without learning the rules of living. He continued his appeal to imagination by describing the game, and referred to "the player on the other side" who is hidden from us:

We know that his play is always fair, just and patient. But we also know, to our cost, that he never overlooks a mistake or makes the smallest allowance for ignorance. To the man who plays well the highest stakes are paid, with that sort of overflowing generosity with which the strong shows delight in strength. And one who plays ill is checkmated—without haste, but without remorse.[3]

More difficult still is the problem of those who are blind because they do not wish to see. "Eating too much? Yes, I know; but I have hard work ahead and must keep up my strength. I am going on a strict diet soon." Or perhaps the truth is too repellent for delicate sensibilities. "Conditions in the slums are terrible; but let's think of pleasant things." It has been very difficult to persuade sufferers from cancer to consult physicians in time. Cancer is too horrible; ignore it. Or the course on which we have set ourselves is too enthralling to abandon. Ludwig says of Napoleon before his invasion of Russia: "Since he cannot refute Coulancourt's arguments, he makes vague answers behind which his

[3] Thomas Huxley, *Lay Sermons, Addresses, and Reviews,* p. 32.

titanic wishes loom." [4] Denial of the facts, excuses, and wishful thinking are defenses against uncomfortable truth. "I didn't do it"; "I am not to blame, I can't help it"; "It is of no consequence anyhow"—these are typical escapes. "What is hard," says William James,[5] "is facing an idea as real."

> How many excuses does the drunkard find when each new temptation comes! . . . It is poured out and it is a sin to waste it; also others are drinking and it would be churlishness to refuse. Or it is but to enable him to sleep, or just to get through this job of work; or it isn't drinking, it is because he feels so cold; or it is Christmas-day, or it is a means of stimulating him to make a more powerful resolution in favor of abstinence . . . or it is just this once, and once doesn't count, etc., etc., *ad libitum*— it is, in fact, anything you like except *being a drunkard.*[6]

Any student knows how many excuses can be invented for cheating in examinations.

To change the name by which we describe an action is one of the commonest ways of avoiding truth. "It isn't cheating; it's only cribbing." Witness the many soft names for petty stealing. Penuriousness may become *caring for one's own household*, prodigality *generosity*, dissipation *being a good fellow*, snobbery *refinement*, or wishywashiness *toleration*.

When mere bluntness cannot be wisely employed to compel one's hearers to accept the right conception, sometimes the truth can be put in an imaginative way that adds sharpness, perhaps also humor, and at the same time makes the dose less objectionable. The story is told of a member of

---

[4] *Napoleon*, p. 376.
[5] *Psychology: Briefer Course*, p. 451.
[6] *Idem*, p. 453. By permission of Henry Holt and Company.

a certain legislature in the Middle West who sought an appropriation of $100,000 for the protection of public health, but could secure only $5,000. One morning he put upon the desk of each legislator a fable which ran like this: A sick mother with a baby was told by her physician that she had tuberculosis and should seek a higher altitude. She had no money, and on application to the state government was told that not a dollar was available to save her and her child from death. At the same time a farmer observed that one of his hogs had symptoms of cholera. He sent a telegram, collect, to the government; and an inspector came next day, treated the hog with serum, and cured it. Moral: *Be a hog!* The $100,000 appropriation was promptly passed.

Perhaps sensationalism is as well justified here as anywhere. Physicians who cannot make their patients face the fact that they endanger health by overeating often declare, "You are digging your grave with your teeth!" A speaker might break the complacency of a community by beginning a speech on fire protection, "With our many firetrap buildings, our complete failure to enforce building regulations, and our poorly equipped fire companies, this town is due for a big fire that will destroy millions of dollars in property and hundreds of lives."

Ridicule is sometimes potent. Comments on the redness of a steady drinker's nose may have more effect than a temperance lecture. The public statement of an outsider in a certain college that it was famous for having the largest gymnasium and the smallest library may have had something to do with the fact that within a few months the trustees resolved that by some means or other a large library should be built.

But if all failures and refusals to face the facts, and all self-deceptions, were to be berated and ridiculed there would be little room for kindly speech. The impersonal explanation, the pointed example or anecdote, may serve better than offensive speech. And if this be called "beating about the bush," remember that it takes a deal of self-righteousness always to go head-on against the faults of others, when there may be an easier, kindlier, and surer way to open their eyes.

Nevertheless there are times for harsher methods. Much depends, as always, upon the relation of speaker and audience. A Yale man may say things to Yale men that it would not be wise for a Princeton man to say to them, lest he awaken a resentment that would give truth a slight chance; for one of the best ways we have of dodging truth is to become angry at the one who tells it to us. But even bluntness and ridicule need not be offensive, especially if they come from one of our own number and are accompanied by good humor. A student described the eating habits of the student body in a way that called forth sheepish grins of acknowledgment; and another won attention to that trite subject, waste of time, by a derisive picture of a typical student day.

HABIT. "The habitual is pleasant," says Aristotle. "Nature—at least that 'second nature' which is habit—calls aloud for the customary performance," says Woodworth.[7] A manufacturer of large experience told me that workmen will put out of operation safety devices attached to machines, although the devices do not make work more difficult and involve but slight change of habit.

It is worth while to recognize difficulties even though there are no certain ways of overcoming them; for one who knows a difficulty is more likely to find a way to meet it, or

[7] R. S. Woodworth, *Psychology*, p. 328. By permission of Henry Holt and Company.

to find a way around it, or to avoid useless attempts. Now there is certainly no sure way to induce others to change habits. Sometimes it is best to attack the habit directly, stressing its evils. When feasible induce your hearers to set up a new habit. Secure, if possible, conduct which necessarily breaks the habit, and set up strong motives for the new way. The student who spoke on waste of time showed not only that the man who makes good use of time has the satisfaction of accomplishment as a reward, but also that he has more leisure, the very thing the waster is greedy of.

Penalties for continuance in a course are among the commonest means of persuasion. Sometimes such penalties as ill health, failure in business, ridicule, disapproval of one's group, ostracism, can be threatened; and sometimes a more definite penalty can be provided. A fraternity that decided that its members were using too much profanity in the house hit upon the expedient of a "cuss-cup" into which a member must drop a nickel for each oath. It proved effective; and one can imagine that members were strict in enforcement, since the nickels went to buy small luxuries for all.

It is well to provide a routine to follow in breaking a habit. Instead of merely telling his hearers to cut down on this and that food, the lecturer on diet will accomplish more by furnishing printed dietaries that they can follow definitely and post conspicuously as reminders. When feasible the persuader will cause his hearers to go through the routine many times. So a voice trainer will not only provide exercises for his students, but will lead them through the exercises again and again, hoping that at least some members of the class will, once accustomed to the routine, follow up with the necessary persistent practice.

Generally speaking, it is better to suggest as little change in habit as will accomplish the object. So the lecturer on health may accomplish more by recommending only moderate exercise, or cutting down by half the consumption of sugar or tobacco, than by more drastic measures. But there is something to be said for a complete break with old habits; and it may be easier, for example, to leave out all coffee than to limit its use. Besides one may get a pleasant feeling of being heroic, and is likely to boast a bit; and both the feeling and the boasting tend to hold him to his course for a time. But there are two drawbacks: first, it is hard to work a person up to the heroic level; and, secondly, it is doubtful if he will remain there long. And the higher the "water wagon," the harder may be the fall.

MOTIVES. We act, or fail to act, or refuse to act, because we wish to gain something, or to avoid something. Motive is so important to persuasion that a special chapter will be devoted to the topic.

MAKE USE OF REPETITION. Napoleon is said to have declared that "there is only one figure of rhetoric of serious importance, namely, repetition." Hitler says in *My Battle*, "You cannot expect people to know what you are talking about unless you tell them the same story over and over again." And that was what he did in the days when he was campaigning for power. Over and over he hammered on the disgrace of the dictated peace, the threat of communism, and the menace of the Jew.

Repetition keeps the desired conduct or belief before the hearer's mind and makes it stick there. It may occur in a single speech, or in successive speeches. It may be in the form of brief set phrases, or slogans, such as "Food will win the war," "Uncle Sam wants you," "They shall not pass." Political speakers go about reiterating in every speech their party's keynotes, as "Turn the rascals out," "The tariff is a tax," "Trade follows the flag," "The American way of life." "He kept us out of the war" had not a little to do with the reëlection of President Wilson in 1916. If the phrase is clever it will be taken up and repeated in conversation and in the press; if not clever, jeers at it as a parrot cry will more than offset its value. To be effective it must both sound well and fit the case. Advertisers know well the force of the multiplied repetition of slogans.

Repeated phrases need not always be so brief as those just cited, though the brief phrase has an advantage in the ease with which it can be remembered and quoted. Candidate Taft in 1908 repeated in most of his campaign speeches a phrase which was the real basis of his bid for election: "I will carry out absolutely unaltered the policies of Theodore Roosevelt." And although his audiences knew he had said it over and over again, they waited for it and applauded it vigorously. But repetition is not limited to set phrases, for there are many ways of saying the same thing (as was illustrated in Chapter VIII). The set phrase avoids the danger that the hearer may fail to identify the idea; but varied statement relieves monotony, and usually also adds something to the idea. But there is no reason why one cannot have the advantages of both. Advertisers show us how when they repeat their slogans in new settings. Those marvels of persistent enthusiasm who mix advertising with radio programs try to do the same thing. So the speech-maker can repeat his set phrases, even in a single speech, provided he gives them new settings to relieve monotony, and he can also put the same idea into varied wordings. Delivery, also, can relieve his repetitions of monotony.

It is not to be assumed, of course, that repetition is necessarily effective. No one would hold up the nagging wife as a model of persuasiveness. Mere harping on an idea will probably cause irritation. And repetition of the less important ideas in a speech tends to diminish emphasis upon the important.

USE AMPLIFICATION. The advantages and disadvantages of brevity were considered in Chapter IX. While there may be great persuasive force in hard, compact statement, often there is need of more copious treatment in order to keep an idea before the hearer's mind until it takes effect. Dr. Austin Phelps, in the midst of an earnest presentation of the argument for brevity, himself produced an example of the value of illustration and amplification; and incidentally suggests one of the chief reasons why a highly condensed expression is sometimes so effective: that it is a striking expression of a belief already fondly held by the hearer:

Many years ago, Kossuth the Hungarian patriot, in an address in the city of New York, expressed the idea that the time had gone by when the people could be depended upon for their own enslavement by standing armies. He compressed it into two words. Said he, "Bayonets think." The words caught the popular taste like wildfire. They took rank with the proverbs of the language immediately. The idea was not new, but the style of it was. It had been floating in the dialect of political debate ever since the battle of Bunker Hill, but never before had it been condensed into a brace of words. The effect was electric. Millions then, for the first time, felt it as a fact in political history. Within a month the newspapers of Oregon had told their readers that bayonets think. Everybody told everybody else that bayonets think. In style it was a minié-bullet: everybody who heard it was struck by it. Such is the force of laconic dialect.[8]

And Senator Beveridge, who also hymned the virtues of condensation, instanced passages from the sayings of Jesus

[8] Phelps and Frink, *Rhetoric: Its Theory and Practice*, p. 139. By permission of Charles Scribner's Sons.

as examples of wise repetition and amplification, including this from the Sermon on the Mount:

Ye have heard that it hath been said, Thou shalt love thy neighbor and hate thine enemy. But I say unto you, Love your enemies, bless them that curse you, do good to them that hate you, and pray for them that despitefully use you and persecute you; that ye may be the children of your Father which is in heaven; for he maketh his sun to rise on the evil and on the good, and sendeth rain on the just and on the unjust.

For if ye love them which love you, what reward have ye? Do not even the publicans the same? And if ye salute your brethren only, what do ye more than others? Do not even the publicans so? [9]

USE CONCRETE AND SPECIFIC LANGUAGE. We have noted in an earlier chapter that concrete and specific language has a stronger hold on attention than abstract and general words. It is also more persuasive. Abstractions are by their nature removed from emotion, which attaches to things, places, experiences, and persons. It is true that some abstractions become so associated with persons and experiences that they acquire strongly emotional connotations, as may be noted in such slogans as "Liberty, equality, fraternity," and "the world safe for democracy." Nevertheless, generally speak-

[9] *Matthew*, vi, 43-47. Senator Beveridge also instanced *Matthew*, xxv, 34-45. A classic example of repetition and amplification is found in the Third Philippic of Demosthenes, which hammers in over and over the assertion that Philip of Macedon is at war with Athens even though Athens does not realize that it is at war with Philip. Coming a long way down, in every sense, Conwell's famous lecture, "Acres of Diamonds," is mainly a series of repetitions and illustrations of the one idea that opportunity is waiting close to every man. Probably no notable speech ever surpassed Clarence Darrow's defense of Loeb and Leopold in copiousness of treatment; but study of the case convinces me that its repetitions and elaborations were mostly wasted.

ing, we care more about persons than about principles, as political campaigns illustrate; and we take more interest in immediate and palpable results than in theorizing about causes.

We may talk of love for mankind, but our genuine feeling is for individuals. You may draw money from the habitually charitable for suffering mountaineer children, but you can draw from more than the habitually charitable for a particular child. The single case is more appealing because easier to see and feel. To urge me to do my duty as a citizen is not so effective as to urge me to go out to-night and work for Thomas Jones for mayor. We do not fight for rights, but for a right. The Revolutionary fathers were not really so much worried about the abstract rights proclaimed by Thomas Jefferson as about the right to trade lumber, wool, and tobacco for molasses and rum in the West Indies. An effective battle cry names a specific goal, as "On to Richmond," "On to Berlin."

Here may be noted again the value of specific example. When Eleazer Wheelock, back in the 1760s, was seeking funds to enlarge his school (later Dartmouth College) for the education, and especially the religious education, of the Indians and the English youth of the colonies, he sent to England Samuel Occum, a full-blooded Indian who under the training of Wheelock had become an eloquent preacher. Occum made a strong impression, and more money was raised than had ever been given to any similar American cause. While we cannot always present so convincing an exhibit, we can often present persuasive examples through narrations, descriptions, models, and pictures.

APPEAL TO IMAGINATION. Close to the topic of concrete and specific diction is that of imagination. Among the sayings attributed to Napoleon is, "Imagination rules the world." "The orator," says an Eastern proverb, "is one who changes ears into eyes." If you would induce a muscular young man who knows nothing of the sport to play football, take him to see a game and let him imagine himself "in there." But if you cannot bring him to see the objective realities, then with word pictures you will strive to make them mental realities.

Sometimes imagination is appealed to in elaborated descriptions, narrations, and analogies. Theodore Roosevelt gave a new meaning to an old word with the following:

In Bunyan's *Pilgrim's Progress* you may recall the description of the Man with the Muck-rake, the man who would look no way but downward, with the muck-rake in his hand; who was offered a celestial crown for his muck-rake, but who would neither look up nor regard the crown he was offered, but continued to rake to himself the filth of the floor.

In *Pilgrim's Progress* the Man with the Muck-rake is set forth as the example of him whose vision is fixed on carnal instead of on spiritual things. Yet he also typifies the man who in this life consistently refuses to see aught that is lofty, and fixes his eyes with solemn intentness only on that which is vile and debasing. Now it is very necessary that we should not flinch from seeing what is vile and debasing. There is filth on the floor, and it must be scraped up with the muck-rake; and there are times and places where this service is the most needed of all the services that can be performed. But the man who never does anything else, who never thinks or speaks or writes save of his feats with the muck-rake, speedily becomes, not a help to society, not an incitement to good, but one of the most potent forces for evil.[10]

[10] From his speech at the laying of the corner-stone of the office building of the House of Representatives, April 14, 1906. The whole speech is in *Theodore Roosevelt*, Vol. XVI, p. 48, and in O'Neill's *Models of Speech Composition*, p. 530. The excerpt is

Since the day of that speech the term *muck-raker* has been potent in discouraging a certain type of reckless speaking and writing.

Ralph Waldo Emerson was thinking, perhaps, of the more tersely put image when he wrote in his essay on Eloquence:

The orator must be, to a certain extent, a poet. We are such imaginative creatures, that nothing so works on the human mind, barbarous or civilized as a trope [figure of speech]. Condense some daily experience into a glowing symbol, and an audience is electrified. . . . It is a wonderful aid to memory, which carries away the image, and never loses it. A popular assembly, like the House of Commons, or the French Chamber, or the American Congress, is commanded by these two powers,—first by a fact, then by skill of statement. Put the argument into a concrete shape, into an image,—some hard phrase, round and solid as a ball, which they can see and handle and carry home with them, —and the cause is half won.

Such images are found in many slogans, as "Remember the Alamo." Some effective phrases do not so much express as suggest images, as "Fifty-four forty or fight," or, "Safety first." The term *child labor*, suggesting woebegone youngsters working at looms while other children play in fields seen from the factory windows, has been a great help to the advocates of measures for the abolition of child labor, and an embarrassment to those who oppose. Would not the cause labeled "conservation of natural resources" have won quicker and more persistent support had it been christened with a less clumsy and abstract name?

The British statesman, Lloyd George, who has rare power

over popular audiences, gave his hearers a strong image to carry home when he told this story of an old Welsh preacher:

He was conducting a funeral service over a poor fellow who had had a very bad time through life without any fault of his own. They could hardly find space in the churchyard for his tomb. At last they got enough to make a brickless grave amid towering monuments that pressed upon it, and the minister, standing above it, said: "Well, Davie, you have had a narrow time right through life and you have a very narrow place in death; but mind you, old friend, I can see a day dawning when you will rise out of your narrow bed and call out to all these big people, 'Elbow room for the poor!'"

Examples already given, both here and in the discussion of illustration in Chapter VIII, prove that vivid imagery lies not alone in magnificent word-painting, such as may be found in Webster's Reply to Hayne; but may be found also in homely form, and is quite as much needed in simple speeches. The speaker who urged the adoption of a new method of traffic control at city crossings had to make vivid to us conditions as they are and as they would be under the proposed system.

EXPOSITION, IMAGINATION, AND PERSUASION. The example just above involves exposition; and there is no more important means of persuasion than clear exposition. A hearer may reject a plan in spite of its intrinsic merits, if it does not acquire reality in his mind and just because of its vagueness seems strange, radical, unpleasant, unprofitable, or dangerous. Exposition reaching imagination must enable the hearer to see the plan working. No speaker should expect intelligent people to adopt a plan of any importance to themselves until he has answered the natural question, "How will this work under such and such conditions?"

MAKE YOUR HEARERS SEE THEMSELVES. The most potent appeal to imagination, whether one wishes to induce or to discourage action, is that which makes the hearer see himself in situations and doing acts. This may cause a man to anticipate a future good so strongly that he will forget the effort, expense, danger, or future evil the course may entail; or it may restrain him by making him realize the consequences. A "strip" cartoon by Briggs, who knew so well our human foibles, shows a man at his desk, away behind on work. The tempter enters armed with golf clubs. Ignoring his victim's protests, he runs on, "Hurry up, put on your coat. Listen, you and I take on Fred and Ray. . . . We'll make 'em look foolish; you're playing a great game. Hurry up, the fellows are waiting." And the victim goes out with a gesture of helplessness. The engineer who can put into the minds of the city fathers a vision of an improved town may win a job; or the leader who can make a people see itself dominant in the world may inspire them to incredible sacrifices.

So make your hearers see themselves happy and successful in the situation you would bring about or in doing the act you urge. Translate duties, or drudgery, or seeming impossibilities into visions. Make the audience of misfits see themselves taking a normal, respected place in society. Make the athletic team see itself returning to an enthusiastic reception. Or make students who would cheat under an honor system see themselves ostracized.

The superiority of expression that is concrete, specific, and imaginative lies in its superior power to fix attention, awaken motives, and cling to memory. But we should not overemphasize any one means of persuasion; any form of expression that does these things will be persuasive.

PREVENTING ACTION. Since the emphasis in this discussion has been upon inducing rather than upon checking or preventing action, it may be well to add a few words upon the latter phase of the subject. Since to cause a man to act, outside the range of his instinctive and habitual conduct, we seek to get and keep his mind on the action as something for him to do, then to keep him from an action we seek to keep his mind off it. And, on the principle that the best defensive is an offensive, the best way to keep his mind off the action is to turn his attention to other conduct. Show him that there is a better way; or that he has better things to do and may well leave this to others. Or show him that it will be better to let conditions work themselves out; most evils cure themselves anyhow; like most sores, "they get well if you don't pick 'em." Why worry? If necessary, impress upon him the difficulty, expense, danger, or impracticability of the course he would follow.

# CHAPTER XIV

## SUGGESTION

We continue in this chapter to consider those hearers who agree that the persuader's proposal is good, or who, having no strong objections or doubts, are rather easily won to agreement; but who yet hesitate, through indifference or inertia, to act.

We distinguished earlier between discourse in which logical connections are stressed and discourse in which they are not stressed. And in considering the second sort of discourse we come to the idea of suggestion. Various technical meanings have been given in recent years to this old word. For our purpose it will suffice to say that when we act on a prompting external to ourselves *without reflection*, we act upon suggestion. We may say in untechnical usage, "Don't suggest it to him," with the implication that he would respond to the suggestion without thinking; but untechnical usage does not necessarily exclude the idea of weighing the pros and cons, while technical usage does. In technical as in common usage the term may imply indirection or hinting, or it may not. In technical usage a direct command is considered suggestion. When a suggestion provokes a reaction contrary to its apparent intent, it is called *contrasuggestion*.

"The working of suggestion," says the psychologist Scott,

"is dependent upon the impulsive, dynamic nature of ideas"; [1] and he expresses this nature in the following laws:

Every idea of an action will result in that action unless hindered by an impeding idea or physical impediment.

Every idea, concept, or conclusion which enters the mind is held as true unless hindered by some contradictory idea.

ARGUMENT AND SUGGESTION COMPARED. In dealing with those distinctly doubtful or opposed, argument seems to be in order; although we are sometimes led to act in defiance of belief.[2] Desire, fear, hate, personal influence, or crowd feeling may overcome reason. But doubters and objectors in a calm state of mind generally require argument.

Even in dealing with auditors who are in substantial agreement with the speaker, he may wish to review the reasons and evidence for his proposal, and thus change a belief held on slight or half-forgotten grounds into a firmly reasoned conviction. But unless familiar and accepted arguments are put in fresh form, one runs the risk of boring his adherents. There is also the risk of awakening doubt where none existed before, since argument indicates the possibility of more than one conclusion. This danger is increased when the speaker falls into the rather common fault of arguing with his adherents as if they were in opposition. I have heard some of my fondest beliefs argued in a way that made me wish to arise and refute them. It

[1] W. D. Scott, *Influencing Men in Business*, p. 37.  By permission of the Ronald Press.

[2] Some say we always believe, at the moment, that what we do is best. That depends upon what meaning we give *belief*. I prefer to make it mean more than the notion of a moment, which may be quite contrary to one's settled conviction. That primitive fear might make me run from a seeming spook does not make me admit that I believe in ghosts.

is more tactful to maintain the air of reviewing what speaker and audience hold in common.

Since argument induces a deliberative rather than an active mood, it should be followed by more impulsive discourse if immediate action is desired; and suggestion may supply that.

The advantages of suggestion are implied in the remarks above about argument. Suggestion, when successful, puts the hearer in a mood for immediate action. This strength becomes a weakness when future action is desired; for although a suggestion may work out at a future time, the probability grows smaller as time passes. It is well, therefore, to provide some immediate outlet for the impulse which a speech creates. If the hearers commit themselves to the course desired, there is a better chance that in the future they will "follow through."

Advertisers provide a coupon for you to "sign and mail today." A speaker may ask his hearers to make a beginning at once by signing a card or a petition, to vote for a resolution, to join an organization, to subscribe now and pay later, to stand up and be counted; or the speaker may at least draw forth vigorous applause for a sentiment which gives rein to the awakened impulse and gains visible assent before there is time for doubt to arise, or for other interests to oust the speaker's suggestion.

VARIATIONS IN SUGGESTIBILITY. Individuals differ greatly in their normal suggestibility, from those who are unable to step over a mark if firmly told they cannot, to those who are disinclined to accept anything on mere statement and who question every proposal however slight. At the extreme are some so contra-suggestible that, in the proverbial saying, they "have to be driven backward like a hog to war."

The more heterogeneous an audience and the less its

members are accustomed to working together, or to working in groups at all, the less suggestible the audience will be. Formerly it was safe to say that farmers were less suggestible than city dwellers; but the statement may be less true to-day since farmers have been brought more into the currents of public opinion, especially by radio, have been drawn into organizations, and also subjected to a deal of propaganda. Bodies of lawyers, scientists, seasoned politicians, or any group composed of those trained to scan all statements are less likely to yield to suggestion than those accustomed to believing and doing what they are told.

DIRECT AND INDIRECT SUGGESTION. If one's hearers are already set for action, the suggestion may be direct and immediate. If they are less ready, it may be necessary to prepare the way, but the suggestion may still be direct. Tact requires that the speaker consider the character of the audience and the nature of his relation to it. A person in authority can speak with more directness than others, as a coach to his squad. Sometimes just an assured manner is sufficient. The book agent uses direct suggestion when he presents form and pencil and says "Sign here." The trick may work; but when we recognize it for what it is, we resent it, for he is assuming a right to dictate which we do not grant him.

This brings us to the fact that the success of direct suggestion depends upon whether the hearer's resistance is high or low. If he is naturally weak-willed, awed by superior intelligence, or is under the influence of authority, of good feeling which makes him dislike to say no, of some emotion such as fear or enthusiasm, or is eager to act, he will accept direct suggestion more readily. But ordinarily it is best to temper one's suggestions with such phrases as, Why not do this? I submit this plan for your approval, The thought occurs to me, It has been suggested, So and So proposes.

Tactlessly used, direct suggestion may act as *contra-suggestion*. One remarks to a contra-suggestible person, says MacDougall,[3] " 'I think you ought to take a holiday,' and although he himself had contemplated this course, he replies, 'No, I don't need one,' and becomes immovably fixed in that opinion." We are all familiar with this sort of perversity, and realize that at times we ourselves are subject to it. Such signs as "Keep off the Grass" invite us to disobey even in our best moments. We often resent a "bossy" manner even in those who have a right to command; and we are pretty sure to in those whose right we do not recognize. While a reasonably confident and positive manner in a speaker is certainly better than a weak and fawning mien, still it is plain that positiveness and bluntness can easily be overdone, and indirect or softened direct suggestion is often better.

Contra-suggestion, however, can be used to further one's ends. It often is in everyday intercourse, and there are many examples in literature.[4] Iago, after subtly leading Othello to believe Desdemona untrue, whispers, "Let her live." And everybody knows how Tom Sawyer got his aunt's fence whitewashed. But contra-suggestion is not, under ordinary condition, so useful to the speaker as the

---

[3] William McDougall, *An Introduction to Social Psychology*, p. 101. By permission of John W. Luce and Company.

[4] Probably the most famous example of the use of contra-suggestion in speech literature is Mark Antony's funeral oration in *Julius Caesar*. It is worth study; but we must remember that it is adapted to the need for quick results on the stage, and addressed to a crowd represented as both very stupid and in a mob-like state of excitement. It would be unwise to assume that such a bald procedure as Antony's could often be employed with the average genuine audience.

other forms; and there is an unpleasing slyness about it that will hurt the influence of a speaker whose use of it is detected by his audience. It has justifiable uses, especially in dealing with the contra-suggestible, the hostile and the very young. The student of speaking should be able to recognize its use by others. The means of checkmating it seems to be direct exposure: This man does not mean what he says; he has his tongue in his cheek. Are you going to let him bamboozle you?

Most useful to the speaker under ordinary conditions, with intelligent audiences little inclined to take orders from him, is *indirect suggestion*. It is particularly effective when we wish an audience to arrive at the desired conclusion with the feeling that it is their own—and nothing is more persuasive than that. The head of a business who throws out ideas in such a way that his colleagues will bring them back embodied in proposals which they present with the pride of creators will have strong coöperation. It is often best for a speaker not to urge his plan, but to present his case so that the desired course will develop in the minds of his audience; and then ask, What shall we do? Or, perhaps, come closer to direct suggestion and ask, Shall we do this? Shall we have a new school house now?

REPETITION AND SUGGESTION. The force of suggestion is increased by repetition, provided interest is sustained; but this topic has been sufficiently developed in the preceding chapter.

AUTHORITY. Direct suggestion in particular is aided by authority; and, first, the authority of the speaker himself. This arises in part from his reputation, from preliminary announcements, and from the chairman's introduction. The speaker can add to his authority by his manner, and add still more by an authoritative treatment of his subject. (The authority of the speaker will be developed in a later chapter.)

Authority can also be utilized by bringing in the support of those looked upon as leaders, past and present. So and So said, So and So stands with us, The fathers intended. All that is necessary is that the person cited be of weight with the particular group addressed. A quotation from a book recognized as authoritative may be effective, especially a quotation with a ring to it. Shakespeare says . . . , and if Shakespeare says it, often we have no disposition to think for ourselves.

Suggestion in positive form is more likely to be responded to than negative suggestion. Says Hollingworth,

> Suggestion is most active at its *positive* pole. Whenever possible, the human mind works in terms of positives rather than negatives. . . . The Old Covenant with its "Thou shalt not" had to be replaced by the New Covenant with its simple positive "Thou shalt." [5]

IMITATION. Notable deeds can be cited to move to imitation. The deeds of "the Fathers" and of this and that hero are the commonest themes of memorial addresses. The deeds of earlier athletic heroes are used to inspire the players of to-day. And there is more than conscious emulation to consider; there is also the tendency to imitate unconsciously conduct that impresses us, whether through direct observation or through dramatic recital.

The speaker is limited in what he can do himself to prompt imitation. He communicates some of his interest

[5] H. L. Hollingworth, *Advertising and Selling*, p. 227. By permission of D. Appleton-Century Company, New York. The statement is repeated in Professor Hollingworth's *Psychology of the Audience*, p. 143.

and enthusiasm, by voice, action, and facial expression.
Sometimes he can do before his hearers what he wishes
them to do, as subscribe to a cause. If he is himself an
embodiment of his cause he is likely to be effective, however
blundering his speech. When in 1918 wounded soldiers,
home to recuperate, spoke in the Liberty Bond campaigns,
the best of civilian speakers felt like taking the back seat.

SOCIAL SUGGESTION. Still greater than the impulse to
imitate individuals is the tendency to yield to environment,
custom, convention, and common opinion; and not merely
from conscious desire for approval and fear of what Mrs.
Grundy may say, but even more from unconscious submission to mass suggestion and social pressure. Says Professor
Ross, the noted sociologist:

Everything we do reveals the pull on conduct exerted by social
pressure. Our foods and drinks, our dress and furniture, our
religious emotions, our investments, and even our matrimonial
choices confess the sway of fashion and vogue. Whatever is
common reaches us by way of example or advice or intimidation
from a hundred directions. In our most private choices we are
swerved from our orbit by the solar attraction—or repulsion—
of the conventional. In public opinion there is something which
is not praise or blame, and this residuum is mass suggestion.[6]

A man obeys this "social imperative," not because he
decides it is wise to obey, "but because he feels he must."
Those who do not obey are the "deliberate criminal and
the moral insurgent."

Old colleges, universities, monasteries, senates, academies, ad-
ministrative departments, army and navy, ancient families and

[6] The quotations are from Edward A. Ross, *Social Control*, p. 148.
By permission of The Macmillan Company, publishers.

quiet neighborhoods become the haunt of traditions that cast a
spell over those who come within their reach.[6]

The speaker who can make his audience feel this social
imperative pushing them in the direction he wishes has a
powerful leverage. This may be most often available to
check conduct disapproved by the community: "That is not
the way we do," or, "It is not being done." But the social
imperative is also available to induce action: "Do this; it is
what is expected of you."

EMOTION. Increase of emotion increases suggestibility,
for when we are emotional we are less likely to demand
proof or to examine closely any statement that is congruous
with our feeling. When filled with desire to see some one
punished we are less likely to question the charge that John
Doe is the villain who committed the crime, or brought
corruption into the city government. Those filled with the
fever of speculation may accept any tip as good. But we
should not think of violent emotions only; an audience that
has been brought into a jolly mood and likes the speaker
is little likely to weigh his statements; and an audience
that has been stirred with desire for a public improvement
is quick to accept the speaker's confident "We can do it."

When a speaker wishes to work through suggestion he
will refrain from argument, and from suggesting alternative
courses, or doing anything to cause reflection. He will speak
in terms suited to emotion, positive terms without the qualifications of careful exposition and argument, in language
concrete, familiar, and imaginative. He will refer much to
events and persons and sentiments that will awaken old
associations.

When William Jennings Bryan swept the Democratic
convention in 1896 and won the presidential nomination,

he used the language of defiance to his opponents, refused all compromise with the "money power," and scorned all admissions of the possibility of the failure of the free coinage of silver to cure economic ills. He referred to the old struggles and triumphs and heroes of the party, and he used many bold figures. The crowning stroke was his conclusion: "You shall not press down upon the brow of labor this crown of thorns; you shall not crucify mankind upon a cross of gold." This delivered with bold picturing gestures had a tremendous effect upon an already excited audience, which contained relatively few experienced politicians and was in revolt against its old leaders. To this day this address is most often called the Cross of Gold Speech. It was not an instance of pure suggestion; but the parts in the form of argument contained nothing which called for reflection or which would not be instantly applauded by the great majority of his audience.

It is unfortunate that examples notable enough to be interesting and to impress the point so often tend to give a false impression. It should not be understood that great excitement, crowds in a mob-like state, and amazing figures of speech are necessary to the working of suggestion, though they do magnify its effect.

EFFECT OF NUMBERS. Every experienced speaker knows that it is easier to move a large than a small audience. A few are more critical than a crowd. Whatever causes us to feel strongly our individuality, our importance as persons, works against suggestion; and "intensity of personality is in inverse proportion to the number of aggregated men." [7] When many are present each shares with others the responsibility of judgment.

[7] Boris Sidis, *Psychology of Suggestion*, p. 277.

ARRANGEMENT OF THE AUDIENCE. But since we cannot always gather a large audience, it is fortunate that the actual number is less important than having the room filled. A hundred crowded into a small room are more suggestible than three hundred scattered over a hall large enough for twice the number.[8] But if you cannot fill your hall, try to bring those present close together at the front. Henry Ward Beecher declared that he would rather speak to a dozen persons close to him and crowded together so that they touch each other, than to a thousand with four feet of space between every two of them. That, he said, would be just the same as an empty room. "Crowd your audience together and you will set them off with half the effort." [9]

But this is often difficult to do. If the chairman is a person of some authority with the audience he may be able to coax them forward; and ushers can be instructed to bring as many forward as possible. But those who enter determined not to come under the influence of the speaker will instinctively keep on the outskirts.

A young woman who had been successful in arguing "Votes for women" in the streets of New York and in other places that would try the courage of most speakers, told me that the worst time she ever had was before a very polite body of people seated around the sides of a room, leaving the center open. And one of my own most painful memories is that of speaking in a long, narrow church before a congregation that refused to come forward past the middle. The reason given for the greater ease of dealing with a

[8] Unfortunately this is offset by the fact that announcement of a large hall will usually bring out more people than announcement of a small one. One needs to do careful estimating in choosing his auditorium.

[9] *Yale Lectures on Preaching*, First Series, p. 73.

compact body is that, when elbow touches elbow, there is a limitation of the movements upon which our sense of individuality partly depends. The members of the compact audience are also more sensible of the reactions of their neighbors to the speaker; and if these are favorable, his influence is multiplied.

The speaker himself must remain unhampered in his movements, so that his individuality will not be cramped and he will have room for the large gestures effective with those in a suggestible state. While Mark Antony remains in the "pulpit" he wishes the crowd close about it; but when he comes down to exhibit the body of Caesar, he waves them back; "Nay, press not so upon me."

UNIFORMITY. Suggestibility is increased when the members of an audience are led to do things together, read a ritual, sing and cheer together, stand up and sit down, laugh, applaud, and vote together. The resolution voted may not be very important, but if it brings out a ringing chorus of Ayes the effect is good. Perhaps music, especially vigorous songs that all can sing, or "sing at," is the greatest unifying force, unless it be laughter. The speaker lets his audience laugh at jokes that all can appreciate, using humor rather than wit that calls for keen thinking; and maybe he turns abruptly to pathos. And when the members of an audience have applauded, laughed, and perhaps sighed a bit in common, each individual feels that those about him are good fellows; and much of his aloofness and reserve is gone, and with it much of his power of resistance.

Sometimes uniform costumes are provided, and this form of "regimentation" tends greatly to increase suggestibility; for it is difficult to keep much sense of personal dignity and responsibility when one realizes that he looks as silly in his regalia as do those about him.

With some obvious modifications, much the same means that can be employed to bring an audience into the mood of good fellowship can be employed to bring an audience into quite different moods; for example, a passion for war.

DESIRABILITY OF INDUCING GREAT SUGGESTIBILITY. We have gradually proceeded from the methods of suggestion that can be used with an audience in its normal state to the means of changing an audience into a *psychological crowd;* that is, a group fused by common emotion and purpose into a high degree of unanimity, and very suggestible. The extreme manifestation of a psychological crowd is a mob.

How far it is desirable or justifiable to go in this direction is a hard question with no definite answer. No complaint can be made against going far enough to remove initial indifference and mere unthinking opposition. As a matter of expediency, it is plain that a suggestible crowd is more easily swayed than a deliberating body; but where deliberation is desired the crowd state is clearly undesirable. It must be remembered, too, that while some who are carried away by suggestion will remain won, others, discovering that they have been carried against their better judgment, will revolt. And in any case, unless the impulse has been firmly connected with the hearers' habitual motives, it is likely soon to fade. The surer way for long-time results, as distinguished from immediate action, is to win by sound argument.

On the other hand, even if the first business is conviction, the time comes when an impulse must be given; and when, if united action is desired, the audience must be brought into community of feeling. On some occasions, too, there is no time for argument; it is suggestion or nothing. And there are times when the mood of the audience will not permit of argument, when the audience is too angry, too hilarious, or too eager for action. And there are times when the audience is so prejudiced that it will not give a fair hearing unless its mood can be softened.

But when we consider controlling people regardless of their reason, we see a serious moral question involved. At this point, as at many others in the study of persuasion, we do well to remember that to influence others is a serious responsibility, whatever the methods employed; but an inevitable responsibility if there is to be any leadership, or if our relations with our fellows are to be other than absolutely passive. I say "whatever the methods employed," for when men are controlled by argument there is the same possibility of misleading and of ruling the weak to their hurt. By employing false data and premises, or by fallacious reasoning from sound facts and premises, one may seem as logical as Aristotle and yet be as false as Beelzebub. In most instances the ethical justification of a method depends less upon the method itself than upon when and how it is used. No one hesitates to use suggestion, even contra-suggestion, with children, or with others incapable of reasoning, whether from natural stupidity or from the mood they are temporarily in.

The most scrupulous speaker needs some knowledge of the methods here suggested if only that he may know how to checkmate an opponent who would change a deliberating body into an unthinking crowd, and how to win back a crowd to deliberation, when that is possible. He needs knowledge of all methods, ethical and unethical, in order that he may fulfil the Scripture, "Be ye therefore wise as serpents and harmless as doves."

REDUCING SUGGESTIBILITY AND CROWD SPIRIT. The means of reducing suggestibility can be drawn from the methods of increasing it. Any hints must be predicated upon the supposition that it is still possible to gain the attention of the audience, either by normal or by sensational means.

Awaken doubts if possible; start an argument on some phase of the subject. Since an over-suggestible audience will not listen to involved argument, questions are useful. The end is good, but is this the best way? Would it not be better to wait until we have more complete information in regard to the other plan? Nothing will be lost by waiting a week. If you get a division of opinion, you break the over-suggestible condition.

If authority has been cited, perhaps as good or greater authority, or more numerous authorities, can be cited in opposition. Against "social pressure" show that other respected communities or groups differ from this.

If there is excess of emotion, the speaker will try to allay it. If the emotion is fear, he will say that there is no reason for panic; the danger has been exaggerated. At worst it is not immediate; and there is no reason why we should not deliberate on the measures to be taken, rather than rush headlong into needless expense, or perhaps still greater dangers. If there is too much enthusiasm for a measure, some "dash of cold water" may check it. The speaker may say that the proposal looks fine, but have you considered the expense, or the risk? Will you risk a sound business on the mere hope of speculative profits? Here are some hard facts that have been overlooked. When justified in so doing, the speaker may make a charge of selfish motives against the proponents of a measure; such as, Do you realize that these men are asking you to pour thousands of dollars into their pockets? The sensational nature of such a charge is likely to break the spell of an advocate's influence, and at least force more careful consideration.

A speaker who feels himself on safe ground with the audience may venture to ridicule the claims made, or to expose the hocus-pocus used on the audience by an opponent. Those who are made to grin sheepishly at themselves will not remain very suggestible. But if the crowd is fully committed to an opposition leader, ridicule is dangerous. Better the tentative approach of Mark Antony, agreeing, at least in part, with the audience. And there is always something one can agree with: Brutus really had fine traits.

Sometimes one can restore the sense of individual responsibility to certain influential persons in a crowd by addressing them by name. Do you, John Roe, approve of this action? Do you, William Winter, realize what this may mean to you? Do you, Tom Nash, mean to tell me you are going back on your past?

One who would outwit a "hypnotic" opponent may have to begin by "out-heroding Herod," ranting a little louder, speaking in more positive and imaginative terms, being more flattering to the audience, the community, and its heroes, or promising greater benefits. Once he has gained some standing, he may be able to talk sense to the audience.

If the crowd state has been fully reached, it will be useless to attempt even simple reasoning. Some sensational statement or action may be needed to get any attention at all. When a mob-like audience refused to listen to Wendell Phillips, he turned away from them and spoke to the reporters. A sudden hush fell and Phillips seized the opportunity to shout, "Howl on; I speak to thirty millions here!" And the crowd kept still. A trick may be justified. In the midst of an audience determined to hoot down the speaker, a tall figure arose and caught an instant's attention. "Well, fellow citizen," the man drawled, "I wouldn't keep still if I didn't want to." The crowd applauded and listened for more. He continued, "But if I were you I should want to!" They laughed and then were quiet.

If the group is far gone in crowd feeling some startling means may be needed to create a diversion, as the cry of "Fire!" or "Police!" Or some popular leader who seems to be on the side of the crowd may be pushed forward to catch attention and then to suggest some harmless outlet for emotion. Eight hundred students in a certain high school, seized by a sudden fancy, refused to return to work after luncheon and proceeded to march around and around the school building with cheers and songs. They refused to listen to their principal when he begged them to return home at least. But when Murphy, athlete and leader, jumped upon a box they listened; and when he shouted, "The Orpheum opens in five minutes; let's go!" they went. That was a hilarious crowd with nothing of importance on its mind.

On the night of Lincoln's assassination a great crowd gathered in City Hall Park in New York and threatened every moment to become a mob, likely to vent its wrath upon certain "copperhead" newspapers. General Garfield was asked to try to quiet the crowd. Stepping out on a balcony, he stood with upraised hands in full sight of the crowd, which surged over to hear his news. This was the news:

Clouds and darkness are round about him;
Righteousness and judgment are the habitations of his throne.[10]

Fellow Citizens: God reigns and the Government at Washington still lives.

The familiar, sacred words, with their great image, caught the crowd and held them long enough to receive the assur-

[10] *Psalms*, 97, 2.

ance that the Government did not fall even with the beloved President; and the danger was over. But had another Mark Antony caught them, he too might have gloated,

> Mischief, thou art afoot:
> Take thou what course thou wilt.

One cannot touch this subject of suggestion and crowd control without realizing the inadequacy and the danger of a brief treatment. Sometimes students become fascinated by the subject and make far too much of it. But the danger is likely to be offset by experience; for, while suggestion, especially in its milder forms, is a useful and legitimate method, the speaker who deals with the average American audience, under normal circumstances, on the assumption that he can manipulate them at will is in line for instructive disappointments. "Suggestions to violate life-long habits, firmly fixed moral feelings, sacred relationships, are impotent even during the hypnotic trance," [11] says the psychologist Hollingworth. Certainly, then, under any conditions a speaker is likely to meet, suggestion will work best when in general conformity to the hearer's desires, tendencies, and habitual conduct; however true it may be that under exceptional circumstances, as when caught by crowd feeling, we may seem to respond in a way contrary to our characters and tendencies.

[11] H. L. Hollingworth, *Advertising and Selling*, p. 234. By permission of D. Appleton-Century Company, New York. The statement is repeated in Professor Hollingworth's recent *Psychology of the Audience*, p. 143.

# CHAPTER XV

## MOTIVES

The matter in this chapter may apply to any of the three
groups, adherents, neutrals, and objectors; for discourse
which touches the listeners' motives may be used to move
to action those who agree, or do not oppose, and also motives may be presented to those who question or positively
oppose, as reasons why the proposed conduct is desirable.

It is misleading to speak, as is often done, of persuasion
as chiefly a matter of "appealing to emotions." That phrase
is too often taken as referring only to pathos, or some large
sentiment such as patriotism, or some strong feeling such
as hate. And the word *appeal* is too liable to be taken to
mean fervid exhortation, or other expression calculated to
bring cheers or tears. But it is already apparent that there
is much in persuasion not suggested by "appealing to emotion"; for example, winning an audience to a candid state
of mind, presenting sober facts, and presenting the best plan
for accomplishing the desired end. Nevertheless, persuasion
is concerned with emotion in many ways, and particularly
emotion in the sense of desire, liking, disliking, fear.

Now we call an effective desire a *motive*. (The word
plainly shows its relation to *emotion*, both deriving from
the Latin *movere*, to move.) We act or refuse to act because we wish to gain something or to avoid something.

We choose one of two desirable courses because desire is stronger in the one direction than in the other.[1]

GENERAL CONSIDERATIONS. However important motives may be in conduct, it does not follow that a persuader should always talk about them as such, even those he is depending upon for results in the particular case. If desire is already strong and needs direction only, then to dwell upon the motives for action may be tiresome. "Let's go!" Again, one's hearers may react habitually, without conscious emotion, to certain stimuli. One need not dwell upon the motive of gain in offering an investment to regular investors. Convince them that the investment is good and motive will take care of itself. Tell a boy that he is wanted to pitch a game of ball, or an audience of workingmen that a strike will bring them better wages, and there is no need of expatiating upon the motives. All they need is assurance that your statement is true, and that there are no weighty objections.

To talk about motives may be even offensive. I shall be offensive to you if I assume that your better nature must be worked up to a good deed which you have been doing regularly, such as subscribing to your favorite charity. Few of us like to be preached at; and many of the most effectual sermons omit the exhortation. The preacher simply makes vice ugly and virtue desirable; or he makes clear the course which clean, honest, generous men will wish to follow; and since most men wish to be clean, honest, and generous, they are likely to respond to the challenge.

---

[1] Some say this is always true, that even when we are conscious of no desire, still desire is working in us. No doubt unconscious desire plays a part in conduct; but still this claim seems to put a strain on the word. It takes a difficult argument to show how some of our

There are times, certainly, when motives need arousing and strengthening, and especially when there are strong competing motives. Unaccustomed investors, fearful of loss, may need to be told about the profits and what they will buy. But even in such cases it does not follow that the speaker need talk about motives as such. There are other ways. The desirability of the result may be pictured; but that is not at all the same thing as talking about the feelings of the audience.

No doubt there are times for the baldest appeals. Much depends upon the character of the audience, the spirit of the occasion, and the relation of the speaker to his audience. We will accept from an acknowledged leader what we might take as impudence from one we consider of less weight than ourselves. A young man would hardly exhort an audience of veterans to patriotism. If he exhorted at all, he would urge the young men present to emulate their elders; and in so doing he might stimulate the veterans to live up to the reputation given them. And it is rash to attempt an open appeal to the higher motives of an audience on a festive occasion.

When familiar motives must be emphasized, care should be taken to avoid triteness. The natural reaction, "Yes, yes, we have heard all that before," does not help persuasion. Indeed, this small resentment may furnish the excuse we like to seize upon as a defense against the call of duty. Probably fresh illustrations furnish the best relief from triteness. Bruce Barton, speaking at a meeting of the Public Relations Section of the National Electric Light Association, brightened up an idea very familiar to his hearers with the old story of Joseph used in a unique way:

attitudes spring from even unconscious desire, and another to show how desire is working when we act on pure suggestion.

Those of you who were brought up on the Bible may have found there some account of his very remarkable business career.[2] . . .

The account of Joseph in the Old Testament . . . tells how he left his country under difficulties and, coming into a strange country, he arose, through his diligence, to become the principal person in the state, second only to the king. Now, gentlemen, the Biblical narrative brings us to that point—the point where Joseph had public relations with all the other ancient nations, while his private relations held all the best-paying jobs—it brings us up to the climax of his career and then it hands us an awful jolt. Without any words of preparation or explanation, it says bluntly:

"And Joseph died, and there arose a new king in Egypt which knew not Joseph."

I submit, gentlemen, that this is one of the most staggering lines which has ever been written in a business biography. Here was a man so famous that everybody knew him and presto, a few people die, a few new ones are born, and *nobody* knows him. The tide of human life has moved on; the king who exalted the friends of Joseph is followed by a king who makes them slaves; all the advertising that the name "Joseph" had enjoyed in one generation is futile and of no avail, because that generation has gone. . . .

If advertising is worth doing at all, it is worth doing all the time. For every day, gentlemen, the "king" dies, and there arises a new "king who knows not Joseph." [3]

HIGHER AND LOWER MOTIVES. Baker and Huntington say[4]:

Choose the highest motives to which you think your audience will respond. If a speaker feels it necessary to appeal to motives

[2] In the *Book of Genesis*.

[3] From the speech entitled "Which Knew Not Joseph." By permission of Bruce Barton.

[4] *The Principles of Argumentation* (1905), pp. 321-323. By permission of Ginn and Company.

not of the highest grades he should see to it that before he closes he makes them lead into high motives. In the *Speech at Liverpool*,[5] even as Beecher showed that his main appeal would be to the interest of his audience in securing a good market, he connected this appeal with the far higher motives of mere justice and the good of humanity. . . . Few men are willing to admit that they have acted from motives considered low or mean. Even if they suspect this to be the case, they endeavor to convince themselves that it is not true. In an audience each man knows those about him see what moves him in the speaker's words and therefore he yields most readily to a motive which he knows is generally commended. . . . Since, then, men yield more willingly to motives generally commended, and since unanimity of action is more easily gained when the highest motives are addressed, this corollary to the suggestion last made may be formulated: The larger the audience, the higher the motives to which appeal may be made.

But if men are uneasy when low motives are attributed to them, it is also true that often they are embarrassed when lofty motives are attributed to them. Large audiences are susceptible to lofty appeals, as Baker and Huntington have said; but we may add as a corollary: The smaller the audience the more embarrassing an appeal to high motives. We all have experienced the half-shamed

[5] The reference is to the speech made by Henry Ward Beecher in an attempt to turn the tide of English feeling which threatened in 1863 to lead to the recognition of the Confederacy. Beecher argued that a free South would offer a much better market for English goods, and also appealed to the English dislike of slavery. The audience was very hostile. It is notable that they jeered his appeals to moral sentiments, but listened while he argued that "pounds and pence join with conscience and with honor." The speech is in G. P. Baker's *Specimens of Argumentation*, p. 154, and in W. N. Brigance's *Classified Speech Models*, p. 40.

feeling which makes us look down our noses when a speaker before a small group talks of our honor or nobility. One has only to think back to the time when some gushing lady called him a noble little lad, right in the presence of the gang. It is a curious fact that we often refuse to admit our highest motives. Few of the young men who went to training camps in 1916 would admit higher motives than desire for fun or physical fitness. If brought to a confession, they would refuse to use such a word as patriotism, and say shamefacedly, "Well, a fellow ought to be ready to do his bit."

And that suggests that effectiveness may depend upon the words used. "To do this is noble and generous," may be less acceptable than the ruder statement, "Not to do this is mean and contemptible." (A student talking to students would put the point more pungently.) Most of us do not, like a European duelist, talk much about our honor.

We are thinking of audiences in workaday mood. In times of stress or excitement (say at an old-time football rally or in a stirring political campaign) audiences will respond to appeals which they would ordinarily receive with grins and blushes. The fact seems to be that English-speaking audiences, though as emotional as any, and perhaps more sentimental than most, do not, under ordinary conditions, relish out-and-out appeals to their feelings. We have to recognize that some speakers, notably some criminal lawyers and evangelists, are able to bring audiences into a state in which openly emotional appeals are acceptable; but these speakers usually have, or create, dramatic situations charged with emotion, and they are masters of the arts of suggestion and stage-setting. It is said, also, that some sections of the country respond more readily than others to openly emotional appeals.

Mind you, I am not saying that emotional appeals cannot, or should not, be made to any audience; I am talking of the open, bald appeal.

Another suggestion in the quotation from Baker and Huntington deserves comment: that our motives are often mixed. Very likely the young men who went to training camps in 1916 were aware that early training might mean commissions if we entered the War. Many who bought Liberty bonds were glad to know that the investment was safe; and the "four-minute" speakers did not omit mention of that feature, although their stress was upon the nation's need. Our motives usually are mixed; but we need not wax cynical about that. Many who bought those bonds had to have a safe investment for scanty savings.

Nor need we hesitate to use motives that are less than noble. If the appeal of philanthropy alone will not move a man to contribute to better housing, should you hesitate to make the appeal of "philanthropy and five per cent"? If a man likes to "run things," and this motive can be transmuted into the action you seek, why not give him a job to do? Those who insist that only the higher motives should be appealed to (and one meets such) are in danger of making themselves hypocrites; for unless they are possessed of a nobility few of us have met, they are themselves moved in part by self-interest.

Whether one should ever appeal to a motive he considers actually base is a difficult ethical question. Would you appeal to a man's hatred of his rival to save him from defeatism? Or check a mob bent on murder by tempting it with plunder in another direction? Not setting myself up as an ethical authority, I make but one suggestion: such questions are the same on or off the platform. Each man must decide them for himself; and no doubt will, according to his character.

There is one other important suggestion to be made in regard to the grade of motives one should appeal to: "Don't take a sledgehammer to kill a fly." If the plain and sufficient reason for voting for John Smith for dog-catcher is that the town needs a good dog-catcher, don't tell me that to vote for Smith is a patriotic duty, even though in essence it may be. Moreover, in many matters no other motive than self-interest should be offered. One hardly urges a boy to go to a certain college on the ground that he will help the college. That would be as bad as offering a petty motive for a difficult or dangerous act.

But there is danger of overstressing self-interest. Do not fear to appeal to the best sentiments of your audiences, though you have to use also a lower appeal. Assume your hearers are better rather than worse than they seem. One is often surprised at the generous sentiments found under the most unpromising exteriors. And it is also true that the same audience that applauds a low appeal will often respond as heartily to a higher.

But one thing is certain: if we cannot meet our hearers on common ground and touch motives to which they will respond, be they high or be they low, we should not try to persuade them. And, in general, we cannot hope for permanent results unless we tie our pleas to motives that are stable, that are the standard, everyday motives of those addressed, rather than to those that move them only under special inspiration.

Do not dictate motives. I pick up a card in a church pew:

As an expression of my appreciation of the services at St. Mark's, I will give $......, etc.

But what if I do not greatly appreciate the services at St. Mark's? And what if I do not consider that the proper motive behind a gift to a church should be my personal gratification? It might be better to mention no motive, but if an appeal is to be made, why should it not touch several motives, to any one of which I may attach my subsequent action? It is true that in some cases there can be but one possible motive; but usually there are several motives to offer. At any rate, it is better, when one can, to avoid insistence upon any one. One can suggest a motive without dictating.

WHAT MOTIVES? To attempt here a complete analysis of human motives would be futile. One might turn to the psychologists who trace all motivation to a few instincts, such as the eating, mating, and playing instincts; but we have to deal with the many desires that have developed from these basic impulses. We may here recall the list of "impelling motives" which I adapted to our study of interest: life, health, property, power, reputation, sentiments, affections, pleasures; and this, although unscientific, may be as useful as any. But no list can be more than suggestive. All we can profitably do here is to consider a few of the motives which speakers most often appeal to, although some, such as desire for property and financial profit, will be passed over as too obvious to need discussion.

DUTY AS MOTIVE. Duty, which falls under the general head of sentiments in the list above, is the hardest worked motive of all. Do not understand from anything I say later that it should not be appealed to, both directly and indirectly. Most of us intend to meet our obligations, as we see them; and we subscribe in the main to the standards of duty to family, friends, employers, employees, institutions, and the state, as these standards are set up by society.

In the summer of 1917 a reporter asked the most successful recruiting sergeant in New York what he found the strongest argument for enlistment. He replied:

"Duty. I tell them more than anything else that this is their country, and that it is up to every man to defend it."

"Do you talk much about the good pay and the chances for promotion and that the government takes good care of them?"

"No, I don't. I find that the idea of the call of duty appeals to more persons than the idea that there is something in it for themselves."

And the editor of the *New York Tribune* commented:

As a matter of fact that was the appeal that won for the Liberty Loan. It was equally the argument that opened purses for the Red Cross. Human nature is a strange mixture. It holds a good deal of everything and a good deal of cantankerousness. Yet . . . there . . . is a fund of fineness and magnificence in the hearts of most humans that no crust of worldliness can disguise or conceal.

Whether we like it or not, despite all the croakers can say, when that stern old recruiting sergeant, Duty, gets us by the collar, there are precious few of us who try to wiggle away.[6]

That may be taken as fundamental truth; yet some qualifications remain to be made. First, the motive should be worthy of the deed. It would have been absurd to ask men to go to the trenches for a soldier's pay; duty was the fitting plea. The second observation is that in wartime we were not living on our usual plane. We believed we had a great cause, and that "every man must do his bit." As a young second lieutenant, coming in to say good-by, expressed it: "It's a dirty job and we hate it; but it just

[6] Editorial page, July 12, 1917. By permission of the *New York Herald Tribune.*

happens to be up to our generation to do it, and here goes." But we are not always on that level; and especially not as regards the simple, everyday duties in which there is no thrill, no adventure, but just nagging insistence.

At any rate, the motive of duty is greatly overworked; and especially, surprisingly enough, by young speakers. One's sense of duty becomes frazzled when he hears a dozen times a day of his duties; and he is likely to say, if he reacts at all, "Well, if I owe so much to my family, my college, my town, to the cause of peace and of preparedness, to my work, and to the football team, I'd better give up and try to do my duty by my tailor, who is threatening to sue."

A speaker attempted to induce us to go out and enjoy the natural beauties all about us. He told us of the benefits in a dry, pedagogical way, and wound up with, "You owe it to yourselves to profit by the wonderful country in which you are living." Even pleasure had become a duty, and an armchair by the fireside looked better than ever. Another told of the fun he had had in woods and mountains, with no *oughts* or *shoulds*. Which was more likely to make a convert? Why not talk sometimes of the pleasures of the course advocated; or better yet, *reveal* them so that we shall wish to share them? And do not conclude with that depressing bromide, "You will find this course both pleasant and profitable"; or worse, "both entertaining and educational." If it should be said, say it some other way.

Speaking at an alumni luncheon Elihu Root said:

I think it is a fine thing for the College that you should come back here. It encourages the President and the Faculty, it incites respect for the institution on the part of the undergraduates; but it is a hundred times more valuable to you who come back and let the memories of youth open up your susceptibilities and align you once more with that "society of educated men" to which you were admitted here. . . . When you come across a fellow graduate . . . who is too busy to come back, do not talk to him about his duty to the College; tell him he is neglecting the opportunity to create for himself the capacity for happiness.

And, I would add, tell him about the grand time you had at your last reunion.

APPROVAL AND ADMIRATION. We desire a good reputation with "our public," be it large or small; but most of us are most constantly affected by desire for the good opinion of those with whom we associate. "What will the neighbors think?" "What will the fellows think?" "What will *they* think?" are queries rarely far from our thoughts. We crave particularly the approval of close associates whom we respect, be they classmates, business colleagues, or fellow bandits; but we shrink from the disapproval of any one, even of complete strangers on the street. Just "It isn't being done" is often a potent remark.

And we wish our community, institution, or country to be approved. Probably with the average man the strongest argument against collecting the war debts was that Europeans were calling Uncle Sam "Uncle Shylock." The speaker who can present evidence to his hearers that their township's neglect of its roads is causing adverse comment by outsiders has a strong argument for improvement.

But we desire more than absence of disapproval; we wish admiration. We will undertake difficult and dangerous enterprises, or contribute money to causes for which we care nothing, for the sake of admiration and reputation. Some can be won to a cause by the chance to be seen associating with prominent people, to sit on a platform, to make a speech, to wear a badge. "You call these toys," Napoleon is said to have retorted to one who ridiculed the crosses of his Legion of Honor; "let me tell you that men are ruled by toys!" But whether swelling egotism be petty vanity or justified pride, that fine feeling can be utilized with great effect to lead us to correct our habits, to work for civic improvement, or to make sacrifices for the state.

This desire also involves institutions to which one belongs. The freshman glows with pride when the team wins, or his visitor praises the library; and the alumnus who remembers nothing but the smells of compulsory chemistry will subscribe handsomely to give Old Siwash the finest laboratory in the land. And this feeling, too, can be used to make us more useful members of society.

EMULATION. We desire to equal or surpass others, not only for the sake of reputation and praise, but also for the feeling of self-consequence. Like the desire for admiration, emulation may also take petty or noble forms, from the desire to have a better car than one's neighbor to desire to provide for the children of one's town an education equal to the best. Emulation may be compounded from boastfulness and public spirit. We must have a better town hall and better lighting than Blankville across the river. It is said that when, back in the 1860s, Agassiz went to the Massachusetts legislature to ask an appropriation to found a museum of research in zoölogy he was given a very cold reception, until he appealed to the pride they might have in a museum superior to any in the great European centers of culture.

Comparison must be made, of course, with some person, institution, or community one's hearers wish to emulate, else one may get the retort, "Who cares what they do?" On the other hand, it is sometimes possible to shame those who fail to equal the despised. "You sniff at X College; but let me tell you that same despised college has a better football team than ours. How long are we going to stand for that?" Few Americans can hear unmoved the truth that several countries we consider inferior have a lower murder rate than the United States.

DESIRE TO "SAVE FACE." This is plainly a matter of reputation, but in a special sense: the desire, not to make a good name, but to escape, through some pretense, the loss of prestige in defeat. We go far to save our dignity and social credit; we seek "alibis" and "outs." It is pleasanter to find that one's studies require all one's time than to admit that the coach said, "You needn't come back." In this matter much depends upon words. A nation may go to war rather than yield to an ultimatum, whereas it might graciously accede to a firm request.

Good persuasion often requires that we provide a plausible way for our hearers to save their faces when they change courses or withdraw from a stand they have taken. There is still value in the old device by which a speaker says, "There are those who mistakenly hold," rather than "You mistakenly hold," or "The old way was once justified, but in the light of present knowledge and under present conditions, we are coming to see that there is a better way." Or "Is there not a better way?" And it is never wise to prove one's hearers wrong in every respect. Go no further than is necessary in that direction; rather let them see that you recognize wherein they are right.

DOMINATION OR DESIRE FOR POWER. The desire to master both things and persons exists in all, though, like all motives, it is stronger in some than in others. We enjoy self-assertion, and especially we enjoy big achievements, chopping down a large tree, operating a machine that multiplies our powers, or, perhaps, bossing an organization small or large. This desire for domination can be used to arouse one's hearers to win games or elections, to build transcontinental railroads, or to subjugate a neighboring people.

However much we are gratified by dominating others, we desire *independence and liberty* for ourselves; and this desire can be utilized to stir us up against subjugation, personal, economic, or political. Our love of independence is the substance of many fervid pleas, of "Give me liberty or give me death!" "Britons never shall be slaves!" or Cassius' artful suggestion to Brutus, "Why, man, he doth bestride our little world like a Colossus!" of the grandiloquent question of Brutus to the Roman populace, "Had you rather Caesar were living and die all slaves, than that Caesar were dead and live all free men?" and of many homelier pleas, such as, "Let's get out into the woods where we can do as we please," and "Are you going to let that upstart boss you around?"

SECURITY. The plea for security seems to be peculiarly potent to-day; security for the old and security for the young, security of employment, security for the unemployed, and security of income; security from disease and suffering, for ourselves and for our families. We are opposed to any measures that threaten our positions and standing in the world, and favor measures that make them more secure.

ADVENTURE AND FIGHT. Opposed to this desire for security is the love of adventure and fight, which inspires explorers and pioneers in every field. The challenge to take a risk is provocative to many; and a sheer joy in fighting, popularly attributed to the Irish, is by no means confined to them. Come on, there's a good fight ahead, a fight against another gang, political faction, competing business, against natural forces and obstacles, for all sorts of causes, a fight for security, and even for peace. And while many of us prefer to fight from the sidelines, still we may encourage whatever promises a combat.

LOYALTY TO INSTITUTIONS. Pride in and loyalty to institutions is a strong motive with many people. Family feeling is strong. The Smiths simply do not do thus and so; the Smiths have always taken the lead in this and that. Similar feelings attach themselves to communities, colleges, fraternal organizations, churches, parties, states, and nations. "For the honor of" is often a potent phrase. Loyalty readily fuses with emulation, and becomes an ambition to equal or surpass rival institutions.

FAIR PLAY. We are quickly moved to resentment if we are shown that we are not receiving fair treatment from employers, colleagues, competitors, or foreign countries. I am more particularly concerned here with the fact that we cannot rest easy under the charge of unfairness in ourselves, and also with the fact that we resent unfairness to others, especially when it is directed toward the under dogs. We detest bullies. "Unfair" has become the standard slogan of picketers. Probably the most effective argument for woman's suffrage was the reiterated claim that women were not receiving a fair deal under man-made laws.

The appeal for fair play can be used in many situations; but I wish to stress its value in meeting prejudice against a speaker or his proposal. When Henry Ward Beecher delivered at Liverpool the speech referred to earlier in this chapter, he faced an extremely hostile audience, composed partly of roughs present for the express purpose of breaking up the meeting. When the uproar threatened to overwhelm him, he shouted, "All I ask is simply fair play!" And for several minutes the interruptions ceased. A Scotch evangelist who went out to preach on one of Chicago's worst corners was hooted and even spit upon by the crowd, who believed him sent by the hated capitalists. "Is not this America?" he cried; "shall I not have free speech?" "Yes," they retorted, "and so shall we!" "But you give me no chance; give me five minutes." The crowd voted that fair and listened.

But we have to face silent as well as boisterous prejudice; and have to open the minds of those who listen only to reject, and upon whose minds arguments and pleas have as little effect as birdshot on an armored tank. Sometimes the plea can be made openly; as:

Ladies and Gentlemen of the jury: The prosecution has brought an imposing array of witnesses against my client, and at this stage of the trial appearances are against him. I ask you, nevertheless, to suspend judgment, as it is your sworn duty to do, until you have heard our side of the case; and I assure you that we shall explain away these appearances, and prove to you that my client is the victim of a conspiracy.

Or the attorney might ask each member of the jury to imagine himself the victim of circumstances and placed in the position of the defendant. Or a speaker might say:

I am aware that some of you look upon my proposal as hare-brained, and even dangerous; but your presence here indicates a willingness to hear it stated by one who understands it. I shall endeavor to misstate no facts and strain no logic; and if I keep that pledge, I am sure you will accord me the grace of a fair hearing. Probably there are some important facts and considerations that have not come to your attention; and possibly my plan has been somewhat misrepresented to you. I have never proposed . . . What I do propose is this . . . Perhaps even this does not meet with your approval; but will you not suspend judgment until I give my reasons?

There may be danger in suggesting that one's hearers are not fair-minded, for they may be priding themselves on their fairness. Are they not listening?—though in truth their listening may be in the spirit of the man who said, "I am quite open to conviction, but I'd like to see the man who can convince me." But however dangerous, the plea for a fair hearing, open or concealed, is often in order. (The discussion of common ground in the next chapter bears directly upon the problem of gaining a candid hearing.)

FEAR. We have emphasized the things men desire; and generally this is the better note to strike. We do not forget, however, that we are much influenced by fear. But we need not here dwell upon this topic, for we should only be putting the reverse of what has been said. We fear the loss of approval, prestige, security, and so on. If our picture of benefits fails to move, we may speak in terms of the losses and dangers that will result from failure to act. And when we speak in opposition to a proposal we naturally dwell upon the dangers of the course proposed, seeking to generate a mood of doubt and fear fatal to action.

STUDY MOTIVES. If there is such a creature as the born orator, one of his marked characteristics must be that he has an instinctive sense of the attitudes, sentiments, and motives of the mass of people; and does not have to calculate them because he shares them. But most of us, too self-centered for that, need to study and plan to meet our audiences on common ground. And this is especially true when our way of life keeps us from close touch with common men. We may say that William Jennings Bryan had a knowledge of human nature by birth and environment as well as by study; while Theodore Roosevelt, less the orator in a conventional sense, but a highly effective speaker none the less, overcame the handicap of having been born "with a gold spoon in his mouth" by deliberately mingling with and studying all kinds of people.

A good way for the student of speech-making to encourage the invaluable habit of observing human nature is to start a list, with brief comment, of the motives he observes in himself and in those about him; and I suggest, in order that the task may not become too laborious for persistence, that he should not attempt strict classification, or mind some overlapping.

# CHAPTER XVI

# PERSUASION AND BELIEF

In the three preceding chapters we have been considering persuasion more particularly in those cases in which our audiences offer only passive resistance. We shall consider now more especially those cases in which there is positive opposition to overcome. It should be understood, however, that the suggestions already made are applicable in great part to the problems now before us, and that the suggestions now to be made are largely applicable to the problems already discussed. But it may be said that, in a general way, we are proceeding from lesser to greater opposition.

A speaker may seek to change a belief of his audience because that belief stands in the way of action he wishes them to take, as when he argues for a political measure in order to win votes for it; or he may simply wish to change their belief regardless of any effect upon conduct, as in arguing before a non-scientific audience for a doctrine of evolution.

SOURCES OF BELIEF. Many of our beliefs we have absorbed from environment—from parents, teachers, and companions—as unconsciously as the head-hunter of Borneo acquired the belief that to capture human heads is the best way to prove his manhood. He simply grew up in a community where the successful head-hunter is honored. So it is with our deepest beliefs, those that have most to do with our characters, beliefs as to what is right and what is wrong, honorable and dishonorable, what is success and what is failure, what is fun and what is tiresome, who should be associated with and who avoided, and many other beliefs affecting our daily lives. Such beliefs, sometimes so deep that we are unconscious of them and never put them into words, are the real major premises of our thinking and acting.

We also acquire beliefs by more conscious experience, to which we may or may not add reflection; as belief that fire burns, that all Chinese are laundrymen, and innumerable beliefs true and false. Then we have beliefs which we have arrived at through the reasoning process. When a partisan concludes that certain policies and candidates are good because they are put forward by his party, the reasoning is rudimentary. From this grade we progress to that in which, after strict investigation and the application of logical principles, we arrive at a genuinely scientific conclusion.

WHY WE BELIEVE. "Every idea, concept, or conclusion is held true unless hindered by some contradictory idea." Consider how much is accepted on appearances, mere "say-so" or suggestion. We usually accept the face of the clock or the word of any passerby as to the time of day. We accept the assertion of the physicist that the speed of light is approximately 186,000 miles a second; and, unless we had some special reason to doubt, we should accept an assertion to that effect from any one who spoke with confidence. If I tell you that Daniel Webster is commonly considered the greatest of American orators, you will probably accept my statement.

"Belief is passive; doubt is active." If to doubt means to question, to test, to demand evidence, then obviously we believe more readily than we doubt; for doubting requires thinking and thinking requires effort. To accept is easier.

Acceptance is also in many cases necessary. I lack time,

ability, and facilities to determine for myself the speed of light, the exact time of day, the price of wheat on the Chicago market, or the purity of the milk I buy. I accept somebody's word, be it right or wrong. And we accept authority for more than facts. Many so-called questions of policy, say the advisability of inflation, involve such complicated masses of evidence and such difficult reasoning that we feel it is better to accept the opinion of one whom we trust than to attempt their solution ourselves. The fact that we may go too far in letting others do our thinking for us does not affect the fact that we do accept very much from others.

So it may be said that if a fact or opinion is suggested to us without objections or doubts in our minds, either because of the source from which it comes or of the way in which it is presented, and if it does not run counter to any of our accepted beliefs, desires, or prejudices, we accept it, at least for the time being.

But if a fact or opinion is presented in a way or from a source which provokes doubt, or if it seems inherently improbable, then it will not be accepted without question. If it is presented hesitantly it will lack the ring of authority; if it comes from a candidate one is opposing it may be condemned by its source; if it runs counter to our established beliefs, as that parallel lines never meet, or that intercollegiate sports are more important than intramural, then it will probably be rejected. Then more than presentation will be required before acceptance is won. If you share the rather common belief that the speeches of Daniel Webster are high-flown, you will not be likely to accept my offhand assertion that, taken as a whole, they are chiefly remarkable for orderliness, clarity, and simplicity. You may put the assertion aside as unimportant, or prejudiced; but if you consider the matter you will wish proof.

### HOW TO WIN BELIEF

It would seem, then, the business of one who would win others to a given view either to present it in such a way that it will be accepted without question; or, if need be, to win from indifference and opposition the grace of a fair hearing, and then to argue away doubts and objections.

GAUGE THE RESISTANCE. The wise speaker will make the best estimate he can of the resistance he faces. In the first place he can *consider the nature of the belief he wishes to change.* It is a mistake to suppose that reasoned opinions are harder to dislodge than those merely accepted. Those are most persistent which have become embedded in one's systems of thought—what one thinks on such subjects as morals, religion, social obligations, politics, and business—and have entered into one's habitual conduct. The persuader, then, has a harder task, generally speaking, when he deals with the more intimate beliefs of his audience than when he deals with those beliefs which relate to matters which touch them only indirectly. It would be much harder to change the belief of business men as to the ethics of a business practice than their belief regarding the independence of the Philippines. It is also true that we are likely to listen less tolerantly to arguments against beliefs we have merely grown into and accepted, than to arguments against those beliefs we have reached by reasoning, and which we realize, in most instances, are not inevitable conclusions.

In the second place, the speaker may ask himself, *Is my prospective audience,* on the whole, *conservative or liberal in its tendencies?* [1]

[1] The terms *conservative* and *liberal* must here be dissociated from special meanings they have acquired in relation to creeds and parties. *Radical* as an antonym for *conservative* is unsatisfactory. It has come to refer to the attitude of one who carries out his beliefs in extreme

There is often difficulty in judging the conservatism of a general audience; but certain considerations may help. It is the common view that the English-speaking peoples do not favor drastic changes. That does not mean that they do not change their practices, and change them extensively, or that they are not leaders in pioneering in every realm; yet it is true that the change in England from an almost absolute monarchy to one of the freest of governments has come about piecemeal and by a long series of compromises. A speaker before most American audiences can hardly expect to win favor for revolutionary changes, even in this era which we look upon as one of rapid change. Americans in general will prefer to tinker up an old system rather than to adopt a new, and the closer the matter comes to their daily lives the greater their reluctance to make a drastic change.

The young speaker, particularly one who has spent four years in a liberal atmosphere and is perhaps filled with enthusiasm for a juster world to be gained soon, will do well to note this tendency to make haste slowly. To ignore it is to furnish a weapon to opponents. Just a sneer at youthful enthusiasm may be enough to ruin his plea. Many even of those kindly disposed to reform simply cannot believe great improvement possible; they have been disappointed too often. "What you say sounds good; but it is too good to be true, human nature being what it is. But maybe we could do something."

It is commonly assumed that we grow more conservative with age; and there is some basis for this assumption. It is certainly true of those who are mere creatures of routine; and many become such at an early age. It is less true of those who are well informed about the past and alert to the

fashion. In this sense Trotsky seems to be more radical than Stalin, but also more conservative in holding to his views on communism.

present. These are not like a freshman who, finding a recently established custom in his college, thinks it is a sacred tradition. They realize that the impossibilities of fifty years ago are the commonplaces of to-day and are not unduly awed by the wisdom of the past. On the other hand, they are not hospitable to panaceas which they know have been tried before and have failed. One man of this type, an economist, described himself as a "conservative radical." To an enthusiast for change, any change, such a man may seem a hidebound conservative; but it does not follow that he is not open to pleas for genuinely progressive measures.

The young may be more adaptable, have fewer set ideas; they are less bound by routine and, having fewer responsibilities, are freer to gamble on change. But touch them on the beliefs that enter into their daily conduct and you will understand why Woodrow Wilson, after years as teacher and college president, indorsed the old saying that a young conservative has the hardest shell of all.

The newer parts of the country are generally thought to be less under the influence of old ideas than the older sections; but we cannot depend upon sectional characteristics, unless it be with reference to particular questions. While the Middle West may be more friendly than New England to political innovations, it is more orthodox in religion. No doubt some communities of long and peaceful existence, like many New England and Southern towns, with numerous old families, complacent local pride, and valued traditions, exhibit a reluctance to change, even a calm disregard for proposals for change, that is the despair of would-be innovators. Such a community may cherish even its nuisances. To suggestions that a change would make for greater beauty, convenience, or efficiency, it may turn a deaf ear, less in opposition than in indifference. Its attitude may be that of the farmer who replied when asked why he did not blast out a rock much in his way, "It has always been there."

Both individuals and communities may be conservative about some propositions and liberal toward others. I have known men of thoroughly scientific attitude in their own fields who were extremely set and prejudiced in their political opinions.

And that reminds us that the tendency to resist change is not limited to the ignorant. The advance of science has been made against the resistance of many scientists. Harvey and Pasteur are familiar examples of those whose discoveries have been condemned. Even the so-called pure scientists hate to change fundamental beliefs. William Patten, noted biologist, wrote in his later years:

The expert, like every one else, once "set" is not easily moved. For he "makes up" his mind as the maid makes up the bed—puts blankets on it and a pillow for his head. Then, let the wind blow as it may, no draft of unwelcome facts can disturb his slumber.[2]

Conservatism may be expected from those who have a goodly stake in the *status quo,* who have property, income, social position, a safe niche which they fear may be disturbed by change, whether or not the immediate proposal affects them directly. And naturally most favorable to change are those who are dissatisfied with their status, who feel that "things could not be worse and might be better."

Thirdly, and most important, *the persuader will wish to ascertain,* as well as may be in advance, *how his audience will react to his particular proposition.* In this he will be aided by the general considerations set forth above, and by the

[2] *The Dartmouth Alumni Magazine,* April, 1926.

further knowledge that resistance is to be expected from those individuals and institutions whose rights and powers are in any way decreased by his proposal. My scientific friend who went into government service assuming that suggestions for more efficient and economical methods would be welcomed soon found that he was becoming unpopular with both his fellow workers and his chief. Efficiency meant smaller personnel, smaller appropriations for the department, and less prestige for its head. The persuader can expect resistance also from those whose habits of thought and action, whose routine, would be affected. They are likely to make themselves believe not only that they would be injured but that their whole institution or community would be damaged with them.

But no one should rely entirely upon general consideration or upon what he guesses are the facts concerning his audience. Whenever feasible he should investigate by means of inquiry and by actually talking with those who are representative of his prospective audience. How far astray one may go is illustrated by what happened to a candidate for the New Jersey legislature. He was sent by his party's speakers' bureau to speak before a branch of the American Workers' Union. He assumed that this was a regular labor union, and launched into a tirade against huge expenditures for the relief of those who had never worked and never wished to work; and then found to his horror that he had been addressing an organization of people on relief. At the election he was the worst defeated of all his party's candidates.

Two observations, which will be developed later, may properly be mentioned here because of their relation to what precedes and what follows: first, the speaker on sizing up the situation will at times find that he is confronted by beliefs that he cannot hope and should not attempt to change; and, second, it is generally unwise, in any event, to prove more than is necessary to his case; or, in more technical language, to take on a heavier burden of proof than is necessary.

WIN A RECEPTIVE ATTITUDE. When you attempt to change a person's belief you usually start with the odds against you. However ready we may be to accept a belief in regard to a subject on which we have as yet no convictions, we ordinarily do not like to change beliefs already adopted. It is an uncomfortable process. Pride in consistency also works against change; and our attitude of resistance may be stiffened by a feeling of resentment, perhaps faint and perhaps stronger, against one who deliberately sets himself to change our minds.

While the presentation of sound arguments is a very important part of winning belief, we have to consider the more emotional phases of the process; because, first, emotion has much to do with determining what are good arguments—that is, what considerations are important—and, secondly, because the soundest of reasoning will not avail if the attitude of the listener is set against the speaker or his conclusion.

A person with a hostile set of mind does not give a fair hearing; he discounts the claims made, he questions the facts, and he challenges the deductions. His whole attitude is *No*. But if we can make our hearers willing to listen fairly, we are well started. If we can make them willing to believe, we are well on our way. If we can make them wish to believe, we have the odds in our favor.

THE APPROACH. It is evident that in the effort to change a resistant to a receptive attitude much will depend upon first impressions. It was Cicero who said that the purpose of an introduction is "to render the audience well-disposed toward the speaker, attentive toward his speech, and open to conviction." Genung lays stress on the "speaker's alliance with his audience," a phrase worth remembering. This relationship is much affected by the speaker's characteristics, a topic that will be treated in a later chapter. We proceed here to other matters important in winning a fair hearing.

AVOID CONTENTIOUSNESS. Sometimes a speaker makes the mistake of emphasizing the difference of opinion between himself and his hearers, and makes his speech a fight from the start. There is point in the humorous exaggeration a story-writer put into the mouth of a character during the campaign for woman's suffrage:

"Mother, you made your first grand mistake in running votes-for-women as a controversy. I don't know a man in my set who understands yet what the arguments against women's suffrage are. But you people labeled it a battle and we are just filling in the mob cues."

A frank answering of objections in your hearers' minds need not be belligerent. You need not go on the warpath. In candid minds loyalty to truth offsets the natural inclination to resist; but even candid minds are with difficulty kept open when the speaker carries a contentious air, especially if there is also a note of superiority and triumph. Ida Tarbell somewhere uses a significant phrase in praising the Canadian leader MacDonald: "He is a convincing speaker whom one does not resent."

DON'T CONDEMN THOSE WHO DISAGREE. One way to avoid contentiousness is to treat with respect the opinions of those who disagree. Avoid the example of a speaker on war: War has no conceivable justification; he who defends war is a fool and a monster. The speech was as unreasonable as war itself. No attempt was made to lead us step by step; offhand we were to rise and rage, or be forever damned.

Not only should we avoid condemning those we hope to win over, but we should refrain from unbridled attacks upon persons we are opposing. There is danger of turning sympathy away from ourselves. Audiences realize that few persons are as black as they can be painted; and good feeling is chilled by ruthless assault. The audience may begin to wonder if the speaker is a well poised individual and can be altogether in the right.

Particularly unpersuasive are abusive epithets. It is an odd fact that a hard name is much more offensive than other words embodying the same meaning. Say, if you must, that an opponent has misrepresented the truth, but do not call him *liar,* unless you wish to start a fight. The offensiveness of an epithet may be greater or less according to the person to whom it is applied. Wendell Phillips, himself an extravagant denouncer who once called Lincoln a monkey, said to Charles Remond when he called Washington a villain, "Charles, the epithet is not felicitous." The fact that Washington held slaves was as offensive to Phillips as to Remond, but he knew that Washington was a sacred memory while Lincoln was as yet in the public mind only a politician. Benjamin Lundy, another uncompromising foe of slavery, held that "the language of cutting retort and severe rebuke is seldom convincing, and it is wholly out of place in persuasive speech."

When Daniel Webster was arguing for the conviction of John Francis Knapp for the murder of Joseph White, he wished to tell the jury that the testimony of both the father and the brother of the prisoner was untrue; but he did not call them liars or perjurers. With the brother he was very severe both in cross-examination and in summation; but he recognized that the young man had been placed in a hard position by the fact that the lives of two brothers might depend upon his testimony. The father was a pitiable figure, recently broken by bankruptcy, and now with two sons under indictment for murder. Denunciation might have turned sympathy against Webster. Of the old man he said:

I find myself incapable of speaking of him or his testimony with severity. Unfortunate old man! Another Lear in the conduct of his children; another Lear I fear in the effect of his distress upon his mind and understanding. . . . Unhappy father, he strives to remember, perhaps persuades himself that he does remember that on the evening of the murder he was himself home at ten o'clock. He thinks, or seems to think, that his son came in at about five minutes past ten. . . . Alas! these are but the swimming fancies of an agitated and distressed mind.[3]

Some terms are offensive *per se;* others may or may not be according to the tone given them or the disposition of the audience before which they are used. "When you call me *that,* smile," said Owen Wister's Virginian. *Respectable* is in some groups a compliment, in others an insult. *Successful politician, Victorian, bolshevik, capitalist, reformer, enthusiast, professor, suave, Yankee* are examples of terms with implications varying with the tone and the company in which they are uttered.

It is true that offensive epithets may be used to label leaders and causes in the hope of deterring the neutral from joining them. In this connection there come to mind such terms as *tory, bourbon, mugwump, copperhead, economic royalist.* Offensive epithets may be used, also, to stigmatize

---

[3] The case is in *American State Trials,* Vol. III, p. 395. Less persuasive is the way in which Webster exaggerates the evidence in the passage from which the excerpt is taken.

conduct the speaker wishes to discourage; as the term *muck-raker* brought into disrepute a certain type of journalist. But it would be hard to find a person who was induced to change his belief by calling him a hard name.

There is no doubt a time for denunciation. Even Jesus did not hesitate to call the Pharisees "extortioners," "whited sepulchers," and "hypocrites." William Lloyd Garrison, leader of the abolitionists, who once went so far as to call the Constitution "a covenant with death and an agreement with hell," answered the remonstrances which his extreme language provoked, "I must be hot for I have mountains of ice all about me." But he and Phillips were agitators, not hoping so much to change the views of their hearers as to keep the slavery question in the public mind and defeat the "conspiracy of silence." But whatever justification there may be for denunciation, we cannot expect those denounced, or those in sympathy with them, to view our proposals favorably. There are times when a man should be knocked down, but not when we wish to bring him into an attitude of "sweet reasonableness."

FIND COMMON GROUND. Usually it is wise not to begin argument immediately, but rather to seek alliance by getting on common ground with those in opposition. The principle runs throughout our subject: To explain a subject to an audience we must meet our hearers on familiar ground and go from what they know to what they do not. To move them to action we must meet them on the ground of common motives. We have considered the necessity of finding a common ground of interest and leading on from this in accordance with the principle of derived interest.

To find a *common ground of interest* is also persuasive. We tend to like a person who shares our interests, as in some sport, hobby, or business; and we are apt to assume that he is a proper sort of man, wise in his general outlook. Consider how casual acquaintances, meeting perhaps on a railway journey, uneasy at first in each other's company, are drawn together by discovering that they have common enthusiasms, have grown up in the same town, have had common experiences, even the same ailments. The more of a stranger a speaker is to his listeners and the further he is from them in occupation and general outlook, the more need he has to touch upon common interests.

Finding common interests will help, as already intimated, in finding *common ground of feeling*. The awakening of old memories or emphasis upon common likes and dislikes may also serve. When on October 2, 1933, President Roosevelt went before the convention of the American Legion, the situation was difficult because of his well known opposition to the bonus the veterans were demanding. Early in his speech he called attention to the fact that he too had had a part in the War; he spent much of his time on ideas that all could applaud; he talked of the needs of the country in that time of depression and pointed out that the interests of the veterans were the same as the interests of other citizens; he stressed the point that a bankrupt government could not discharge its obligation to the needy and restore prosperity; he heartily agreed that veterans suffering from wounds or in ill health because of war service must be cared for; and he spent very little time in telling them, what presumably he went there chiefly to tell them, that "no person, because he wore a uniform, must thereafter be placed in a special class of beneficiaries over and above all other citizens." It cannot be recorded that the Legion ceased its agitation for the bonus; but the speech was well received and was considered a success because in a very difficult situation the President succeeded in voicing a firm opposition without awakening resentment.

When in 1912 Theodore Roosevelt was leading great numbers of Republicans into the Progressive or "Bull Moose" party, an Old Guard Republican, in striving to hold them back, would attempt to meet them on a common ground of feeling, dwelling upon the historical glories of the Grand Old Party and its heroes; and then point out that the probable result of their defection would be the triumph of the common foe, the Democrats.

Stories are often used to banish initial strain and produce a feeling of friendliness. Hostility can hardly survive the sharing of emotion; and especially is it blown away by a gust of laughter. And here we find, perhaps, the only justification for the use of stories and other materials not applicable to one's subject; but it is much more skilful to establish a common bond of interest and feeling out of the materials which also serve to introduce the subject.

The third phase of common ground is *common ground of belief*. The three phases blend, of course, as in the President's speech to the Legion. Good feeling results when the audience sees that the speaker's views are in some respects in harmony with their own; and this tends to the belief that his present proposal is not, after all, impossible. Also it is a bit of a wrench to stop agreeing with a man with whom you have gone some way in harmony. Once heads are nodding in assent they tend to go on nodding.

When Wendell Phillips addressed the Phi Beta Kappa Society at Harvard, he had before him an exceptionally distinguished and conservative audience, in which were many who disapproved of him as a reckless agitator. Barrett Wendell says:

A good many went to hear him with much curiosity as to what he might say, and apprehension that they might have to disapprove it by silence at moments which to less balanced minds might seem to call for applause. In the earlier parts of his oration they found themselves agreeably surprised: he said nothing to which they were unprepared to assent, and what he said, he said beautifully. They listened with relief and satisfaction; when the moment for applause came, they cordially applauded. So the oration went on with increasing interest on the part of the audience. Finally when some fresh moment for applause came, they applauded as a matter of course.[4]

And so finally they applauded Russian Nihilism and the assassination of czars.

The fact that common ground can be, and probably was in this instance, used somewhat slyly, does not make it a less legitimate method. It is, indeed, at the basis of all constructive discussion. In most cases people differ less than they suppose. It has been said that there never was a war that could not have been prevented by honest men come together for frank discussion, meeting each other on common ground and making mutual compromises. That is overstatement; but nevertheless there was wisdom in the man who, when invited by another to "talk over our differences," replied, "No, let's talk over our agreements."

When Abraham Lincoln was first inaugurated the Confederate government had already been formed; but the question of secession was still at issue in the border states. In these states were many, especially the former Whigs, who, while alarmed at Mr. Lincoln's attitude toward slavery, were still reluctant to leave the Union. In his inaugural address Lincoln made slavery almost an incidental

[4] Barrett Wendell, *English Composition*, p. 243. By permission of Charles Scribner's Sons.

question and put his stress upon his oft-expressed view that
the paramount issue was the preservation of the Union.
Almost immediately he attempted to relieve the fear of
Southerners that "their property and their peace and their
personal security are to be endangered. . . . I have no purpose, directly or indirectly, to interfere with the institution
of slavery where it exists." The Constitution provides for
the return of fugitive slaves, and he intends to abide by the
Constitution in all respects. He is then ready to take up
the question of secession; and he argues that the Union was
intended to be, and is by its nature, perpetual (familiar
Whig doctrine), and expresses his determination to maintain
it, peaceably if possible. Only the people can change the
nature of the government; and he is quite willing that
amendments to the Constitution shall be made, even one "to
the effect that the Federal government shall never interfere
with the domestic institutions of the States, including that of
persons held to service."

In your hands, my dissatisfied countrymen, and not in mine,
is the momentous issue of civil war. The government will not
assail you. You can have no conflict without being yourselves
the aggressors. . . .
I am loath to close. We are not enemies, but friends. We
must not be enemies. Though passion may have strained, it must
not break, our bonds of affection. The mystic chords of memory,
stretching from every battlefield and patriot grave to every living
heart and hearthstone all over this broad land, will yet swell the
chorus of the Union when again touched, as surely they will be,
by the better angels of our nature.

The passions of the hour being what they were, it was
probably too late to prevent war, unless Lincoln would make
concessions which he felt to be impossible. There was an

"irrepressible conflict" which had with difficulty been held down for years. The extremists of neither side were pleased with the address; but sober-minded lovers of the Union everywhere could unite upon it. The description of its preparation given by Nicolay and Hay, Lincoln's biographers, makes it clear that Lincoln studied every phrase and, up to the last feasible moment, made changes in the hope of conciliating and holding in the Union a part of the South.[5]

Finding common ground is helpful not only in forming an alliance between speaker and audience but also in securing harmony among factions of the audience itself. When in December, 1876, George William Curtis spoke at the New England dinner in New York, the country was tremendously excited over the question of whether Hayes or Tilden had been elected President, a controversy which carried with it the possibility of civil war.[6] Curtis faced passionate partisans of both sides. The discreet way would have been to avoid the question on this festal occasion; but Curtis would not. Before the end he had those distinguished and normally reserved men standing on chairs and cheering his demand for a peaceful, lawful settlement. He enlivened the early part of his address with humor, and said many pleasant things about their common mother, New England; he talked of the New England spirit, which he found to be "liberty under law."

It provides us a lawful remedy for every emergency that may arise. . . .

The voice of New England, I believe, going to the capital, would be this, that neither is the Republican Senate to insist upon

---

[5] See *Abraham Lincoln: A History*, Vol. III, Chapter XXI.
[6] C. R. Lingley, *Since the Civil War*, p. 52.

its exclusive partisan way, nor is the Democratic House to insist upon its exclusive partisan way, but Senate and House, representing the American people and the American people only, in the light of the Constitution and by the authority of the law, are to provide a way over which a President, be he Republican or be he Democrat, shall pass unchallenged to his chair.[7]

Edward Everett Hale, who heard the speech, wrote:

Those three hundred men of mark in New York went home that night, and went to their businesses next day, to say that a court of arbitration must be established to settle the controversy. In that moment of Mr. Curtis's triumph, as I believe, it was settled.

If you read the whole speech you will find that Curtis not only started on common ground, but that he never left common ground; and yet he brought two heatedly differing factions into enthusiastic agreement. Probably the chief reason for the amazing outburst of approval was that as he neared his suggestion, his hearers *saw for themselves* that this was the only possible stand for sons of New England to take.

The usefulness of common ground is not limited to cases where antagonism exists. Henry Ward Beecher has put the case well. He tells how as a boy he never hit anything with his gun until his father showed him how to take aim. When he became a preacher he failed for two years to get results from his sermons. Then he reviewed all the sermons of the apostles:

And I studied the sermons until I got this idea: That the apostles were accustomed first to feel for a ground on which the

[7] George William Curtis, *Orations and Addresses*, Vol. I, pp. 247f. By permission of Harper & Brothers.

people and they stood together; a common ground where they could meet. Then they heaped up a large number of the particulars of knowledge that belonged to everybody; and when they got that knowledge, which everybody would admit, placed in proper form before their minds, then they brought it to bear upon them with all their excited heart and feeling. This was the first definite idea of taking aim that I had in mind. "Now," said I, "I will make a sermon so." [8]

The results of his first sermon following out this idea were so marked that he adds, "I never felt so triumphant in my life. . . . I said to myself, 'Now I know how to preach.'"

The speech by Curtis, Lincoln's First Inaugural, and the address by Booker T. Washington, to be discussed presently, all illustrate the fact that common ground is not, as is sometimes assumed, useful only in the early part of a speech. It is only more conspicuously useful there. In every effectual argument there must be, indeed, elements to which both parties agree.

There are times when the common ground is too evident to need elaboration, or even statement; but in any case it is well for the speaker to think out its boundaries so that he will make no false assumptions of agreements that do not exist, or fail to take advantage of those that do.

EXPLANATIONS AND ELIMINATIONS. In order to determine how much is agreed upon, to get rid of matter which has no proper part in the argument, and so to come to the real points at issue, if any remain, it is often important to clear the ground by explanation. Some listeners may be in opposition simply because the proposal has not been properly explained to them. Sometimes it will have been deliberately

[8] *Yale Lectures on Preaching*, First Series, p. 11.

misrepresented by opponents. Racial, sectional, or other prejudices may have been aroused. A "whispering campaign" may have been carried on to make people believe that sinister forces are at work. "Red herrings may have been dragged across the trail." If the drive is against corruption in the city government, the grafters will be sure to raise the cry that "the fair name of our city is being besmirched" by the revelations and the wicked reformers are seeking personal aggrandizement.

During Washington's second administration the country became greatly excited over the British treaty negotiated by John Jay. Even after its ratification an attempt was made in the House of Representatives to defeat the treaty by refusing to pass the laws necessary for carrying it into effect. Fisher Ames made the most notable speech for the treaty, in the course of which he said:

We hear it said that this is a struggle for liberty, a manly resistance against the design to nullify this assembly and to make it a cypher in the government; that the President and the Senate, the numerous meetings in the cities and the influence of the general alarm of the country, are agents and instruments of a scheme of coercion and terror to force the treaty down our throats, though we loathe it, and in spite of the clearest convictions of duty and conscience.

It is necessary to pause here and consider whether suggestions of this kind be not unfair in their very texture and fabric, and pernicious in all their influences. They oppose an obstacle in the path of inquiry, not simply discouraging, but absolutely unsurmountable. They will not yield to argument; for as they were not reasoned up, they cannot be reasoned down. . . . While this remains it is vain to argue.[9]

[9] E. B. Williston, *Eloquence of the United States*, Vol. I, p. 426. This speech will repay study. It is notable for the way in which the speaker philosophizes about the problems of argument, as well as

But there may be misunderstanding that is not due to passion or misrepresentation. Often, of course, your audience has not heard of your proposition in advance. Sometimes the best way to clear the ground and arrive at a common understanding is to set forth the *history of the question*. The proposition that the United States had no right to let American ships pass through its own Panama Canal free of charge, while demanding payment from the ships of other nations (a lively question back in Wilson's administration), struck many as absurd on the face of it; but when an affirmative speaker set forth the series of treaties by which we acquired the right to build the canal at all, the absurdity disappeared, and his audience was ready to meet him on the common ground that we should abide by our treaties. The issue then became a matter of construction of the treaties.

*Definition of terms* is often needed. It is common experience that disputes often arise from the lack of common understanding of words; and that when each party learns what the other really means, the disagreement is over. "Oh, if that is what you mean," says a disputant, "I agree with you." Especially do such words as *democracy, temperance, socialism, fascism* need definition. If you assert that a British subject is freer than an American citizen, you will do well to explain what you mean by freedom. Recently I heard the discussion that followed an address by a European lawyer in which he had argued that the European way of deciding cases in accordance with natural law is better than our way of following precedent. But as he was either unwilling or unable to tell us what he meant by "natural law," we never did reach the point of intelligent discussion.

---

for other qualities. We are told that the young Daniel Webster committed its thirty-eight pages to memory.

A dictionary definition may serve the purpose, but often it will not.[10] If you are discussing an old age pension system, the dictionary will not help you to explain whether you mean $200 a month for all over sixty, or $30 a month for those without other income, and who have no children to support them; whether you would permit pensioners to retain such property as they have, and whether the system should be state, federal, or both.

CONCESSIONS AND ADMISSIONS. One of the most unpopular men I know never concedes anything. To the simplest claim he demurs; to the assertion of the most obvious fact he retorts, "That is your opinion." He insists that you make all the six-inch putts of argument.

No means of finding common ground, removing distrust, and establishing good feeling is more important than making concessions. We dislike one who would prove us altogether wrong, leaving us without a leg to stand on, and giving us no chance to save our faces. Instead of admitting he is right, we ignore his proof, become sullen, seek small flaws in his argument, or take refuge in calling him names. But if the speaker will be generous in admitting that we have some right on our side, we shall be ashamed to be less generous with him. Concessions provoke concessions; but if the speaker, like Charles Sumner, thumps the table and roars, "There is no other side," we shall certainly get our backs up.

However effective with their own partisans, those advocates of the New Deal are not the most effective in winning new adherents who ridicule all conservative ideas, scoff at the "founding fathers," the Constitution, "rugged indi-

[10] A valuable illustration of this problem, and its solution, will be found in Baker and Huntington, *The Principles of Argumentation* (1905), pp. 24ff. This illustration involves the word *statesmanlike*.

vidualism," and the "horse-and-buggy days"; denounce business men, flout the idea that the states could solve some of our problems, and demand a complete abolition of old methods. Nor are those the most effective defenders of the older order who attack President Roosevelt as an incipient fascist who is bankrupting the country, destroying American character and institutions, and seeking to become a dictator. Such advocates only intensify the opposition.

Those advocates of woman's suffrage were most effective who admitted that woman's best place was in the home and urged that women needed the ballot to protect their homes and children. And those advocates of prohibition won most votes who did not view with horror the sinfulness of every drink, but argued that the industrial and social welfare of the country required that even moderate drinkers should sacrifice their desires in order that the evils of intemperance might be abolished.

What one cannot honestly concede, he can, if it is not necessary to his argument, ignore, or "admit for the sake of argument," and thereby escape unnecessary contention. To overstate one's case, on the other hand, to claim everything, to refuse to admit what is true, and even to insist upon claims that have some validity, but are open to effective assault, is to lay one's self open to damaging rebuttal. In his defense of Father Damien, Robert Louis Stevenson says:

> Damien has been too much depicted with a conventional halo. . . . It is the least defect of such a portraiture that it makes the path easy for the devil's advocate, and leaves for the misuse of the slanderer a considerable field of truth. For the truth that is suppressed by friends is the readiest weapon of the enemy.

Taking on too heavy a burden of proof by conceding nothing and claiming everything is one of the commonest faults of the inexperienced arguer. He is constantly being taken up on such assertions as "There are no good corporations," "The present system is absolutely wrong," "The proposal is completely vicious," "This remedy will wipe out the entire evil," "Preparedness always leads to war"; and rebuttal of his overstatements often blinds his audience to the truth he may have on his side.

The man who concedes nothing may rally his partisans and be a good "rabble-rouser," but he is not likely to succeed in winning over objectors or neutrals. Of these he tends to drive the unthinking into hostility, or greater hostility, and to cause the thoughtful to doubt his fairness and soundness.

An admission may not only be a good way to impress an audience with one's candor, but may serve also to take the wind out of an opponent's sails. In his defense of Loeb and Leopold, Clarence Darrow replied to the prosecution's taunt that the defendants had pleaded guilty because they did not dare to go before a jury:

Your Honor, that is true. . . . We did plead guilty because we were afraid to submit our case to a jury. . . . I am aware that a court has more experience, more judgment, more kindliness than a jury.

A famous speech that illustrates several of the above suggestions, skilful use of common ground, concession and admission, and the ignoring of contentious matter not necessary to his theme, is the address of Booker T. Washington at the Atlanta Exposition. "This was the first time in the entire history of the Negro," says Washington,[11] "that a member

[11] From *Up From Slavery* by Booker T. Washington, p. 211; copyright, 1900-1928, reprinted by permission of Doubleday, Doran & Company, Inc.

of my race had been asked to speak on the same platform with white men and women on any important national occasion"; and he remembered that he had been a slave. There had been much opposition to the invitation. The auditorium was packed, the greater part of the audience being Southern whites, with a considerable number of Northern whites, and a good many Negroes. Washington agreed heartily with his white neighbor who had said to him, "I am afraid you have got yourself into a tight place."

When I entered the room, there were vigorous cheers from the coloured portion of the audience, and faint cheers from some of the white people. I had been told, while I was in Atlanta, that while many white people were going to be present to hear me speak, simply out of curiosity, and others who would be present would be in full sympathy with me, there was a still larger element of the audience which would consist of those who were going to be present for the purpose of hearing me make a fool of myself, or, at least, of hearing me say some foolish thing, so that they could say to the officials who had invited me to speak, "I told you so." [12]

He began with an assertion of the importance of the Negro to the South; but at once took the edge off this by thanking the managers for the large part they had given the Negroes in the exposition. He admitted that in the early days of freedom the Negroes had tried to begin at the top; and he urged upon his brethren that they must rise by industry, and right there in the South which, whatever her sins, gives the blacks a fair chance in business. They must learn the dignity of labor. He urged upon the whites that they should not turn to foreign labor, but should depend

[12] *Idem*, p. 215.

upon the faithful race that had hitherto done the work of the South.

We shall stand by you with a devotion that no foreigner can approach, ready to lay down our lives, if need be, in defence of yours, interlacing our industrial, commercial, civil, and religious life with yours in a way that shall make the interests of both races one. In all things that are purely social we can be as separate as the fingers, yet one as the hand in all things essential to mutual progress.[13]

This analogy, reinforced by an upthrust ebony hand with wide-spread fingers which closed into a fist, produced a sensation; for it touched upon the tenderest spot in Southern thought upon the race problem and flashed into imagination the possibility of coöperation without social mingling. The implied concession came as a great relief to many; he was not going to say some foolish thing. And many who had been hostile responded generously.

The passage also paved the way for delivering, what could not have been acceptable earlier, a solemn warning that the blacks must be treated with justice, lest they inevitably pull the South down with them. But this he immediately relieved with a humorous reference to certain venial faults of the Negroes just out of slavery. But read the whole speech. Note how his advice to his own people is a means of getting on common ground with the whites; and how he is on common ground nearly all the time.

While very tactful, this is no truckling speech. Note that, besides the warning mentioned, he does not say the blacks are not worthy of social recognition, only that they can

[13] *Idem*, 221. The speech can be found also in Baker's *Forms of Public Discourse*, p. 210, O'Neill's *Models of Speech Composition*, p. 509, and Brigance's *Speech Models*, p. 8.

remain distinct. He does not say that they will be content to remain at the bottom, only that they must begin there. They should not bother about social rights; rather they should make themselves worthy of them. "No race that has anything to contribute to the markets of the world is long in any degree ostracized." [14] After the great moment he could say almost anything.

How much better, how much more helpful to his people, than a speech of complaint and defiance. When he had finished, Governor Bullock, who had introduced him in a most non-committal fashion, rushed across the platform to shake his hand; and Clark Howell, the influential editor of the Atlanta *Constitution*, telegraphed a New York paper:

I do not exaggerate when I say that Professor Booker T. Washington's address yesterday was one of the most notable speeches, both as to character and as to the warmth of its reception, ever delivered to a Southern audience. The address was a revelation. *The whole speech was a platform upon which blacks and whites can stand with full justice to each other.* (Italics mine.)

President Cleveland wrote, "Your words cannot fail to delight and encourage all who wish well for your race."

MAKE THE INTRODUCTION TO YOUR ARGUMENT FAIR AND IMPARTIAL. If you have given an untrue history, distorting or omitting important facts, if your definitions are warped, or your concessions are unreal, you will be open to the charge of trickery, and will deserve the discredit of exposure. Even the man who is plainly bigoted and prejudiced will make a better impression than one who under the pretense of fairness attempts to deceive his audience. The best opinion is that, if only on the ground of expediency, even honest par-

[14] *Idem*, p. 223.

tisanship should be excluded from the introduction of an argument with the unconvinced. Much emphasis has been placed by Lincoln's contemporaries upon the fairness with which he would state the facts and the issues in a lawsuit, frequently alarming his client lest he give his case away.

If a speaker has gained the good will of his audience, he will wish to retain it and take them with him emotionally as well as intellectually, as he proceeds step by step beyond his initial common ground. He may have to argue, but will still wish to avoid contentiousness. If he does so he can still have a reasonable hope that his argument will at least be listened to; and that is much.

# CHAPTER XVII

## BELIEF—THE ARGUMENT

When the common ground is well marked out, explanations made, immaterial matter excluded, and concession carried as far as is wise, then the real matter in dispute, the issues, if any remain, should be evident; and argument, in some form or other, is in order.

IMPORTANCE OF SOUND ARGUMENT. I cannot here attempt a complete and systematic treatment of a subject that fills weighty treatises by jurists and philosophers and occupies the major portion of textbooks devoted to argumentation. Most of the available space will, therefore, be given to consideration of the adaptation of arguments to audiences and the winning of open-minded attention to them. Some consideration will be given also to a few methods of proof which seem particularly to need attention in speech-making, either because so much used or because so often badly used. Attention has already been given, in Chapter V, to the analysis and briefing of arguments; and numerous works will be found in almost any school or college library which elaborate the logic of argument.[1] And, after all, most of the prospective users of this book are daily exposed to training in straight thinking, the detection of fallacies, and the handling of evidence, including the use of statistics.

[1] For a simple treatment of those phases of the logic of argument most important to speakers see Winans and Hudson, *First Course in Public Speaking*, Chapter XII. For more elaborate treatments see Winans and Utterback, *Argumentation*, and numerous other works.

I should greatly regret being understood as putting a low estimate upon the importance of sound logic and evidence. Sound argument is important, first, because the speaker owes a high duty to himself and to his audience to argue as truly as he can. In the second place, expediency coincides with duty. In most assemblies the stronger minds control; in the long run they are likely to formulate opinions and determine action. These stronger thinkers resent attempts to control them in defiance of their judgment; and they will not often yield until the demands of reason have been satisfied. If a triumph is gained over reason, reason will reassert itself. The triumph of Wendell Phillips (mentioned in an earlier chapter) in making a cultured and conservative audience applaud Russian Nihilism was more amusing than lasting. On the evening of the same day President Eliot made a speech "vigorously rejecting Phillips's doctrine and exposing the essential fallacy of his discourse."

There often will be some one at hand to expose attempts to befog reason; if not some other speaker on the same occasion, or on a later occasion, then perhaps a newspaper writer, or some hard-headed man on the street or in the club. Opponents will look for every weak link; doubters will ask "Why?" and "What is the evidence?" "A political opinion that has been shaped by salestalk," says Professor Sheffield, "in the minds of more or less passive hearers is shallow and fitful. 'Things that are put over,' says E. C. Sunderman, 'don't stay put.' " [2] *Argument to be surely effective should be both persuasive and sound.*

THE FUNDAMENTAL OF ARGUMENT. Every belief arrived at by reasoning acquires its validity in the mind because it seems to be consistent with beliefs already held, beliefs in facts and in principles. At the basis of every effective argu-

[2] *Training for Group Discussion,* p. 65.

ment, then, we must have beliefs already accepted by the hearer as true, or as probably true; or beliefs that the speaker can show are true, or probably true.

We have to add "probably true" because in most of the questions a speaker deals with there are elements of uncertainty. One may, of course, believe absolutely that the present Russian government is the best possible government for Russia, that Mars is inhabited, or that college education pays in dollars and cents; but since none of these propositions can be demonstrated, thinking people will not hold them as absolute truths. And from probabilities only probable conclusions can be drawn. Still, if the probabilities are strong and if several probabilities point in the same direction, then the conclusion may be very convincing, even, in the language of criminal law, beyond a reasonable doubt. It may be strong enough to act upon, as in many of the affairs of life we have to act without certainty, as often in voting, or as in business one must act upon less than certainty as to future supply and demand.

If the arguer can base his arguments upon beliefs or premises already accepted, well and good; then he has only to impress those premises—if there seems need of that—and to show that his conclusion is bound to follow. But often he has to support one or more of his premises by further argument.

It should not be understood that all the foundations of an argument need be even stated. If you were arguing with the city council that the time has come when it is necessary to have a paid fire department, you would not ordinarily need to lay down the major premise that the town needs adequate fire protection; though you might wish to state it as a take-off for your argument; and you might even wish to elaborate it if you judged that the city fathers were not sufficiently impressed with this truth. You would probably enunciate the minor premise that the volunteer system is not providing adequate protection; but you might leave the councilmen to deduce this for themselves from your story of badly handled fires. And even the conclusion might be so obvious that you would not put it into words. That is, all the terms of an argument may be left implicit, though more often minor premise and conclusion are made explicit.

By whatever method of argument one proceeds, his argument will be an attempt to combine into logical wholes certain general principles and specific facts. Some of these will be already accepted by his hearers, some may be in the opinion stage, accepted as probably true, and usually some he will have to substantiate. These last he can substantiate, perhaps, by evidence which is already in the possession of his audience, and which he combines and brings to bear on his points; some may be accepted on his authority, and others will have to rest upon the authority of those whom he can cite.

AUTHORITY: *Its use.* We have noted that authority and precedent may serve as suggestions on which we act without deliberation. But often belief rests consciously upon authority and precedent; hence we have to consider their place in argument.

"Our strongest beliefs are always in persons," says Harry Emerson Fosdick. We may accept authority for facts, as that the population of X City is 75,000. We may accept authority for opinions, as that for such a city the managerial type of government is best. We usually accept authority for such a conclusion as that malaria is carried by mosquitoes, or that the census figures indicate certain tendencies in our population. And while objection may be made that in accepting conclusions we are letting others do our thinking for

us, yet as a matter of fact we do accept them; and in all but
the simpler forms of reasoning, we must. Not one person
in a thousand knows what to do with a batch of statistics
concerning "hidden taxes." Even the experts still disagree
about the causes of the World War, and perhaps always
will.

Even scientists and experts cannot "prove all things";
and the best most of us can do is to choose our authorities
with care. It is certainly true that often the best a speaker
with limited time can do is to establish some of his claims
upon the dicta of the best authorities available.

Authorities chosen should be such as will satisfy the
demands of honesty in argument and withstand attack and
will also impress the audience with their weight.

The purely logical value of a man's authority rests upon
his information, judgment, and integrity. He should have
had unusual opportunity for learning the facts and for forming a judgment. The fact that a man belongs to a given
profession does not make him an authority on all its problems. A criminal lawyer may know less of the law of real
property than a dealer in real estate who has never opened
a law book. A college professor's conception of the
philosophies and methods of education may be limited to
the little he has observed in his own narrow work. A man
who was in a certain battle probably knows less about what
actually occurred than a later student of the event.

Given a weighty authority, it is important to know that
the expression you wish to cite from him represents his
matured and deliberate judgment. Woodrow Wilson, the
Governor of New Jersey, withdrew the opinion of Woodrow
Wilson, the Princeton scholar, on direct primaries. Was
your scientist expressing a deliberate judgment after careful
investigation, or was he perhaps giving rein to his fancy, or

"making the front page" with some startling announcement, or possibly speaking facetiously, as Dr. Osler spoke when he caused much agitation by declaring in an after-dinner speech that all men should be chloroformed at sixty. Book covers do not change error into truth; but we are rightly more impressed by a statement carefully prepared and given permanent form in a book or a carefully edited review than by one in an interview or an offhand speech.

It is well to note, too, whether the authority was speaking an unbiased opinion. If he spoke as a partisan, an advocate, as a man with a grievance, or if his opinion was paid for, we discount his utterance, even though we believe him an honest and capable man. The opinion of neither a munitions maker nor an ardent peace advocate can be quoted with authority on preparedness.

There are, of course, many works that will be accepted as practically final authority on facts. A standard work on physics, *The Statesman's Year Book*, the *Encyclopedia of the Social Sciences*, and such standard reports as those of the Interstate Commerce Commission furnish facts that cannot easily be questioned.

Unless a quotation cited as authority is such that its source will be generally recognized, the speaker should state its source so that it can be readily found by one who wishes to look it up, as "On p. 64 of Fowler's *Dictionary of Modern English Usage*, the author says . . ." Such phrases as these are to be condemned: Competent authorities agree, It has been established. And this condemnation is especially valid if there is any reason why the speaker might be tempted to misquote.

It is better to quote the exact words of an authority, when feasible, than to paraphrase. Often a debater may profit by demanding the originals of an opponent's paraphrases; for even the most honest arguer is apt to color such restatements with his own views, or to omit qualifying clauses or context. There are times, of course, when strictness is not necessary and also times when citations must be reduced in length. There may be a conflict between exactness and desire to avoid cluttering up one's speech. When in doubt be exact, for at best the paraphraser makes himself to some extent the authority.

If one follows out the preceding suggestions as to the use of authority, he may reasonably hope to satisfy the demands of sound, honest argument and to be as safe from damaging rebuttal as may be; although it is not to be understood that authority will often bring a claim to the point of demonstration.

Nor will the best of authority, quoted in the most correct fashion, necessarily impress a particular audience. Several other considerations enter here.

Is your authority known to your audience as an authority on the point at issue? It is true that the statements and opinions of some men are of weight on a variety of subjects, and the unthinking will accept them on almost anything; while the more thoughtful will feel that men of such poise, wisdom, and impartiality are not likely to express themselves except upon valid grounds. I should not like to limit authority to experts, certainly not as to many problems of everyday life and human relations; but careful thinkers will realize that on some matters only an expert who has investigated, perhaps experimented under rigidly controlled conditions, can speak with authority. And the thoughtful will recognize that authority in one field does not extend to all. Because a man is a marked success in building automobiles or in tracing the stars, it does not follow that his opinions on education and politics are more important than those of other intelligent people.

Is the emotional attitude of your audience favorable to your authority? The fact that a man is of a certain party, church, or school of thought, or is connected with certain causes, may add to or subtract from the weight of authority that is rightfully his. In spite of his ability and exceptional experience there was a time when some would not have accepted the authority of Theodore Roosevelt for anything, while others would have taken his word as gospel on any subject whatever.

Does your authority, though lacking popular reputation, hold a position, or is he associated with some achievement, which will give him authority in the public mind? The statement that your authority was chief engineer of the Golden Gate Bridge would give him authority on bridge-building. The name of Carter H. Harrison may mean little to readers of this book; but when told that he was for three terms Mayor of Chicago, they will admit that he could speak with a good deal of authority on city government.

Has your authority been given credence by opponents? This question does not imply that any authority used by an opponent must be accepted by them forever after; still if your opponent has put much stress upon an authority he is at least embarrassed in repudiating that authority later. In his Cooper Union address Lincoln turned the tables neatly upon Senator Douglas and his "squatter sovereignty" doctrine:

In his speech last autumn at Columbus. . . . Senator Douglas said: "Our fathers, when they framed the government under which we live, understood this question as well, and even better than we do now." I fully indorse this. . . . It simply leaves the inquiry: What was the understanding those fathers had of the question mentioned?

Lincoln then proceeded to review the records of those fathers and came to a conclusion in harmony, not with the position of Douglas, but with his own:

The sum of the whole is that of our thirty-nine fathers who framed the original Constitution, twenty-one, a clear majority of the whole, certainly understood that no proper division of local from federal authority, nor any part of the Constitution, forbade the federal government to control slavery in the federal territories; whilst all the rest probably had the same understanding.

If some one says it is not possible to use authorities in a short speech with so much care as is indicated, the first answer is that most of the suggestions above relate to the choice of authorities, and there is no reason why the choice cannot be as careful for a short as for a long speech. Indeed, there is an added reason for care in the fact that in a short speech one cannot use many authorities. The second answer is that often an authority can be introduced at once adequately and briefly. When you say, "General Grant states on page 503 of his *Memoirs* . . ." you have said enough; not that General Grant is always final authority, but that nothing more would add to the weight of your citation. The third answer is that there is no good in citing authorities that will not be accepted as authoritative. You are only laying yourself open to attack.

Please understand that I have been talking of authorities as such, of quotations used as proof of something that needs proving. That is quite a different matter from quotations used only because they say admirably what you wish to say, or because their style and their authors' names add something of distinction and impressiveness to your speech.

*Opposing authorities.* The suggestions above furnish methods of attacking authorities used against you. You should not be awed by the authorities your opponent uses, however imposing they may be. It may be unwise to attack some authorities by denying their weight, as the Bible or the Founding Fathers; but it is usually possible to attack an opponent's interpretation of a passage from such sources, or the application he makes of it. Often it can be shown that the words of an authority were used in a technical sense, or with reference to circumstances quite other than those under discussion. Do the words of Washington in warning a feeble and unformed nation against entangling alliances have any application to the United States of to-day? Shakespeare is quoted on all sorts of problems; but it is possible to point out the difficulty of knowing when he speaks his own opinions. Did he, for example, indorse Hamlet's sentiments on suicide?

If one is sure of his ground he may attempt the refutation of almost any authority. This he should do modestly, but without apology, either bringing forward equal or greater authority for his own position, or setting forth facts and arguments which overcome the great man's dictum. We must, however, take cognizance of the risk of laying one's self open to such a sneer as, "He thinks he knows more than Washington!" Often it may be best to ignore imposing authority rather than to emphasize its importance by attack. Just go ahead with your case.

When confronted with authorities not very imposing in the eyes of your audience, the situation is less difficult. The problem is to judge whether they make impression enough to be worth your time, or the risk of giving them importance through attack. If some man is put forward as authority who is not well known and whose claim to authority is slight, the simple question, Who is this man Smith? may destroy his effect; or one may proceed to show how slight is his weight. Unless you know his pretensions are flimsy, however, you run the risk of an effective rejoinder, and your attack will have emphasized his importance.

The question of prejudice should be especially noted. The intimation that an authority is biased is so destructive of his influence that the charge is often made without good reason; but this should not deter us in a clear case from questioning an authority on this ground. If Macaulay were quoted on a question involving some dispute between Whigs and Tories in English history, it would be effective to quote in reply this from Woodrow Wilson:

Macaulay the Whig, subtly turning narrative into argument, and making history the vindication of a party. The mighty narrative is a great engine of proof. It is not told for its own sake. It is evidence summed up to justify a judgment. We detect the tone of the advocate, and though if we are just we must deem him honest, we cannot deem him safe.[3]

I have been speaking of the authority of individuals. We are affected also by group and public opinion, and in many matters to a greater extent than by expert opinion.[4] Experiments by psychologists seem to indicate that the influence of group opinion is markedly greater in changing beliefs about marketable products, probably greater as regards beliefs about such matters as language, music, and morals, and perhaps greater as regards beliefs about all sorts of debatable

[3] *Mere Literature and Other Essays*, p. 168. By permission of Houghton Mifflin Company, publishers.
[4] H. L. Hollingworth, *The Psychology of the Audience*, p. 151.

questions. Certainly, while such generalizations must have many exceptions, it is safe to say that when one can show that public opinion, or the opinion of the group to which one's hearer belongs, or the opinion of a group which he respects is contrary to the belief he holds, the effect will be strong.

The authority of the speaker himself will be discussed in a later chapter.

PRECEDENT. Precedent, or literal analogy, is somewhat of the same nature as authority; but goes beyond it in establishing, not only that a certain course is thought wise, but that it also works well in practice. The following shows the two methods together:

Yarmouth College permits its students to play baseball in summer for pay. Why should not this college do the same? President Jones of Yarmouth, whom you will recognize as a man of high ideals in education, said at page 10 of his annual report last year, "I think it better that students should play summer baseball openly, under proper restrictions, than that they should play in spite of prohibition, deceiving the authorities by various subterfuges. I believe our present policy is working well."

Most of the "safe and sane" members of an audience will be resistant until they learn that a plan you are advocating has been in successful operation in some respected community. Until of late it has hardly been possible to argue before most American audiences that United States courts should be deprived of the power to declare laws unconstitutional; but information that in most of the countries of the world the courts do not have this power would usually open the way at least for discussion of the proposition.

The prestige of the persons or communities furnishing the precedent counts for much. An argument for a change in social customs based upon the ways of the Chinese would have little effect upon the average American, for he assumes that the Chinese are "outlandish." Much, as always, depends upon the group addressed. There are groups to whom the fact that English aristocrats do thus and so is sufficient to overcome reluctance to change; while other groups would be turned by the same information in the opposite direction.

An arguer runs the risk of damaging rebuttal if he cites precedents in which the conditions are not in essential points similar to those in the case in hand. The fact that a fairly homogeneous city of 100,000 people, with no difficult industrial problems or distressing slums, has succeeded with the commission form of government goes but a little way toward proving that the same type of government would succeed in New York City. That the honor system is working well in a small college hardly begins to prove that the system would be good in a large and amorphous city university.

Back in the days when expansion was a live issue, a college debater argued for it on the ground that the United States had come to greatness by expansion. True, retorted an opponent, but always on this continent, and into regions that could be carved into sister states—a very different thing from holding subject territory on the other side of the world.[5]

The speaker arguing for expansion was attempting to use that most effective form of the argument from precedent which consists in showing that we ourselves have done practically what is now proposed, or that the new doctrine is really an old belief in new form. Governor Lehman of

[5] This instance is also a good illustration of the value of admission and avoidance of unnecessary burden of proof, discussed in the preceding chapter.

EXAMPLE 365

New York, calling upon his party to support his measure permitting municipalities to furnish gas and electricity to their residents, said in answer to the objection that the measure was radical, that on the contrary countless municipalities in the country had been operating gas and electric plants for more than forty years. There had been a plank in the Democratic state platform demanding the full right for municipalities to own and operate their public utilities as far back as 1918 when Alfred E. Smith first ran for Governor. This, Governor Lehman said, was orthodox Democratic doctrine.

EXAMPLE. Close to precedent is example; so close, indeed, that some instances can be called either. But we are now concerned with examples brought forward, not as models to be followed, but as instances to prove a generalization. For example, George William Curtis (in a speech from which an excerpt is given under Analogy in Chapter VIII) answered the charge of Wendell Phillips that college-bred men have failed to do their part as leaders of reform by giving example after example of college-bred men who have been in the forefront of the battle.

It cannot be claimed that the many examples Curtis gives *demonstrate* his contention; but their cumulative effect is strong. How many examples are necessary to satisfy the thoughtful listener depends upon the nature of one's proposition. The assertion that the railways of the country are losing money on their passenger service would require the listing of a large number of railways, with proof that they are losing on their passenger service; and these roads must be typical, not hand-picked to prove the point but representative of the various types of roads and of the different parts of the country. Still more satisfactory would be a compilation of the figures for all the railways of the country.

For universal statements, such as "Every planet in our solar system revolves in an elliptical orbit about our sun," every instance must be considered. One instance of the spontaneous generation of life would destroy the belief that life always comes from life. In general, a speaker should be careful of inviting the retort that his examples are only "the exceptions that prove the rule." And the more settled the belief one is seeking to change, the greater the need of cumulating examples.

The treatment of illustration in Chapter VIII is applicable to the presentation of examples and precedents.

# CHAPTER XVIII

## WHEN OPPOSITION IS STRONG

The matter presented in this chapter might properly have been included in the two preceding chapters; but it has seemed both simpler and less discouraging to keep back for a time consideration of those instances in which change of belief can be accomplished only with great difficulty, or perhaps not at all.

There are beliefs which the speaker cannot hope to change. Perhaps, strictly speaking, any belief can be modified by imposing evidence and authority, or worn away by the attrition of new environment and experience; but some beliefs, for the purposes of immediate argument, must be accepted as fixed, no matter how strong the case brought against them. If we change the old poser, "What happens when an irresistible force meets an immovable object?" into, What happens when a perfect argument meets a fixed belief? the answer is that the argument gets the worst of it.

Even though we do yield such a belief to an unanswerable argument, the chances are that we shall be back at the old stand to-morrow; because the old belief is so entangled with other beliefs, sentiments, and habits, that it is very hard to remove. It was the Aristotelian belief that of two bodies of equal density the larger will fall the faster. Galileo tested this theory by dropping two balls from the Leaning Tower of Pisa. They reached the ground simultaneously; but the learned witnesses, who had been trained to look to

Aristotle as the source of all wisdom, went home to compose treatises proving that their master was right.

Some of our most stubborn beliefs we are hardly aware of; some we may not like to admit, and some we hold only in emotional states, as that the umpire is always against our team. Others we are frank to affirm at any time. Of the following some may not seem to a particular reader to belong in the class of unchangeable beliefs; but I believe that all are fixed for large groups. No implication is intended as to the truth or falsity of any of these statements:

To grow large is a grand thing for a town, or other institution.

Acquired characteristics are never transmitted to offspring.

A college course should last four years.

The chief good of college is to be found in the courses (or in the activities).

Most of the men in X College are "smoothies."

Parents have a right to rule their children.

Parents cannot understand the new generation, which is quite different from theirs.

Human nature cannot be changed.

If a policy is democratic it is good.   Or if liberal.

The intelligent have a right to ride on the backs of the less intelligent.

Taxation without representation is tyranny.

A man is innocent until proved guilty.

All Americans are "dollar crazy."

No gentleman will engage in retail trade.

An early winter means an early spring.

One should exact "an eye for an eye."

It is disgraceful to be out of style; to carry food to the mouth with a knife; to refuse to take a dare; to refuse to fight when called a liar; to strike a woman.

A man should kill the seducer of his wife or daughter.

In time of danger the rule must be women and children first.
The captain must be the last to leave a sinking ship.
A man should endure obloquy rather than tell on a woman.

No doubt it is a social good that some beliefs are fixed;
but the problem for us is what to do when we come up
against a belief that cannot be changed, at least not within
the limits of our opportunity.  The answer is that we must
take it as we find it, and either use it or ignore it.  "There
is no use in butting your head against a stone wall."  When
you come to an immovable obstacle, you can utilize it where
it is, or go over or around it.

If it has already been undermined, and only looks immovable, that is another matter.  The Monroe Doctrine is
an example of a belief once too firmly established in the
American mind to be budged by argument.  When in 1903 a
team of college debaters had to argue against a resolution
that sounded like the Monroe Doctrine, they did not dare
to proceed until they had made a strong argument to the
effect that the resolution did not state the original doctrine,
but a recent extension of it.  To-day the doctrine is debatable; if, indeed, in its former meaning it is still existent.

But if Bostonians still feel that, in the words of Oliver
Wendell Holmes, "Boston is the hub of the solar system;
you could not pry that out of a Boston man if you had the
tire of all creation straightened out for a crowbar," then,
when you are talking to Boston, admit it, or keep off the
subject.  After all, men of widely differing sentiments and
opinions can work together.  Of two wealthy alumni asked
for a subscription for a new college library, one may feel
that the library is the most essential feature of a college;
and he responds liberally.  The other may feel that the
"life" is the only important feature and that the old library

is quite good enough; but when he learns that his college is being jeered at for having a huge gymnasium and a tiny library, he too may subscribe liberally, for the reputation of Alma Mater is dear to him.

One man who supports slum clearance for humanitarian reasons may be heartily backed by another who believes the inhabitants of the slums worthless flotsam, but also believes the slums a danger as a breeding place of disease, crime, and revolution; and by still another who hopes that abolition of the slums will increase the value of his real estate. It is unnecessary to change the views of any of these. But if you are unwilling to meet your hearers where they are willing to come, let them alone where they are. One is never ("well, hardly ever") bound to open his mouth at all.

But if you do try, keep in mind that to persuade a man is largely a matter of *identifying* the opinion or course you wish him to adopt with one or more of his established beliefs or customary courses of conduct.

STRONGLY HELD BELIEFS. Whether a speaker should accept a given belief as immutable or attempt to modify it will depend, of course, upon the belief, the audience, and the entire situation. I shall here proceed to certain methods which are particularly important in dealing with strong convictions; but I do not mean to imply that they are not also applicable in dealing with beliefs of any degree of firmness.

Even a strongly held belief can be overwhelmed by another still stronger. We are told that when the question of adopting the national Constitution was before the Massachusetts convention, Samuel Adams was strongly in opposition, and his support was gravely needed. So there was held a large meeting of shipwrights and mechanics, who sent a delegation, headed by Paul Revere, to tell Adams that the common people were for the Constitution. He yielded his opposition because he had, says McMaster, "a strong faith in the hard sense and patriotism of the people." [1]

This example suggests the value of influential authority in dealing with embedded beliefs. Reluctance to give genuine, open-minded attention may yield to respect for a great name, or for a group. In some instances very striking facts may serve the same purpose. The man who opposes reform because he complacently believes this the best of all possible worlds may be jarred into attention by the facts regarding the slums a few blocks from his mansion. The belief that machines are a prime cause of unemployment might, perhaps, be dented by a cumulation of such instances as this: When the linotype, enabling one man to do the work of five, was put into use in 1889, the population of the United States was approximately 61,000,000. By 1929 the population had nearly doubled. In 1889 there were engaged in the printing industry 50,000 people. By 1929 there were 281,000, to say nothing of the vast increase in the numbers of those in allied industries such as paper-making.

ARGUMENT WITHOUT ARGUING. It is particularly wise to avoid the appearance of controversy in dealing with strong beliefs. And this brings us to a consideration important regardless of the nature of the beliefs we wish to change.

It is possible at times to avoid contentiousness by casting one's argument into the form of narrative, description, or exposition. These forms are commonly employed in the introduction; and may, in many cases, be carried into the body, and even quite through the speech. We are familiar with plays, histories, and biographies that are in effect arguments. Thomas Huxley's lecture, "A Piece of Chalk," in

[1] J. B. McMaster, *History of the People of the United States*, Vol. I, p. 479.

which he traced nature's eon-long process of manufacturing a familiar mineral, was a powerful argument for evolution, with the least possible conflict with the religious ideas of his audience.

When William Howard Taft came home after some years as Governor of the Philippines, he was sent out in the campaign of 1904 to defend the acts and policies of our government in the Islands. Bitter charges had been made of American cruelty and mismanagement. Taft simply told, largely in narrative form, what had been done, explaining the problems and how they had been solved. He did not seem to argue, defend, or extenuate; he just told us, and in such an interesting way that we listened intently. Mr. Taft said, with his famous chuckle, "My friends tell me this isn't a stump speech at all"; but I still think it was the most effective stump speech I ever heard.

A simple exposition of the human spine, by a professor of anatomy, was another effective argument. Not in word, tone, or look was there a suggestion of controversy; yet if a hearer was mindful of the claims of a certain school of medicine, he realized that those claims were being deftly overturned.

Whether there were fallacies or misleading omissions in any of these speeches I am unable to say; but flaws would have been quite as probable if the arguments had been cast in argumentative form.

Again, the mold for an argument may be description. A very effective argument for intramural sports was made by a former Rhodes scholar who was asked by a college paper to describe sports at Oxford. There was not a trace of argument in the form of his article; indeed, one was not sure the writer had an argumentative purpose. But he put the prestige of Oxford back of the intramural idea and showed us how a university renowned for its athletes gets along without ballyhoo, paid coaches, and most that we have come to associate with intercollegiate contests.

To argue through narration, description, and exposition does not necessarily take more time than through the argumentative form, unless one chooses to cast out of the latter concrete and illustrative matter. The non-argumentative forms are superior in suggesting minor points that one has not time to develop, and also in impressing ideas upon the hearer's memory. Whether the impressions will be sharp enough and the conclusion evident enough depends upon how well the story is told; but it is always possible to sum up in a way which puts them beyond doubt. Probably in the majority of cases it is better to restate arguments and conclusions in explicit terms before ending the speech; and that is especially true when the "wish to believe" is against the speaker; for it is easier to dodge an unpleasing conclusion that is implied than one put into definite terms.

When it is possible to induce one's audience to draw for itself the desired conclusion as the inevitable conclusion, the method we are considering has been called the *this-or-nothing* plan. Certainly those are great moments when the speaker sees his audience rushing ahead of him to his goal. Conclusions so reached will be held more enthusiastically and persistently than those to which an audience is marched, or perhaps dragged, by more obvious logic. Unfortunately the speaker does not deal with many questions to which there is an inevitable answer. And this is particularly true in arguing questions of policy. There is usually more than one good way to go, and a speaker has done well when he has brought his audience to agree that his way is somewhat the better, very well indeed if the audience was hostile to his plan in the beginning. Nevertheless, the general idea of inducing an audience to draw its own conclusion is excellent.

The process of elimination (discussed in Chapter V under Patterns of Analysis, and the core of the this-or-nothing plan) is not, of course, limited to arguments thrown into other than argumentative forms. Whatever form one uses, he may argue away other conclusions before presenting his own, and so prepare his audience to see that his is either superior, or the only conclusion reasonable. This was the plan used by President Wilson when, in April, 1917, he went before Congress to ask for a declaration of war against Germany. He first disposed of the only alternatives, armed peace or submission; and so, he held, war was inevitable.

ORDER OF ARGUMENT. It is not always wise to attack at first conclusions other than the one we wish to establish; and never so unless we are sure we can do so convincingly, for we may succeed only in raising obstacles. In such a case it is better to proceed at once to make our own plan as attractive as possible.

Whether one should come at once to the specific aspect of his proposal has to be decided in the light of conditions. The more natural order seems to be to state first the general ideas upon which the proposal is based; and this will be a persuasive order if the general ideas are in the nature of common ground. But there are times when the specific proposal will be more welcome. Most people will listen more readily to a particular plan for social betterment, such as old age pensions, than to a general discussion of social wrongs, which may sound radical. But if the early part of a speech describes concrete conditions in a way to awaken a desire for a remedy, then the audience may be ready to consider a remedy that at first would have seemed extreme.

Or perhaps some attractive feature of a proposal may be put forward early in the speech. The proposed removal of the city and county buildings from the old site would leave a large space for a much needed, and at the same time attractive, parking space. One seeking to secure the adoption of an expensive coaching system will have less trouble in convincing the Athletic Council that the money can be found, if he first convinces them that the system will bring athletic supremacy. "Hope springs eternal" that we can do what we greatly wish to do.

*Rate of progress.* To proceed too rapidly with those reluctant to accept one's proposal weakens persuasion, just as truly as too slow progress may dull the enthusiasm of the eager. There is need of time for the strangeness of a proposal to wear off and for its attractiveness to work into imagination. There may be danger of boring trained thinkers with too slow progress; but inexperienced speakers are far more likely to go too fast than too slow. Or perhaps it would be better to say that they fail to discriminate what may be passed over rapidly because easy, familiar, or already accepted, from what should be dwelt upon because difficult, strange, or hard to accept.

Sometimes it may be possible to employ a method of Benjamin Franklin's. This master molder of public opinion used to begin, he tells us in his *Autobiography*, not by calling a meeting of the citizens of Philadelphia and asking them to accept his proposal at once, but by accustoming the public mind to his plans by prolonged newspaper discussion before calling his meeting. But, as noted before, it is possible to have repetition and restatement in the single speech. And as Mr. Dooley says, "I'll belave onything atall if ye'll only tell it to me aften enough."

ASKING FOR MORE THAN ONE EXPECTS TO GAIN. It is sometimes wise to begin with mild suggestions and gradually add to them, a method not unknown to salesmen. Again it may be better to set forth a proposal in its most startling form; and then, when opposition has grown up, to relieve anxiety by suggesting various modifications and limitations which make the proposal less extreme than it seemed. This may be a good way of winning attention; but it may cause misunderstanding and open the way for misrepresentations which will be hard to eradicate from the popular mind. The method may also gain for one the reputation of being "unsafe."

OPPOSITION ARISING FROM PREJUDICE. Near the beginning of our consideration of persuasion it was pointed out that one strongly resistant group is composed of those whose opposition is due to prejudice, rather than to understanding and deliberation. As regards this group there is but little to add to what has been said. The hardest part of dealing with the prejudiced is to gain a fair hearing. Sometimes a speaker can reach them through authority and precedent which shows that after all the "right people" have indorsed the proposal, or that it is actually working in some respected community. Indirectness of approach may be necessary, holding back the real proposal and putting much stress on common ground, until the prejudiced hearers are assured that, in some respects at least, the speaker is a sensible fellow to whom it may be well to listen.

OPPOSITION ARISING FROM SELF-INTEREST. It was also pointed out that, generally speaking, the most difficult opponents of all are those who see in the speaker's proposal a threat to their comfort, position, or income. If they can be induced to listen at all, perhaps their fears can be relieved by an exposition of the proposal. People tend to fear most the things they do not understand. Perhaps they can be brought to see that they will not be affected at all, or even that they will be benefited. A man who fears that federal regulation of Wall Street will hurt his holdings may be assured that such regulation will insure him greater security and fairer treatment.   And it is always possible that many in an audience have a sense of fairness and honor that will compel them to yield to the plea of the greater good for the greater number.   The chief difficulty is not that all men are completely selfish; but rather that they do not listen gladly to proposals that seem to threaten their personal interests.   Once their minds are open there is always hope.   Indeed, the gaining of open-minded attention is the most constant problem in persuasion.

# CHAPTER XIX

## THE SPEAKER HIMSELF

One of the most important elements in persuasiveness is the impression made by the speaker himself. His personal influence depends upon his reputation, the mastery of his subject which he manifests, his skill in presenting his proposal, and his attitude and personal characteristics. Some of these matters affect more particularly his authority, or the confidence his hearers feel in his trustworthiness; and others affect more particularly the friendliness of the audience toward him and their consequent willingness to give ear to his ideas.

The persuasive use of authority has already been discussed. But, after all, the speaker is himself the chief authority. When an audience goes out saying, "That sounds good, but I don't know," it may be that the speaker's contention has been too difficult or too novel for immediate acceptance, or it may be that the audience doubts the speaker's trustworthiness. The average listener realizes that a speaker can talk plausibly while misstating his facts, warping his precedents and authorities, juggling his logic, or resting his argument upon premises that are false. Although some hearers may not be able to detect the flaws in his argument, they usually do not fail to gauge his general reliability. But whether they judge him as he speaks, or assess him in terms of a previous impression, it is a matter of high importance to the speaker whether they hold toward him a doubting or a trusting attitude, and whether they look upon him as a man competent to tell them the truth, and disposed to tell them the truth because he is a man of integrity; hardly less important, indeed, than their attitude toward his proposal itself, and often more important.

AUTHORITY OF THE SPEAKER AND COMMON GROUND. We have noted earlier that a speaker gains prestige with us when we find that he shares some of our interests, feelings, and beliefs. He needs particularly to gain this prestige when his way of life marks him as different from his audience. The business man may feel that an artist is not to be trusted in "practical" affairs. He may also doubt that any reformer is "safe and sane"; and the reformers have shown a distrust of business men. Country folk may distrust the "city slicker," and city folk tend to look down upon a "rube." We give our greatest confidence to him who shares our own general outlook, especially when his advice touches a matter which directly concerns us.

The suggestion is not that an artist should attempt to talk of business to business men, or that a city man should attempt to talk of farming to farmers. Unless at home in these topics either may bungle his attempt to bridge the gap between himself and his hearers, and, by bringing derision upon himself, lessen rather than increase his influence with them. Rather the speaker should touch upon problems and experiences common to all men. Recently I was introduced to an artist and felt that conversation was difficult; but when he said he had just come from a ball game, I relaxed and felt that we could sit down for a "good visit." Whatever a man's way of life he shares the common life; or, if he has "lost the common touch," he should not attempt to speak outside his own precious circle.

PREPARATION AND AUTHORITY. Our confidence in a speaker is enhanced when we feel that he "knows what he is talking about." We are especially pleased to know that experience and investigation have made him an authority on his subject. We may like to hear any well informed man speak on conditions in Russia; but we are especially eager if told that the speaker has lived many years in Russia and has studied her history and politics.

Unless the speaker's qualifications are a matter of common knowledge, it is often desirable that the audience be told of them. This may be done by a discreet chairman who, without puffery, makes a statement adding to the speaker's prestige. The chairman's words should be controlled by a decent restraint; many times an audience goes out feeling peevish toward a speaker who has had an introduction he failed to justify. There is no good reason why a speaker may not state his own qualifications, provided he does so without either boasting or self-depreciation. This may be done openly; for example,

For the past fifteen years I have lived in Spain, engaged in a business which has brought me into contact with all classes of her people. I have been interested in studying her history and her politics, and have done my best to understand the present struggle. I do not profess to know all about it; but I hope to throw some light on this confused subject.

Sometimes the facts which give the speaker authority may be brought out indirectly, as when an explorer says, "The division I was in charge of was stationed at this point." "Down in my home state of Alabama" might give weight to the words of a Southerner on the race question. A student in a class may need no special introduction; but at times the force of his remarks would be increased by letting his audience know that he has more than book knowledge of his subject. If he has had experience as a foreman he may well let this be known when he speaks on a labor problem.

The fact that a speaker comes forward at all should be announcement that he is reasonably well qualified. Happy is the speaker who has established a reputation for fulfilling the expectation of his audiences in this respect.

EXAGGERATION AND AUTHORITY. One's standing as a person of judgment and probity is weakened by the habit of rash and exaggerated statement. "That terrible sanity of the average man is always watching you," says Barrett Wendell.[1] If you habitually overstate, all your claims will be discounted. "Yes, Smith is a great talker and I like to hear him go it," says the average man as he goes out; "but you can't believe more than half he says." At the time when Governor Sulzer of New York was impeached, a student made a speech lauding the Governor to the skies and painting his enemies as monsters of iniquity. A classmate, asked to comment, said, "It was a good speech, but I was not in the least convinced." Was it, then, a good speech? Reasonableness of attitude may not produce talk that sounds so strong; but it accomplishes more than does exaggeration, certainly more in winning over the doubtful and the reluctant.

Exaggerated statements breed misunderstandings. Even if understood as exaggeration when spoken, they may appear in a different light when quoted, or perhaps misquoted, and so they may gain for their author a reputation for untrustworthiness. They play into the hands of opponents. *Falsus in uno falsus in omnibus*, though an exaggeration itself, is a proverb readily accepted. Facts and authorities can be

[1] *English Composition*, p. 271. By permission of Charles Scribner's Sons.

used with damaging effect against the exaggerator. "The gentleman says that the cruel injustice of the white man has all but driven the red man from his native land; but So and So, the well known authority, says that there are more Indians in America to-day than when Columbus landed." And the audience is likely to overlook the essential truth in the exaggerated statement.

The agitator is usually a reckless exaggerator. There is a place for him in our scheme of society, for he awakens public interest in conditions that need attention; but the Lincolns and Roosevelts, not the Phillipses and Coughlins, win the masses in the end and carry through changes.

It is not possible to emphasize both sides of a truth at once, and in vigorous statements overemphasis is almost inevitable. Indeed, the preceding paragraphs, taken alone, exaggerate the evils of exaggeration. Postiveness is an element in authoritativeness. If a speaker is not sure of his ground, his hearers are little likely to accept his conclusions. The way to gain positiveness, however, is not to make reckless assertions, but to make sure of your ground. Obey both parts of the injunction, "Be sure you are right, and then go ahead."

A painful degree of accuracy is not required. The sum of $987,569 may be spoken of as a million, unless the particular case calls for exactness. Honesty in public as in private discussion depends upon the understanding of one's hearers. Hyperbole, or exaggeration understood by both parties as such, may be effective in arousing one's adherents who need no argument but may lack ardor. It is the natural language of emotion. But whatever uses extravagant statement may have, it has little place in sober discussion aimed at changing belief.

UNDERSTATEMENT AND AUTHORITY. We are now ready to note that understatement is often more forceful and weighty than overstatement. Few men have ever spoken with as great authority as Daniel Webster. After one of his short speeches a hearer was heard to remark, "He didn't say much, but every word weighed a pound." No doubt his authority lay much in his personality, which seems to have made a tremendous impression; but one element is thus explained by Marsh:

It was a maxim of Webster's that violence of language was indicative of feebleness of thought and want of reasoning power, and it was his practice to understate rather than overstate the strength of his confidence in the soundness of his own arguments, and the logical necessity of his conclusions. He kept his auditor constantly in advance of him, by suggestion rather than by strong asseveration, by a calm exposition of considerations which ought to excite feeling in the heart of both speaker and hearer, not by an undignified and theatrical exhibition of passion in himself.[2]

Wendell Phillips, that "infernal machine set to music," showed in his oration on Toussaint L'Ouverture, Negro liberator of the blacks of Santo Domingo, that he knew the value of restraint in expression, even in a speech which must have impressed many in 1861 as a marvel of exaggeration:

Let us pause a moment and find something to measure him by. You remember Macaulay says, comparing Cromwell with Napoleon, that Cromwell showed the greater military genius, if we consider that he never saw an army till he was forty; while Napoleon was educated from a boy in the best military schools

[2] G. P. Marsh, *Lectures on the English Language*, p. 235. It is evident to one who studies the evidence in Webster's jury cases along with his summation speeches, that his own language is often most violent when he has least to base his assertions upon.

in Europe. Cromwell manufactured his own army; Napoleon at the age of twenty was placed at the head of the best troops Europe ever saw. They were both successful; but, says Macaulay, with such disadvantages the Englishman showed the greater genius. Whether you allow the inference or not, you will at least grant that it is a fair mode of measurement. Apply it to Toussaint. Cromwell never saw an army till he was forty; this man never saw a soldier till he was fifty. Cromwell manufactured his own army—out of what? Englishmen—the best blood in Europe. Out of the middle class of Englishmen—the best blood of the island. And with it he conquered what? Englishmen—their equals. This man manufactured his army out of what? Out of what you call the despicable race of negroes, debased, demoralized by two hundred years of slavery, one hundred thousand of them imported into the island within four years, unable to speak a dialect intelligible even to each other. Yet out of this mixed and, as you say, despicable mass, he forged a thunderbolt, and hurled it at what? At the proudest blood in Europe, the Spaniard, and sent him home conquered; at the most warlike blood in Europe, the French, and put them under his feet; at the pluckiest blood in Europe, the English, and they skulked home to Jamaica. Now if Cromwell was a general, at least this man was a soldier.[3]

Had Phillips expressed the conclusion that one is bracing himself against—that Toussaint was a greater military genius than Cromwell, greater even than Napoleon—one's judgment would reject the claim in spite of the plausible argument. But hearing the mild assertion that Toussaint was a soldier, one is prompted to exclaim, "Nay, he was much more!" We see here the reasons for the force of

[3] From "Toussaint L'Ouverture" in *Speeches, Lectures and Letters,* First Series. By permission of Lothrop, Lee & Shepard Co. Perhaps in the conclusion of the passage quoted, Phillips carries understatement too far and seems a bit affected.

understatement: a sense of relief that the claim is not too great to accept and a prompting to assert more than one would accept from the speaker.

Do not indulge much in the exclamatory style, the besetting sin of some "inspirational" preachers. From the stump, too, one hears speeches for which the "scare mark" (!) is the only appropriate punctuation. No doubt this style has its uses as occasional relief and in the expression of strong emotion; but it easily runs into the style described as the "feeble forcible."

Back in the time of the World War I heard a man who had recently returned from near the front. He was greatly stirred by his experiences, and we responded somewhat to his earnestness; but the effect was much lessened by his constantly telling us, in the most exclamatory terms, how greatly the horrible scenes had moved him, rather than telling us plainly what had moved him. I also heard Hendrik Van Loon tell of his war experiences. They were not nearly so shocking in fact; but he had the skill to tell us what he had seen. This he did interestingly, even at times humorously, and without any expressions of horror; yet the after impression was a strong disgust for modern warfare. Simple vividness was sufficient.

HUMOR AND AUTHORITY. Humor was discussed in an earlier chapter with reference to interest. Its relation to the speaker's authority is still more important. One may take pleasure in the reputation of being a humorist, but it is less pleasant to discover that people refuse to take one seriously. Mark Twain felt so keenly the limitations which his reputation as a humorist imposed that he first published his life of Joan of Arc anonymously, lest it be taken as a joke. There are comedians on the stage eating their hearts out because, when they attempt serious parts, the public still insists that

they are funny. Chauncey M. Depew was a serious gentleman, president of a great railway system, once a prominent
candidate for the Republican nomination to the presidency.
He delivered many serious speeches; but his fame as an
after-dinner speaker was so great that when he spoke on the
stump his hearers would barely tolerate his arguments and
wished he would hurry on from story to story. He himself said to Edwin C. Hill[4] that his reputation as a humorist probably cost him the presidency. Garfield told him that
the nation would never trust a joker.

Genung says of college students:

I have seen men whose rising to speak on any topic before
their classmates only produced a broad grin, the broader as the
speaker attempted to be more earnest. These men had been
too content to be class buffoons; and when they assumed the
solemn rôle their classmates judged that their specific gravity
was too light to sustain such character, and they would have
none of it.[5]

Yet the argument in regard to humor in persuasion is
not all one way. We have already noted that humor has its
uses in winning attention, in making a point stick, and also
in relieving any initial strain. There is little reason for
going to the extremes of the late Senator Beveridge, who
seems to have held that humor should never be employed
in any speech of serious purpose. One hardly knows what
to make of his saying—

To find a joke in Webster would be an offense. . . . Lincoln's Gettysburg Address, his first and second inaugurals, his
speech beginning the Douglas campaign and his Cooper Union

---

[4] Told by Mr. Hill in a speech on the air, November 18, 1937.

[5] J. F. Genung, *Practical Elements of Rhetoric*, p. 451. By permission of Ginn and Company, publishers.

address in New York, are, perhaps, the only utterances of his that will endure. Yet this greatest of story tellers since Aesop did not adorn or deface one of these great deliverances with a story or any form of humor.[6]

Turn to Webster's Reply to Hayne, considered the greatest of American speeches, and by many the greatest in modern times. Its purpose and occasion were intensely serious. Hayne had attempted to array the South and the West against the Northeast, and secession and civil war were in the making; yet this speech begins humorously and has several humorous passages. Some of them are grim, even savage; but they are plainly meant as humor and probably were intended to relieve somewhat the strain of the situation, as well as to lessen the authority of Webster's opponent by making him a bit ludicrous, and perhaps to brace the courage of his own supporters. If you turn to the latter part of the speech you will find a passage which would fill two pages of this book, in which, after a long and severe argument against the constitutionality of nullification, Webster draws a picture of Hayne at the head of the militia of Charleston, South Carolina, attempting to put nullification into practice at that port. Hayne's troops are represented as worried lest resistance to the laws of the United States may be treason.

"These tariff laws," he would repeat, "are unconstitutional, palpably, deliberately, dangerously." "That may be so; but if the tribunal should not happen to be of that opinion, shall we swing for it? We are ready to die for our country; but it is rather an awkward business, this dying without touching the ground! After all that is a sort of hemp tax worse than any part of the tariff."

[6] Introduction to *Modern Eloquence* (1923), Vol. I, p. xxxix. By permission of P. F. Collier & Son Corporation.

Mr. President, the honorable gentleman would be in a dilemma, like that of another great general. He would have a knot before him which he could not untie. He must cut it with his sword. He must say to his followers, "Defend yourselves with your bayonets"; and this is war—civil war.

One is glad to have stress laid on the fact that Lincoln's speeches are serious and not marred by the clownishness sometimes attributed to him. Beveridge conveniently rules out Lincoln's debates with Douglas, although they are much studied to-day. In them one finds numerous places where Lincoln has made humor effective for his argument, but no places where he has yielded to the temptation to be amusing for the sake of the laugh only. There are few stories and these briefly put. If the Springfield speech with which he opened his campaign against Douglas did not provoke a broad smile at one point, then I do not understand the speech. And one will look long to find a better example of wit used to destroy a slippery fallacy than this from the Cooper Union speech:

But you will not abide the election of a Republican president! In that supposed event, you say, you will destroy the Union; and then, you say, the great crime of having destroyed it will be upon us! That is cool. A highwayman holds a pistol to my ear, and mutters through his teeth, "Stand and deliver, or I shall kill you, and then you will be a murderer."

Apparently some do not realize that humor may be used with serious purpose; and that while it may be a tyrannical and ruinous master, it may also be a useful servant. If the people will not trust a joker, we must note that there is a vast difference between a man who sometimes jokes, and one who comes before them as primarily a "funny man."

Much, as always, depends upon the situation in which

one finds himself. Of course Lincoln did not attempt humor in his inaugurals and in the Gettysburg Address. It would have been as much out of place as in a psalm. Much depends, too, upon the quality of the humor. Resort to low-grade humor or buffoonery will not add to one's influence. Sarcasm will not tend to win over opposition; and if too savage may turn sympathy away from the speaker toward the object of his shafts. And few things are less likely to enhance prestige than the futile attempts of one who has no wit. For such it is fortunate that there are few, if any, situations in which one must be humorous. Geniality will suffice.

But we need not condemn ourselves to solemnity because we recognize the danger of frivolity. As a rule students in my classes are much too solemn.

SINCERITY AND AUTHORITY. Nothing is so destructive of confidence in a speaker as suspicion of his sincerity. The commonness of the device, detestable when dishonest, of charging hypocrisy against an opponent proves the importance of a reputation for sincerity. If it be suspected that a speaker is ready to sell his persuasive powers, that he will advocate a measure for the sake of private gain, or that he is driven to one side or the other by pique, as when a man changes his party after failure to secure a nomination, at once his influence wanes.

The best way to be believed sincere is to be sincere. A speaker should not permit himself to declare a belief that he does not hold. Apart from the question of common honesty, he cannot afford to develop the insincerity which is bound to show in the tones of his voice and in other subtle ways; just as it shows in the tones and manner of a salesman who for a considerable period has sold goods he does not believe in. A self-respecting man will not permit himself to be used as a mere mouthpiece, except when he, or the situation itself, makes it clear that he is speaking only as the representative of another.

The best way to resist unfair charges of insincerity is to deal fairly with one's public and build up such a reputation as will itself refute the charge. A reputation for cleverness may commend one to rogues; but there is far more persuasiveness in the reputation of one of whom it is said, "Whether you agree with him or not, you can bank on it that he tells you what he means." It is not often best to proclaim one's own sincerity, unless one has been attacked on that score,[7] and not always then. One may, if he feels the need, set forth facts which indicate his sincerity without specifically raising the issue. Too much insistence upon one's sincerity may provoke the retort of Hamlet's mother: "The lady protests too much, methinks."

One meets at times the belief that a public speaker has some peculiar license to misstate facts and advocate beliefs he does not hold. This is a dangerous doctrine, subversive of all integrity in public speech. It is not the view of audiences. They will agree with the fiery words of Demosthenes to Æschines:

What greater crime can an orator be charged with than that his opinions and his language are not the same? Such is found to be your character. And yet you open your mouth and dare to look these men in the face.

PERSONALITY AND AUTHORITY. There is an element in the power of a speaker, sometimes referred to by the misleading term "personal magnetism," which can be recognized rather than cultivated directly. Such men as Alcibi-

[7] As had Demosthenes when he delivered his masterpiece "On the Crown," and Webster when he summed up in the Knapp-White case.

ades, Mahomet, Luther, Mirabeau, Napoleon, Clay, Webster, Brigham Young, Stonewall Jackson, and Theodore Roosevelt have exercised upon their fellows a fascination not readily explained. We may make such mystery of it as we will; but probably their spell has been due to combinations of quite understandable characteristics, some of which I am discussing in this chapter. They have also been men of imagination and able to put visions into the minds of their followers; and they have had an insight into human nature that has enabled them to touch effective motives. They have been men of positive character, knowing with certainty what they wished to bring about; and they have been masters of the technique of persuasion.

Personal appearance is no doubt an element in impressiveness. The tall, well-proportioned man has an advantage. But Webster, "the godlike Daniel," though spoken of as a giant, was really of only moderate height; and Stephen A. Douglas, called the "Little Giant," a leader of rare influence whether before the people or in the Senate, was less than five feet in height. Since we cannot by taking thought add to our stature, discussion of height is of no value, except as it gives opportunity to say to those who lack physical impressiveness: Do not worry about the lack. And do not try to increase your height by "standing on your dignity." Don't call attention to your lack by a strut. Real dignity of bearing, however, can be gained by developing self-respect, courtesy, and physical and mental poise.

Emerson, in his essay on Eloquence, touches a matter to some extent within our control:

Perhaps it is the lowest of the qualities of an orator, but it is, on so many occasions, of chief importance—a certain robust and radiant physical health.

I shall not attempt to tell you how to develop physical vitality; but I point out that the passage just quoted suggests the desirability of coming to the platform in good condition, rested and with reserves of nervous and physical energy on tap. Often physical exercises shortly before speaking will aid in releasing the energy one has.

We should not be discouraged to find that we are not great personalities. Some of us will never "sway the listening thousands," but we can make the most of the gifts we have. "The race is not always to the swift, nor the battle to the strong." Every experienced teacher has seen sadly handicapped students surpass their more gifted classmates. One can develop some of the qualities that enter into personality, and one can be a sincere, straightforward gentleman on the platform. Beyond this one can let personality take care of itself—unless, indeed, one may need the services of a psychiatrist; in which case one should make sure that he consults a highly skilled practitioner.

SELF-CONTROL AND AUTHORITY. It is a truism that to be master of a situation a man must first be master of himself. We instinctively turn for guidance to men of poise, who are unruffled under provocation and calm in a crisis; not to those who are calm from indifference, but to those who under strong feeling yet remain masters of their powers. Such a man on the platform will be able to speak with an authority never granted to one whose control is easily destroyed. He will be better able to think of the right thing to say at the time when it should be said, to judge the mood of his audience, and in every way to adapt himself to the situation.

Poise is a quality which comes from long practice; and it will not come to one on the platform as a spontaneous acquisition. But one will be helped for the single speech by thorough preparation, and by the self-forgetfulness which accompanies a strong interest in one's subject and purpose. Physical poise also is a help to mental. The rest is mainly experience.

FAIRNESS AND AUTHORITY. In the chapter on Motives I spoke of fairness as something to be appealed to in the hearer. Here I speak of it as an element in the speaker which adds to his hearer's confidence in him. Willingness to grant the worth of the valid arguments of the opposition gives the impression that a speaker is honest and trust-worthy; and, instead of weakening his case, is evidence that he has confidence in it. The persuader is an advocate, and is expected to present his side strongly; but he can still be fair.

In order to be fair, first be reasonable. Instead of shut-ting your mind to the case of the opposition, consider it candidly. Intolerance is characteristic of immaturity in argument.

MODESTY AND AUTHORITY. There is a conflict of opinion between those who hold that a speaker should speak with the utmost assurance and those who hold for a more modest attitude. Senator Beveridge said:

Not one immortal utterance can be produced which contains such expressions as, "I may be wrong," or, "In my humble judgment," or, "In my judgment." The great speakers, in their highest moments, have always been so charged with aggres-sive convictions that they announce their conclusions as ultimate truths. They speak "as one having authority," and therefore, "the common people hear them gladly." [8]

---

[8] Introduction to *Modern Eloquence* (1923), Vol. I, p. xxxvii. By permission of P. F. Collier & Son Corporation.

But wise old Ben Franklin tells us in his *Autobiography* that as a youth he practised the Socratic method of argument (a question method which tends to the discomfiture of opponents by compelling them to admit themselves wrong); but he goes on to say—

I practised this method for some years but gradually left it, retaining only the habit of expressing myself in terms of modest diffidence, never using when I advance anything that may possibly be disputed, the words *certainly, undoubtedly* . . . ; but rather say, I *conceive,* or *apprehend,* a thing to be so and so; *It appears to me,* or *I should not think it so and so, for such and such reasons;* or *I imagine it to be so,* or *It is so, if I am not mistaken.* This habit, I believe, has been of great advantage to me when I have had occasion to inculcate my opinions and persuade men into measures. . . . I wish well-meaning and sensible men would not lessen their power of doing good by a positive, assuming manner, that seldom fails to disgust, tends to create opposition, and to defeat most of those purposes for which speech was given us.

We may add to Franklin's list two other expressions that tend to make the hearer scan our arguments with severity: *I shall prove to you absolutely,* and *I have proved to you beyond question.*

Following Franklin's policy, I shall not attempt to lay down any positive rule in this matter. In leading a mass of men already somewhat suggestible and largely in agreement with the speaker, the positive assertion may be better; but in winning over thinking men Franklin's way is usually better, though it need not be carried always to the extreme he suggests. However much truth there may be in Beveridge's contention, one is not often a "great speaker in his highest moments," delivering "immortal utterances."

Lincoln, whom Beveridge credits with having delivered such utterances, often spoke with humility, and he habitually took pains to give reasons for his conclusions. In the Gettysburg Address and his inaugurals he spoke with unassuming dignity, as the President, but as one who rather minimized than magnified his authority. He never used the *ex cathedra* manner.

However much we like a speaker to know his own mind, we resent strut or bullying. Franklin said, "Firmness carries weight; a strut never does." Some who make excellent arguments let creep into their voices a note of superiority which says, "Now is n't that clever?" and "Have n't I shown you how foolish you are?" Others have a bulldozing note of "You must take it from me, for I know and you don't." It is hard for such men to be "convincing speakers whom one does not resent." They often provoke the resentful comment, "He thinks he knows it all."

*Due modesty does not require the speaker to apologize* for his unworthiness to speak before his audience, or upon the subject chosen. No doubt there are times when apologies are appropriate, but in general they should be avoided. Apologies for lack of preparation are especially objectionable. If an audience forces one to speak without opportunity for preparation, no apologies are called for. Apologies under other circumstances may imply that the speaker does not think his audience worthy of his best efforts. Often these apologies spring from the silly desire to pose as a clever impromptu speaker. They are a way of bragging, "See what I can do without half trying!" In general, one should not attempt a theme he is not qualified to speak on before the given audience. Having accepted an invitation, he should make as good preparation as he can, and then no apology is needed.

SELF-RESPECT AND AUTHORITY.  If arrogance is objectionable, even less persuasive is the air of one who holds himself
too cheaply.  No audience will respect a speaker who does
not respect himself, and seems to be begging them to tolerate him and his ideas.  One may be sure that such an attitude
did not go with Franklin's modest phrases.  No suggestion
regarding modesty, courtesy, or tact should be taken to
mean that a speaker should fawn upon his audience.  An
audience respects manliness above all things, and has more
regard for a good fighter than for a devotee of "soft soap."
We may recall here the speech of the former slave, Booker
T. Washington, at the Atlanta Exposition; a speech at once
respectful and self-respecting.  I heard him speak before a
great audience at the University of California.  His attitude was entirely free from the bumptiousness sometimes
seen in a man who has climbed from a lowly to a high
position, and also free from any touch of subserviency.

Self-respect demands, among other things, that although a
speaker must avoid stiff reserve, he should not sacrifice his
personal dignity, or descend to low jokes or buffoonery.  I
am glad to believe that not even expediency justifies the
sacrifice of one's dignity before the American electorate.
It was reported in the campaign of 1936 that the kissing of
babies was no longer winning votes.  One wonders if it ever
did win more than it lost.  A certain wealthy and dandified
young man became a candidate for Congress in a New York
State district.  He put away his fancy vests and went among
the farmers in a scarecrow costume.  They snowed him
under at the polls.

RESPECT FOR AUDIENCES.  Many of the suggestions of
this discussion of persuasion will be easily followed by the
speaker who has a genuine respect for his audience.  "I think

that is just about the right stuff for such an audience—just a little hokum," said a young speaker, as we came away from a political meeting in a village. But it seemed to me that his speech had been a failure. It was an audience not strongly partisan in his favor; but one made up largely of those who were wondering if they would stick to their old party or follow Theodore Roosevelt out of it. They wished help with their problem. They had looked at the young man steadily, made polite response at the end, and had gone out quite as well aware as he that he had given them hokum. However humble the individual members, almost any audience deserves respect. Give them your best. Your audience may be slow. It probably has not thought through your subject, and it may not be capable of taking many new ideas in rapid succession; but do not mistake slowness for stupidity, or small schooling for ignorance.

It is difficult to tell the truth about audiences in cold print without giving an essentially false impression. It is true that men in general are not thinkers, in the stricter sense of the term. They may be controlled at times by emotion and suggestion, in defiance of reason; and they have strong prejudices. At times they are swayed by dema-gogues, are subject to panics, and form mobs. Still their emotions are often true guides; and their inherited opinions and many of their prejudices are, after all, the product of the experience of the race and not altogether bad stand-ards of conduct. Moreover, there are in almost any audi-ence superior men whose conclusions in the long run are likely to control. They may or may not be educated in a formal way, but native ability and experience have given them a wisdom not guaranteed by diplomas.

Not often has a speaker just cause to feel himself superior

to his audience. Lincoln, when asked the secret of his success as a popular debater, replied: "I always assume that my audience is in many things wiser than I am, and I say the most sensible things I can to them. I have never found that they did not understand me." Edward Everett Hale told a group of students that the least educated man in an audience can conceive of a better speech than the speaker can make. He might have added that this least educated man has probably heard better speeches than the speaker can make.

Lord Bryce, a most competent observer, says in his chapter on "The Nature of Public Opinion," that while nineteen out of twenty persons do not think out public questions for themselves:

It is not that the nineteen persons are incapable of appreciating good arguments, or unwilling to receive them. On the contrary, and this is especially true of the working classes, an audience is pleased when solid arguments are addressed to it. . . .

The chief difference between the so-called upper, or wealthier, and the humbler strata of society is, that the former are less influenced by sentiment and possibly more influenced by notions, often erroneous, of their own interest. . . .

Where the humbler classes have differed in opinion from the higher, they have often been proved by the event to have been right and their so-called betters wrong. . . . Ordinary education, even the sort of education which is represented by a university degree, does not fit a man to handle these questions, and it sometimes fills him with a vain conceit of his competence which closes his mind to argument and to the accumulating evidence of facts. . . . In the less educated man a certain simplicity and openness of mind go some way to compensate for the lack of knowledge. He is more apt to be influenced by the authority of leaders; but as, at least in England and America, he is generally shrewd enough to discern between a great man and a demagogue, this is more a gain than a loss.[9]

Senator Jonathan P. Dolliver, who at the beginning of this century was one of America's strongest political speakers, wrote:

Whoever would deal with the modern American mass-meeting must put into the preparation of his speech time and labor without stint or grudging. . . .

The time has come in the United States when no community is so remote that it does not demand a high order of public speaking. . . . The stump speaker of today has a good many competitors, and it behooves him to bring his audience fresh knowledge, or at least the old, familiar knowledge dressed up so that its friends will be glad to renew its acquaintance. . . .

The democracy of England and America is no fierce mob bewildered by the babble of tongues or the scribble of pens.[10]

If this was true in 1901, how much more true to-day when in the humblest and remotest homes are heard the best speakers of the world.

Do not, above all things, patronize or "talk down" to any audience. If the wheedling, circumflexed tones of the fawning speaker are objectionable, still more so are those which imply, "My dear good people, it must be a real treat to have me come and enlighten your ignorance."

You should use words familiar to your audience; but this in no case requires poor or childish English. The King James version of the Bible has few words not plain to the

---

[9] From James Bryce, *American Commonwealth*, Vol. II, p. 250. By permission of The Macmillan Company, publishers.

[10] *The Saturday Evening Post*, May 25, 1901, p. 7. By permission of the editors.

simplest man; yet it is called a "well of English pure and undefiled." Austin Phelps said:

Patrick Henry thought to win the favor of the backwoodsmen of Virginia by imitating their colloquial dialect, of which his biographer gives the following specimen from one of his speeches: "All the larnin upon the yairth are not to be compared with naiteral pairts." But his hearers, backwoodsmen though they were, knew better than that; and they knew that a statesman of the Old Dominion ought to speak good English. They were his severest critics. The common people know good English when they hear it; they understand it; men crave it who never use it. In their unconscious criticism of a speaker, his right to their hearing depends on his ability to say something worth their hearing; and one of the first evidences they look for of that ability is that he speaks better English than they do.[11]

Respect for audiences must be felt. We reveal in our speech many things we would not, and perhaps are unconscious of—peevishness, egotism, weakness, contempt. The snob will show himself in his speech as well as the hypocrite.

COURTESY. Any exhibition of boorishness upon the platform will discredit the speaker, while the speaker who is courteous can say stern things with impunity. Cutting remarks may sometimes be justified, but are rarely persuasive. Bad temper should not be mistaken for righteousness. It would be a good rule never to say anything about an opponent that you would not say if you were alone with him; but, on the other hand, there are personalities, harmless enough in private, that are in bad taste on the platform. Young debaters sometimes violate good taste by aiming at

[11] Phelps and Frink, *Rhetoric; Its Theory and Practice*, p. 17. By permission of Charles Scribner's Sons.

each other remarks that pass as humor in everyday intercourse, but which in public seem sheer insolence. Do not mistake a laugh cheaply won by blackguardism for genuine approval.

Your audience especially deserves courtesy. Its members have paid you the compliment of giving you their time. In particular you should not trespass beyond the time allotted to you, either by those in charge or by common understanding.

Courtesy does not demand cheap, insincere compliments either to audience or community. A gracious and sincere compliment is welcomed anywhere; but no intelligent audience will be won by strained flattery. The audience may applaud perfunctorily, as in duty bound; but applause accompanied by knowing looks and the nudging of neighbors is not evidence of persuasive effect.

Courtesy does not demand those elaborate welcomes and thanks which are becoming customary in intercollegiate debates, since we have been learning so much, good and bad, from visiting English teams. Less preliminary palaver and more sustained courtesy throughout a debate would be better.

Nor does courtesy demand a final "I thank you." There are times when a speaker does owe thanks for a hearing, and then he should express them in less perfunctory fashion; but in most instances, while the audience has paid the speaker a compliment by attending, the speaker, if he has done his duty, has paid the debt. Usually the "I thank you" has as little meaning as the "thanks" of a clerk in the post-office when you buy a penny stamp.

GENIALITY. Far more important than humor is good humor, or geniality. It is a foil for the attacks of an opponent and one of the surest means of winning over a hostile audience. It is a quality that enables a speaker to meet all sorts of situations with good temper.

One of the worst things a speaker can do ordinarily is to show irritation. A trick of debaters and advocates is to provoke an opponent into a display of wrath. This decreases his authority with his audience and causes him to make damaging statements. There is great force in righteous indignation when a strong man, for proper cause, boils over; but do not have a low boiling point.

Interruptions from the floor may try the temper of a speaker; but if he keeps good-natured he can usually be sure of the sympathy of the audience, who will not demand a very high grade of answer. If he loses his temper he will usually find himself in their bad graces. In the campaign of 1900 I heard Mr. Bryan speaking before a large, and largely hostile, outdoor audience. The University Republican Club was present in force and gave Mr. Bryan an unmerciful heckling. To every question he came back with ready answer, not profound, but good enough for the situation; and all with his beaming smile. I cannot report that we all went away converted; but I believe we did go away with increased liking and admiration for the man who had gone through that ordeal without "blowing up."

While many of us can never succeed as wits, we can all cultivate geniality. Young speakers, in particular, need to cultivate it. That it can be cultivated is evidenced by the case of a young man much criticized for the severity of his manner, who reached the point within three months where a man hearing him for the first time said, "What a very genial speaker that young man is!" And he had not accomplished this by smirking or by putting on geniality, but by developing a genuinely genial attitude toward his hearers.

# CONCLUSION 403

We have come to the end of our study of persuasion so far as this book goes; but it is a study that has no ending. If you have developed your intelligence on the subject so that you will go on learning from experience, your time has been well spent. If you have acquired only a few rules and dogmas, your time has been largely wasted. You will never become persuasive by rule. If you have differed with me at some points, that is your privilege. Indeed, if you have not differed with me now and then in a subject which deals with so many uncertain elements, I fear you have not become as intelligent as I hoped. But whether you agree with this or that suggestion is of slight importance in comparison with your ability to solve the problems that may confront you.

# CHAPTER XX

## FURTHER STUDY OF DELIVERY

In Chapter II we examined, in a somewhat general way, the action of the speaker's mind during delivery. It became evident that a high degree of attention is called for; and in later chapters we considered what can be done to build up ideas so that attention to them shall be as easy as possible, even effortless. In this chapter I wish to return to the subject of delivery. If one delivers speeches prepared in accordance with the suggestions of the chapters on Interest, he will presumably come to have the "keen sense of communication" set down in Chapter II as one of the prime essentials of good delivery; but something remains to be said of the other, the "full realization of the content of your words as you utter them," and especially something more definite with reference to the action of the mind in relating idea to idea.

To attend to an idea means that one holds it in the focus of consciousness, excluding for the time the swarm of other ideas and sensations that constantly bid for attention. We can think clearly and definitely only one thing at a time. We cannot attend to all the thought of even a short speech at once, or of the ordinary paragraph, or of any but the shortest sentence. We can hold in mind a summary of a speech; but the summary is only the thought generalized, without its definite, specific phases. If we are to have definite thinking, we must also focus, or center, upon each successive detail.

But it does not follow that at a given instant we are oblivious of all but the one idea, as an isolated thing. Just as when one focuses his eyes upon a dot at the center of a circle, he is still aware of the white background and of the fact that it is the center of a circle; so when one fixes attention upon an idea he is still aware that it is related to other ideas which form its background and its margin. Moreover, having focused upon an idea, the mind turns to the relations of that idea to other ideas. So we may say that the speaker's mind should dwell definitely upon successive ideas, and also maintain a sense of their relations.

CENTERING AND PHRASING. The term *centering* has been used to indicate this momentary focusing or prolonging of attention upon an idea until it stands out in relief from other ideas. By a *phrase* we mean a word or a group of words containing such a part of the thought as the mind focuses upon, or what amounts to the same thing, containing a center of attention; and by *phrasing* we refer to the action of the voice in marking a phrase, whether by pause, or by change of rate, pitch, or tone color. (The term *phrase* is not to be confused with the grammarian's use of the same word.) It is convenient to treat centering and phrasing together; for, by definition, every phrase embodies a thought center and there is a phrase for every center. There should be no difficulty in keeping the terms distinct when we consider that centering is a mental action while phrasing is a matter of words and delivery. To avoid a common misunderstanding, note here that every word of a sentence is a part, or the whole, of some phrase; and centering is not limited to the main ideas of a speech.

The physical manifestation of centering is *emphasis,*

whether this be shown in increased force, pause, inflection, or other manner. *Centering and emphasis are not synonymous terms;* when you center you use your mind; when you emphasize you use your voice, or other means of expression. Emphasis is the result of centering. While true emphasis is of high importance, we shall say little of it as such; for the term too strongly suggests a mechanical application of force. We shall do better to think and speak of the mental act of centering; and we should make sure that our emphasis springs from alert thinking and a keen realization, as we speak, of the relative importance of ideas and of their relations.

Please note that nowhere in this chapter is it suggested that you should first decide what words are emphatic and then apply stress to them; and that nowhere in speaking of pause, inflection, or tone color, is there any intention of suggesting mechanical as opposed to mental action. The difference may be illustrated thus: One working by the mechanical method decides that in the sentence, "Are you going downtown to-night?" the word *to-night* is emphatic; and then consciously applies stress to that word. One working by our method holds in mind the meaning he wishes to convey, and then trusts the conception to prompt the right emphasis, as in conversation. If he finds difficulty in securing right expression, he sharpens his thinking, perhaps saying to himself, "Not to-morrow night but to-night." What shall it profit one who reads—

> And Death, whenever *he* comes to me
> Shall come on the wide, *unbounded* sea—

to have it pointed out to him that the italicized words do not chiefly bear the thought of the couplet? He knows that as well as his critic, if he has any understanding at all. His trouble is reading without thinking. What he needs is the habit of keeping his mind constantly alert as he reads.

Centering and phrasing are *not fixed and unchanging:* they vary as one's conception of a passage varies, as the context varies, or as the speaker conceives the content to be more or less easy or difficult to his hearers.

Note how the centers shift in Emerson's sentence, "If I should make the shortest list of the qualifications of an orator, I should begin with manliness," according to whether we assume that there has been no preceding discussion, or that there has been a discussion about orators, or statesmen, or soldiers, or about the qualifications of orators, or lists of qualifications.

That phrasing and centering are variable should not lead one to assume that they may be left to chance, habit, rhythm, or the necessities of breathing. It is important that the speaker think in the true units so that he may convey the true units to his audience. Confused centering means confused thinking on the part of the speaker, which will cause confused expression and, therefore, confused understanding on the part of the hearer.

The youth who declaimed: "My name is Norval on the Grampian Hills—my father feeds his flock a frugal swain," did not mean to imply that his name was different in the Lowlands, and had only his slovenly thinking to blame when some of his puzzled mates thought he said his father fed a flock of frugal swine. One may not often fall into results so plainly absurd as that, but centering as absurd in fact is common enough. And strangely enough, bad centering is nearly as common in delivering the speaker's own matter as when interpreting another's. Whenever the attention slips from content and relations are forgotten, the voice may run units together, or halt and break up units, and so throw upon the hearer the burden of analysis or perplex him utterly. But when the mind alertly notes each point, the voice will guide the hearer's attention aright and listening will be easy.

*How much centering?* We should center, not merely upon the major ideas of a sentence or paragraph, but also upon each detail which is necessary for a true grasp of the thought, passing over those which serve their purpose while remaining in the "fringe of consciousness." Another way to put it is that we should focus upon each part of the thought we wish the minds of our hearers momentarily to dwell upon. How long attention will dwell upon each part of the thought depends upon its importance in the speaker's mind. The time may vary from a hardly appreciable instant to several seconds.

This leads us to consider *certain common faults*. First is the fault of *centering too infrequently*—attempting to take and give the thought in too large units. This is the fault of one whose mind skims over the surface, taking only a bird's-eye view. The result is that neither speaker nor hearer is able to grasp the thought definitely, or gain more than a general understanding.

But the more serious fault, akin to this, is *failure to center long enough and firmly enough* upon each phrase. The chief reason a beginner usually speaks too fast is that he does not think enough as he goes. This results in vagueness of delivery and indistinctness of impression upon the hearer. He may have understood clearly in preparation, he may have a sort of understanding as he speaks, but his mind is not taking a firm grasp upon the meaning. He should train himself to *dwell sufficiently upon each phrase to have a distinct impression* of it. While some points must be subordinated to others, still whatever is worth saying at all is worth saying firmly.

Further, it is necessary to take time so that the audience may have time to think. There is need for the deliberation that is characteristic of most experienced speakers. There is little good, however, in simply trying to go slow; the effort often results in even greater rapidity. The speaker who talks too rapidly should impress upon himself the importance of gaining distinct impressions, of full realization of the content of his words, and of giving his audience time. He should fix firmly in mind the truth that his audience cannot move as rapidly as he can. They are not so familiar with his line of thought. If they are to see the pictures suggested, compare his statements with their experience, they must have time. In particular he should impress upon his mind the truth that he fails unless he provokes reaction in his hearers, and causes them to relate his words to their knowledge, beliefs, and experience. In brief, the too rapid speaker should think more, and give his hearers time to think more.

We must now consider faults the opposite of those just discussed: *focusing too frequently and unduly prolonging attention upon minor ideas*. It is possible, for instance, to find significance in almost every word of the sentence referred to above: "*If—I—should* make—the *shortest* list—of the *qualifications*—of an *orator—I*—should *begin*—with *manliness*." The delivery there indicated would be, of course, very tiresome to the hearer, and no one idea would stand forth; but delivery only a little less laborious is sometimes heard. The fault is particularly bad when a speaker marks off a word or a group of words which offers nothing for the mind to rest upon; as "About one third—of our country—was originally covered—with the most magnificent forest."

One cannot really think "about one third" alone.  The true unit is "About one third of our country."  The rest is a single picture readily taken in at one mental glance.  And it is undesirable that one's hearers should try to think "was originally covered" by itself, lest they think of the wrong covering, as the sea.

The more analytic the mood and the more difficult the ideas, the more numerous the centers tend to be, and the longer each will be dwelt upon; but if a speaker finds that his sentences force him to continued labored delivery, he should consider if his composition is not too condensed. The fault, however, more often lies in failure to realize, while speaking, the true units of thought.

There is also to be noted a sort of *false centering* which occurs at such words as *but, and, that, which, are,* and other connective and introductory words, which should ordinarily blend with what follows.  In this sentence (taken from the selection "Who is to Blame?" printed farther on in this chapter), "The party cries, for which he is responsible, are, 'Turpin and Honesty!' 'Diddler and Reform!' " there is nothing in the word *are* to hold attention, and in alert speech the word will blend with what follows.  There are times when attention should dwell upon the relations which these words represent, but such times are rare.

This false centering is sometimes due to conventional reading habits, or to an erroneous belief that we should "mind our pauses," meaning the punctuation.  But punctuation is only to aid readers and has nothing to do with delivery.  A punctuation mark may or may not coincide with the end of a phrase; as in, "Oh, yes, I am young, I know; but youth, Sir, is not my only crime."  False phrasing most often arises from wandering attention or inability to think what comes next.  Instead of pausing till he has a grip on his next clause, the speaker begins, "But—" and then, like the parson in "The One-Hoss Shay," "stops perplexed at what the—Moses—is coming next."

On the whole, the fault of centering too little is more common than that of centering too much. What is needed is complete understanding of each idea, large and small; but with this must go an appreciation of the relative importance of each in the speech. This involves, as we have seen, a keen realization of the relations of idea to idea. With such a realization, one is in a fair way to speak with correct emphasis, pitch, rate, tone color, and, in particular, with proper inflection.

RELATIONS OF IDEAS. Some are principal ideas, some subordinate; some are related as cause and effect; some are repetition or echo, some new thoughts; some are contrasted with others, some are concessive rather than in support of the main thought, and so on through all possible relations of ideas to each other and to the central theme.

*Distinguish principal and subordinate ideas.* Much poor work, showing peculiarly in bad centering and consequent false emphasis, is due to failure to discriminate values. Attention should vary with degree of importance. This does not mean the absolute value of an idea, but its value in its place with reference to the larger thought one is expressing. The effect upon delivery of unduly prolonging attention upon ideas that deserve some attention, but yet are subordinate, is much the same as focusing upon possible points that should be left in the background. Take this sentence: Since it is true that our affairs are in such a desperate state, it behooves us to consider what measures should be taken. Now assuming, what the construction indicates, that the first clause states a fact already agreed upon, then it should receive less attention than the second. Yet many speakers, seeking to be very forceful, impressed by the fact stated in the first part, and perhaps caught by the strong word *desperate*, would pound upon the subordinate and thus obscure to some extent the—at the moment—more important major clause.

*Distinguish echo and new idea.* The word *new* here has no reference to novelty or originality, but refers to an idea that has not appeared before in the particular discussion. *Echo* is the felt recurrence of an idea already expressed. The echo may or may not be in the same words as the part referred to. It most frequently refers to the immediately preceding, but may refer to any preceding part. Almost any sentence in a speech may be considered a link in a chain, reaching both forward and backward. It is this interlinking which gives firmness of structure, and where it is absent the style is abrupt and liable to be disjointed. When the echoes are not clearly distinguished, delivery will also be disjointed and lacking in coherence. They have been called the "connective tissue" of language.

A fine example of coherence through echo—coherence in composition, which should result in coherence in delivery—is found in the Gettysburg Address. Analyze for new idea and echo the first four sentences:

Fourscore and seven years ago our fathers brought forth on this continent, a new nation, conceived in liberty, and dedicated to the proposition that all men are created equal.

Now we are engaged in a great civil war, testing whether that nation, or any nation so conceived and so dedicated, can long endure. We are met on a great battlefield of that war. We have come to dedicate a portion of that field, as a final resting place for those who here gave their lives that that nation might live. It is altogether fitting and proper that we should do this.

But, in a larger sense, we can not dedicate—we can not consecrate——we can not hallow——this ground. The brave men, living and dead, who struggled here, have consecrated it, far above our poor power to add or detract. The world will little note, nor long remember what we say here, but it can never forget what they did here. It is for us the living, rather, to be dedicated here to the unfinished work which they who fought here have thus far so nobly advanced. It is rather for us to be here dedicated to the great task remaining before us——that from these honored dead we take increased devotion to that cause for which they gave the last full measure of devotion——that we here highly resolve that these dead shall not have died in vain——that this nation, under God, shall have a new birth of freedom——and that government of the people, by the people, for the people, shall not perish from the earth.[1]

Note in particular how *might live* echoe*s endure*. Then turn to the last sentence of the speech and note the many echoes from the early part; and note especially how the last phrase, usually read with flat dulness, is charged with meaning by the echo of *endure* in *shall not perish from the earth*. Throughout this speech, and indeed, throughout any well knit composition there are numerous——one might almost say, innumerable——echoes, the recognition of which, although they may not be so notable as those referred to, is necessary for informing the voice with the true meaning.

That the new idea must be recognized is too obvious for illustration. In the majority of cases, it is the new idea which for the moment is of chief importance; it is the one

---

[1] This copy of the Address is taken from a facsimile of what William E. Barton, in *Lincoln at Gettysburg*, p. 111, pronounces the sixth and last copy made by Lincoln. The punctuation is not according to rule, not even according to the rules of his time; but I believe it furnishes a better cue to his phrasing than does a formally correct punctuation, for a speaker, and especially a speaker not trained to the niceties of composition, tends to punctuate by ear.

now to be impressed. The echo, on the other hand, is already in mind and is often given chiefly for the purpose of keeping relations clear. Nevertheless, it may be, in a given case, the most important part of a sentence, as in the case of repetition for emphasis. In the sentence, "For prosperous labor, industry, and commerce, three conditions are necessary: first, liberty; second, liberty; third, liberty," the third *liberty* is meant to be the most significant; if the significance diminishes with repetition, then repetition is worse than useless. The echoes, noted above, in the Gettysburg Address, *might live* and *shall not perish,* are certainly large with meaning.

A new idea is not necessarily important, though it usually should have some attention. When Lincoln said, "Now we are engaged in a great civil war," the fact of war was too obvious to need much attention, though a "new idea"; but the new idea of *testing* free government was a major point. So while this method of analysis is an aid in our study, neither it nor any other method can relieve us from the use of our brains.

The term *echo* is hardly adequate, though the one ordinarily used. Many a phrase which contains a back reference is really an amplification, or a restatement with so much added meaning and force that the feeling of reference is not prominent, although present. To echoes should be added *restatements* and *amplifications*. And there are also instances of restatements where the back reference is entirely lost. Echo or not echo is a question of fact; that is, the question is not, Might not a word or clause refer back, but Does it?

*Note the contrasts and comparisons.* Not often is there failure to do this when the two parts are very close together; but there often is failure when they are separated by matter which causes the speaker to forget the first half.   Take this passage:

In a rural community such as this country was a hundred years ago, whoever was nominated for office was known to his neighbors, and the consciousness of that knowledge was a conservative influence in determining nominations.   But in the local elections of the great cities of today—elections that control taxation and expenditure—the mass of the voters vote in absolute ignorance of the candidates.

Very commonly those attempting to interpret this passage fail to remember what is said in the first sentence of knowledge on the part of the voters, when they reach "absolute ignorance" in the second sentence.   And, incidentally, for the same reason they fail to note that "candidates" echoes "whoever was nominated for office."   Lively thinking is required to bring out all the relations in those two sentences.

*Does the thought look forward?*   Most of the thought relations need no discussion here, but there is one other that should be noted because of its bearing upon a common fault—that of dropping the inflection at nearly every pause, giving a limping effect.   Now, speaking generally, a downward inflection is our instinctive way of indicating a degree of completeness in the thought; while an upward inflection indicates that the mind is looking forward rather than resting upon what is at the instant being said.   I hear a reader declaring—

> I never was on the dull, tame shore'—
> But I loved the great sea more and more'—
> And backward flew to her billowy breast'—
> Like a bird'—that seeketh its mother's nest.

Now presumably the reader does not wish to make his author say he was never on shore, or that he flew like a bird;

but either the words are just dead words to him, or he has a bad habit.

Try this: If you try to convince me that inflation is a sound economic policy, I have no patience to listen to you; but if you are trying to say that inflation is an heroic remedy for a desperate condition, I will hear your argument. Here the voice would naturally rise at all pauses save those at the semicolon and the period; and at the semicolon there is not the same sense of completeness as at the period.

The fault referred to is evidently that of one who fails to keep alert to the relations of his ideas, and especially to the forward relations. He sees each point in isolation, and to him each stop is a terminal. A good remedy is to practise much upon passages that strongly demand the forward look; as

> The hills,
> Rock-ribbed, and ancient as the sun; the vales
> Stretching in pensive quietness between;
> The venerable woods; rivers that move
> In majesty; and the complaining brooks
> That make the meadows green; and, poured round all,
> Old Ocean's gray and melancholy waste,—
> Are but the solemn decorations all
> Of the great tomb of man.

Sometimes the fault has grown into a habit so strong that it will not yield to "mental treatment" alone; and then the inflections should be drilled up arbitrarily, till the ear grows to demand them. What is said of the treatment of this fault may be applied, in principle, to the treatment of any other delivery faults that persist very long after good mental action on the platform has been attained.

There is the correlative fault of rarely letting the voice

fall, even at the end of sentences. Such delivery, an approach to intoning, lacks positiveness and directness. It is due to taking too cursory a view, failing to center definitely enough. But it is sometimes an affectation. It is common among stump speakers. The practice of sustaining all inflections, though employed by some eminent speakers, and sometimes defended as a means of making the voice carry over very large audiences, is, I believe, rarely justified, and it quickly establishes a bad habit. It seems to be going out of vogue.

It is true that words delivered with a falling inflection are often weak or even inaudible; and this is highly undesirable because these words, especially the final words of a sentence, are usually the most important. Delivery in which endings weaken will be weak in total effect. The cause of this weakness, however, is not that there is any necessary connection between falling inflection and falling force; but that the speaker's attention does not stick to the point he is expressing, but too soon goes forward to the next. If he will bring the point to completion with sustained attention, his voice will usually maintain carrying power.

NOTE WHAT'S "BETWEEN THE LINES." All expression in words is elliptic; reader or hearer is constantly supplying something beyond what is put into words. In speaking expressively we supply much by inflection, emphasis, pause, and tone. The simple words, Are you going out to-night? can have innumerable implications; as, You know you ought not, Good, I'm glad of it, What will So and So think? How about that exam. to-morrow? It's all right with me, I am indifferent; just making conversation, If you go we're through. Often the unspoken questions of the audience are implied in answers by the speaker; and often language leaves to delivery the expression of the ideas lying in such phrases as, *however, therefore, I concede, I submit, I protest that, to be sure, what do you think of that? I am strong for this idea, I don't think much of this, It's absurd, What of it? I challenge denial, We all know this, Don't you see?* Practise speaking some simple sentence, as This is a fact, with these implications added.

Less obvious implications are also common. Not one per cent of those who have tried to interpret the passage concerning elections, quoted above, have clearly noted that the contrast is not completed, even with a context plainly showing that the main point of the contrast is left to implication: In the great cities of to-day the voters vote in absolute ignorance of the candidates, *and so there is not, as in the country, a sufficient check on bad nominations.* Huxley, after pointing out that, if success and happiness depended upon a game of chess, we should prepare earnestly to win the game, continues: "Yet it is a very plain and elementary truth, that the life, that the fortune, and the happiness of every one of us, and more or less of those connected with us, do depend upon our knowing something of the rules of a game infinitely more complicated and difficult than chess." Now there is undoubtedly an implication, beyond what is put into definite words, that while we should work very hard for that hypothetical chess game, we prepare for this other game (the game of life) very casually. This implication, too, is usually missed, and for the same reason in both cases: that there is so much else to attend to. Yet the real tang of these passages is lost unless these implications are clearly in the mind of one who speaks them. The speaker, then, must train his mind to alertness in speaking, so that it can not only focus upon the particular point he is uttering and play forward and backward over related ideas, but also note even the unexpressed ideas.

How all this can be done. At this stage students have said, "How is it possible to attend to so many things at once, especially when one is addressing an audience?" The question is natural, but rests upon a misunderstanding. I do not mean that you should be saying to yourself, This is the main idea, This is an echo of such and such a passage. That would be but little better than to be saying, This word is emphatic, and, I must pause here. But I do mean that you are to be *sensible* of values and relations as you speak. The better your preparation and grasp, the easier your task. For a beginner to control his mind sufficiently may not be easy, but for this control he must work and practise. But after all, what is urged upon you must be practicable, for it is only what we do in a wide-awake conversation. We are striving only to reproduce and accentuate upon the platform the mental activities of conversation.

*Pause*. The secret of success in carrying on all the complex process is pause. The rapid turning of attention from the particular idea to its relations and to the audience all becomes possible when we take time. There is hardly a beginner who does not need this advice: *Train yourself strictly to the habit of pausing until the next thought and its relations are clearly grasped by your mind,* before giving it to your audience. And do not forget that that requirement is not met by grasping the bare intellectual content of your words. You must recognize the full significance of the thought, and that includes the emotional content also. Remember also that while the speaker needs time to think what is to be said, the audience needs time to think of what has been said. "Speech is silvern; silence is golden," says the proverb, and silence is never more golden than in the midst of speech.

Do not fear your pauses will be too long. What may

seem to a beginner a long wait will really be very short. When your mind is doing its proper work in your pauses, they will not seem long. Do not fear that drawling will result from deliberate pausing. When it is not intentional, drawling is the sign of a listless or of a too introspective state of mind, and not the expression of alert thinking.

Do not confuse pause with hesitation. We pause to think; we hesitate because we cannot think. Nothing is more tiresome to an audience than a hesitating, halting delivery. It seems to be due chiefly to beginning a clause without a firm forward-looking grasp of it.

Hesitation is especially annoying when the gaps are filled with *urs* and *uhs*. Grunting is no part of thinking. Heed the plea of Oliver Wendell Holmes:

> And when you stick on conversation's burrs,
> Don't strew your pathway with those dreadful *urs*.

Pause gives opportunity for breathing, but a speaker should never stop simply to breathe. To do so is to let physical necessities tyrannize over mental processes. So far as consciousness is concerned, pause should be only an opportunity to think. Still, breathing is an important matter. A well controlled, sufficient supply of breath is necessary to a well supported tone and helps to steady the nerves. A speaker should cultivate the habit of utilizing the pauses for breathing, and particularly should he avoid going so far as to be compelled to gasp for breath. The opportunities are always sufficient, without interfering with the thought movement.

*Summarizing* will be found very helpful; first, because to make a good summary one must have the clearest understanding; and, secondly, because if you put into your summary just the right turn of the thought, the real point of view and the true emphasis, and fix these in your mind before you rise to speak, you will be aided greatly in giving to each part its due importance and in relating each to the whole. A summary is like a bird's-eye view: by omitting details it makes clearer the relations of parts. Many speakers who deliver individual sentences well fail in giving due value to each part as related to the whole. Summarize your speech, then, as a whole, and summarize each paragraph. Make these brief and clear-cut, in order that they may be easily carried in mind. Of course one's subject sentence and main heads constitute a summary, with the connectives a bit more elaborated; although if one makes his summary very long it loses much of its value. It should be easily "portable."

*The amplified paraphrase.* When you have gained some mastery of your speech, in its details and as a whole, you will find it an excellent practice to go, silently at first, through the *thought chain* time after time, until you can, without reference to notes or manuscript, proceed through the entire speech without mental wandering, at once individualizing each point and seeing it in its relations. In this practice, it is well to throw in, especially into the transitions, those phrases that have been described as lying between the lines, and which, while not necessary to expression of the thought when delivery is fully adequate, will serve to accentuate in your mind both the relation of idea to idea and the emotional significance of each.

Then practice aloud with the additional words inserted. Then say the speech with these words inserted only mentally; and finally speak without trying to "think in" particular words, but making sure that you still fully realize the significances the added words have stood for. It will be found that this practice, by inducing deliberation and sharpening realization, will do much to increase expressiveness. Incidentally, the practice will tend to aid memory, for memory usually fails at transitions.

For practice a selection is fully as good as your own speech. The use of the amplified paraphrase can be shown in a selection already used for illustrative purposes.

## WHO IS TO BLAME?

1  Public duty in this country is not discharged, as is often
2  supposed, by voting.  A man may vote regularly, and still
3  fail essentially of his political duty, as the Pharisee who gave
4  tithes of all that he possessed, and fasted three times in the
5  week, yet lacked the very heart of religion.  When an Ameri-
6  can citizen is content with voting merely, he consents to accept
7  what is often a doubtful alternative.  His first duty is to help
8  shape the alternative.  This, which was formerly less neces-
9  sary, is now indispensable.  In a rural community such as this
10  country was a hundred years ago, whoever was nominated
11  for office was known to his neighbors, and the consciousness
12  of that knowledge was a conservative influence in determin-
13  ing nominations.  But in the local elections of the great cities
14  of to-day, elections that control taxation and expenditure, the
15  mass of the voters vote in absolute ignorance of the candi-
16  dates.  The citizen who supposes that he does all his duty
17  when he votes, places a premium upon political knavery.
18  Thieves welcome him to the polls and offer him a choice,
19  which he has done nothing to prevent, between Jeremy
20  Diddler and Dick Turpin.  The party cries, for which he is
21  responsible, are "Turpin and Honesty!" "Diddler and Re-
22  form!"  And within a few years, as a result of this indiffer-
23  ence to the details of public duty, the most powerful politician
24  in the Empire State of the Union was Jonathan Wild the
25  Great, the captain of a band of plunderers.  I know it is said
26  that the knaves have taken the honest men in a net, and have
27  contrived machinery which will inevitably grind only the grist

28 of rascals.  The answer is, that when honest men did once
29 what they ought to do always, the thieves were netted and
30 their machine was broken. . . . To say that in this country
31 the rogues must rule, is to defy history and to despair of the
32 republic.

33    If ignorance and corruption and intrigue control the pri-
34 mary meeting, and manage the convention, and dictate the
35 nomination, the fault is in the honest and intelligent work-
36 shop and office, in the library and the parlor, in the church
37 and the school.  When they are as constant and faithful to
38 their political rights as the slums and the grogshops, the pool-
39 rooms and the kennels; when the educated, industrious, tem-
40 perate, thrifty citizens are as zealous and prompt and unfail-
41 ing in political activity as the ignorant and venal and mis-
42 chievous, . . . then, but not until then—if ignorance and
43 corruption always carry the day—there can be no honest
44 question that the republic has failed.  But let us not be de-
45 ceived.  While good men sit at home, not knowing that there
46 is anything to be done, nor caring to know; cultivating a feel-
47 ing that politics are tiresome and dirty, and politicians vulgar
48 bullies and bravoes; half persuaded that a republic is the con-
49 temptible rule of a mob, and secretly longing for a splendid
50 and vigorous despotism—then remember, it is not a govern-
51 ment mastered by ignorance, it is a government betrayed by
52 intelligence; it is not the victory of the slums, it is the sur-
53 render of the schools; it is not that bad men are brave, but
54 that good men are infidels and cowards.[2]

[2] From "The Public Duty of Educated Men" by George William
Curtis, in *Orations and Addresses*, Vol. I, p. 261.  By permission of
Harper & Brothers.  This selection is not perfect and is far from
being the best passage in the speeches of Curtis; but out of the hundreds I have tested I have never found one better adapted to drill in
delivery, or one that stands up better under the severe test of intensive
class study.  Its usefulness is by no means limited to the exercise
described just above.  It can be used for working out in practice all
the suggestions of this chapter.

I will now insert in the first paragraph some of the implications that occur to me. No doubt your interpolations would differ from mine, but that is immaterial, provided they are consistent with the meaning of the passage. (The series of dots in the passage below stand for words in the original paragraph which are here omitted to save space. They do not indicate that these parts of the original should be omitted in practice speaking.)

Public duty in this country is not discharged, as is often supposed, by voting. A man may vote regularly [taking the utmost pains], and still fail essentially of his political duty, as the Pharisee [you know the story—the Pharisee who boasted that he] gave tithes of all that he possessed, and fasted three times in the week, yet lacked the very heart of religion. [Voting is necessary, of course, but] when an American citizen is content with voting merely [and does nothing else], he consents to accept what is often a doubtful alternative. [Doesn't that square with your experience? What should he do, you ask? Why,] his first duty is to help shape the alternative. . . . was known to his neighbors [how terribly well they knew him!], and the consciousness of that knowledge was a conservative [or restraining] influence in determining nominations. But in the local elections of the great cities of to-day, elections [mind you] that control taxation and expenditure, the mass of the voters vote in absolute ignorance of the candidates; [and so there is not the same check as in the country on bad nominations. Why, with such blind voting] the citizen who supposes he does all his duty when he votes [(How can he be so dumb?) actually] places a premium upon political knavery. [See our respectable, well meaning citizen coming to vote! In many cases] thieves welcome him to the polls. . . . "Diddler and Reform!" [So gullible they think us!] And within a few years [I am not talking theory, but facts], . . . . the most powerful politician in the Empire State of the Union [the state with the greatest wealth, population, and political power] was [a man who might justly be called] Jonathan Wild the Great [Boss Tweed, I mean], the captain of a band of plunderers [as truly as ever was the old master of London thieves]. I know it is said [the cheap excuse is common] that. . . . . The answer is [fact against theory; you can't get away from it] that when honest men did once [to that very Tweed] what they ought to do always, the thieves were netted and their machine was broken. To say [as you practically do] that in this country the rogues must rule, is [both] to defy history, and [what is vastly more serious] to despair of the republic.

Go through the second paragraph in the same way. In particular, add a clause to make more evident the transition to the second paragraph; insert words to bring out more sharply the relation of the second sentence to the central idea (a matter easily confused), and note the implied conclusion of this sentence; develop what we might be deceived about, and add touches to dramatize a bit the first part of the last sentence. Then practise the selection as suggested above.

MONOTONY OF DELIVERY. Monotony is a fault so common that it is worth while to point out here that it is due fundamentally to failure in discrimination, to drifting; and that it is not likely to exist where the true value and character of each idea is recognized and relations are clearly discerned; provided there be emotional as well as intellectual discrimination. Monotony may also be due to repression, an unwillingness to speak out. And monotony may grow into a habit which calls for very direct treatment. An excellent method—good regardless of whether one is usually monotonous or not—is to practise on passages notable for variety, such as the long quotation from Carlyle in Chapter IX, and the selection from Curtis just used. The exercise described under the preceding heading is a strong antidote for monotony. A sharp interchange in a dialogue is also good for the purpose, since it calls for keen discrimination. First, get a thorough understanding of the passage you are working on, and then, keeping always a clear sense of meaning, practise until you have expressed that meaning completely. It is well in such practice to go beyond adequate expression and exaggerate; and then tone down.

HOW TO WORK. The methods set forth in this chapter can be most advantageously practised by the beginner with a written speech or a selection. But they are, in part, quite as applicable to an extemporaneous speech; that is, a speech prepared and outlined, but not fixed in phraseology. Let there be the most complete understanding of each detail and of the relation of idea to idea, and then let there be speaking, with deliberate, complete thinking. Do not try to "make a speech," but only to command the thought and to express it; first as to one person (to an actual person if you have a patient friend), and then to a larger and larger number.

THE ELEMENTS OF EXPRESSION SUMMARIZED. To make expression clearer and stronger, accentuate mental processes which are the natural cause of expression. Proper pausing and phrasing will spring from recognition of the successive thought units; and length of pause and rate of utterance will be regulated by the relative values which the mind assigns to each step. From centering will spring emphasis, which will be due emphasis, if the relation of part to part is clearly in mind. Recognition of relations will prompt true inflections.

Change of pitch arises from discrimination of ideas and values; climax, from a sense of the development of the thought and feeling; and change of tone color, from change of attitude, as from the explanatory to the argumentative mood. Where these elements of expression exist, monotony is impossible. It should be understood that this analysis is but a rough one; the various elements may combine in countless ways. Expression is too complex a matter for brief analysis; if, indeed, complete analysis be possible.

# CHAPTER XXI

## GESTURE

Gesture is the communication of thought and feeling through posture and movement, including facial expression.

The brief treatment of gesture at the end of Chapter II should be reviewed at this point. The subject was introduced into that chapter to encourage gesturing from the beginning of your practice, and because gesturing is a help in gaining the communicative spirit. Two other reasons were given for developing one's ability to gesture: first, that gesture is a useful means of expression; and, second, that you cannot keep from gesturing if you try. Gesture was not urged as a means of making a fine appearance, for that view of the matter may lead to affectation, and certainly does tend to self-consciousness. Nevertheless it is true that a speaker who makes easy and expressive gestures will make a much better appearance, and at the same time will attract less attention to his person than one who holds himself rigidly or slumps into inactivity.

GESTURE AS A MEANS OF EXPRESSION. Any man who has really striven to communicate his ideas and feelings knows the inadequacy of words; and gesture, although more limited in range, is often a quicker, plainer, and stronger means of expression. A motion toward the door, a shrug, a lifted eyebrow—what words can equal these gestures?

Gesture is particularly adapted to the expression of attitude and feeling. It is used also to express facts and ideas apart from feeling, as that the statue was so high, or that there are two opposing principles; but here the use of gesture is obviously limited. Words, which have developed along with ideas, are, generally speaking, the better expression of them. But through posture, action, and facial expression the speaker expresses effectively his degree of earnestness, his attitude toward the idea presented, whether he accounts it trivial or important, acceptable or objectionable, pleasing or disgusting, whether he is eager or doubtful, mocking or serious, hesitant or confident, and so on through the range of feelings and attitudes.

Whether he wishes to gesture much or little, no speaker can afford to leave latent his powers of gesture, or to run the risk that when he does gesture, perhaps in spite of himself, he will attract attention to his awkwardness, or the risk that nature will show her rebellion against restraint in aimless, fidgety movements that will detract from rather than add to his effectiveness.

First stage of gesture training. Gesture training should proceed by stages, although these cannot be sharply separated. In the first stage one should seek to encourage the native impulse to gesture, and get to doing something. This impulse is no more, and no less, of a mystery than the impulse to express in any way. It is in you and will make you gesture if you do not suppress it, or have not attenuated it by long suppression.

Perhaps you say, "I have tried, but I feel no impulse; if I make a gesture it is just by main strength and awkwardness." My first question then is, Have you really wished very much to express yourself and to impress your audience? My second question is, Have you gained a state of poise that encourages the working out of the impulse? Or do you stand clutching a desk as your last friend, or perhaps in the attitude of a weary horse at a hitching post? Or do you clinch your hands behind your back, or hold them tense at your sides, while you stand rigid as a tin soldier? Or do you stick your hands deep into your pockets as if holding fast to your last nickel? If you do any of these things you do not give the impulse a chance. You have not gained poise or the free but firm attitude of a self-controlled man who has business with his hearers.

*Helpful exercises.* You probably need exercises to help you in gaining poise and free, coördinated action. Now exercises may be, and usually are, silly movements in themselves, as are the exercises of musicians, athletes, and soldiers; but anything that helps is not silly. Those suggested below are of little use unless practised persistently, for it is not to be expected that a little practice will overcome bad habits. If you will practise in a room filled with fresh air, you will find these exercises restful after study.

These exercises are not gestures, and it is not desirable that you should practise on a "handy set" of gestures. A great variety of movement is possible to the speaker, and a great variety should be practised until all natural movements seem natural. After the few exercises offered are mastered the student should have no difficulty in inventing variations.

1. Stretch and yawn very thoroughly.

2. Lift your hands high and walk about on your toes.

3. Stand erect and let the head sink forward on the chest; then let the shoulders droop, and the arms hang limp. Now slowly fold the spine from the top downward, being sure that the head leads at all times. Do not bend the knees or strain the muscles of the legs. Unfold the body, being sure that the movement begins at the hips, that the head follows, and that the arms and shoulders come gradually into the normal position.

If these directions are followed, the head will be the last part of the body to assume an erect position. Faults to be avoided in the execution of this exercise are, in folding, a hinge movement at the hips with a straight back, and, in the unfolding movement, cramping the neck and lifting the shoulders, thereby making it necessary to let them drop at the completion of the exercise.

4. Standing or sitting erect, let the head drop forward on the chest as if you were asleep; relax the jaw, tongue, eyelids and facial muscles. Focus the attention at the base of the neck behind, being sure that there is no unnecessary muscular exertion, and slowly lift the head to a normal position—the mouth at this point should be open at least an inch—then let the head back as far as possible, then bring it forward to an erect position.

If in this exercise you feel like a drooling idiot, that will be all to the good.

5. From the forward position of the head described in Exercise 4, slowly roll the head around, describing as large a circle as possible. Neck muscles not necessarily used should be relaxed. The pivotal point is at the base of the neck. Repeat in reverse direction. Let the head feel as if it would roll off if it were not tied on.

6. *a.* Stand erect, with the weight forward, arms lifted straight to the front, palms down. Let the arms fall lifelessly to the side and swing as a result of their own momentum.

*b.* Place the arms parallel above the head with the palms in, and let them fall.

*c.* Extend the arms to a lateral horizontal position, and let them fall lifelessly.

*d.* Make the arms flop about like the arms of a loose-jointed doll. Let the muscles controlling the arms be completely relaxed, and produce the flopping by a movement of the body.

*e.* Let another person flop your arms about without the slightest interference from you. If he lifts them up and lets go, they should fall like stuffed sacks tied to your shoulders.

*f.* Place the arms as in *c;* let the fingers relax, then the fore-arm, bending at the elbow, then the upper arm.

*g.* Reverse *f,* beginning by lifting the shoulders slightly. Energize the muscles of the upper arm, with the forearm pendent; energize the muscles of the forearm, then of the wrist, and lastly of the fingers.

You should now be pretty well rid of stiffness, and ready for exercises to bring you into a position of activity combined with poise.

7. Sit in an armless chair of fair height, without touching the back, with head erect, feet resting easily but squarely on the floor, arms relaxed in the lap, and the chest expanded but not strained. (Expansion should be in all directions; not merely forward with contraction at the back.) Move gently forward and back and from side to side, until the position is found in which the body seems to remain erect with the slightest effort. This may take repeated trials.

8. Keeping the feeling of poise gained in Exercise 7, stand easily erect, with the heels together, letting the toes find a comfortable position with the weight well forward on the balls of the feet. Focus the attention at the notch of the sternum and slowly rise on the toes, and at the same time lift the arms to a lateral horizontal position; sustain until there is something of the feeling of lightness one has when up to the armpits in water, then return slowly to the former position, keeping the weight well under control. Do not push the hips forward or let the body rest back on the heels.

9. Take the position described in Exercise 8 and slowly move toward the right until the weight is wholly on one foot and the other foot rests lightly on the floor. Place the free foot as far as possible to the left without disturbing the body or stiffening the leg, then slowly move the body toward the free foot until the weight is well over it, and it has become the supporting or "strong" foot. Place the free foot forward and slowly move the

weight forward over it.   Place the foot now free to the side and move the weight over it; move the foot now free back, and transfer the weight.   The movement can now be made in any direction.

Now for some exercises involving coördinated movements:

10.  *a*. Standing with the weight on one foot, place the free foot at the side, and the arm of the same side across the body till the finger tips touch the opposite shoulder; then simultaneously unfold the arm to a lateral horizontal position and cross the strong foot with the free foot.   Reverse and repeat.

*b*. To Exercise *a* add a pivotal action of the head from side to side in the direction that corresponds to the movement of the foot and in opposition to that of the arm.

11. Stand with the weight on one foot, arms lifted and the tips of the fingers touching the chest.   Step firmly forward and at the same time unfold the arms to a lateral horizontal position. Carry this unfolding movement out to the very tips of the fingers and see that the body is well supported on the forward foot.

Repeat, starting with the weight on the other foot.

Repeat, unfolding the arms at an angle of about forty-five degrees from the horizontal.

12.  *a*. Stand erect, slightly forward on the right foot, stretch the right arm forward and describe with the hand a figure eight lying on its side.   Move the hand in the direction indicated by the arrows in the accompanying cut.   Let the movement be

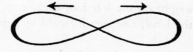

initiated at the shoulder; but strive for the feeling that the tips of your fingers are drawing the figure in the air.

Do not exaggerate the sidewise sway of the body, but let the body respond easily to the movement of the arm.

Repeat with the left arm; then with both arms; then with the arms moving in opposition to each other. Make the figure now large and now small.

*b*. Repeat the figure with the arms extended laterally, first with either arm, and then with both arms.

*c*. Repeat occasionally with the movement in opposition to the arrows.

This movement, which is described as the Greek curve and is said to have been practised in ancient times, is, I believe, the best single exercise ever invented. Properly done it involves every joint in the body, all working in unison.

13. *a*. Stand with the weight on the left foot and place the right foot slightly forward in a relaxed condition; focus the eyes on a definite point to the right, turn the head till it faces in the same direction; place the right foot slightly behind the left and transfer the weight back on to it, and at the same time relax the left, which should be allowed to adjust itself. Do not lift it. The eyes, head, body and feet should now face directly toward the point first selected.

*b*. With the weight on the right foot back, turn the eyes to the right to a definite point, then the head; turn the left heel out by pivoting on the ball of the foot, and immediately follow this action by transferring the weight to the left foot. Let the right foot adjust itself.

Repeat *a* and *b* alternately until a complete circle has been made; then reverse.

*c*. With the weight on the left foot back, turn the eyes to the right, and then the head, and step forward by replacing the right foot.

*d*. With the weight on the right foot forward, look to the left, turn the head, and step forward to the left. Movement may now be made from any position in any direction. These exercises should be practised until great facility in moving in any direction is attained.

Now if you say there is nothing remarkable about these movements, you are quite right. They are simply the movements a well poised person makes in turning. Still you may need to practise them.

Now after faithful practise, and immediately after practise, try again speaking something with vigor. If still no gestures come, try again lifting your arms to encourage the impulse. Or say very positively, "I will not do it," and at the *do* bang the desk, not gently but hard enough to hurt your hand. You may substitute for "do it" other words, as "I will not go to that party," or any act you can think of that you positively object to. If after hitting the desk a few times you do not have a sensation that is not the pain in your hand, then I lose my wager. Please do not think I wish to make table-thumpers of you; but just to get started.

Or try this: Take an object in your hand and show it to your imaginary audience, with some remark such as, "Can you see what I have here?" and extend it so they can see better. A quarter or a half-dollar is excellent. Put the coin as near the tips of your fingers as you can and handle it well. Step forward as you extend it. Ask them, "Who wants my quarter?" Take in with eyes and movement all parts of the audience, and act as if you would give the money to any one who would come forward. Make up a speech about it: "Ah, gentlemen, this is money. That's what we are all out for; money! Greatest stuff in the world." And lift it up for their admiration. Or turn noble, and exclaim, "Money; filthy lucre! who would give his life for that?" and put it from you.

Now borrow another coin, of a different design, and extend one on each hand—always taking in the whole audience—and ask, "Which design do you think better? This one has the full-length figure of Liberty, and this only her head. Which do you think the more artistic?" One can go on endlessly with such nonsense. The advantage is that the movements come more naturally with objects in the hands.

Now put aside the coins, and make talk of a somewhat analogous character about ideas: "Will you accept this proposal? Or do you think the other plan is better? I think the first proposal is splendid, and worthy of a great organization; but the second seems to me disgracefully cowardly." Use exaggerated terms. You will be likely to make much the same motions you did with the coins; for by origin gestures are largely metaphors in action. For example, primitive man stuck up his nose at an offensive smell, and then he stuck up his nose at an offensive idea. He threw out his arms to indicate that he would not resist the approach of another, and we still express welcome in the same way.

If you still grow rigid before an audience, I suggest three things to help in overcoming this tendency: 1. Go through the exercises as near the time of your speech as possible. 2. Have something in your speech which will take you to a blackboard or a chart where you will point out details. This will put you into motion without that almost guilty feeling that you are gesturing. 3. Be sure to have parts in your speech that should be said with unusual vigor.

SECOND STAGE OF GESTURE TRAINING. We will now assume that you can gesture after a fashion, and that you have to some degree conquered your self-consciousness, so that you can make a motion without stopping your mental processes. Perhaps you have not had to go through the first stage, but literally took to gesture as do ducks to water.

Or perhaps the exercises and the attempts you have made have in some measure brought you back to nature. Is this all that can or should be done? We have to consider (1) that it does not follow from the fact that gestures should come from the prompting of nature that nature will make them all they should be; (2) that it is doubtful if you have completely overcome restraint, and (3) that it is probable that because of restraint, timidity, or tight muscles you have developed some bad habits. For example, it is rather probable that you have developed a very few favorite gestures which, because you have a comfortable feeling in making them, you make so often that they lose meaning, and at the same time keep you from making others.

One who has reached the point where he can gesture with some freedom may safely consider what he is doing and how he can improve. This may cause a degree of self-consciousness; but it is better to settle with some things at once rather than to keep one's faults and mannerisms which all the time may be becoming more firmly fixed.

Get before a large mirror and learn from "the only honest man." Do not be afraid of the sneer at the "looking-glass orator." Many experienced speakers make use of the mirror; and you, I assume, are beginners. I am not asking you to practise the gestures of a speech you are to deliver, but only to practise so that when you come before an audience you will not have to think of how you gesture.

Now question yourself a bit: Do your gestures express something? Do you feel that your hand is talking to the audience? Does it seem to say, Note this point in particular; or, This is of little account; or, This is displeasing; or, This is fundamental; This is noble, inspiring; Put this idea from you? These and many other things your action can say, and you should begin to feel it is speaking.

Try now to express shades of meaning. Say with your hands: This is a fact. This is a fact, but I am indifferent to it. This is a fact; make what you can of it. This is a fact and you must accept it. This is the most fundamental fact of all. Yes, that is the fact, I regret to say. Work in all sorts of moods and mental attitudes.

I append a list of sentences for practice. Some of them can be conceived in various moods; for example, "Look out" may be anxious, threatening, humorous, or gently chiding. Some of the ideas can be expressed by posture alone; more will require both posture and action. Use your whole physical being, and make it act as a unified mechanism. It will not be difficult to make an additional list of your own.

White Hall is across the campus.

These two ideas are at opposite poles.

Note this.

On Fourth Avenue luxury, on Third Avenue dire poverty.

I wash my hands of the whole affair.

My friends, we must face this crisis together; we are all in the same boat.

Welcome to our little home. Welcome to our city. Welcome to our shores.

I'd like to see you prove it. I challenge you to prove it.

I believe I am in the right.

I see that I have been in error.

I can see one, two, three, . . . four, five . . . yes, six planes in the air.

They started toward the west; now they have swung to the extreme east.

Take it away.

Get that idea out of your mind.

Listen! Look out!

Everybody up!

If you come any closer I'll knock you down.

We must get into this campaign and fight.

So this is Boston!

I plead with you for tolerance.

Leave the room.

We will fight to the end.

I give up.

Up, guards, and at them!

The bird flew up and up till at last he passed from sight.

Do you see that man—I think it's a man—away over there on the mountain?

The great pinnacles of the mountains towered about him, inclosing him in a vast solitude.

Turn to the selection, "Who Is to Blame?" in the preceding chapter, and go through it gesturing freely. Try, for instance, to express in action the idea that the story of the Pharisee is familiar (You all know the story); and in the last sentence, suggest first the indifference of the "good men," then their positive contempt, and then drive home the sweeping denunciation. The selection from Carlyle in Chapter IX offers good opportunity for gesture.

Keep on at the effort to express an idea or feeling until you have some success. Use the method of trial and error; depend upon vivid conception rather than upon planning particular movements. And do not think you must always picture something. All the time keep your body in a condition to encourage gesture, poised and free.

THIRD STAGE OF GESTURE TRAINING. It is true, however odd it may seem at first thought, that one should not think of how to make gestures until one can make them. Even if a small child were capable of receiving such instruction, it would not be wise to begin teaching him to walk by explaining the mechanism and methods of walking. We first learn to walk, not how to walk. When we think how we walk, we walk badly. Nevertheless it is possible to improve our walking, running, and other natural actions by taking thought.

You have now in some measure got back to nature, and have convinced your muscles that the ban on their instinctive response to impulse has been lifted. You have recaptured the feeling that you talk through action. If these assumptions are true, you may venture to seek improvement by a closer examination of the mechanism of gesture.

Confining your attention for the moment to the part of the hand and arm, observe that gesture is not a single, straight-arm motion, but a composite. First there is the preparation. The hand does not go from your side directly to the point of completion, but is lifted, perhaps a great deal and perhaps very slightly. At the side the hand should be free from all impulses, but in the preparation it should not be limp, although somewhat relaxed. Then follows the stroke, down, up, sidewise, or at any of the possible angles, though not usually across the body; rather from the center outward, for that gives a larger and more communicative effect. At the completion of the gesture *every* joint is completely opened, though not rigidly, down to the last finger joint. Let all the joints work together and avoid a final jab. The hand and arm should simply open completely and firmly.

Do not get the idea that the hand must be doing something all the time. It may at times remain in the preparatory position calling attention to a point to come. After the stroke the hand may remain firmly in the position it has taken, holding attention to the point it has emphasized, until at the end of a pause the next idea is taken up. This will be true generally where the thought is positive or deliberative. But when one does not wish to hold attention to the idea, as when it is waved aside as unimportant, there is no appreciable rest.

In any case, the hand and arm should drop or pass into preparation for another gesture without attracting further attention. To avoid attracting attention to the way your hand comes down, let it fall before or after, not during a pause. Do not double up your fist in dropping your arm. The way to get away from a completed gesture is to forget it; and the way to forget it is to think of the next point. It helps the beginner to turn to another part of the audience, as it is nearly always proper to do. A slight turn (and be sure the turn involves your whole person, not just your head, or your body above your feet) just as you begin the next phrase will take your attention and the eyes of your audience off the gesture; and your hands will come down without either stiffness or floppiness.

Never, unless for some very special reason, look at your own gestures; look at the people you are trying to impress the idea upon. If you do this they will rarely be conscious of your gesture as gesture, though they will feel its force. Ideally the audience should be no more conscious of your gestures than of your lip and jaw movements. It has been said of many notable speakers that they did not gesture, or gestured very little, when as a matter of fact they made many gestures, but gestures so expressive that only their significance impressed the audience.

There are usually many places in a speech where a wide-awake speaker will have an impulse to step forward, where the thought is particularly positive and direct. Such movements are expressive gestures; and may or may not be accompanied by arm movements. Frequently one steps toward the left or the right side of his audience, perhaps as he takes up a new point. Such movements may be a sort of paragraphing. They may also help a speaker get away from a completed climax, or a certain feeling or attitude, even from a high pitch of voice. The change may help in getting a new start, nearer the colloquial, and relieve both speaker and audience from the tiresome effect produced by a speaker who stands stock-still.

Beginners often ask, How can I respond to the impulse to step forward frequently without walking off the platform? There is really no danger of stepping off; but it is not pleasant for an audience to see a speaker pacing back and forth on the very edge of the platform, or leaning over in a frustrated attempt to come forward. A man of good bearing can easily step back while speaking, but he rarely has to give the matter attention. Being free in his movements, his feet adjust themselves under him as he turns from side to side. These movements may carry him forward or backward. The dropping-back of one foot after the other may carry him back a considerable distance in a single sentence, yet no one notices. Ordinarily these adjustments are slight, and the beginner must not suppose that he should be constantly moving about. Often the first freedom shows itself in restless movements, which make the observer want to cry out, "Stand still!"

Now try these exercises:

Stand facing left with right arm extended to the left; turn to right letting the arm turn with the body.

Again, same position, swing arm alone to right.

Stand facing right with right arm extended right; turn to left leaving arm unmoved.

Stand facing left with both arms extended left; turn to right leaving left arm unmoved and letting right arm swing with body.

Put in no strokes with hands at all, but let them freely

open.  Note the large sweeping character of these movements.  Turn the last into a real gesture with the words:
"My friends, we must all face this problem together."  Be
sure to let your eyes sweep over the whole of your imaginary audience in a way which says, "I mean every one of
you."

Here are a few more questions by means of which you
can criticize yourself:  Do your arms swing from the
shoulder?  Are your elbows free from your sides?  Does
every joint from shoulder to finger tip have a part in your
gesture?  Do your finger tips describe curves, rather than
make angles or thrusts?  Does your body respond by moving now with, now from the hand?  Do you in moving forward, backward, or sideways with a gesture, really respond
from head to foot, rather than tip and twist with your feet
stuck to the floor?  Does your bodily response prevent
straining of your arms backward?  Do your arms swing
freely into all ranges, high and low?  Do they at times
swing high in preparation?  Do they start soon enough to
permit a free, full motion?  Do your gestures, generally,
freely reveal the opened palms?  (Do not try to hold the
fingers in any position, and especially do not hold the thumb
down.)  Do your hands sometimes take a prone position?
Can you straighten your arm and open your hand at the
finish of a gesture without a jerk or stab?  Is the stroke
of your gesture finished on the accented syllable of the
emphatic word?  Do your gestures disappear without flour-
ish, doubling of the fist, or any other motion which catches
the eye?  Do you avoid stepping one foot over the other as
you move right or left, especially as you leave the platform?  All these questions you should be able to answer
in the affirmative.

KINDS OF GESTURE. At the stage of work which we now assume, we shall be aided by a rough classification of gestures. It is made, however, not so much for its own value as because it furnishes a convenient way of giving certain suggestions and warnings. One should have attained a good deal of freedom in gesture before considering these; for in the early part of his work he should not trouble himself about absurdities, but rather dare to be absurd.

*Locative gestures*. First, we will notice gestures which indicate place, with reference either to visible objects or to imagined objects. Sentences for illustration: This is the picture I refer to. "On they went, charging up that fearful path, eleven against seventy."

Suggestions: Avoid unnecessary pointing; as in saying, You and me. It is unnecessary to indicate the seat of the emotions as in either heart or stomach every time one refers to a feeling. Beware of unfortunate pointing; as when one indicates that the good sheep in his audience are on the right and the bad goats on the left, or whirls upon the chairman as a dastardly villain. But note that much depends upon where the speaker looks. Since the audience follows the speaker's eyes more than they do his hand, they are not likely to turn to an individual when the speaker says dramatically, "Thou art the man!" unless he both points and looks at some unfortunate. Do not look *fixedly* at any point within easy range of your hearers' eyes, unless you wish them to look there also. They will not often turn, however, to a point toward the back of the room. Do not look at a blackboard, chart, or picture unless you wish your audience to look there at that moment.

Do not look at a commonplace object, such as a white wall, within easy range of their eyes, when you wish them to imagine a scene. What they actually see checks their imagination. "They bore their hero back to the little village where he first saw the light, back to the little cemetery on the hill, and they buried him there," declaimed a student; and he pointed with two hands and looked at the floor. Ever since that hero has lain buried in a hole cut through the dusty old matting in front of that platform. You will observe that looking definitely limits imagination. When one says, From north to south, meaning merely great distance, and looks at a certain point as north and another as south, he confines the distance within the room. There should be in such a case an indefinite sweep of look and action, which suggests, As far as you like. It is unnecessary in most cases, unless one is in the locality referred to, to pay strict attention to points of the compass; but having indicated the right as east, it should remain east to avoid confusing the picture; as, for example, in describing a battle. Do not confuse the literal with the figurative. One should not intimate that "the great heart of the universe" is within his thorax.

In spite of all these "don'ts" the locative gesture may be helpful in pointing out literal objects and in tickling the imagination of the audience when one is describing scenes and actions. Many of the absurdities referred to are due to trusting to mechanical plotting rather than to a true imaginative conception. And the same remarks may be applied to absurdities touched upon below.

*Illustrative, or picturing gestures.* We have these in the simplest form when gestures accompany such sentences as, The cloud was this shape, He walked like this, Throw down that bauble, He stretched forth his hand. The illustrative gesture attempts to do for speech in a limited way what an illustrator does for written words. It may sometimes stimulate imagination far more, but has obvious limitations.

Illustrative gesture may also do for language what the figure of speech does: it is at times metaphorical, as when one speaks of a lofty ideal, or a foundation principle.

Suggestions: Do not attempt the impossible. Sometimes dramatic gestural description is attempted that is too complex, even when truly carried out. Sometimes the fault is simply inadequacy, as when a preacher held up his own pudgy forefinger in saying, "the finger of God." The same preacher (who had been a "boy elocutionist" and had not outgrown it) once made a spiral upshoot with his hand to indicate—no, not a roman candle—the ascension of Christ! This seems blasphemy in action; but it sprang from the notion that gesture must constantly picture.

Do not reduce the figurative to the literal. This point is not easy to state, and has been overstated. When it is said that we should never use "those gestures which indicate a literal carrying out of the figurative language," this might be understood as denying our most primitive use of gesture, and as forbidding one to make a wry face when one speaks of a "bitter pill," or as a criticism on the Crow Indian who told me the sermon we had listened to was a "high-up talk," with hand held above his head. Perhaps it is sufficient to say, keep always in mind the fact that a figurative statement is figurative. Also, be careful with faded metaphors. A speaker extended his arm when he mentioned "the arm of a crane." I saw a debater, describing what he considered the repeated encroachments of England upon the Transvaal, move down the platform one step for each encroachment.

The speaker should remember that he is not an actor. He has not even a tin sword to draw. He may *suggest* drawing an imaginary sword; but when he proceeds to thrust it through an imaginary foe, wipes it and returns it to its scabbard, he is just absurd. I saw a young man, clad in a dress suit, reciting a lullaby, and cuddling an imaginary baby in his arms while he crooned to it. Had he wished to be funny, he would have been a success. To provide paraphernalia is usually rank absurdity. When the great orator Burke, wishing to defy his enemies in Parliament, drew from his bosom an actual gauntlet and hurled it upon the floor, he was laughed at as he deserved.

Distinguish also the narrator from the impersonator; there is a difference between telling about another's deeds and speaking in his person. Fulton and Trueblood [1] tell how a prominent reader acts out these lines from Whittier's "Maude Muller":

> She stooped where the cool spring bubbled up,
> And filled for him her small tin cup,
> And blushed as she gave it, looking down
> At her feet so bare, and her tattered gown.

He stoops low and dips at the water, stands up and tries to blush as he hands the cup, "and looks down directing the attention of the audience to his own feet which are not 'bare' and to the 'tattered gown' which is not there."

When speaking the actual words of another, impersonation in tone and action may be carried further; as in telling a story with a dialogue. Note also that when an audience is aroused they will accept extremes at which in the beginning they might laugh. A classmate of mine "brought down the house" by accompanying the opening words of his declamation, "Roll back the curtain of history," with a magnificent, double-armed sweep. We were watching him critically as he began; but later, had he succeeded in arousing us, we might have accepted his gesture without a thought. Some go as far as to say, make no gesture in your opening

[1] *Practical Elocution*, p. 338.

words: you are too self-conscious, and your audience is not yet interested in your subject.

*Suggestive gestures* are frequently better for the public speaker than those more fully illustrative. If Burke had made a movement just suggesting the throwing down of a gauntlet, the imagination of his hearers might have formed a vivid image of the act, with no hint of absurdity. As an over-elaborate stage setting may check imagination, so elaborate gestures may also.

*Manifestive gestures* is another classification that has been made. This is hardly a necessary classification, but serves to emphasize the use of gestures to manifest our feelings toward an object or idea; as when one tosses off a proposal as of no account. These are suggestive in character, but also partake of the nature of

*Emphatic gestures.* These are the most serviceable gestures of all for the speaker. They are the last to be thought of by one going mechanically to work to determine his gestures, for they do not necessarily suggest any picture at all. Often a beginner, with a false idea of how to begin, says, "There aren't any gestures in that speech," which is equivalent to saying, There is no force in it. All gesture is emphatic in nature, but this term is applied to the plain gesture which simply says, What I say is true. It may move in any direction and have much variety. The principal suggestion to be made is to avoid the habit of making the same movement all the time or gesturing too constantly; for either of these habits soon destroys all effect from gesturing. Where every idea is emphasized, nothing is emphasized. For the rest, the general training advised should suffice. Any speaker who is in earnest will make emphatic gestures.

CONCLUSION. It is difficult to discuss gesture on paper without making the matter seem mechanical. But if you will follow out the course of training as laid down here, persistently working at each stage without hurrying on to the next, you should become able to gesture normally and effectively, without the necessity of giving the matter a thought, although it may always be best occasionally to observe yourself as a safeguard against bad habits. If you insist on working mechanically, you will have a much poorer chance of arriving at easy effectiveness. If you refuse to work at all, you are likely to limit much your powers of expression, or to do many awkward and absurd things which detract from the force of your speaking.

The most important thing about gesture is not how much you gesture, or even how you gesture, important as these considerations are; but are you on the platform free to gesture, in a condition that encourages response to impulse? If you are you will probably gesture pretty well. And this condition being one of physical alertness will encourage mental alertness and vigor of speech. Not much can be expected of one who is either rigid or slouchy.

PLATFORM MANNERS. It will be appropriate here to comment upon certain movements upon the platform that, though not strictly gesture, do make their impression upon the audience. Platform manners are to be learned chiefly by observation; but a few suggestions may relieve the embarrassment of beginners.

We may say that a speaker should be a simple, unpretentious gentleman on the platform; but that hardly finishes the matter. To say that a man who "has something to say which he very much wishes to say," will conduct himself properly, is to utter a half truth. The matter is of some importance, for every move a speaker makes from the time he is first noticed by the audience may affect the success of his speech. Perhaps people ought not to judge him by his appearance; but many will, and decide that they do or do not like him, or have confidence in him, before he speaks a word. And he may be under temptation to carry off his "nerves" with a swagger or a slouch, or to take on an excuse-me-for-presuming air. To step forward, without attracting any attention to how he does it, but with an air which impresses upon the audience, "I have business with you," is to make a good start. Nothing will help so much in this as to be conscious of having something to say worth saying, and to lose self-consciousness by thinking of the purpose of speaking. Add to this, modesty, self-respect, and respect for the audience, and a speaker will probably bear himself well; provided he has developed physical poise.

A few "don'ts" are in order: Don't follow a big curve in walking forward; and don't, on the other hand, stride down the back of the platform and turn front with a military swing. "A straight line is the shortest distance between two points." If open to you, follow this line to a position well forward. If you can do so without twisting your neck, look at the audience as you come forward. The position of the chairman, and perhaps other persons on the platform, may interfere with carrying out these suggestions.

The chair is to be recognized with a "Mr. Chairman," or a bow, or both. Be deliberate over this recognition and speak in a firm tone. It helps you in maintaining self-possession, in finding your voice, and also in gaining the "sense of communication." The salutation may be given from the side of the platform, or one may walk to the front and then turn to the chairman. The audience too should be recognized. To say "Ladies and Gentlemen," is not only good form: it helps the speaker strike the conversational note, provided he makes the salutation genuine. The objection some make to the use of this salutation by a student speaker seems to me to spring from a feeling that his speaking is necessarily unreal. It is, of course, good form merely to bow. But one hesitates to use the word "bow," so suggestive is it of the profound obeisances which, however appropriate for actors and musicians, are certainly absurd for public speakers. If the young speaker will always think of his bow as a genuine salutation, such as he might give an individual for whom he has respect, he will not go far wrong. He will almost certainly go right, if he has gained good bearing.

There should be some form of leave-taking, usually a bow at the end.

# CHAPTER XXII

## VOICE AND SPEECH [1]

The speaker uses the mechanism of voice and speech much as a musician uses the piano or violin. Like the musician, the speaker is bound by the limitations of his instrument, but he is also free to develop its capacities to the utmost. The skilled musician controls the instrument as a whole, and uses it to express his musical ideas, but he can do so only after many laborious hours of attention to timing, bowing, fingering, listening to the accuracy of his pitch, and other technical details of his craft. Similarly, the skilled speaker uses the mechanism of voice and speech to express his ideas, and uses it subconsciously as a whole, but only after practice in the control of breathing, voice production, resonance, and articulation. All of us get some of this practice, in our daily lives, but many of us acquire faulty habits of voice and speech, and few of us develop the capacities of the mechanism to anything like their full extent. This chapter is designed to help the speaker develop greater effectiveness in the management of his voice and speech.

BREATHING. The mechanism of breathing, which supplies the energy consumed in speech, consists of the bony structure of the chest, the muscles which do the work, and the lungs and passages through which the air moves. The individual vertebrae which compose the spinal column can

---

[1] This chapter was written by C. K. Thomas of Cornell University.

be felt as a line of small bumps down the back. The upper end of the sternum, or breastbone, can be felt at the notch of the neck; from here it can be traced downward slightly more than half way to the waistline. From the bottom of the sternum the rib arch can be felt extending downwards toward the sides; the individual ribs, however, connect with the spinal column at a somewhat higher level than their attachment to the sternum. These bones resemble a flexible birdcage whose expansion enlarges the chest in inspiration, and whose contraction contracts the chest in expiration.

The floor of the chest consists of an important muscle called the diaphragm, which is attached to the sternum, to the rib arch at the side, and in back to the spinal column at a point somewhat lower than its front attachment. The diaphragm, which is dome-shaped, rests on the upper organs of the abdominal cavity. As it contracts, it pushes the abdominal organs down and forward, thus distending the waistline; at the same time it helps raise the lower ribs. It is thus the most important muscle of inspiration. As the diaphragm and other muscles enlarge the chest, the air pressure within the lungs is reduced to the point at which atmospheric pressure will force air in from the outside. In expiration, the ribs fall back of their own weight, the elastic recoil of the distended lungs and body wall helps the contraction, and the muscles of the abdominal wall may be used to force the abdominal organs up against the diaphragm and lower surfaces of the lungs, thus producing the forced expiration needed for speaking and singing.

Ideally, the lungs should be allowed to expand easily in all three diameters by allowing both chest and waistline to expand moderately during inspiration. In expiration it is best to support the tone against sudden fluctuations in breath pressure by slightly delaying the lowering of the chest, and using the muscles of the abdominal wall to control the outgoing breath. To develop this control it is useful to practise exhaling in two separate movements: first, by contracting the waistline; second, by lowering the chest. When he has mastered this technique, the speaker should practise maintaining the chest in the high position for two or three breaths, controlling inspiration and expiration by means of the diaphragm and abdominal muscles.

In quiet breathing, inspiration usually takes about half the time, expiration most of the remainder, and there is a short period of rest before the next inspiration. In speaking, however, one must inhale quickly and exhale slowly; at the end of the phrase there should be a short expiration as the chest is lowered, and a short rest period of the sort that one takes automatically in quiet breathing. If the speaker inhales as soon as he has completed the phrase, or if he inhales no more deeply than in quiet breathing, the vocal quality will deteriorate into a gasp. The habit of inhaling just deeply enough to "come out even" at the end of the phrase can be developed if the speaker pays attention to the problem at first.

VOICE PRODUCTION. Though the speaker can directly control breathing, resonance, and articulation, he has no direct control of voice. The movements of the vocal cords in the larynx are produced by involuntary muscles, and the speaker is limited to the indirect control maintained by the hearing mechanism. The ability to hear accurately and distinctly is consequently of the greatest importance to the speaker, and the structure of the larynx of minor importance.

Essentially, the larynx is a valve at the top of the windpipe in which the vocal cords form shelves extending from front to back on either side. The cords lie close to the side walls in ordinary breathing, to provide a maximum of space for the passage of air between them. When the breath is being compressed for a cough, however, the cords come into contact with each other and prevent the escape of air. When the cords come so close together that their edges are set into vibration by the air escaping between them, this vibration is transmitted to the escaping air, and is heard as voice.

The frequency, or pitch, of the vocal sound depends principally upon the tension of the vocal cords; control depends on hearing. The structure of the sound wave, however, also includes higher frequencies which cannot ordinarily be heard individually, but which, in their total effect, determine the quality of the sound. These harmonics, or overtones, result from the vibration of the vocal cords in fractional segments at the same time that the vibration of the whole cord is producing the fundamental tone.

The passages of the throat, mouth, and nose modify both the volume and quality of the complex vocal sound as it comes from the larynx, but have no appreciable effect on the frequency of the fundamental tone. Various parts of these passages exert a selective influence on the overtones, emphasizing some and suppressing others; this action, known as resonance, is responsible for the good or bad quality of the sound as heard by the listener. Since the speaker can control the adjustments of throat, mouth, and nose, it is important for him to understand the structure and action of these passages.

The throat, or pharynx, is a muscular tube lying directly in back of the larynx, mouth, and nose. Vocal sound passes back from the larynx into the pharynx, and then up to the mouth or nose. Large swallowing muscles alter the diameter of the pharynx, but the vocal use of these muscles interferes with good voice production; the speaker should learn to keep them relaxed by means of the exercises at the end of this chapter.

If the student examines the back part of his mouth in a mirror, he will see that the roof of the mouth ends in a small hanging tip, known as the uvula, and that the whole back part of the roof, known as the soft palate, moves up and down as he makes various sounds. The soft palate, which is connected by muscles to the skull above and to the tongue and pharyngeal wall below, is a muscular partition between the mouth and the upper pharynx. When the soft palate rises and moves slightly backward, it prevents air and sound from getting into the upper pharynx and nose; when it lowers and touches the back of the tongue, as at the end of *hung*, it prevents the air and sound from getting into the mouth, and sends them out through the upper pharynx and nose. For most English sounds, this valve to the upper pharynx is closed, and the sound comes out through the mouth. Only for the consonants in *meaning* does the sound normally come out through the nose. Many people are unable, however, to make this sharp distinction between nasal and oral sounds. If the soft palate is inadequate to close the opening to the nose, as in cleft palate, some sounds are impossible, and others take on an abnormal nasal quality. Cleft palate, fortunately, is rare. Many people, however, have allowed the muscles to become weak and inactive, so that the upward and backward movement is insufficient to close the valve for oral sounds; this inactivity leads to an excess of nasal quality, for which exercises are given at the end of the chapter. At the other extreme, obstructions within the nose or upper pharynx, such as the swollen mucous membrane of the common cold, or the development of excessive adenoid tissue or other growths, make the proper production of nasal consonants impossible; *meaning* sounds very much like *beadig*. Removal of the obstruction is the only cure; afterwards, the speaker often discovers that he has substituted an excess of nasal quality for a deficiency, because active use of the soft palate formerly had no effect, and he had no incentive to develop control. He can develop this palatal activity, however, with the exercises already mentioned. Except for the valvular action of the soft palate, the speaker has no control over the size or shape of the upper pharyngeal and nasal cavities, and consequently no control of nasal resonance.

SPEECH. Unlike the pharynx and nose, the mouth can be adjusted in many ways for the demands of speech. Lips, teeth, cheeks, tongue, jaw, gum ridge, and hard and soft palates all help in the production of speech sounds. All these structures can be readily located by the tip of the tongue or by a mirror. The line between the hard and soft palates cannot easily be seen, but can easily be located by the tip of the tongue.

The tongue, which occupies the entire floor of the mouth, is attached to the chin bone and to the hyoid bone in the neck, the latter acting as a connecting link between tongue and larynx. The phonetician arbitrarily divides the tongue into several regions according to the parts of the roof of the mouth which lie opposite them when the tongue is at rest: the tip, which lies against the front teeth; the sides, which lie against the side teeth; the blade, which lies against the upper gum ridge; the front, which lies against the hard palate; and the back, which lies against the soft palate. Reference to these arbitrarily chosen regions makes possible the analysis of the articulation of speech sounds.

CONSONANTS. Though it is convenient to retain the traditional classification of vowels and consonants, the student should realize that no sharp line of demarcation exists between the two classes. In a drawling pronunciation of the phrase *see you*, or *you will*, the vowel of the first word gradually changes to the consonant of the second. In *will*, the vowel gradually changes to the final [l]. The traditional classification of vowels as freer and more open sounds than consonants thus breaks down, and it is more satisfactory to think of speech sounds as formed with various degrees of freedom and openness from the completely stopped consonants of *pact* to the open vowels of *oh* and *ah*.

Six English consonants are formed by completely stopping and compressing the breath; a slight explosion of voice or breath usually follows the compression. To produce the stop, the soft palate must be raised, and there must be a complete obstruction at some point in the mouth. If the vocal cords continue to vibrate during the stop, the result is one of the voiced stops in *bagged;* if the cords stop vibrating, the result is one of the voiceless stops in *pact*. If the soft palate is lowered and the obstruction in the mouth maintained, one of the three nasal consonants in *meaning* will result. For these nine consonants, three positions of the mouth are necessary: the obstruction may be made by closing the lips, by raising the tip of the tongue to the upper gum ridge, or by raising the back of the tongue to the soft palate, as in the following diagram:

|  | Lips | Tip | Back |
|---|---|---|---|
| Voiceless stops ........... | [p ] | [t] | [k] |
| Voiced stops ............. | [b ] | [d] | [g] |
| Voiced nasals ........... | [m] | [n] | [ŋ] |

Since English spelling is notoriously a confusing guide to English sounds, the symbols of the International Phonetic Association are used in this chapter, and are enclosed in square brackets. The phonetic symbol has the advantage of a fixed meaning. In the chart above, [g] always represents the consonant in *egg*, never the consonant in *age*. The symbol [k] represents the consonant spelled in various ways in *cake*, *kick*, and *ache*. *The symbol* [ŋ] represents the final consonant in *long*, *sing*, and *tongue*; [ŋ] also occurs in such words as *think*, *lynx*, and *anxiety*. In *finger*, *angle*, *prolongation*, and other words, *ng* represents [ŋg]; in *danger*, *ungrateful*, and other words, the nasal consonant is [n]. The relations between [ŋ] and [ŋg] are usually puzzling to foreign speakers, particularly to those with Slavic or Jewish backgrounds; such people can benefit from the *ng* exercises at the end of the chapter. Speakers with an English background are not so likely to confuse [ŋ] and [ŋg], but are quite likely to substitute [n] for [ŋ] in such words as *eating*, *nothing*, and *length*; this substitution, popularly known as "dropping the *g*", is usually considered substandard on any but the most informal occasion.

Another important group of consonants is that of the fricatives, which take their name from the audible friction which results when the breath stream is forced through a narrow opening. With the exception of [h], these consonants are in pairs, one of which is voiced, the other voiceless, as in the following diagram:

|  | Lip teeth | Point teeth | Front gums | Rear gums | Glottis |
|---|---|---|---|---|---|
| Voiceless fricatives .... | [f] | [θ] | [s] | [ʃ] | [h] |
| Voiced fricatives ..... | [v] | [ð] | [z] | [ʒ] | |

The letters *f* and *v* are reasonably phonetic in character, since they usually correspond to the sounds [f] and [v]; *of* is exceptional in being sounded with [v]. Both [f] and [v] are formed by placing the lower lip against the upper teeth and forcing breath through the spaces between the teeth.

Both [θ] and [ð] are spelled *th*, as in *thin* [θɪn] and *this* [ðɪs]. Each is a single sound formed by placing the tip of the tongue against either the back or the lower edge of the upper teeth and forcing breath through the spaces between the teeth. They are thus very similar to [f] and [v], with which they are often confused in childish speech. Because of unfamiliarity, rather than of inherent difficulty, [θ] and [ð] are usually troublesome to foreigners, who tend to substitute [t] or [s] for [θ], and [d] or [z] for [ð]. Exercises for this difficulty will be found at the end of the chapter.

The sibilants [s] and [z] require the most delicate adjustment of any English consonants. Though slight differences of articulation are possible for the individual, and though differences in the structure of different mouths sometimes makes differences in articulation necessary, the sounds are normally formed by forcing the breath through a narrow aperture between the blade of the tongue and the upper gum ridge, and then against the teeth. For proper articulation, the tongue must be somewhat stretched from back to front, the sides must be in contact with the side teeth, and the tip may be placed in back of either the upper or the lower teeth, provided that it is not in contact with either the upper teeth or the cutting edges of the lower teeth. Most Americans rest the tip against the lower gums.

Most difficulties with [s] result from getting the tip of the tongue too close to the cutting edges of the teeth; the resulting [s] hisses too loudly. If the tongue actually touches the cutting edges, a variety of [θ] will result. If the tip comes in contact with the upper gum ridge, the breath must escape around the sides of the tongue, or through the nose; a faulty [s] results in either case. Difficulties with [z] parallel those with [s], but since voice accompanies [z] and helps to cover up the faulty quality, these difficulties are not ordinarily so noticeable. Exercises will be found at the end of the chapter.

The principal difference between the articulation of [s-z] and of [ʃ-ʒ] is that for the latter pair the tongue is drawn slightly further back in the mouth, and is spread laterally, so that the breath is sent forward in a broad stream instead of being concentrated. The most familiar spelling of [ʃ] is *sh*, as in *ship* and *fish;* other spellings represent it in *sugar, mission, pressure, nation, gracious,* and many other words. The spelling for [ʒ] is usually *s*, as in *pleasure* and *vision;* occasionally *z*, as in *azure;* occasionally, in words of recent French origin, *g*, as in *rouge.* These two sounds also occur as parts of the compound consonants [tʃ], as in *church, itch,* and *future;* and [dʒ], as in *gem, judge, soldier,* and *education.* Ordinarily native speakers have little trouble with the four sounds [ ʃ-ʒ-tʃ-dʒ ], except for the confusion caused by the irregular spellings.

The aspirate [h] may also be considered a fricative, though the audible friction is slight. It has no special tongue position, but assumes the position of whatever sound is to follow it; the frictional element seems to be produced in the larynx. A proper use of [h] is essential to good, unaffected speech. At the beginning of stressed syllables it is usually pronounced, though it is silent in a few such words as *hour, honest,* and *exhaust.* But when, in the middle of words, it comes at the beginning of an unstressed syllable, it is normally silent, as in *shepherd, prohibition,* and *annihilate.* Any attempt to sound [h] in these medial unstressed positions is likely to sound forced, as it so often does on the radio. Similarly, when *he, his, him, her, has, have,* or *had* are unstressed in the middle of a phrase, [h] should not be sounded. In the sentence, "He hit him on the head," there should be no [h] in *him;* in the sentence, "John would have run after him if he had not been exhausted from his labors," no [h] should be heard unless one of the words with initial *h* is stressed.

Finally, there is a miscellaneous group of consonants which are acoustically intermediate between vowels and consonants, and which are sometimes called semivowels. The words *woo* [wu] and *ye* [ji] illustrate two of them, the consonant in each word being closely akin, both in formation and sound, to the vowel which follows it; [w] and [j] are always followed by vowels. In such words as *what* [hwɑt] and *hue* [hju], most people use a closely blended combination of [h] and the semivowel; others omit [h], and pronounce these words the same as *watt* and *you.* Though opinions differ, one will probably be criticized less if he retains [h] in these two types of word.

The consonant [l] is a voiced continuant, formed by placing the tip of the tongue against the upper gum ridge and sending voice around one or both sides. English has two main varieties; initial and pre-vocalic [l], whose quality suggests that of the vowel *ee* [i], occurs in such words as *lit*, *close*, and *explain.* Final and pre-consonantal [l], whose quality suggests that of the vowel *oo* [u], may be heard in such words as *till*, *cold*, and *apple.* Between vowels, as in *silly* and *hollow*, American [l] may be of either type, but is more often of the final type. Use of the final type in the initial position leads to muffled speech, and should be avoided. In some foreign types of English, the exclusive use of one or other of these [l] sounds adds to the foreign flavor.

Initial [r], as in *read, broke,* and *stream,* is a weak semivowel formed, in America, by raising the tip of the tongue toward the upper gum ridge, or the middle of the tongue toward the line between the hard and soft palates. Medial [r], as in *carry* and *moral,* is ordinarily formed in the same way, though a few Americans and many Englishmen briefly touch the gum ridge with the tip of the tongue; this tapped [r] suggests [d] to many Americans, and is often condemned as an affectation. Final [r] as in *far, farm,* and *father,* may be a weaker version of either of the two main varieties, or may be omitted entirely.

Many speakers, though by no means all, in New England and New York City omit [r] except when a vowel follows without a pause; such people omit it in *far* and *farm,* but often retain it in *far away.* This use of [r] as a link between vowels often leads to such pronunciations as *idear of it* and *vanillar ice cream,* pronunciations which are usually considered substandard.

In the Southern states, final [r], and even medial [r], is somewhat more likely to be dropped; consequently *far, far away, idea of it,* and even *very* and *Carolina,* are often pronounced without [r]. Retention of the intervocalic [r] of the last two words is, however, an aid to distinctness. Since usage varies, the student should realize that inclusion or omission of final [r] is irrelevant to questions of good speech.

A common substitute for [r] in the initial and medial positions is a sound resembling [w]. Since this is usually caused by excessive lip action and insufficient tongue action, the adult whose speech is otherwise normal can usually correct it by keeping the lips spread and as nearly immobile as possible, and by preceding [r] with [t], [d], [θ], or [z]. Exercises will be found at the end of the chapter.

VOWELS. For most consonants the position of the tongue and other speech agents is fixed within definite limitations; to remove the tongue from contact with the roof of the mouth for [t] or [ŋ] is to change these sounds to other sounds. Vowel positions are not so definitely fixed; the tongue is not braced against some other structure in the mouth; slight variations from the normal, or average, position for a given vowel may be unnoticed by the casual listener, though many of them are evident to the trained listener. The positions described hereafter must therefore be taken as average, rather than as true in every instance.

Three positional factors determine the formation of all English vowels; a fourth factor helps to determine some of them. If the student alternates the words *sack* and *sock* he will notice that the tongue is bunched further back in the mouth for *sock*. If he alternates *sack* and *sick* he will notice that the mouth is wider open, the tongue lower, and the angle of the jaw wider for *sack*. If he alternates *sick* and *seek* he will notice, if he observes closely, that the muscles of the tongue feel more relaxed for *sick* than for *seek*. These three factors: forward and backward position of the tongue, height of the tongue, and degree of muscular tension, combine to differentiate English vowels; the fourth factor, degree of lip-rounding, affects a few vowels, and in America its effect is highly uncertain.

The vowels [i] and [ɪ] are formed with the tongue bunched high in the front part of the mouth, [i] with tense muscles, [ɪ] with lax. Commonly known as "long *e*," [i] occurs in the stressed syllables of such words as *bee, beating, grieve, seize, people,* and *police.* Commonly known as "short *i*," [ɪ] occurs in the stressed syllables of such words as *give, city, busy, pretty, women, here,* and *clearing.* In the unstressed syllables of such words as *busy* and *cities,* the vowel usually sounds intermediate between [i] and [ɪ]. Rather than complicate the record with a third symbol, most phoneticians record this vowel as [ɪ], thus: *busy* [bɪzɪ], *cities* [sɪtɪz]. The unstressed vowel of such words as *sitting* and *rubbish* is, however, not the intermediate vowel, but the ordinary [ɪ]. A few words, such as *been, creek, breeches, idea,* and *sacrilegious,* may be heard with either vowel; either is considered normal. The most common substandard pronunciation of these vowels is to pronounce them with the tongue too far back in the mouth, with a blurred effect. *Will* then sounds too much like *wool,* for instance; [ɪ] is more subject to this distortion than [i].

The vowels [e] and [ɛ] are mid-high and front, [e] tense, [ɛ] lax. Commonly known as "long *a,*" [e] occurs in such words as *say, pane, raid,* and *veil.* Commonly known as "short *e,*" [ɛ] occurs in such words as *get, guest, fair,* and *any.* In such words as *measure* and *pleasure,* [ɛ] is the usual vowel. Some people regard [e] as substandard in these words.

The vowels [æ] and [ɑ] are low and lax, [æ] front, [ɑ] back. Commonly known as "short *a,*" [æ] is the characteristic vowel of *cat;* in such words as *carry, carriage,* and *marry,* many good speakers replace [æ] with [ɛ], though by others the substitution is regarded as substandard. Commonly known as "broad *a,*" [ɑ] is the characteristic vowel of *calm* and *cart.* In such words as *ask, dance, half, path,* and *command,* the usual American vowel is [æ]; the usual vowel in the south of England is [ɑ]. Some Americans, notably in eastern New England and eastern Virginia, use a compromise between [æ] and [ɑ], the vowel [a], which is low, half-front, and lax. This compromise [a] is not widely spread, and is usually used inconsistently by those who consciously set out to acquire it after childhood. Such people usually fail to use it in the less familiar words, such as *command*, and use it improperly in such words as *bad* and *land*. In some sections of the country a rural substitution of [a] for [æ] may be heard in such words as *alley* and *balance*, *carry* and *wheelbarrow*; this is substandard. In New England [a] is frequently substituted for [ɑ] in *calm*, *cart*, and *father*. Opinions differ as to the propriety of the substitution.

The vowels [ɒ] and [ɔ] are low and back, and usually involve some lip rounding; [ɒ] is lax, [ɔ] tense. The vowels [ɑ-ɒ-ɔ] form an acoustic series, all three members of which may be heard in the pronunciation, by different speakers, and sometimes by the same speaker, of such words as *log*, *gong*, *mock*, *orange*, *horrid*, and *forest*. The first syllable of *forest* is, for some people, identical with *far*; for others, identical with *for*; still others use the intermediate [ɒ]. Such words as *not*, *rob*, and *pond* vary between [ɑː] and [ɒ]; *soft* and *long*, between [ɔ] and [ɒ]; [ɑ] and [ɔ] are much the more common. The vowel [ɒ] is most common in Pennsylvania and New England, but many people do not use it at all. Since variations within this group are on the standard level, nothing will be gained by changing [hɑrɪd] to [hɔrɪd] or vice versa.

The vowel [o], in *rode*, *boat*, *shown*, *though*, and *sew*, is mid-high, back, and tense, with lip-rounding. Ordinarily it causes little trouble to the native speaker, though in the middle Atlantic states from New York City to Baltimore the tongue may sometimes be pushed too far forward. In *more*, *course*, *story*, and the like, some speakers use [o], some [ɔ]; both forms are standard.

The vowel [v], in *cup*, *love*, and *rough*, is mid-high, lax, unrounded, and confined to stressed syllables. According to some phoneticians, it is a central vowel, but the evidence seems a little stronger that it is produced in about the same position as [o]. The substitution or approximation of [ʌ] for [o] in such words as *home, stone, only,* and *won't* is fairly common in New England, and is occasionally heard elsewhere; outside New England the substitution is usually considered substandard.

The vowels [u] and [ʊ] are high and back, with lip-rounding; [u] is tense, [ʊ] lax. Both occur with the same spellings: [u] in *do, fool, soup,* and *rude;* [ʊ] in *wolf, foot, could,* and *put.* In some parts of the country, notably in the South, [u] is produced with the tongue further forward, so that the vowel acquires some of the quality of [i]. Some people regard this variation as substandard. A few words, of which *broom, coop, hoof, roof, room, root, soon,* and *soot* are the most common, occur in standard speech with either [u] or [ʊ]. Before *r,* as in *poor* and *tour,* [ʊ] is the normal vowel; lowering the vowel to [o] or [ɔ] is usually considered substandard. In the unstressed syllables of such words as *gradual* and *usual,* [u] weakens to a vowel which is acoustically intermediate between [u] and [ʊ], but which most phoneticians record as [ʊ].

The combination [ju], commonly known as "long *u,*" occurs initially and after [p-b-m-f-v-k-g-h] in such words as *use, puny, beauty, music, few, view, cube, gules,* and *huge.* In stressed syllables after [r-l-tʃ-dʒ], as in *rule, lewd, chew,* and *June,* only [u] occurs. After other consonants, as in *enthusiasm, tune, due, new, suit,* and *presume,* good usage varies between the limits of [u] and [ju], but [u] is the usual American form. Before *r,* [ju] weakens to [jʊ], as in *pure* and *secure;* in unstressed syllables, as in *argument, circulate,* and *mercury,* it may be weakened still more. In *column, coupon, percolator,* and *Marguerite* [j] occurs only in substandard speech, by a false analogy with such words as *volume, cubic, circulate,* and *argument.*

The vowels [ɜ] and [ə] are mid-high, with the tongue bunched in the central position, approximately underneath the line between the hard and soft palates; [ɜ] is tense, and used only in stressed syllables; [ə] is lax, and used only in unstressed syllables. Speakers who omit final and preconsonantal [r] pronounce *further, murmur,* and *perverse* as [fɜðə], [mɜmə], and [pəvɜs]; speakers who use the [r] may say [fɜrðər], [mɜrmər], and [pərvɜrs], or may blend [r] and vowel into a single, [r]-colored vowel. Either the inclusion or the omission of this [r]-coloring is acceptable in good usage. In the neighborhood of New York City and in some parts of the South, [ɜ] is lengthened into the diphthongal form [ɜɪ], which is indicated in popular respelling as *foither* [fɜɪðə] and *moimer* [mɜɪmə]. In New York, this diphthong is considered substandard; in the South, opinions differ.

Aside from its use in syllables with *r,* the mid, central, lax [ə] is widely used in unstressed syllables, and has a wide variety of spellings, as in *above* [əbʌv], *broken* [brokən], *bacon* [bekən], *status* [stetəs], and *gracious* [greʃəs]. Similarly, when such words of limited thought content as *an, and, but, can, could, has, must, of, some, than, us,* and *was* occur in unstressed positions within the phrase, [ə] normally replaces the stronger vowel of the stressed pronunciation. The avoidance of [ə] in unstressed positions leads to the "feeble forcible" type of monotony, and is no more a sign of good speech than the use of obscured vowels in stressed positions.

DIPHTHONGS. A diphthong is not a succession of two sounds, but a single gliding sound within the limits of a single syllable; the phonetic symbols represent the approximate terminal points of the glide. In English there are three principal diphthongs: [ɑʊ] in *how* and *house*, [aɪ] in *my* and *mine*, and [ɔɪ] in *boy* and *boil*. All three vary somewhat in good usage, but the forms [æʊ] for [ɑʊ], [ɒɪ] for [aɪ], and [ɜɪ] for [ɔɪ] are usually considered substandard. The excessive weakening of the end of the diphthong, which is fairly common, should be avoided, since it leads to indistinctness.

The vowels [e] and [o] are often diphthongized as [eɪ] and [oʊ]. Some speakers do so in all words; others use a relatively pure vowel when it is short, as in *gate* [get] and *goat* [got], but diphthongize the longer vowels in *gay* [geɪ] and *go* [goʊ]. Either form is acceptable, but foreigners will usually sound less foreign if they always diphthongize these two sounds.

In such words as *peer, pair, pour,* and *poor,* those who replace [r] with [ə] use the diphthongal pronunciations [pɪə], [pɛə], [pɔə] or [poə], and [pʊə]. After [ɑ] and [ɔ], [r] may be simply dropped; after other vowels, [ə] should replace it.

SPEECH. Though good speech, or standard speech, is a favorite topic of argument, many of the arguments are futile because of the assumption that goodness or correctness of speech is analogous to that of an arithmetical solution. The notion that there is but one correct pronunciation of a given word and that the dictionary is final authority for that pronunciation is still current, but fortunately not so current as it used to be. The authority of the dictionary in matters of pronunciation rests on the intelligence and skill with which its editors have ascertained the facts of educated usage. Some dictionaries have been much more successful in this than others. The ultimate authority must always be the habitual usage of respectable, educated speakers whose speech is accepted as normal in the community. It is therefore evident that standard speech does not mean uniform speech; what sounds normal in one large section of the country may sound slightly exotic in a different section. The Southerner may readily concede that the speech of a particular New Englander is good, even though it differs in many details from his own. Even in single communities some variation may either attract no unfavorable attention or pass entirely unnoticed: one speaker may use [s] in *discern, greasy,* and *transit;* another, [z]; friends may use [ɑ], [ɒ], or [ɔ] in *orange, horrid,* and *moral,* without damage to their friendship. Attempts to improve speech by seeking uniformity of speech are thus likely to be no more than a waste of time.

On the other hand, much can be done to improve substandard speech and substandard voice without aiming at the false goal of uniformity. Every section of the country has its good speech and its bad speech, its good voices and its bad voices. Some bad qualities are more characteristic of one section than of others; some are general. All can be improved without leaving the framework of good speech in the section in which the speaker lives.

Harsh, nasal voices are common in all parts of the country; attention to relaxation, and to control of the soft palate, is worth most speakers' time. Close, muffled pronunciation, which confuses the vowel of *will* with that of *wool,* the vowel of *wear* with that of *were,* and the vowel of *good* with that of *gird,* can be made more incisive. The diphthong of *pound* can be pronounced with enough energy to prevent confusion with *pond;* the frequently lost [t] of *mountain* and *little* can be restored. All such details can be improved if the speaker trains himself to use slightly more than a minimum of energy, and the greater effectiveness of his speech will more than repay him for the time and effort consumed.

## SELECTED EXERCISES

### Relaxation:

1. While standing erect, raise the arms to the level of the shoulder, and let them drop to the side. Eliminate muscular control as fully as possible. Repeat the drop several times, from the shoulders, and also from above the head.

2. Alternate clenching the teeth and pronouncing "ah" [ɑ] with the mouth somewhat more open than usual.

3. (a) While standing erect, let the head drop quickly on the chest; don't lower it, but let its own weight do the work. (b) Close the eyes, relax the facial muscles as much as possible, keep the eyes shut, and make sure that the lips and teeth are not quite shut. (c) Raise the head slowly and steadily, avoiding all jerky movement; let the jaw hang loose; think about yawning; move the head as far back as is comfortable. (d) Return the head slowly to the position on the chest; don't use muscular force to close the jaw; it will close itself. (e) Repeat the exercise several times before leaving it; the jaw should open wider with continued practice.

### Breathing:

1. While walking briskly on level ground, time the breathing by allowing three steps (two with one foot, one with the other, not three with each) for each of the four stages of the breathing cycle: (a) inspiration, (b) a brief holding of the breath, (c) expiration, and (d) a brief pause before the next breath. Continue for not more than a hundred paces at this rate. Practise frequently for several days, then increase the rate to four steps for each stage, and eventually to six or seven. Keep within the range of ease at all times. The exercise will aid in the control of deeper breathing.

2. Place one hand on the chest, the other at the waistline, so as to make sure that expansion occurs at both places during inspiration, and contraction at both places during expiration. (a) Inhale and exhale slowly, expanding and contracting chest and waistline together. (b) Expand chest and waistline together as you inhale; contract the waistline before contracting the chest. (c) Expand chest and waistline together as you inhale; keep the chest expanded while you control two or three consecutive breaths with the waistline alone. (d) Keep the chest expanded as you whisper "ah" [ɑ]; lower the chest when the sound is finished; repeat with other vowels; later sound the vowels on a sustained pitch.

*Nasality:*

1. Alternate [z] rapidly and vigorously with *ah* [ɑ]: *zah-zah-zah-zah-zah-zah-zah;* then alternate [z] successively with *aw* [ɔ], long *o* [o], *oo* [u], *ee* [i], long *a* [e], short *e* [ε] and short *a* [æ]. These are the vowels of *sock, saw, soap, soup, see, say, set,* and *sat.*

2. Alternate [z] vigorously, but not so rapidly, with [m], [n], and [ŋ]; avoid using any vowels in this exercise.

3. Alternate rapidly and vigorously [zɑnɑzɑnɑzɑnɑzɑnɑzɑ]; use equal force for every syllable; repeat with the other vowels of exercise 1.

4. Practise the following sentences twice: first read the sentence carefully in the normal way; then read it while you hold your nose to prevent the escape of air through it; repeat until all feeling of breath pressure in the nose, and all audible muffling, is eliminated:

There is a good show at the theatre to-day.
This is the place where the boy was last observed.
Where did you put the book I gave you for your birthday?
The flag fluttered with the breeze at the top of the pole.

*Exercises for "ng":*

1. The following words contain the combination [ŋg]; be sure to include [g] vigorously enough for it to be clearly heard: *finger linger single mingle tingle England English distinguish extinguish angle anger dangle languor anguish longer longest prolongation stronger strongest bungle jungle hunger younger youngest.*

2. The following words contain the single sound [ŋ]; pronounce the words slowly; prolong [ŋ] slightly; keep the muscles of the tongue relaxed, particularly at the end of [ŋ], so that there will be no suggestion of [k] or [g]: *thing bring sing wing hang sang rang bang song long wrong lung sung hung tongue length strength things brings hangs bangs gongs songs lungs tongues singing bringing ringing hanging banging clanging longing gingham singer ringer hanger singsong songster youngster Springfield Birmingham.*

3. Carefully distinguish [ŋ] and [ŋg] in the following sentences:

The longer the youngster angled, the greater grew his anguish.
The hangman strangled the strongest man.
His fingers tingled as he was washing them in the morning.
He distinguished the bird by the markings on its wings.
While the fire was burning they mingled with the throng.
While extinguishing the light he heard something banging.
The singer sang English songs in Springfield and Birmingham.
Nothing that he was doing in the jungle was wrong.

*Exercise for "th"* [θ-ð]:

This sound is made while the tongue is being pulled back from between the teeth. It may be voiced, as in *this,* or voiceless, as in *thin.* Unless the tongue is far enough forward at the start of the sound, voiceless *th* will be replaced by *t* or *s,* and voiced *th* by *d* or *z.*

1. [t-θ]: *tin thin, tank thank, taught thought, tie thigh, team theme, tick thick, torn thorn, tug thug, tree three, true through,*

*trill thrill, tread thread, boat both, bat bath, hat hath, rat wrath, mitt myth, toot tooth, suit sooth.*

2. [d-ð]: *dare there, dense thence, dough though, den then, day they, die thy, dine thine, doze those, breed breathe, laid lathe, seed seethe, read wreathe, ride writhe, side scythe, bayed bathe, wide withe, needer neither, ladder lather.*

3. [s-θ]: *sin thin, sank thank, sought thought, sigh thigh, sick thick, seem theme, saw thaw, sum thumb, surd third, sing thing, song thong, sink think, symbol thimble, sundered thundered, moss moth, truce truth, miss myth, lass lath, pass path, worse worth, Norse north, force forth, gross growth.*

4. [z-ð]: *breeze breathe, lays lathe, seize seethe, rise writhe, size scythe, bays bathe, wise withe, close clothe, teasing teething.*

5. Think the thought through till you find the truth.

The thunderstorm came either from the north or the south.

Father went bathing on the other side of the thicket.

They withdrew from the room since they could not breathe.

This is the third time she has lost the thimble.

There on the heather the brothers saw three feathers.

### Exercises for [s]:

The sound is made by raising the sides of the tongue and forcing the breath through a narrow groove along the middle of the tongue. The tip of the tongue must be turned slightly downward, so as not to interfere with the narrow stream of breath, and must not be placed too near the teeth. The tip may be placed either on the lower gums or near the upper gums, and the whole tongue should be pulled slightly further back.

1. *see sit say set sat sob saw sun soap soot soon sir sigh soil.*

2. *speak spin spade sped span spar spot spawn spun spoke spool spur spy spoil spout lisp grasp cusp leaps tips caps coops.*

3. *scheme skin skate sketch scalp scar scot score skull scope school skirt sky scout risk desk ask dusk peeks picks bakes necks, axe barks box talks ducks oaks books dukes irks likes.*

4. *smear smith smell smack smash smart smock small smug*

*smudge smother smuggler smoke smolder smooth smirk smile smite.*

5. *sleep slip slay sled slap slot slut slow sloop slur slouch slight whistle wrestle castle jostle hustle else false pulse.*

6. *sneeze snip snail snare snag snarl snob snore snub snow snipe snooze listen hasten fasten lesson prince fence dance dunce.*

7. *lease miss lace less pass loss fuss dose loose ice mouse fierce pierce farce horse course purse worse terse hearse.*

8. *steel still stay step stand star stop stall stun stone stood stoop stir style stout stream strip stray strap strut stripe.*

9. *east list haste lest last lost dust host roost first hoist.*

10. *eats its gates bets bats carts cots nuts ports coats puts roots hurts bites bouts quoits.*

Special care will be needed in the following word-lists to avoid blurring of consonants. Dashes indicate that the preceding sound should be slightly prolonged before you move quickly to the next sound; the breath stream should not, however, be interrupted:

11. *lis—ps, gras—ps, cus—ps, ris—ks, des—ks, as—ks, hus—ks, feas—ts, lis—ts, res—ts, cas—ts, cos—ts, rus—ts, hos—ts, roos—ts.*

12. *heath—s, myth—s, death—s, hearth—s, fourth—s, fif—th—s, six—th—s, seventh—s.*

13. The salesman sold the sample of silk to the spinster.

Six strong steeplejacks ascended to the summit.

A sudden storm scattered the sail boats.

The silver spoons spilled from the sideboard.

The spy spoke softly to the policeman.

Mists and severe frosts descended on the sixth of December.

Seven eighths of the strawberries were spoiled in transit.

## Exercises for [r]:

1. Prolong [z], and gradually pull the tongue back from the gum ridge toward the hard palate; hold the tongue close to the roof of the mouth till the sound changes to [r]. Then, somewhat more rapidly, practise: *zree, zray, zrah, zraw, zroh, zroo, zry, zrow, zroy.*

2. Practise rapidly, trying to make *thr* [θr] with a single impulse: *three reed, thrill rill, thread red, thrash rash, throttle rotten, throng wrong, thrush rush, throw row, through rue, thrice rice.*

3. Practise rapidly, trying to make [tr] with a single impulse: *tree reed, trill rill, train rain, tread red, trash rash, trot rot, trust rust, troll roll, true rue, trice rice, trout rout, Troy Roy.*

4. Practise rapidly, trying to make [dr] with a single impulse: *dream ream, drill rill, drain rain, dread red, dram ram, drum rum, drove rove, drew rue, dry rye, drowned round.*

5. Practise more slowly; use the lips vigorously for [w], but keep them as inactive as possible for [r]: *weed reed, will rill, wane rain, wed red, wax racks, won run, walk rock, wove rove, woof roof, wise rise, wound round.*

## Exercises for distinctness of vowels:

1. The stressed vowel should be a clear, sharp "short *i*" [ɪ] regardless of the spelling: *bewildered, brilliant, built, children, clearly, dreary, ears, equivalent, experience, fear, fierce, hear, here, hill, imperial, inferior, little, living, lyrical, material, merely, miracle, mirror, mysterious, nearer, period, pillar, political, pretty, quiver, rear, rigor, river, serious, shrill, silver, spirit, still, superior, Syracuse, village, weary, which, whip, wilderness, will, willow, window, winter, wisdom, wish, withered, year, yearling.*

2. The stressed vowel should be a clear, sharp "short *e*" [ɛ] regardless of the spelling: *air, America, area, aware, bear, berry, bury, chairs, dwell, elegant, fell, fellow, friends, hair, health, help, heron, inherit, intelligence, left, level, Mary, merry, perilous, rare, rebel, relevant, relish, reverent, scarcely, scare, self, spell, square, sterile, swell, terrible, there, theirs, twelve, vary, very, wealthy, wear, welcome, well, where.*

## Exercises for the diphthong [ɑʊ] in "how" and "house":

The diphthong should begin with the [ɑ] of *calm* rather than with the [æ] of *cat*. To pronounce it properly, keep the tongue bunched in the back part of the mouth, repeat [ɑ] several times, then make a quick glide to [ʊ] or [u], rounding the lips vigorously as you end the diphthong. Listen attentively while practising, to prevent recurrence of the substandard diphthong.

1. Repeat rapidly; take breath only at punctuation marks: *ah ah ah ah ow, hah hah hah hah how, bah bah bah bah bough, cah cah cah cah cow, nah nah nah nah now, vah vah vah vah vow, ahl ahl ahl ahl owl, aht aht aht aht out, ahr ahr ahr ahr hour, pond pond pond pond pound, prod prod prod prod proud, shot shot shot shot shout, fond fond fond fond found.*

2. Practise more slowly; if you mispronounce a word, practise it with [ɑ], as in the first exercise: *how cow now bough vow thou scow prow plow vouch out ounce oust owl hour pound proud shout found mouse mouth mound bound round town down rouse crouch noun browse sound gown howl house scout brown loud count frown couch spout south growl hound clown our fowl sour shower tower power towel vowel mountain fountain allow endow carouse amount account surround pronounce.*

3. Practise slowly; correct each mistake before going ahead:

The south wind howled around the mountains.
The hound bounded up the mountain.
The grass was brown on account of the drouth.
The woman bought a brown gown in the big town.
The owl on the bough saw the cow on the ground.
A large amount of flour lay on the ground.
The clown ran around the tower.
The plowman heard the sound of cowbells from the south.
The scout was drowned in a pond at the edge of the town.

## Bibliography

W. A. Aikin, *The Voice* (New York, Longmans, Green & Co., 1920).

A. I. Birmingham and G. P. Krapp, *First Lessons in Speech Improvement* (New York, Charles Scribner's Sons, 1922).

G. Dodds and J. D. Lickley, *The Control of the Breath* (New York, Oxford University Press, 1925).

J. S. Kenyon, *American Pronunciation*, 6th ed. (Ann Arbor, Michigan, George Wahr, 1935).

G. P. Krapp, *The Pronunciation of Standard English in America* (New York, Oxford University Press, 1919).

T. W. Mills, *Voice Production*, 4th ed. (Philadelphia, J. B. Lippincott Company, 1913).

G. O. Russell, *Speech and Voice* (New York, The Macmillan Company, 1931).

# APPENDIX

## PARLIAMENTARY PROCEDURE

A CHART PREPARED AND TESTED
BY
PROFESSOR S. L. GARRISON
*Amherst College*

## CLASSIFICATION AND QUALIFICATIONS OF MOTIONS COMMON IN PARLIAMENTARY PROCEDURE

| Rank or Order of Precedence | General Class | Description of Motions and Questions | May interrupt speaker? | Must floor be got by introducer? | Seconder required? | Debatable? | Amendable? | 2/3 vote required? | Subject to reconsideration? |
|---|---|---|---|---|---|---|---|---|---|
| 15 | Main | The Main Motion or Question Itself | | * | * | * | * | | * |
| 14 | Subsidiary | Motion to Amend | | * | * | * | * | | * |
| 13 | | Motion to Postpone Indefinitely | | * | * | * | | | * |
| 12 | | Motion to Commit, Recommit, or Refer | | * | * | * | * | | * |
| 12 | | Motion to Postpone to a Day Certain | | * | * | * | 2 | | * |
| 11 | | Motion to Close Debate (Previous Question) or to Limit Debate | | * | * | | | * | ?. |
| 10 | | Motion to Lay on the Table | | * | * | | | | |
| 9 | | Question of Consideration (Objection to Consideration of Motion) | * | | | | | * | |
| 8 | Incidental | Division of Question | | * | * | | * | | * |
| 8 | | Method of Consideration | | * | * | | * | | * |
| 8 | | Reading of Papers | | * | * | | | | |
| 8 | | Suspension of Rules | | * | * | | | * | * |
| 8 | | Withdrawal of Motion | | * | * | | | | |

| | | | | | | | | |
|---|---|---|---|---|---|---|---|---|
| 7 | Extraneous | Motion to Reconsider | [3] | | [3] | * | * | * |
| 7 | | Motion to Rescind (or Repeal or Expunge) | | * | * | * | [4] | * |
| 6 | Privileged | Appeal from Ruling of Chair | * | * | * | [5] | | * |
| 5 | | Rise to Point of Order (or Information or Parliamentary Inquiry) | * | * | | | | * |
| 4 | | Question of Privilege (a) concerning a member; (b) concerning the assembly | * | | | | | |
| 3 | | Motion to Take a Recess | | * | * | | | |
| 2 | | Motion to Adjourn | | * | * | * | | |
| 1 | | Motion to Fix Time of Reconvening (or of Next Meeting) | | * | * | [6] | * | * |

[1] A negative vote to *lay on the table* may be reconsidered, but not an affirmative vote; in the latter case, a motion to *take off the table* is the proper procedure. According to most authorities, the motion to *lay on the table* takes precedence over a motion to close debate.

[2] A motion to *limit debate* may be amended, but not the motion to *close debate* (moving the *previous question*); the motion to *limit debate* is debatable if made as a main motion.

[3] A motion to *reconsider* may interrupt a member who has the floor in order to prevent action on the motion to be reconsidered; consideration of the motion is postponed until the floor is clear. The motion to *reconsider* is not debatable if the motion to which it is applied was not debatable.

[4] A motion to *rescind* requires a two-thirds vote unless previous notice has been given of the particular *motion to rescind*.

[5] An *appeal from the ruling of the chair* is not debatable if it relates to decorum, violation of rules, order of business, or an undebatable motion.

[6] A motion to *fix the time of the next meeting* is debatable if not offered as a privileged motion; it is then treated like any other main motion.

# INDEX

## A

Activity, interest in, 150.
Amplification, 191, 278; see Brevity.
Analogy, 166, 241.
Analysis, and briefing, Chapter V, 85; patterns of, 88; in exposition, 230.
Antithesis, 211.
Approach to audience, 112, 331, 350.
Argument, analysis in, 88; briefs for, 93, 95; place in persuasion, 256, 352; and suggestion, 287; in winning belief, Chapter XVII, 352; importance of, 352; fundamental of, 353; authority, 355; precedent, 363; example, 365; without arguing, 371; order of, 374; rate of progress, 375; against prejudice, 376; against self-interest, 376; see Belief.

## B

Baker, G. P., quoted, 80; Baker and Huntington, quoted, 307.
Baldwin, C. S., quoted, 206, 210.
Barton, B., quoted, 307.
Beecher, H. W., 61; Liverpool speech, 308 n., 319; quoted, 61.
Belief, Chapters XVI-XIX, 323-403; sources of, 323; why we believe, 324; gauging resistance, 326; conservative or liberal, 327; receptive attitude, 331; the approach, 331; denunciation, 332; common ground, 335; explanations and eliminations, 342; definition, 344; concessions and admissions, 345; fixed beliefs, 367; see Argument, Opposition, Persuasion, Speaker Himself.
Beveridge, A. J., quoted, 70, 386, 393.
Bible, quoted, 279.
Brevity, 196; see Amplification.
Briefing, Chapter V, 85; briefs for arguments, 93, 95; for exposition, 98; tests of, 99; subject sentences, 99; main heads and subheads, 104; clearness and coherence, 105; phrasing refutation, 109; compared with outline, 116, 118.
Brooks, P., quoted, 79.
Bryan, W. J., delivery, 21; style, 183; Cross of Gold speech, 294; geniality, 402.
Bryce, J., quoted, 398.